THE STOIC ORIGINS OF ERASMUS' PHILOSOPHY OF CHRIST

ROSS DEALY

The Stoic Origins of Erasmus' Philosophy of Christ

UNIVERSITY OF TORONTO PRESS
Toronto Buffalo London

Toronto Buffalo London
www.utppublishing.com
Printed in Canada

ISBN 978-1-4875-0061-0 (cloth)

Printed on acid-free, 100% post-consumer recycled paper with vegetable-based inks.

Library and Archives Canada Cataloguing in Publication

Dealy, Ross, author
The stoic origins of Erasmus' philosophy of Christ / Ross Dealy.

(Erasmus studies)
Includes bibliographical references and index.
ISBN 978-1-4875-0061-0 (cloth)

1. Erasmus, Desiderius, –1536 – Criticism and interpretation. 2. Jesus Christ. 3. Stoics. I. Title. II. Title: Erasmus' philosophy of Christ. III. Series: Erasmus studies

B785.E64D42 2016 199'.492 C2016-904332-0

This book has been published with the help of a grant from the Federation for the Humanities and Social Sciences, through the Awards to Scholarly Publications Program, using funds provided by the Social Sciences and Humanities Research Council of Canada.

University of Toronto Press acknowledges the financial assistance to its publishing program of the Canada Council for the Arts and the Ontario Arts Council, an agency of the Government of Ontario.

Funded by the Government of Canada
Financé par le gouvernement du Canada

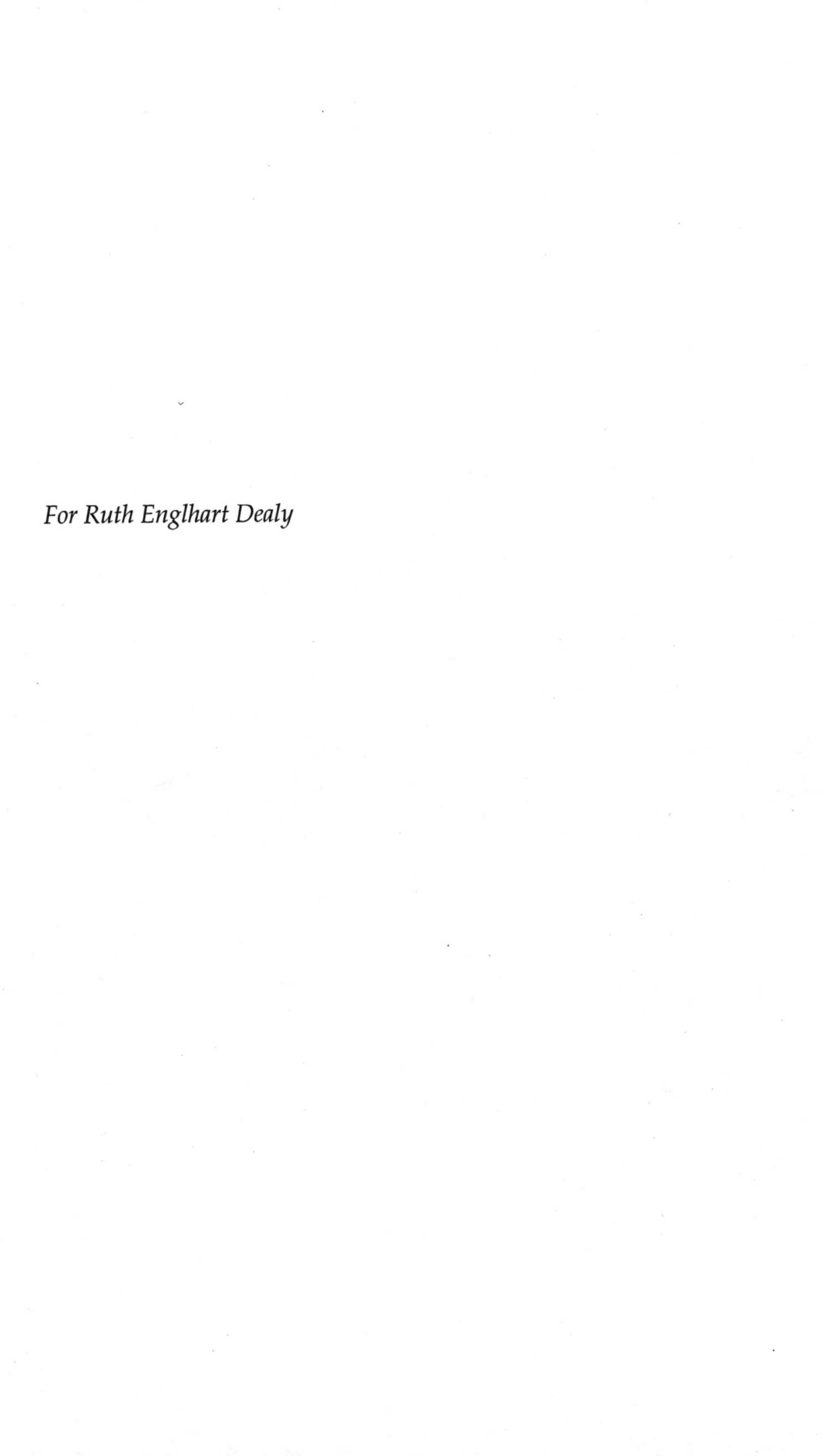

For Ruth Englhart Dealy

Contents

Preface

Research does not always follow a straight path. In my case two years travelling by motorcycle from the Arctic Circle to the tip of South America and throughout Africa as an undergraduate (1952–6) led to an interest in the impact of the intellectual history of Europe on the larger world. Ford Foundation grants later allowed me to spend two years in Europe researching in the Archive of the Indies (Seville, Spain) the influence of Thomas More and Erasmus in the Spanish New World, particularly on Vasco de Quiroga, which resulted in a dissertation on this subject (1975). What followed was a decades-long conviction, based on deep and independent analysis, that something is fundamentally wrong with accepted interpretations of the thought of More, as seen in his *Utopia* (1516), and of his friend Erasmus. It was *Utopia* that first impelled me to study Erasmus. How did More's mind work as he went about composing *Utopia*? Was there somehow a connection to the thinking of Erasmus? Against all odds I ultimately came to see that Erasmus' war writings, free-will writings, and *The Praise of Folly* and More's *Utopia* reflect a set way of thinking, but for years I was unable to discover the basis of this thinking. Only detailed analysis of Erasmus' earliest writings finally provided the answer – which is what the book at hand is about.

Along the way I have profited from positions at the University of Wisconsin-Marinette, Brown University (one year as Curator of Books in the John Carter Brown Library and one year as Visiting Scholar), and St John's University in New York City. I am particularly indebted to St John's in that those in charge overrode various countervailing forces and allowed time to continue research, including a research leave. As for individuals, no one has influenced my interest in research more than

Professor Gerald Strauss at Indiana University. Not of little importance has been the enduring support of my life partner Ruth Englhart Dealy, whom I met so memorably in her hometown, Aschaffenburg, Germany.

Thanks also to Suzanne Rancourt, Executive Editor of the Press, for her patience. I appreciate as well the editorial assistance of Barbara Porter and Miriam Skey and earlier (locally) Wayne Losano. Immensely helpful have been the insights and suggestions of two anonymous readers.

Abbreviations

Ac.	Cicero, *Posterior Academics*
Allen	*Opus epistolarum Des. Erasmi Roterodami.* Ed. P.S. Allen, H.M. Allen, and H.W. Garrod. 12 vols. Oxford, 1906–58
ASD	*Opera omnia Desiderii Erasmi Roterodami.* Amsterdam, 1969–
Ben.	Seneca, *De beneficiis* (On Benefits)
Brev.	Seneca, *De brevitate vitae* (On the Shortness of Life)
C.N.	Plutarch, *De communibus notitiis adversus Stoicos* (On Common Conceptions)
CWE	*Collected Works of Erasmus.* Toronto, 1974–
CWM	*The Complete Works of St. Thomas More.* 15 volumes. New Haven, CT, 1963–97
D.L.	Diogenes Laertius, *Lives of the Philosophers*
De ira	Seneca, *De ira* (On Anger)
De or.	Cicero, *De oratore* (On the Orator)
Disc.	Epictetus, *Discourses*
Ep.	Erasmus, *Epistolae* (Letters)
Ep.	Seneca, *Epistulae morales ad Lucilium* (Moral Letters to Lucilius)
Fin.	Cicero, *De finibus bonorum et malorum* (On Moral Ends)
GCS	*Die griechischen Christlichen Schriftsteller.* Berlin, 1897–
Gellius	Aulus Gellius, *Noctes Atticae* (Attic Nights)
H	*Desiderius Erasmus Roterodamus: Ausgewählte Werke*. Ed. Hajo Holborn and Annemarie Holborn. Munich, 1933
Inv.	Cicero, *De inventione*
LB	*Desiderii Erasmi Roterodami opera omnia.* Ed. J. Clericus. 10 vols. Leiden, 1703–6

Leg.	Cicero, *De legibus* (On the Laws)
LS	*The Hellenistic Philosophers*. Ed. A.A. Long and D.N. Sedley. 2 vols. Cambridge, 1987
Off.	Cicero, *De officiis* (On Appropriate Actions)
Olin	*Christian Humanism and the Reformation: Selected Writings of Erasmus.* Ed. and trans. John C. Olin. New York, 1965
Op.	Poggio Bracciolini, *Opera Omnia*
Or.	Cicero, *Orator* (Orator)
Ot.	Seneca, *De otio* (On Leisure)
Par.	Cicero, *Paradoxa Stoicorum* (Stoic Paradoxes)
PG	*Patrologia graeca*. Ed. J.-P. Migne. 162 vols. Paris, 1857–66
PL	*Patrologia latina*. Ed. J.-P. Migne. 221 vols. Paris, 1844–64
Princ.	Origen, *De Principiis* (On First Principles)
Sent.	Peter Lombard, *Sententiae in IV libris distinctae*
ST	Thomas Aquinas, *Summa theologiae*
T	Tracy, *Erasmus of the Low Countries.* Berkeley, 1996
Tr.	Seneca, *De tranquillitate animi* (On Peace of Mind)
Tusc.	Cicero, *Tusculan Disputations*

THE STOIC ORIGINS OF ERASMUS' PHILOSOPHY OF CHRIST

Introduction: A Philosophy beneath the Rhetoric

How did Erasmus' mind work? For decades scholars have focused on the rhetorical makeup of his mind, his relation to the rhetorical tradition and within this context his thought on religion.[1] Humanists are considered rhetoricians, not philosophers, and Erasmus was a humanist. Humanists sometimes made use of ideas found in various philosophies but not, we are shown, in any systematic way. They tended to see the ideas that interested them in rhetorical terms and to make them fit particular rhetorical needs. And Erasmus was unquestionably a great rhetorician. He wrote extensively on rhetoric and brilliantly displayed his rhetorical skills in works such as *The Praise of Folly* and *Colloquies.* Erasmus not only taught and employed rhetoric, he thought, it is contended, in rhetorical terms. In proof that the very matrix of his mind was rhetorical, scholars have uncovered, for one thing, a "rhetorical theology."

This book reveals something radically different. There was a set way of thinking beneath the rhetoric. Erasmus' mind was framed by a particular ancient philosophy. That philosophy was not Platonism, currently the rage among humanists, but Stoicism. Never recognized, Erasmus early on grasped the meaning and importance of the Stoic two-dimensional mindset. What interested Erasmus about Stoicism was not odd tidbits gathered from here and there but the core *katorthoma/*

1 In his *Erasmus in the Twentieth Century,* Mansfield concludes: "The recovery of his reputation as a religious thinker and the recovery of his connection with the rhetorical tradition are the two great achievements of Erasmus scholarship in the second half of the twentieth century" (223).

kathekon (and, closely related, *honestum/indifferens, honestum/utile*) frame of thought. Employing his unparalleled philological skills he correctly defined the meaning of *katorthoma* and *kathekon* – something the philologist Angelo Poliziano (d. 1494) was unable to do – in his 1501 edition of Cicero's *De officiis*. His 1499 debate with John Colet at Oxford shows that he had been systematically employing Stoic concepts, particularly *oikeiosis*, even earlier. He had become deeply attached to the Stoic mindset not simply because his philological skills allowed him to see a new way of conceptualizing reality but, most of all, because it answered very consciously to deep-seated mental, physical, social, and religious problems. He was to transfer this way of thinking to the very heart of Christianity. Indeed, "the philosophy of Christ" for which he is known was not built from rhetoric, as is commonly believed, but from this philosophy.

Erasmus worked out this two-dimensional but unitary way of thinking and placed it at the very core of his outlook in the most crucial years of his intellectual and emotional development, beginning around 1497. Therewith he brought to life an outlook that had not been recognized or employed since late classical times. Unlike previous humanists he grasped and was deeply affected by the Stoic focus on human nature, including natural instinct (*oikeiosis*), and the way two seemingly opposite types of value combine. Throughout *De taedio Iesu* (1501) and the *Enchiridion* (1503) he insistently and consistently rewrites Christianity and the authors with whom he deals – including fathers of the church, scholastic theologians, "devotionalists," and humanists – in terms of his new way of seeing himself and the world. His sources in particular were Cicero's *De finibus, De officiis*, and *Tusculan Disputations*, and Aulus Gellius' quotes and illustrations in *Attic Nights* of the arguments found in Book 5 (now lost) of the *Discourses* of Epictetus. Even where he very consciously revises Stoicism – on emotion – he was not motivated by, or even thinking about, ancient Peripatetic criticism. Nor does he here discard the essential categories of Stoic thought. Supported by his own experientially based philosophic analysis he simply transfers emotion from its governance by Stoic reason (*ratio*) to Stoic natural instinct (*oikeiosis*).

It is noteworthy that Erasmus was not at this time interested in the writings of Seneca. In a letter of 1523, he states that before age twenty (1486 or 1489?) he had preferred Seneca over Cicero and indeed could not bear to read Cicero at length, but after age twenty he had reversed his assessment.[2] One could say, that is, that Erasmus came to prefer Cicero's rendering of Stoicism far above the Stoic writings of Seneca that he had read. *De taedio Iesu* and the *Enchiridion* bear this out.

Outlines of the Stoic *katorthoma / kathekon* mindset and "the philosophy of Christ"

So what is the *katorthoma / kathekon* way of thinking from which Erasmus early on built his "philosophy of Christ"? The Stoics describe with these words two types of value, one perfect and the other imperfect, one unbending and the other bending. Both types of value are encompassed by their fabled wiseman. On the bending side, everything the wiseman does is "an appropriate act," *kathekon* (Latin *officium*) (*Fin.* 3.20) – a word first used by Zeno himself (335–262 BCE) (D.L. 7.108). An appropriate act is "an act so performed that a reasonable account can be rendered of its performance" (*Fin.* 3.58) or, stated otherwise, "an act of which a probable reason can be given" (*Off.* 1.8).[3] Even those not wise can and sometimes do carry out appropriate acts. In contrast, however, the Stoic wiseman at all times acts appropriately – "selecting," employing reason, courses of action that are most in accord with nature and rejecting, employing reason, those that are contrary to nature.

Remarkably, the wiseman's selections do not in themselves contribute to virtue. Selecting is simply essential to his character and activities, his virtue and happiness (*Fin.* 3.58–9). He always acts appropriately because not to do so would be to abolish virtue itself (*Fin.* 3.12). What the wiseman has that others do not have and cannot have is *katorthoma*, or "right action" (*rectum factum*, *Fin.* 3.45). An act carried out with a virtuous disposition is a "right action," whereas the same act done without a virtuous disposition – by those not wise – is not virtuous. In Seneca's words: "The same act may be either shameful or honorable: the purpose and the manner make all the difference" (*Ep.* 95.43). Every right act (*katorthoma*) is also an appropriate act (*kathekon*) and every appropriate act *(kathekon)* is for the wiseman – though never for others – a right act (*katorthoma*).

Critics in the ancient world, vigorously supported by Plutarch (d. 120 CE), berated Stoics for – unlike all other schools – setting up two ends,

2 *Ep.* 1390. Allen 5, 340/103–8, CWE 10, 99/113–17.

3 Translations are from printed editions found in the bibliography, unless otherwise stated.

one being that which is obtained by *katorthoma* and the other being that which is obtained by *kathekon* (*C.N.* 1070F–1071B). Responding to these objections, Antipater (2nd cent. BCE) compared the operation of the wiseman's mind to that of an archer (*Fin.* 3.22). To accomplish his primary goal – the end, the ultimate good – the archer does everything in his power to obtain the secondary goal – hit the target. But the degree to which the secondary goal is accomplished or not accomplished has no bearing on the primary goal. So, in fact, Antipater held, the two types of value converge; they do not contradict each other.[4]

Honestum (Greek *καλόυ*, D.L. 7.100), moral worth, is what the perfect wiseman, unlike other humans, possesses. *Honestum* is "something that, even though it be not generally ennobled, is still worthy of all honour; and by its own nature, we correctly maintain, it merits praise, even though it be praised by none" (*Off.* 1.14).[5] *Honestum* is the sole good. As the Stoic Cato states in *De finibus*, "The essential principle not merely of the system of philosophy I am discussing but also of our life and destinies is that we should believe moral worth (*honestum*) to be the only good" (3.26). In calling virtue *honestum*, Zeno "denoted a sort of uniform, unique and solitary good" (*Ac.* 35). Virtue, including the four cardinal virtues (wisdom, justice, temperance, and fortitude), is inherent to *honestum*, as is reason itself (*Fin.* 2.48). "Haec ratio perfecta virtus vocatur eademque honestum est" (*Ep.* 76.10). Reason, virtually indistinguishable from nature, proves that *honestum* is the only good (*Fin.* 3.75). The wiseman is at all times perfectly happy because he has a fixed inner orientation towards the good, *honestum* (*Fin.* 3.26).

Zeno also argued that things neither good (*bonum*) nor bad (*malum*) are "indifferent," *indifferens* (Greek *adiaphoron*) (*Fin.* 3.53), and that some of these indifferents are "preferred" and others "rejected" (*Fin.* 3.15).[6] Of the indifferents, some have positive value, others negative value,

---

4 Agreeing with Antipater, Striker concludes: "It is simply wrong to assume that there can be only one reference-point of all action." See "Antipater, or the Art of Living," *The Norms of Nature*, 203 and 204. And yet Antipater still fails to explain, Long and Sedley note, "how it can be rational to make happiness depend upon aiming at objectives whose attainment is irrelevant to happiness" (LS 410).

5 Andrew R. Dyck points out that prior to the arrival of Stoicism the ideals *honestum/honestas/honestus* were "rarely used and of vague significance in the Roman political vocabulary." See *A Commentary on Cicero, De Officiis*, 31.

6 "*Indifferens*" is a word that occurs for the first time in Cicero's works. See Powell, "Cicero's Translations from the Greek," in *Cicero the Philosopher*, 296.

and others are neutral (*Fin*. 3.50). Positive values comprise things such as health, beauty, wealth, fame, and freedom from pain (D.L. 7.102). Negative values comprise things such as ill health, pain, and poverty.

Another core Stoic doctrine is that of "*oikeiosis*," which means something like "self perception" or "orientation to oneself." In Chrysippus' words, "The dearest thing to every animal is its own constitution and its consciousness thereof" (D.L. 7.85). Cicero Latinizes *oikeiosis* as "*sensus sui*" (*Fin*. 3.16). Invented, it appears, by the Stoics, no comparable concept is found in Plato or Aristotle.[7] All animals, humans included, exhibit at birth a self-preservation and (logically secondary to it)[8] self-love instinct. Self-preservation is "a primary impulse of nature" (*Fin*. 3.16) and as such will relate to types of appropriate actions (*kathekonta*) and eventually, with the advent of reason, *katorthomata* (*Fin*. 3.20–4). In exemplifying natural instinct at birth, Seneca avers that it is not experience, which teaches only slowly, that makes a young chicken fear a cat and not a dog. The skills of bees and spiders were not taught. No matter how dumb animals may be, they are all equally clever at living. As for humans, every one of us knows that something stirs our impulses – but we don't know what it is (*Ep*. 121.20–4, 13).

Note the tie of the Stoic outlook to both the nature of the individual and the nature of the universe. Diogenes Laertius quotes Chrysippus in his *Lives of the Philosophers* as follows:

> The end may be defined as life in accordance with nature, or, in other words, in accordance with our own human nature as well as that of the universe ... The virtue of the happy man and the smooth current of life are found when all actions promote the harmony of the spirit dwelling in the individual man with the will of him who orders the universe. (7.88)

The dynamism and tension in the Stoic unitary but two-dimensional mindset is brought out by the Stoic Epictetus (d. 135 CE):

> (Material things) must be used carefully, because their use is not a matter of indifference, and at the same time with steadfastness and peace of mind,

7 See Long, "Hierocles," 250. Cf. Pembroke, "Oikeiosis," 132–41, and Gill, *The Structured Self in Hellenistic and Roman Thought*, 36–46. *Oikeiosis* also has an important social dimension.

8 Long, "Hierocles," 254.

> because the material is indifferent ... It is, indeed, difficult to unite and combine these two things – the carefulness of the man who is devoted to material things and the steadfastness of the man who disregards them, but it is not impossible. Otherwise happiness were impossible. (*Disc.* 2.5.7–9)

Depending on the standpoint, that is, material things are either of no importance or – what popular modern referrals to Stoicism miss – all important. At every instant the wiseman combines both standpoints. Material things are indifferent, but not with regard to the wiseman's use. The wiseman is steadfast and confident regarding internal things, moral right, but careful and cautious regarding material things. Based on rules, he decides what actions regarding material things are the most appropriate (or not appropriate) at the same time as he holds firm to moral right. In short, the wiseman's outlook is not either/or (other than holding that the opposite of *honestum* is *turpe*) but unitarily both/and.

A new humanist mindset

Erasmus not only recognized the spirituality of *katorthoma*, the double meaning of *indifferentia*, the unique importance of natural instincts at birth, *oikeiosis*, and surrounding everything the unitary both/and frame of thought, he worked out these concepts in terms of his own life and Christianity. Deeply motivated by his youthful mental and physical suffering and his conviction with the help of Stoicism that this suffering had been needless, brought about by a failure to recognize that the traits he was born with are ineradicable, Erasmus was determined to show in *De taedio Iesu* that Christ himself was racked by ineradicable natural instincts – while at one and the same time contemplating the divine. In *De taedio Iesu* and throughout the *Enchiridion* he works out *oikeiosis* and other Stoic concepts within Stoic two-dimensional but unitary *katorthoma/kathekon* and *honestum/indifferens* ways of thinking. Therewith he inextricably binds together the worldly and the non-worldly, the mundane and the spiritual, the active life and the contemplative, action and reason, individual nature and universal nature, emotion and rigid precepts.

Previous humanists, most of them Italian, had made hardly anything of the words *katorthoma* and *kathekon* and the thinking surrounding them – such as *oikeiosis*. They could have learned much from the technical discussions found in Cicero's *De finibus*, Diogenes Laertius' *Lives*, and many other available sources, but such discussions were largely beyond their interests and mental capacity. Humanists were by training rhetoricians and unlike Cicero were mere novices in philosophy. What they most admired about Cicero were his writings on rhetoric and his active life. They were, it is true, interested in his *De officiis*, a philosophical work that relates to worldly affairs, but even here they had made little or nothing of the encompassing Stoic *honestum/utile* theme, the fact that *honestum* and *utile* are not rhetorical words but philosophic words, unitary both/and words that go back to Zeno and Chrysippus.[9] Not unlike medieval thinkers, who like them held *De officiis* in high regard, they were able to focus on various theses within the work but the author's overall outlook and purpose was beyond their grasp. Their blindness to the Stoic unitary both/and mindset also blinded them to Cicero. They did not see the degree to which Cicero admired Stoicism (albeit questioning and reworking some doctrines, such as *apatheia*) and that *De officiis*, his most original work, is fundamentally Stoic. They did not see that Stoicism is worldly as well as otherworldly, bending as well as unbending, and as such, directly applicable to contemporary affairs.[10]

And yet, the Stoic *katorthoma/kathekon* model – and related doctrines – existed. But when would someone see or take an interest in this model? How could it ever be a humanist? In Cicero's books on philosophy rhetoric serves philosophy (even if rhetoric in certain ways influenced philosophy) – philosophy does not serve rhetoric. Is it to be believed that a humanist would come along who would put rhetoric in the service of the Stoic unitary both/and mindset – as distinct from placing pieces of Stoicism in the service of rhetoric? Even more improbable, what would ever impel a humanist to apply the Stoic *katorthoma/kathekon* way of thinking to his own life and the society and intellectual/religious climate that surrounded him?

---

9 For the Stoic Panaetius, whose views Cicero worked out in Books 1 and 2 of *De officiis*, the *utile* was a criterion for judging actions – related to *kathekon*. On employment of the term in Stoicism and especially Panaetius' usage, see Dyck, *A Commentary on Cicero, De Officiis*, 353–4 and 492–3.

10 Perhaps, states Dyck, "Cicero's major contribution to Roman political thought is his radical identification of *honestum* and *utile*, with the consequences worked out in detail in Off. 3." "Ironically, it is in Book 3, where Cicero boasts of his independence of sources (3.34) and where the scale of values can ostensibly be either Stoic or Peripatetic (3.33), that the rigor of the older Stoa reasserts itself (cf. *ad* 3.62–3, 97–115, 119)." See *A Commentary on Cicero, De Officiis*, 33 and 37.

But these improbabilities actually happened. Erasmus set in play a profound shift in the humanist mindset. Cicero developed 250 years of Stoicism within a Roman context and Erasmus, 1500 years later, applied Stoicism to yet another psychological, social, intellectual, and religious setting. What Erasmus brought to the table was not just a collection of ideas but a way of thinking that had not been recognized for a thousand years. There is a reason why the *Enchiridion* was to become so popular – even if understood in limited ways – and why scholars have been so perplexed as to why this was the case. *De taedio Iesu* and the *Enchiridion* are not as has been thought mere rehashes of traditional views. They are radical books in that they lay out a new way of looking at oneself and at larger issues. Erasmus stated that he was setting forth a new type of spiritual "warfare" and he did just that.

What is most important about Erasmus' employment of Stoicism is not that it shines a light, which it does, on a heretofore hidden link in the history of philosophy. However much he admired key Stoic doctrines, Erasmus was not writing as a philosopher for philosophers. Nor, unlike previous humanists, was he writing simply for a coterie of intellectuals. He had in mind something he considered incomparably more important. The *Enchiridion* and many of the writings which followed were designed to have a large religious relevance and appeal and they in fact significantly impacted the religious, social, and political development of Europe. Through these works Stoicism played a role in Renaissance history that has been little seen.

Modern research on Erasmus: Vacillations between worldly and non-worldly

Concentrating on the Stoicism represented by the humanists they study, historians of the Renaissance have seen almost nothing of the two-dimensional but unitary way of thinking.[11] What specialists on Erasmus see is not unitary both/and thinking, Stoic or otherwise, but something that appears to be the opposite, an Erasmus who vacillated – guided above all by rhetorical methodologies – between contradictory poles of thought: non-worldly and worldly, spirit and flesh. Bruce Mansfield alludes to this perception of a vacillating mind where he concludes, in

11 See, for example, Jill Kraye's summaries, "Stoicism in the Renaissance," and "The Revival of Hellenistic Philosophies." See also her "The Humanist as Moral Philosopher."

his *Erasmus in the Twentieth Century: Interpretations c 1920–2000* (2003), "There are well-founded arguments that he distinguished sharply between spirit and flesh and was in a kind of inner retreat from the world. There are equally well-grounded views that he exalted natural gifts and natural powers and cherished the ordinary lives of men and women in the world" (226).

Answers to this apparent polarity have been sought, deeper research reveals, in the wrong places. Rhetoric, lack of scholastic logic, devotionalist influences, Platonism, and personality cannot account for the way of thinking found in *De taedio Iesu* and the *Enchiridion*. These writings are throughout explained by Stoicism, a philosophy that does not vacillate between worldly and non-worldly but is all about the oneness of two radically different types of value.

Erasmus' use of non-Stoic sources

Erasmus' referrals to non-Stoic authors in *De taedio Iesu* (1501) and the *Enchiridion* (1503) have not, in truth, been analysed. Since Erasmus seldom criticizes the sources he refers to, researchers have simply assumed that he is merely adding a rhetorical flourish to accepted and traditional views. As a consequence *De taedio Iesu* has been largely ignored and though often discussed the *Enchiridion* has been subjected to rather little study. And one can understand why Erasmus' 1499 trip to England, which spawned these works, has appeared to be "unremarkable" and why a mystery has surrounded his "sudden transformation from rootless Latin poet to northern Europe's most influential scholar and inspirer of religious reform."[12] What the book at hand will demonstrate is that Erasmus' 1499 trip was eminently remarkable, crucially important for understanding his early motivations, the nature of his writings, and indeed his entire life. Nor is there a mystery regarding his "sudden transformation" from poet to scholar and inspirer of religious reform.

Close analysis of the sources Erasmus refers to with regard to particular issues opens up his writings – and his mind. It is precisely the contrast between the statements and meanings of the writings directly in front of him and his own theses – what he does with these

12 See Nauert, "Rethinking 'Christian Humanism,'" 175. There is no direct referral to *De taedio Iesu* in either Tracy's *Erasmus of the Low Countries*, or Mansfield's *Erasmus in the Twentieth Century*.

writings – that shows most clearly what he is doing and what his thinking is about. Erasmus corrects these authors – consciously and consistently and systematically – in terms of a particular way of thinking and particular doctrines. In *De taedio Iesu* and the *Enchiridion* he rewrites with all diligence Origen, Gellius, "Colet," Bonaventure, and Socrates (as well as authors who figure less prominently, such as Augustine and St Bernard) in terms of Stoic *oikeiosis* and the Stoic unitary (*katorthoma/kathekon, honestum/indifferens, honestum/utile*) frame of thought – and in the process revolutionizes long-standing views of Christ and Christianity and the human predicament.

Nor does Erasmus swing carelessly or fitfully, in rhetorical fashion, from one source to another without a clear plan. He uses the sources he brings in, however diverse, to develop step by step a thesis. Although a casual reading does not show this, his mind is set. He knows where he is going. Whether mentioning Plato or Origen or St Paul or a passage in the Bible or, now and then, some literary figure, he does not simply state a view and go on to the next. He very consciously revamps these sources, either directly or contextually, to make them fit a set way of thinking and outlook – one moulded by Stoicism.

Plato had become the vogue in late fifteenth-century Europe, gravitating out from Florence, and readers of the *Enchiridion* have repeatedly held that here, more than in perhaps any of his writings, Erasmus sees Christianity in terms of Platonist one-dimensional other-worldly ideals. A core proof given is that Erasmus mentions Plato more often than any other pagan. What has not been seen, however, is that without exception Erasmus places Plato's outlook within a Stoic frame – on the unbending side. From cover to cover the work is built from Stoic or Stoic-based sources. Cicero had sometimes referred to Plato in his philosophical works and so too does Erasmus, but he does not think in terms of Plato's transcendent view of truth anymore than had Cicero.[13]

---

13 As Julia Annas comments, "The ethical discussions of Cicero's time assume that our ethical aims are limited to the fulfillment of our human nature; they are all naturalistic, in a common understanding of that term. Plato does not appear as a participant in these debates because his most striking claim is that the virtuous person should 'become like God', transcending human nature as much as he can [she cites *Theaetetus* 171d–177c]. This idea does not fit into Hellenistic ethical debate at all, though it was to have a great future in later antiquity." See *On Moral Ends* [*De finibus*], ed. J. Annas and trans. R. Woolf, xxii.

Themes

Part I ("The Fifteenth-Century Background: One-Dimensional Stoicism within Either/Or Mindsets") shows that humanists prior to Erasmus never thought in Stoic two-dimensional but unitary terms – much less expressed interest in Stoic *oikeiosis*. Due in particular to their educations and worldly activities they saw in *De officiis*, published in 1465, either/or, *honestas* or *utilitas* arguments as distinct from *honestum/utile* arguments. This either/or mindset was pervasive, as in their debates over "Epicurean or Stoic," "Stoic nobility or inherited nobility," "active life or contemplative." Leonardo Bruni had an acute mind but he too little grasped (he favoured Aristotle) the Stoic *kathekon/katorthoma*, active/contemplative, bending/unbending frame of mind. The many humanist "mirror-for-princes" treatises advocate for princes Stoic-type precepts, based on Seneca's *De clementia*, but here too nothing is seen of the larger and more authentic two-dimensional Stoic way of thinking. Even Machiavelli in his criticisms of these treatises, in *The Prince*, nowhere recognizes the Stoic *honestum/utile* mindset – a mindset that could be considered an alternative to his thesis.

Part II ("Erasmus' Two-Dimensional Stoicism") works out the following theses. (1) Erasmus' *On Contempt of the World*, written around 1485–8, and other writings prior to his debate with John Colet at Oxford in 1499, portrays a Christianity that is about making either/or choices – flesh or spirit, worldly or non-worldly, active life or contemplative life. Nothing relates to the Stoic unitary both/and mindset. (2) Scholars have given diverse definitions of Erasmus' "philosophy of Christ" but no one imagines that Erasmus was ever thinking of a true philosophy. (3) Analysis of Erasmus' 1501 edition of *De officiis* reveals an unprecedented grasp of the meanings of *katorthoma* and *kathekon* and of the importance of Stoic thinking on natural instinct (*oikeiosis*). (4) In his preface to *De officiis* Erasmus recognizes that Stoicism is not so much about the solutions to particular social, political, and intellectual problems as about how to go about solving such problems. And he was determined to apply this method to the world he knew. (5) Erasmus deeply grasped the religiosity of Stoicism and *De officiis*. (6) His 1509 motto appears to have been Stoic inspired. (7) One reason scholars have considered *De taedio Iesu* of little importance is that they have misread statements of Erasmus at the beginning and end of the work. (8) Contrary to the widely held view that Erasmus' later complaints about his youth were for various reasons largely made up, detailed consideration of all the evidence shows the seriousness of his mental and physical suffering in his youth and, more than this, that he became deeply attached to Stoicism as a direct result – which analysis of *De taedio Iesu* will further confirm.

Part III ("Stoic Natural Instinct and Christ's Fear of Death, *De taedio Iesu*") shows that the debate between Erasmus and Colet at Oxford in 1499 was over the nature of Christ's Passion, a subject that had been tied for a thousand years to conceptions of the nature of Christ and of Christianity. While Colet held that Christ could not have feared death Erasmus argued that he was overwhelmed by fear. Chapter 1 analyses Erasmus' reasons for contending that the Stoics consider fear of death a natural instinct and assesses the relationship of his arguments to the ancient sources. Having concluded, with the help of Stoicism, that natural instincts and character traits are given at birth and vary greatly, Erasmus questions the meaning of bravery. Is bravery really about overcoming one's nature? Can bravery be ascertained by merely observing a person's physical and/or mental reactions to danger? Do natural disabilities decrease or increase one's opportunities for virtue? Chapter 2 shows that Erasmus emphatically rejects, based directly on the Stoic *honestum/indifferens* mindset, the views of the Greek father Origen (d. 255) on the nature of the soul. The soul does not tie itself to either spirit or flesh. It has a substantive and independent existence in-between spirit and flesh. Soul is comprised of natural instincts, things that are "indifferent." Chapter 3 details Erasmus' argument that martyrs may have experienced a joy that wipes out natural instincts but Christ was not a martyr. Building on the Stoic two-dimensional mindset Erasmus shows that Christ experienced *unitarily* incomparable fear and incomparable joy (Stoic *gaudium*, not *alacritas*).

Part IV ("Larger Philosophical Issues"), chapter 1, reveals the differences between the views of Colet expressed at the actual debate and the "Colet" Erasmus refers to in *De taedio Iesu*. Though Colet the person knew nothing about Stoicism, Erasmus has "Colet" argue orthodox Stoic views against his corrections of Stoicism – "my Stoics." Chapter 2 works out Erasmus' objections to the Stoic contention that the wiseman's involuntary physical or mental reactions to such things as a bolt of lightening do not indicate fear in that his reason immediately overcomes the initial "pre-emotion." What these discussions of "pre-emotion" miss, Erasmus shows, is emotion that comes about internally. Gellius' story about the Stoic in the typhoon does not prove what Gellius thinks it proves in that the Stoic was demonstrably unable to overcome his fear before the typhoon subsided – and during this time reason could do nothing. Chapter 3 points out a relationship between Christ in Gethsemane and the Stoic in the typhoon. Christ's fear was overwhelming and it was not overcome but lasted as long as he was alive – and yet the other side of his soul remained at one and the same time serene, at one with reason and the contemplation of heaven.

Part V ("Correcting a Thousand Years of Christology") describes the thinking of patristic and scholastic theologians on Christ's Passion and Erasmus' carefully worked out rejections of their arguments. Chapter 1 delineates Jerome's thinking on pre-emotion, which he inherited from Seneca and Origen, and the changes inaugurated by scholastics such as Peter Lombard, Bonaventure, and Aquinas. While Jerome had contended that Christ only "began" to be sad and thus never suffered full-blown emotion, scholastics demonstrated, based on complex logic-based "distinctions," that Christ's pre-emotion was brought about and governed by reason. Chapter 2 describes the ways in which Erasmus argues – against Jerome and Bonaventure directly – that Christ suffered full-blown emotion. While the church fathers and scholastics had not realized that their thinking on pre-emotion was originally derived from the Stoics, Erasmus fully understood and yet he was determined to show that Stoic thinking is here misguided in that talk about pre-emotion from external happenings covers up emotion that is actually a natural instinct (and found in Stoic *oikeiosis*). In being a human Christ suffered from emotions such as fear from the very beginning, even in the state of innocence. Reason had nothing to do with his fear of death, a fear greater than ever experienced by a human. In his Passion Christ demonstrated (expanding the Stoic mindset) that he "could be both willing and unwilling, both dread and desire the same thing in equal measure and at one and the same time."

Part VI ("Beyond Devotionalist Assumptions") considers the larger social and religious environment in which Erasmus lived. Could it be that Erasmus was simply reflecting in some way a view of the Passion embedded in late medieval culture, not least relevant being his youthful contacts with the Devotio Moderna from 1475 to 1493? Leaving aside Erasmus' Stoic mindset, a fundamental difference is that the devotionalist accounts of Christ's death emphasize in graphic detail his physical suffering. Erasmus goes out of his way to reject the view of the Passion represented by St Bernard, who was extremely popular among fifteenth-century devotionalists, and to tie Bernard with Colet. In emphasizing the physical suffering of Christ and Christ's overcoming of emotion Bernard advised working one's way upward from flesh to spirit and mystical union with God.

Part VII ("Spiritual Warfare: Christianizing *Katorthoma/Kathekon*: The *Enchiridion militis christiani*") shows that the *Enchiridion* is all about Christianizing for ordinary people the Stoic mindset. Unlike *De taedio Iesu*, the *Enchiridion* was written as an advice book and was to have a Europe-wide impact, especially on the Reformation inaugurated by Luther and on the social/political/religious environment that would emerge in England with Henry VIII's separating of the Church of England from Rome. And yet *De taedio Iesu* and the *Enchiridion* have in common the fact that they both build directly from Erasmus' youthful existential problems and the resolution of these problems by Stoicism. Demonstrating again the deep-seated nature of these problems and the degree to which they affected his outlook, Erasmus corrects in the *Enchiridion*, in terms of his new understanding of natural instinct and its relation to Christianity, Origen and Socrates on the origins of human diversity at birth and Socrates' fable of the good and bad horses. Nor, against a view everywhere accepted, does Erasmus see himself as having a modest and gentle disposition or as even favouring dispositions like modesty and docility. And yet Erasmus shows throughout that Christianity is an extension of the Stoic two-dimensional mindset – only one side of which relates to natural instinct and worldly situations as such.

Although the beginning of the *Enchiridion* closely correlates with the tone and wording at the beginning of *De officiis*, the arguments in the work swirl around core theses of the Stoic wiseman as set forth in *De finibus* in particular. While Erasmus emphasizes the oneness of the *honestum* and the *utile*, as in *De officiis* 3, his primary focus is on the oneness of *katorthoma* (virtue, reason, spirit, intention) and *kathekon* (seen as *indifferentia*) as in the old Stoa and *De finibus* 3.

The "soul" is found on the indifferent side of this unitary both/and mindset. Against the theologians (not least being Origen), as well as contemporary Neoplatonists (such as Marsilio Ficino, greatly admired by Colet), the soul is not simply a decider between two opposites, flesh and spirit (Stoic *turpia* and *honesta*, vice and virtue, bad and good); it has an independent and material reality. As in Stoicism, things "intermediate" and "indifferent" comprise everything in the world that is not *turpe* or *honestum*, carnal or spirit. Having no connection with either flesh or spirit, the soul "constitutes us as human beings," "seeks what is necessary," and is "the life-giving element." Substantive, inclusive, and variable, the soul is at the very core of what it means to be human. The indifferents that the soul first needs to deal with are the particulars of one's own body and mind.

"Spirituality" has no meaning in itself. Whether one's life is at any particular moment spiritual or not depends entirely on the degree to which one works out two opposite but inseparable types of value, one unbending the other bending. Over and over Erasmus refers to the mindset required as a type of "warfare." Note what this warfare is not.

(a) It is not about the traditional opposition (as with, in their own ways, Origen and Colet) between Christian ideals and worldliness.
(b) It is not about rhetorical debate between two opposed but more or less equally viable positions, between for example *honestum* and *utile* or contemplative life and active life, as in fifteenth-century humanism.
(c) It is not about the one-dimensional and mystical "ascent to God" represented by the Neoplatonism gyrating out from Florence, inspired in particular by Ficino.
(d) It is not about the logicizing "distinctions" of scholastics, such as Thomas Aquinas, by which the validity of actions – such as, for example, physical warfare – is decided on.

The model and frame is through and through Stoic. Holding high and unbending Christ's absolute precepts (such as charity and the denial of warfare) entails working out things that are not absolute in appropriate real world ways, ways that are also inherent to Christ's teachings and inseparable from one's hold on the absolutes.

As in Stoicism "intention" is a crucial factor in this mindset and accompanying course of action. Erasmus had deeply grasped, first demonstrated in his editing of *De officiis*, the inherency of intention to *katorthoma*. An act carried out with a virtuous disposition is a "right action" (*rectum factum*) whereas the same act done without a virtuous disposition is not virtuous. Purpose and manner are critical components of a "right action." The Christian takes over where the Stoic wiseman leaves off in that this purpose and manner – motivation, intention, spirit – is about faith in a revealed truth as well as the virtue and reason that reigns in the universe. It is a fault, argues Erasmus, to perform a good action – whether a religious ceremony or any other positive worldly action – lacking a spiritual purpose.

In short, analysis of the *Enchiridion* reveals that Erasmus transfers the Stoic unitary two-dimensional mindset to Christianity and that this is what he is thinking about when he states in a 1504 letter that the work is about "fixed procedures." Evil exists (cf. *turpe*) and contrasts with spirit (cf. *honestum*) but Christianity, "the philosophy of Christ," is not fundamentally about this either/or choice but about a unitary *indifferens/spiritus* mindset.

The conclusion sums up the main theses and then points out that many of Erasmus' writings that followed *De taedio Iesu* and the *Enchiridion* need to be restudied. There is reason to believe that many works considered "rhetorical" (one obvious example being *The Praise of Folly*) are in fact built from a philosophy. In illustration of the point it is shown that *Ecclesiastes* (1535), one of Erasmus' last works, is about the rhetorical tools needed in preaching and yet the goal is not built from rhetoric but from Stoic philosophy. The influence of the *Enchiridion* in the sixteenth century was phenomenal and it was understood and employed in many ways but one thing seems evident: no one (other than, I will demonstrate elsewhere, Thomas More) clearly recognized the sources of Erasmus' thought or the larger meaning of the work.

PART I The Fifteenth-Century Background: One-Dimensional Stoicism within Either/Or Mindsets

Two Propositions:

(1) No humanist prior to Erasmus ever truly grasped or employed the Stoic two-dimensional but unitary (*katorthoma/kathekon, honestum/indifferens, honestum/utile*) frame of thought.
(2) Within this frame – or even outside it – no previous humanist ever focused on or employed Stoic thinking on natural instinct at birth (*oikeiosis*). The standing of these propositions is of more than esoteric interest. Historians know that it is impossible to validly evaluate thought outside of context and are thus interested in the personal, social, political, intellectual, and religious contexts in which thought emerges. Changes in the meaning and relationships of words such as *honestum* and *utile* may denote far-reaching shifts both in mindset and society. In this regard, was Erasmus' outlook just a continuation of common assumptions – or something radically different? Only analysis of previous humanist theses and arguments can make the differences, to be revealed in Parts II–VII, stand out.

Fifteenth-century humanists, proponents of the *studia humanitatis* – rhetoric, grammar, poetry, history, and moral philosophy – were commonly employed as schoolmasters, professors of literature, court poets, political secretaries, ambassadors, chancellors, and high-level civil servants.[1] Considering on the one hand their training and on the other their

1 See Kristeller, *Renaissance Thought*. On the educational interests, goals, methodologies, and professional duties of earlier humanists, such as Lovato dei Lovati (d. 1309) and Albertino Mussato (d. 1329), before even Petrarch (1304–74), see Witt, *In the Footsteps of the Ancients*. Paul F. Grendler describes the grammar and rhetoric taught in the fourteenth-century university in *The Universities of the Italian Renaissance*, 199–205.

employment it may not seem surprising, as often noted, that humanist thinking could and did vacillate greatly. The rhetorical need to suit an argument to place, time, and situation (*De or*. 3.210–12) and in that way to prove, to please, and to sway (*probare, delectare, flectere*) (*Or.* 69) was directly applicable to the worldly functions of many humanists.[2] They used their rhetorical skills to respond to particular social, political, economic, intellectual, and emotional factors.[3] And we can see why the same person would sometimes argue one position only to argue something else at another time or in a different context. In Bruni's "Dialogue to Pier Paolo Vergerio," for example, Niccoli attacks Dante, Petrarch, and Bocaccio in Book 1 only to retract and praise them in Book 2.[4] Nor did humanists espouse a singular political ideology.[5] For them, worldly endeavours required adaptability, not expertise in consistent or systematic thinking.[6] In short, there is good reason why humanist thought is often shifting, ambiguous, ambivalent, confusing, or contradictory.

It was within this rhetoric-based milieu that humanists turned the pages of Cicero's philosophical works. They were much impressed by the harsh and unbending side of the Stoic wiseman epitomized in Cicero's *Paradoxa Stoicorum*, published in 1465, but saw little of the worldly side of this wiseman, evident in his unbending/bending way of dealing with personal, social, and political affairs. To the extent they considered *Paradoxa Stoicorum* by itself, it is not difficult to understand their misperception. *Paradoxa Stoicorum* is but a short caricature of the wiseman.[7] The wiseman presented here has nothing in common with the

---

2 Building on ancient practices, humanists focused on types of persuasion (logos, pathos, ethos), branches of oratory (judicial, deliberative, epideictic), the various categories (invention, argument, style, memory, delivery), the parts of a speech (exordium, narration, partition, confirmation, refutation, conclusion), and rhetorical devices (such as alliteration, amplification, and synecdoche). Cf. Kennedy, *Classical Rhetoric*; Murphy, *Renaissance Eloquence*; Vickers, *In Defence of Rhetoric*; and Wood, "The Teaching of Writing in Medieval Europe."

3 Writings on the nature and importance of eloquence by Petrarch, Salutati, George of Trebizond, Valla, Agricola, Pico, and sixteenth-century humanists, including Erasmus, are found in Rebhorn, *Renaissance Debates on Rhetoric*. Kathy Eden shows that *style* was central to humanist expressions of inmost feelings in letter writing, evidenced by Petrarch, Erasmus, and Montaigne. See *The Renaissance Rediscovery of Intimacy*.

4 See *The Humanism of Leonardo Bruni: Selected Texts*, 63–84.

5 Regarding Hans Baron's contrary thesis, see among many works, Hankins, "The 'Baron Thesis' after Forty Years," and *Renaissance Civic Humanism*.

6 On the relationships between rhetoric and the development of social and political theory in the early fifteenth century, see Skinner, *The Foundations of Modern Political Thought*, esp. 1:101–12.

7 On Cicero's purposes in writing *Paradoxa Stoicorum*, see Baraz, *A Written Republic*, 131–6.

assumptions and practices of ordinary folk. Only the wiseman is noble, good, happy, virtuous, rich – lacking even a penny, subject to no authority, unconquerable, immune to emotion. Contemptuous of what goes on in the world of affairs, the wiseman considers everyone else foolish and insane, not free but slaves, and sees all sins as equal.

And yet humanists had at hand a plethora of texts that detail the unitary both/and nature of Stoic ethical thought, epitomized by the wiseman.[8] Among these works were Cicero's *De finibus*, *De officiis*, *Tusculan Disputations*, *De legibus*, *Academica*, and *De natura deorum*; Seneca's many essays, such as *De constantia sapientis*, *De vita beata*, and *De tranquillitate animi*, and *Letters* (*Epistulae morales*); Diogenes Laertius' *Lives of Philosophers*; Epictetus' *Enchiridion* and *Discourses*; Plutarch's lengthy discussions of Stoicism in his *Moralia*, especially *De Stoicorum repugnantiis* and *De communibus notitiis contra Stoicos*; and, not least, the quotations, summaries, and illustrations of Stoicism in Aulus Gellius' *Attic Nights* (*Noctes Atticae*).[9]

Paul F. Grendler reveals that Italian Renaissance Latin schools gave little attention to Cicero's philosophical works, ignoring not only *Paradoxa Stoicorum*, *De finibus*, and *Tusculan Disputations* but even *De officiis*. The focus was on rhetorical rules and definitions and letters.[10] At the universities, fifteenth-century humanist professors concentrated on Latin poetic and rhetorical texts. Grendler lists the poetical and rhetorical works taught from 1458 to 1469 by Cristoforo Landino at Florence and by Angelo Poliziano, from 1480 to 1494 (which includes a number of works by Aristotle). At the University of Rome, by way of exception, Martino Filetico incorporated into his teaching between the 1470s and 1490s Cicero's *Paradoxa Stoicorum*, *Tusculan Disputations*, and *De officiis*.[11] However, Grendler does not show that *De finibus* was ever studied in fifteenth-century Italian universities.

Paradoxa Stoicorum and *De officiis*, published together in 1465, were the first works of classical literature printed.[12] Not without significance,

8 "The question which comes first, theory or practice, is not relevant to the Stoics, because philosophy is always inextricably linked to one's being in the world and in society." See Reydams-Schils, *The Roman Stoics*, 90. Cf. D.L. 7.130.

9 On the availability of these and many other relevant authors, such as Sextus Empiricus or Dio Chrysostom, see Hankins and Palmer, *The Recovery of Ancient Philosophy in the Renaissance*.

10 Grendler, *Schooling in Renaissance Italy*, 216–17.

11 Grendler, *The Universities of the Italian Renaissance*, 237–9.

12 See Ronnick "The Raison d'Être of Fust and Schoeffer's *De Officiis et Paradoxa Stoicorum*, 1465, 1466."

Paradoxa Stoicorum, with its harsh, one-dimensional, and counter-intuitive depictions of the wiseman, went through more editions (69) before 1500 than even *De officiis* (64). Since *De officiis* emphasizes the worldly side of Stoicism and *Paradoxa Stoicorum* the hard and abstract side, one could imagine those responsible for the printing had in mind the both/and nature of Stoicism. But this was clearly not the case. I know of no instance where a humanist compares the one-dimensionality of *Paradoxa Stoicorum* with the two-dimensionality of *De officiis*, the distorted view of the wiseman in the former and the unitary *honestum/utile* way of thinking focused on in the latter. *De officiis* was something of a textbook for humanists,[13] as it had been for many medieval thinkers, but the Stoic frame of the work was outside the humanist purview.

At the beginning of *De officiis* Cicero points to the Stoic focus on nature and the self-preservation instinct (1.11–14) and emphasizes that the book is framed by the Stoic way of thinking. Regarding this way of thinking he explicitly refers to the Greek words *katorthoma* and *kathekon* and states that they embody the difference between "absolute" duty, that which is "right," and "mean" or "ordinary" duty (1.8). He also points to the particular influence of the Stoic Panaetius on the first two of the three books. Near the beginning of Book 3 he discusses the frame of thought of the fabled Stoic wiseman and states that his goal is to adapt this outlook to the lives and understandings of ordinary humans (3.13–17). Throughout Book 3 he shows – "in perfect harmony with the Stoics' system and doctrines" (3.20) – that anyone who thinks the issues of life are to be seen in either/or terms, either *honestum* or *utile*, simply does not understand fundamentals. The *honestum* cannot be separated from that which is actually *utile* and that which is actually *utile* cannot be separated from *honestum*. Against Peripatetics and common opinion it is not the case that something can be *honestum* and not *utile* or *utile* and not *honestum*. The *honestum* and the *utile* (as distinct from that which is only apparently *utile*) are two very different types

13 Nearly 700 manuscript copies have been located, the overwhelming majority dated to the fifteenth century. See Winterbottom, "The Transmission of Cicero's *De Officiis*." Half of Jones' *Master Tully* describes the transits of Cicero's writings before their arrival in England. In *Humanism, Reading, and English Literature 1430–1530*, Wakelin shows the contexts within which Cicero's writings were read in England and how they were read. On the influence of *De officiis* from Cicero's death to 1500, see Walsh, *Cicero: On Obligations* xxxiv–xliv; Dyck, *A Commentary on Cicero, De Officiis*, 39–44; and Zielinski, *Cicero im Wandel der Jahrhunderte*.

of value but they are inseparable. This unitary both/and is not simply an abstract moralistic ideology; it has to be worked out anew, Cicero demonstrates, in every situation. On one side various and complex aspects of *honestum* (including not only reason per se but wisdom, justice, greatness of spirit, and decorum) have to be distinguished and applied and there is always a possibility that there are two morally right courses that have to be differentiated. On the other side, complex distinctions have to be made regarding various or unique circumstances and the most appropriate response. Does a particular course of action only appear to be *utile* or is it actually *utile*? Then too one must hold in mind that a decision will also need to be made should two actions both be *utile*.

But again, where do previous humanists see or take interest in the larger philosophic meaning of *De officiis*, not to mention the *katorthoma/kathekon* background? Far from building on Petrarch's interest in the Stoic wiseman, particularly his doctrine of *apatheia* (freedom from emotion), humanists who followed increasingly tended to ridicule Stoicism. Like Petrarch they saw little of the Stoic two-dimensional way of thinking and virtually nothing of the *katorthoma/kathekon* mindset and natural instinct at birth. They saw a Stoicism that consists of little more than rigid and abstract doctrines and often placed this outlook in an either/or frame opposite worldliness and the active life.

Petrarch in his tract "How a Ruler Ought to Govern His State" (1373) refers at one point to the dictum of Cicero, "the most learned and wisest of men," that "Nothing can be useful that is not at the same time just and honourable" (nihil esse posse utile, que non idem iustum honestumque sit) but illustrations are lacking and we are left with the belief that this is nothing but moralizing.[14] His "Dialogue on Pain" in *Remedies for Fortune Fair and Foul* portrays, like so many of his writings, a vacillating either/or frame of thought with Stoic reason (person Ratio) on one side and pain as an emotion (person Dolor) on the other.[15] Charles Trinkaus shows that Petrarch – followed by Salutati, Bruni, Valla, and other humanists – oscillated between contradictory positions, between emotion and reason, the internal and the external, subjective and objective, experienced truth and revealed truth, his own professional career

14 See Kohl and Witt, *The Earthly Republic*, 63, and Petrarch, *Opera omnia*, 1:429.

15 See *Petrarch's Remedies for Fortune Fair and Foul*, ed. and trans. Rawski, 3:267–91, 4:440–55.

and the lives of monks, pride in his worldly achievements and contemplative truths, a sense of self and an eschatological vision.[16]

Ronald Witt quotes from the letters of Coluccio Salutati (1331–1406), Florentine chancellor 1375–1406, the following statement:

> For who, I ask, without the writings of the ancients, with nature alone as a guide, will be able to explain with sufficient reason what is honest (honestum), what useful (utile) and what is the meaning of this battle of the useful and honorable? Doubtless nature makes us fit for virtues and secretly impels us to them but we are made virtuous not by nature but by works and learning.[17]

Although Witt does not tie this statement to Stoicism, much less *De officiis*, a relationship seems apparent.[18] Note the referral not only to *honestum* and *utile* but to "nature alone" as guide and the fact that nature "secretly impels," which is the Stoic "inborn seeds of virtue" theme (semina innata virtutum) (*Tusc*. 3.2).[19] But where does Salutati develop the meanings or apply this thinking to particular intellectual or worldly issues? In seeing *honestum* and *utile* as involving a "battle" he is not seeing them as Cicero saw them, as unitary, but conceptualizing a rhetorical debate between opposed positions, *in utramque partem*. Perhaps knowledge of some aspects of Stoicism increased during the fifteenth century but where is there a grasp of the two-dimensional but unitary Stoic frame of mind, one obvious exemplification being *De officiis* 3?

For a better understanding of the difficulties humanists had in seeing the Stoic *honestum/utile* mindset, let us look more closely at the place of *honestas* and *utilitas* within rhetoric. Within the three classical types of oratory – judicial, deliberative, and demonstrative (or epideictic) – the ancients had set forth various topics for discussion, particularly

---

16 See "Themes of a Renaissance Anthropology," 393, and *The Poet as Philosopher*, 89. Compare McClure, *Sorrow and Consolation in Italian Humanism*, 72, and Zak, *Petrarch's Humanism and the Care of the Self*, 158; also Mazzotta, *The Worlds of Petrarch*.

17 Witt, *Hercules at the Crossroads*, 69–70. The quote is from *Epistolario di Coluccio Salutati*, ed. Francesco Novati (Rome 1891), 1:106 (dated 1369).

18 The basis of Witt's assertion elsewhere that Stoicism influenced Salutati more than any other philosophy is unclear. It appears that Witt may be relating only particular statements in Books 1 and 2 of *De officiis*. See *Hercules at the Crossroads*, 64 passim.

19 Nature's greatest service, states Seneca, is "that Virtue causes her light to penetrate into the minds of all; even those who do not follow her see her" (*Ben*. 4.17.4).

important being *honestas* (honour) and *utilitas* (utility).[20] Orators would support one approach or the other, but not both in the same speech. In considering a particular issue, what course of action would be the most advantageous or, on the other side of debate, what would be the most honourable path? Or, by chance, could *utilitas* and *honestas* not be in conflict? Deliberative rhetoric tended to consider *utilitas* the ultimate end whereas demonstrative rhetoric considered *honestas* the ultimate end.[21] Throughout the Middle Ages and the Renaissance the two main textbooks for such issues were Cicero's *De inventione*, which he wrote as a teenager (92–88 BCE), and the pseudo-Ciceronian *Rhetorica ad Herennium* (85–80 BCE).[22] A complete copy of Quintilian's massive *Institutiones oratoriae* (c. 96 CE) was discovered only in 1416 and intact copies of Cicero's mature works, *De oratore* and *Orator*, appeared only in 1421.[23] *Rhetorica ad Herennium* focused on expediential factors and has been related to Machiavelli's *The Prince*,[24] while *De inventione* was more moralistic in tone. *De inventione* allowed that expedience (security) could override the moral on certain occasions, but this should not be the goal.[25]

Not at odds with fifteenth-century humanists they study, modern researchers have often failed to clearly distinguish rhetorical meanings of *honestas* and *utilitas* from philosophic meanings. John F. Tinkler, for example, does not look for or notice – in an often cited article – any difference in humanists' employment of *honestas* and *utilitas* in rhetoric

20 On the practice and theory of the three types of rhetoric in the classical world, see Kennedy, *A New History of Classical Rhetoric*. On their use in humanistic circles, see O'Malley, *Praise and Blame in Renaissance Rome*, esp. 36–51.

21 See Tinkler, "Praise and Advice," 204, and Cicero, *De inventione* 2.12–13, 155–75, *De oratore* 2.333–49, and *Topica* 91. Cf. however Virginia Cox, "Machiavelli and the *Rhetorica ad Herennium*."

22 See Monfasani, "Humanism and Rhetoric"; Ward, "From Antiquity to the Renaissance"; and "Renaissance Commentators on Ciceronian Rhetoric."

23 Note Matthew B. Roller's comment on Quintilian's *Institutes* 3.8.22–47: "Though the basic *divisio* he specifies for *suasoriae* nominally sets the *honestum* against the *utile*, he notes repeatedly that courses of action advocated fundamentally on the basis of utility must also be claimed as morally right, or at worst indifferent; they must never be conceded as morally wrong." See "Color-Blindness," 112. See also Ward, "Quintilian and the Rhetorical Revolution of the Middle Ages"; Monfasani, "Episodes of Anti-Quintilianism in the Italian Renaissance"; and Walzer, "Quintilian's 'Vir Bonus' and the Stoic Wise Man."

24 See Virginia Cox, "Machiavelli and the *Rhetorica ad Herennium*." Aristotle's *Rhetoric*, which was little known, also emphasized expediential factors.

25 Cicero, *De inventione* 2.156 (against Aristotle's view) and 2.174–5.

and their understanding of the meaning of *honestum* and *utile* in *De officiis*.[26] Seeing *De officiis* 3 in terms of Quintilian's rhetoric Victoria Kahn holds that Stoic *honestas* has nothing to say regarding real world effectiveness (*utilitas*).[27] Without doubt Cicero employed his rhetorical skills in composing *De officiis* but *De officiis* is a work on philosophy and here *honestum* and *utile* are built (even if augmented by rhetoric) from the thinking of Zeno and Chrysippus.[28]

Anthony Long notes that even contemporaries of Cicero would have been more familiar with the conflict between *honestas* and *utilitas* discussed in rhetorical works such as Cicero's *De oratore* (2.335) than with the definition of *honestum* and the uniting of the *honestum* and the *utile* found in *De officiis*.[29]

Not philosophers but rhetoricians: Rhetorical debate *in utramque partem*

One aspect of the humanist rhetorical approach to problem solving, also imported from classical practices, was the dialogue. The dialogue form allowed rendering of opposed positions, *in utramque partem disserere*. A negative consequence of dialogic thinking was that it allowed the trivialization of serious philosophical issues. Although Cicero had employed the dialogue in his books on philosophy (such as *De finibus*) as well as those on rhetoric (such as *De oratore*), humanists, unlike Cicero, had no significant philosophical training or expertise. Lacking a grasp of the differing suppositions, methodologies, and teachings of the various ancient philosophies, pitting a superficial grasp of a thesis

---

26 Tinkler, "Praise and Advice," 192.

27 Kahn, "*Virtu* and the Example of Agathocles in Machiavelli's *Prince*," 247.

28 Paul O. Kristeller, along with Hans Baron the most influential Renaissance historian of the twentieth century – trained in philosophy, particularly Plato – displays little knowledge of Stoic thought. "Where questions of virtue and vice are not involved the Stoic sage is allowed and even encouraged to follow expediency. With virtue and vice often limited to a few ultimate decisions, the sway of expediency becomes very large indeed, and the Stoic moralist, while continuing to be rigorous in theory, may turn out to be lax, if not selfish, on most practical questions." See *Renaissance Thought II*, 36. Cf. his *Greek Philosophers of the Hellenistic Age*, 30–1, 84.

29 Long, "Cicero's Politics in *De Officiis*," 218 n. 13. On the difference between Augustine's *uti* (or *usus*) and *frui* (or *fruitio*) and Cicero's *utile* and *honestum* and the evolution of thought on the *res publica* up through the fifteenth century, see Kempshall, "*De Re Publica* 1.39."

found in one philosophy against a superficial grasp of a thesis found in another philosophy in a rhetorical debate *in utramque partem* often did little to advance understanding. Humanist assessments of Stoicism exemplify these shortcomings. Within their dialogues, David Marsh points out, "the group often mocks or isolates dogmatic rigidity, represented in the person of an intractably 'Stoic' interlocutor out of touch with practical realities."[30] Placing the unbending side of Stoicism within a rhetorical context, it was easy not to see or take seriously the bending side of the Stoic wiseman's mindset, much less the relationships between the two sides.

Epicurean philosophy or Stoic philosophy?

The most sustained and brilliant dialogue in opposition to Stoicism was Lorenzo Valla's *De voluptate* (*On Pleasure*) (1431–49), in later editions titled *De vero falsoque bono*.[31] Influenced by Quintilian's *Institutio oratoria*, Valla looked at issues not from the standpoint of philosophy but, very consciously, as a rhetorician (cf. 2.29.12; 3.11.6).[32] Rhetoric for him included everything that involves being a human. In three books the work ridicules Stoics and their *honestum* (represented by Catone) in favour of an Epicurean-rooted pleasure philosophy (represented by Vegio). Explicitly rejecting Cicero's siding with Stoicism against pleasure philosophy, in Book 2 of *De finibus* and elsewhere, Valla shows that it is in fact pleasure and self-interest that willy-nilly govern all of life. There is all the difference between the way Stoics imagine humans should act and the way, by nature, they actually do act. The actions of even the most important worldly proponents of *honestum*, such as Cato and Scipio, were in fact self-interested. They obtained great pleasure from being heroic (2.3.3). It is silly to put country above personal advantage. Once you are dead your country is dead to you (2.1.5). It is better to save oneself than a hundred thousand people (2.1.7). "We should not fight against the crowd, as the Stoics do, but go along with it, as with a rapid river" (1.46.2). In the creation of cities and states, "no prince, administrator, or king

30 Marsh, *The Quattrocento Dialogue*, 11.

31 Valla, *On Pleasure/ De voluptate*, and *De vero falsoque bono*.

32 See Gerl, *Rhetorik als Philosophie*. Richard Waswo sees Valla as a forerunner of Ludwig Wittgenstein in that both see epistemology as one with the ordinary use of language. See *Language and Meaning in the Renaissance*, 88–113, esp. 103–4.

was ever chosen unless men expected great advantage from him" (2.32.1). Laws and concepts of justice have come about because of their usefulness to people, not because of any abstract truth (1.33.2). "You may cheat, deceive, or defraud someone in a contract; however, you should do it craftily and subtly" (2.27.3). Prudence "consists in knowing how to procure advantages for yourself and avoid what is disagreeable" (1.33.1). Kindness can be very advantageous. Life is about pleasure, not the rigidity and death advocated by the morose and marble-like Stoics (2.2.1–3). Illustrating the point, Valla spends a good deal of time on sex. The breasts and body of a nude female are beautiful (cf. 1.20.2).[33] What does it matter whether one makes love to one's wife or, provided there are no unacceptable consequences, a lover? (1.38.1). If a woman gets raped there is no sense in her killing herself (2.4.4). Honour as such is ridiculous. *Honestum* has no reality or meaning (cf. 1.35.1, 2.15.2). Not only is the hard side of Stoicism denied and ridiculed, the bending side goes unmentioned and, apparently, unnoticed. Passing over the role of indifferents in Stoicism and the fact that some are preferred and others dispreferred, Stoics are lambasted for not (like Aristotelians) allowing goods of the body and external goods (1.16.1). Although at one point Stoics are censured for "saying that the advantageous derived from the virtuous" (dicentes utile ab honesto manare) (2.32.9), there is no recognition of the both/and dynamics of Stoic thought.

In the third book Valla attempts to go beyond the views of both the Stoic Catone and the Epicurean Vegio. Raudense, a Franciscan monk, shows that the hope and faith of Christianity change everything. The beauty of women is trifling in comparison to heavenly beauty. The heavenly state will be the highest pleasure of all (3.23.5–9). Notwithstanding the introduction of Christianity, *honestum* is still seen in terms of pleasure, delight, and joy. Pleasure in this world is a stepping stone to pleasure in the hereafter. Christian pleasure *(voluptas)* motivates Christian *honestas*, not the other way around.[34]

33 Valla's emphasis on the pleasure of sex and the beauty of the female body appears to go beyond that of Epicurus and the Epicurean Lucretius (d. 55 BCE). On the latter, see Brown, *Lucretius on Love*.

34 Cf. Lorch, *A Defense of Life*, 263. *De voluptate* plays a central role in Charles Trinkaus' rendering of "*theologia rhetorica*." See his *In Our Image and Likeness*, 105–50.

Stoic nobility or inherited nobility?

While Stoicism was most commonly ridiculed,[35] Niccolo Niccoli (d. 1437) supported Stoicism. But how did he understand Stoicism and what was his motivation? Famous for his collecting of ancient works, the evidence for his Stoicism is found in a dialogue, "On Nobility" (*De nobilitate*) (1440), written by Poggio Bracciolini (d. 1459).[36]

Opposing Lorenzo Medici, Niccoli employs Stoicism in arguing against inherited wealth and a variety of current and past ideals of nobility. Custom and common opinion, he contends, are out of sync with Stoic philosophy. After a referral to things that are "good" or "evil" or "indifferent" that seems to conflate *honestum* and *turpe* with preferred indifferents and dispreferred indifferents (75, *Op.* 72–3), we are informed that nobility, as commonly understood, has no place in any of this. Goods of the body (such as health and beauty) and external goods (such as wealth) do not denote true nobility and neither, surprisingly, do goods of the mind. "Prudence makes one prudent, wisdom makes one wise, justice makes one just, temperance makes one temperate" but none of these, as such, makes one noble. True nobility is found in virtue alone (*a solis virtutibus*), not – and this is the central point of his argument – in family, country, or ancestors, and not in honours, deeds, or public offices (82, *Op.* 78).[37] When pressed Niccoli does not deny the possibility that a wealthy person can have virtue but thinks this would be rare and in any case cannot be passed on to offspring (79). Virtue must be "the controlling principle" in winning honours and public offices (83). Truth and reason alone constitute virtue and true nobility. The Stoics considered Plato the source of their view that nobility is found only in the virtue of the wise and that, "honor, which is stable and enduring, is the highest good and rules our conduct, while fortune is fleeting" (83).[38]

---

35 See McClure, *Sorrow and Consolation in Italian Humanism*, 100–3, 136–9.

36 See Bracciolini, "On Nobility" in *Knowledge, Goodness, and Power* and "De nobilitate" in *Opera Omnia*.

37 On Niccoli's equating of virtue and nobility and the fact that this theme was to become a humanist commonplace, as for example with Alberti (d. 1472), Landino (d. 1498), and Platina (d. 1481), see Skinner, *Visions of Politics*, 224–9, and *Foundations*, 1:82.

38 Niccoli cites Diogenes Laertius on Plato's four categories of nobility (6.72) (83). *De officiis* 1.15 ties *honestum* with Plato's statement that "if it could be seen with the physical eye, it would awaken a marvellous love of wisdom" (*Phaedrus* 250d).

In response, Lorenzo Medici cites Aristotle on the importance of things such as wealth and health for virtue and contrasts Stoics. For Stoics, "generosity is a disposition of the mind, not a deed" (82). Like a philosopher hidden in his study, "virtually unknown even unto himself," Stoics like Niccoli lead "a lonely, destitute existence, since it does not advance the society and community of people" (87).

To which Niccoli replies that one can be noble without involvement in worldly affairs. Learning tied to virtue, even if one leads an isolated life, can result in knowledge of what things should be desired and avoided (87).[39] "What need has virtue of external aid when, content with its own resources and wealth, it excels all other things?" (88) (cf. *Fin.* 3.75, *Par.* 6). At the conclusion we learn that besides being the truest view (cf. *Tusc.* 5.82), Stoic virtue can be more useful than other philosophies in everyday life. But how, we may wonder? How can perfect, abstract, and unbending virtue help humans in their day-to-day activities? Seeing Stoicism in one-dimensional terms, Niccoli imagines that in simply putting aside common ideas of nobility humans would discard the laziness evident in accepting what they are born with and be motivated to seek true nobility, as well as happiness and immortality, by right action (89, *Op.* 83).

Nowhere does Niccoli take up the Stoic distinction between appropriate actions (*kathekonta*) and the right actions (*katorthomata*) inherent to virtue. What Niccoli conveniently passes over is the fact that wealth and money-making are, in Stoicism, not denigrated. What matters – Erasmus would see – is only how wealth is treated and how one makes money. Making money by trickery or craft is not expedient, for it destroys the very basis of civilization, "the law of nature," "a bond of fellowship uniting all men" (*Off.* 3.69). While wealth separated from *honestum* quickly turns into vice, wealth tied to *honestum* results in worldly attitudes and practices that are at one and the same time truly expedient and truly honourable.

> As for property, it is a duty to make money, but only by honorable means; it is a duty also to save it and increase it by care and thrift (*Off.* 2.87). "When a man enters the foot-race," says Chrysippus with his usual aptness, "it is his duty to put forth all his strength and strive with all his might

39 Cf. Bruni, n. 71 below.

to win; but he ought never with his foot to trip, or with his hand to foul a competitor." (*Off.* 3.42)[40]

Niccoli quotes (85) Seneca's statement in Letter 44 that "the mind makes us noble," but Seneca does not here argue against nobility as an institution. What Seneca emphasizes is that nobility does not depend on one's profession or position in life. Niccoli's opposition to inherited wealth and inherited position may be important, historically considered, but it was not Seneca's concern (albeit he advises living simply, *Tr.* 8.9). And in tying Plato so closely to Stoicism Niccoli misses the uniqueness of both Stoicism and Plato.[41] In short, he may have glimpsed, as represented by Poggio, some of the pins that make up the Stoic way of thinking but he had not deeply absorbed the Stoic *honestum/utile* frame of mind. He wanted to depose inherited wealth and status and the "laziness" of those who had such, and Stoicism provided a tool. As represented by Poggio, his Stoicism was primarily motivated by his animosity towards a certain segment of society.[42]

Unlike Niccoli, Francesco Filelfo (1398–1481) brings in Stoicism in support of the noble class, in his *Oratio* and *Commentationes* (1440s). Nobles must seek honour in a world where expediency, calculation, and self-interest (epitomized in his mind by Cosimo de Medici) is more and more the rule. While the discussants note that for Stoics *utilitas* has a secondary value deriving from the pursuit of *virtus*, Palla holds to the contrary that right actions are not necessarily both beneficial and virtuous and decides to argue only in terms of abstract and one-dimensional

40 A.A. Long points out that Aristotle, the Epicureans, and the Cynics all assume that some individuals will be property owners but with Stoics, property ownership, since Chrysippus, served "as the foundation for a theory about the common interests and rights of all human beings." See "Stoic Philosophers on Persons, Property-Ownership and Community," 18. Regarding Stoicism and *De officiis* on property, see Erskine, *The Hellenistic Stoa*, 103–22, 210; Neal Wood, *Cicero's Social and Political Thought*, 11, 68, 105–19, 131–2; and Long, "Cicero's Politics in *De Officiis*," 233–40. Long sees the discussions of society and property in *De officiis* as a continuation of the conclusion to Cato's discussion of Stoicism in Book 3 of *De finibus* (233).

41 Politian (Poliziano) (1454–94), it may be noted, translated the Stoic Epictetus' *Enchiridion* (1479) and yet, in defending Epictetus from the attacks of Bartolomeo Scala, argued on various grounds that Plato inspired the work. Jill Kraye discusses and translates Politian's Letter to Bartolomeo Scala in *Cambridge Translations of Renaissance Philosophical Texts I*, 192–9.

42 Cf. Rabil, *Knowledge, Goodness, and Power*, 61.

virtue – the happy man's *recta ratio*, divorced from political affiliations.[43] Rather than arguing about whether the *honestum* or the *utile* should be sought, he declares, at one point, that they are both found in the ineffable good that is the divine mind.[44]

Active life or contemplative life?

Nor do we find anything of the Stoic unitary contemplative/active life in fourteenth- and fifteenth-century discussions. Salutati's discussions, for example, range over the entire active/contemplative spectrum. They may have had value in opening up various avenues of thought, but considered from the standpoint of consistency or logic they are very weak. His most insistent support for the active life is found in *De nobilitate legum et medicine* (1399), important historically because, according to Witt, Salutati was "the first thinker of the early Renaissance even to suggest that the active life of the layman could be equal or superior to the contemplative life of the monk."[45] Debating whether law or medicine is the more useful, Salutati comes down heavily on the side of law. Law relates to the active life and the lawyer, in carrying out his functions, not only benefits this world but earns salvation in the next world. The physician, on the other hand, deals with speculative matters, in seclusion, and attempts to benefit not society as a whole but individuals. Missing, however, is an ultimate resolution, a definitive statement regarding the relationship of the active and contemplative lives.[46] *De seculo et religione*, written earlier (c. 1381), but at a time when the author was already deeply involved in governmental affairs, far from arguing for a secular life condemns it.[47] A friend is advised to love God and poverty and to hate the world and riches. Highest sanctity and merit are found in the life of religious and his friend should submit to a harsh monastic existence. A letter of 1398, on the other hand, takes more of an intermediate position. But even here there are major problems. Salutati contends that a choice must be made between the active and contemplative lives and yet he himself finds no solution.[48] At one point we

43 See Blanchard, "Patrician Sages and the Humanist Cynic," 1150–9.
44 See Filelfo, *On Exile*, 2.151.
45 Kohl and Witt, *Earthly Republic*, 90.
46 Cf. Witt, *Hercules at the Crossroads*, 425.
47 Trinkaus, *In Our Image and Likeness*, 662–74.
48 Witt, *Hercules at the Crossroads*, 350, 351.

learn that worldly actions, such as serving family, friends, and country, can be stepping-stones to heaven while in another location we are told that the person living the contemplative life inevitably has worldly contacts, as evidenced by Christ himself.[49]

With much greater cogency, Valla argues in *De voluptate* that the contemplative life must be seen in terms of the active. With regard to the wisdom that is contemplation, even Aristotle is not spared. Aristotle did not understand, any more than Stoics, that contemplation is not a static and heavenly felicity but a type of labour and activity. Contemplation is "a progressive process of learning, which we sometimes call interpretive reflection and sometimes invention, which is proper to men and not to gods" (2.28.9). The contemplation represented by *honestum* must likewise be brought down from its pedestal and entirely recast in terms of rhetoric and the active life.

But perhaps a more common referral to the contemplative life among early fifteenth-century humanists had not so much to do with Franciscan ideals or reconceptualizing contemplation in terms of the active life as distinguishing the life of learning from involvement in governmental affairs. In his *De Infelicitate Principum* (1440), Poggio has Niccoli argue that all princes, whether good or bad, are unhappy and from this standpoint praises scholarly retirement, seen as the *vita contemplative.* Learning is the only way to *virtus*.[50]

Later in the century otherworldly conceptions of the contemplative life weighed heavy for two interrelated reasons. The political environment in Florence and elsewhere became more autocratic and rigid – which meant less important roles for humanists – and Neoplatonism came to be a very dominant intellectual force among humanists. Inspired in particular by Marsilio Ficino's unprecedented translations from Greek of all of Plato's works (published 1484) and his voluminous discussions and commentaries on Plato's writings, Neoplatonism spread from Florence to other areas of Europe, including England. Ficino saw Plato in spiritualist and mystical terms, influenced in particular by Plotinus but also Dionysius the Aeropagite, Proclus, and Augustine. He considered Plato entirely superior to Aristotle and even more superior to the scholastic employment of Aristotle. As exemplified by his *Platonic*

49 Salutati, Letter to Peregrino Zambeccari, in Kohl and Witt, *Earthly Republic*, 93–114 at 110, 112.

50 See Kajanto, "Poggio Bracciolini's *De Infelicitate Principum*."

Theology: On the Immortality of Souls (1482), he focused his thinking on the spiritual ascent to the highest good, seen as the vision of God, and the immortality of the soul.[51] He did not see Plato's message as complex and multisided and developmental but one-dimensional and normative. James Hankins points out that in his translation of *Gorgias* he interprets the sharp interchanges between Socrates, Gorgias, and Callicles as mere playful sparring, covering up Plato's real, albeit hidden, views.[52]

Although some of these humanists may have believed that Neoplatonist beliefs could affect by osmosis worldly and political actions, this was little demonstrated.[53] According to Kristeller, the leading Platonists "tended to reduce all ethical questions to the single task of attaining the contemplative life."[54] In line with this argument, the Neoplatonist Cristoforo Landino (1424–1504) lectured on *Tusculan Disputations* early in his career (in 1458) and saw this work as related essentially to the contemplative life. His lectures in the years that followed were exclusively concerned with poetry and rhetoric.[55] And it is only within a Neoplatonist frame that he has several humanists compare the merits of the active and the contemplative life in his *Disputationes Camaldulenses* (c. 1474).[56]

In short, fourteenth- and fifteenth-century humanists were concerned with the opposed or comparative merits of the active and contemplative lives. Their outlooks had little in common with the Stoic unitary contemplative/active, active/contemplative way of thinking.[57]

Bruni favoured Aristotle

Florentine chancellor from 1427 to 1444, Leonardo Bruni is noted for his appreciation not only of Cicero the author but of Cicero the man of affairs and republican. And yet how closely had he actually read Cicero's

51 Ficino, *Platonic Theology*. The editors outline Ficino's arguments in volume 6, 319–26.

52 Hankins, *Plato in the Italian Renaissance*, 1:53–8, 327, 330; 2:394–6. See also Ficino, *Marsilio Ficino: The Philebus Commentary*, ed. and trans. M.J.B. Allen, 22.

53 Cf. Field, *The Origins of the Platonic Academy of Florence*, 191, 260, and Hankins, *Plato in the Italian Renaissance*, 1:294–6. On the relation or nonrelation of Ficino's thought to the Medici autocracy, see Mahoney, "Marsilio Ficino and Renaissance Platonism," 241–4.

54 Kristeller, *Renaissance Thought II*, 35.

55 Field, *The Origins of the Platonic Academy of Florence*, 242–7.

56 See Lackner, "The Camaldolese Academy."

57 Nor do the many discussions of the active and contemplative lives in Vickers, *Arbeit, Musse, Meditation* consider relationships to the Stoic both/and way of thinking or describe comparable ties between the active and contemplative lives.

extensive writings on philosophy and Stoicism in particular? In "Cicero *novus*" (1416) he discusses Cicero's speeches and letters and reconstructs his political involvements, but regarding Cicero's philosophical works states only that he was the first to expound philosophy in Latin.[58] Discussing in the same year his reasons for translating Aristotle's *Ethics*, alleging that previous translations such as that of Robert Grosseteste (d. 1253) were barbarous, he brings in at one point the word *honestum*. What word, he asks – missing the distinctiveness of the Stoic meaning – could be more common? Seneca, the Stoic, says all goods should be referred to it and "we often say, 'All virtuous actions are contained in the *honestum*.'" Immediately he launches into a sustained criticism of Grosseteste for confusing the Greek equivalent of *honestum* (*kalon*) with the Latin word *bonum*.[59] In "An Isagogue of Moral Philosophy" (1425) he refers to Stoic *honestum* and points out that for the wiseman virtue is in itself sufficient for happiness, no matter the poverty or pain that may befall him and that bodily or external advantages or disadvantages are not evil. He connects *honestum* with an act done virtuously, laudably, well, bravely, with self control, nobly, properly, beautifully (cf. *Fin.* 2.45–50, *Off.* 1.14) – but without discussion.[60] Nor does he mention the inherency of reason and nature to *honestum*. Allowing that Stoicism is a "manly" doctrine, he doubts at the same time its truth and turns to his real interest, the moral views of Aristotle, whose *Nicomachaen Ethics* he had earlier translated and discussed at some length. Referring to Peripatetic views, he distinguishes three types of goods: goods of the soul, bodily goods, and external goods. After stating that happiness is the greatest and most important of the goods of the soul, he correctly distinguishes between Peripatetic "goods" and "evils" (271) and Stoic advantages (*commoda*) and disadvantages (*incommoda*) (i.e., "preferred" and "dispreferred" indifferents) (272). Further on, however, he holds, in line with the revisionist argument set forth in Books 4 and 5 of *De finibus*, that the differences between the Peripatetic and Stoic positions are merely verbal (273). Likewise, Epicureans, Stoics, and Peripatetics all say, we are told, virtually the same thing regarding the highest good. Referring to Aristotle's distinction between intellectual virtues (relating to apprehension of truth) and moral virtues (actions and dispositions)

58 See Fryde, "The Beginnings of Italian Humanist Historiography," 550.

59 Bruni, *The Humanism of Leonardo Bruni*, 215.

60 Bruni, "Isagogicon moralis disciplinae," in *Leonardo Bruni Aretino*, 20–41 at 26.24–7. Translated in *The Humanism of Leonardo Bruni*, 267–82 at 271–2.

(274), and between universal or perfect justice and particular justice (279), he says nothing about the Stoic distinction between *katorthomata* (right actions) and *kathekonta* (appropriate actions), possibly believing, as does Lapo da Castiglionchio in 1438, that the Stoics simply followed Aristotle's thinking.[61] With Aristotle, moral virtue is a "mean" between excess and defect (274) and, thus, *prudentia* is a fleeing from extremes. Surprisingly, he equates "prudential," as a "mean," with "right reason" (*recta ratio*), failing to understand or at least point out that right reason is a theme central to Stoicism and has a very different meaning (281, Bruni, *Schriften* 38).

Hans Baron – ever so influential – has shown at length that humanists such as Bruni were moving away from Stoicism, which they equated with Franciscan ideals of poverty and contempt for possessions,[62] and towards more worldly outlooks regarding wealth, marriage, and worldly betterment in general.[63]

One could imagine that in taking pride in being a man of affairs, Bruni would have seen and been interested in the Stoic unitary worldly/non-worldly, bending/unbending frame of mind. But such was not the case. The *honestum/utile* political goals of *De officiis* 3 were directly relevant[64] yet Bruni saw nothing of this. He strongly identified with Cicero's involvement in affairs of state, rhetorical interests, and writings, but did not grasp Cicero's mindset, a mindset that had been moulded above all (even though he was an adherent of the Academic school) by Stoicism. Therewith Bruni did not grasp that *De officiis* 3 is not so

61 Lapo da Castiglionchio the Younger states, as a matter of fact, that Cicero follows Aristotle's distinction between intellectual virtues and moral virtues in referring to "middle duties" and *katorthomata* in Book 1 of *De officiis*. See Celenza, *Renaissance Humanism and the Papal Curia*, 53–5.

62 Baron, *In Search of Florentine Civic Humanism*, 1:162, and *The Crisis of the Early Italian Renaissance*. Writing before the flowering of studies of ancient Stoicism, Baron saw Stoicism in one-dimensional abstract terms not unrelated to the views of the humanists he studied, which resulted in contradictions regarding the meaning of *De officiis*. See, for example, his interpretation of Matteo Palmieri's *Vita civile* (1430s), where sometimes he judges *De officiis* in terms of Cicero the non-worldly Stoic (*In Search of Florentine Civic Humanism*, 1:147, 234–5), and at other times in terms of Cicero the worldly non-Stoic or anti-Stoic (ibid., 1:125).

63 On the benefits of wealth see Bruni's introduction to his translation of the *Economics*, then attributed to Aristotle, in *Humanism of Leonardo Bruni*, 305–6, *Schriften*, 120–1. On the essentiality of marriage, see his notes to the *Economics*, in *Humanism of Leonardo Bruni*, 312–15.

64 See n. 8 above.

much a demonstration of particular courses of action as an illustration of the methods, two-dimensional but unitary, by which issues need to be addressed (*Off.* 1.59).

Unlike Bruni, Cicero and Seneca saw their own deep involvements in political affairs as inseparable from a higher two-dimensional outlook. Cicero's decisions and activities in the months and years that preceded his beheading are instructive. His letters, which reveal his sincere beliefs and feelings, show him in the years 50–49 debating with himself incessantly regarding whether to join Pompey or Caesar or neither and holding in hand ideals very comparable to those set forth in *De officiis*. At one point, for example, he speaks contemptuously of Caesar for espousing mere expediency (*utilitas*) without *honestas*.[65] Note also M.R. Wright's comment on Cicero's explication of Stoicism in Book 3 of *De finibus*: "The three philosopher-politicians involved in the book – Cicero who wrote it, Cato the propounder of the ethics involved, and Brutus to whom it was dedicated – did not avoid practical involvement, but defended the Republic unto death."[66] While counsellor to the nefarious emperor Nero and involved in the hurley-burley of court life, Seneca set forth work after work describing Stoic *honestum/utile* truths, including wise courses of action for a ruler – ending in his forced suicide in 65 CE. In *De tranquillitate* Seneca advises Serenus to do what Zeno, Cleanthes, and Chrysippus advocated but did not carry out (1.10) and be as active as possible in worldly affairs and not withdraw if he comes face to face with rampant chicanery and evil (3.1–5). Although retreat is sometimes necessary, one must retreat only gradually and without surrendering principles (4.1). Impressed by Seneca's emphasis in some works on the active life and his use of military metaphors, Neal Wood has considered the possibility of an influence on Machiavelli, in particular his *The Prince* (1513).[67] For good reason Wood does not consider an influence on Bruni. Bruni saw little of Stoic worldliness and determination, much less a militaristic, unitary both/and, mentality. James Hankins sees Bruni's celebration

65 See Brunt, "Cicero's *Officium* in the Civil War," 15. See also Griffin, "Philosophy, Politics and Politicians at Rome," and, though related to modern issues, Vaughn, "Cicero and Mario."

66 Wright, "Cicero on Self-Love," 193. In *De finibus* Cato states that "the wiseman should desire to engage in politics and government" (3.68).

67 Neal Wood, "Some Aspects of the Thought of Seneca and Machiavelli."

of the glory won by knights and condottieri in defending the liberty of Florence as merely a reflection of civic religion.[68]

Bruni marvelled at Cicero's ability to be a man of letters and involved in the active life and yet did not grasp what it was that held his writings and life together. "If you read his books and works, you would never think he had the leisure for a public career. On the other hand, if you consider his deeds, his controversies, his occupations, his battles, in both the public and private sector, you would think he could have had no time left for reading and writing."[69] Similarly, in his "Lives of Dante and Petrarch," more read by humanists than any other early fifteenth-century work,[70] Bruni admires Dante above Petrarch in that Dante was involved in politics and worldly affairs as well as being an intellectual.[71] But this literature/public affairs duality is not what Cicero focuses on in *De officiis*.

There is all the difference between the ability to perform two activities, one intellectual the other worldly, one literary and one public affairs, and a deeply thought out two-sided but unitary philosophic mindset. *Honestum* is no more "literary" than is *utile* and *utile* is no more "public affairs" than is *honestum*. Nor does this Stoic mental stance comprise on one side a wisdom consisting of hard truths and on the other a rhetoric that relates these truths (bending them if need be) to worldly practices.[72] Since the Stoic mindset is worldly as well as abstract this means that the

68 Bruni, *History of the Florentine People*, 1:x.

69 Bruni, "The New Cicero" (*Cicero novus*), in *Humanism of Leonardo Bruni*, 184–9 at 187; *Schriften*, 113–20 at 115.

70 Baron, *In Search of Florentine Civic Humanism*, 1:133. Hankins shows that Bruni was "the best selling author of the fifteenth century." See *Humanism of Leonardo Bruni*, 45.

71 See Bruni, *Humanism of Leonardo Bruni*, 85–100; *Schriften*, 50–69. Bruni holds that even when Cicero was involved in the contemplative life, reading and writing were for serving his country and other humans – which was precisely the way he also judged Aristotle's purposes. See Hankins in Bruni, *Humanism of Leonardo Bruni*, 264. Cf. Cicero, *Off.* 3.1–2, and Baraz, *A Written Republic*. See also Seneca, *Tr.* 4.8, *Ep.* 68.2, *Ot.* 6.4–5, *Brev.* 18.2.

72 Long ago Jerrold Seigel argued – a thesis that has had a long life – that philosophy is by its nature anti-civic and that rhetoric is by its nature practical and civic and that this was the way Cicero saw it followed by Petrarch and other humanists (resulting in all sorts of contradictions). See Seigel, "'Civic Humanism' or Ciceronian Rhetoric?" 35 and 36, and *Rhetoric and Philosophy in Renaissance Humanism*. In a related argument, Victoria Kahn has contended that rhetoric is concerned, exclusively, with worldly practices and worldly prudence. See her *Rhetoric, Prudence, and Skepticism in the Renaissance*.

rules of implementation are written into the philosophy. Rhetoric must take account of the worldly rules as well as the accompanying abstract precepts.

"Mirror-for-princes" treatises and the one-dimensional Stoicism Machiavelli criticized

In considering the proposition that no humanist prior to Erasmus ever truly grasped or employed the Stoic unitary both/and – *katorthoma/kathekon, honestum/indifferens, honestum/utile* – frame of thought, many scholars may think, prima facie, that the humanist *speculum principis* or "mirror-for-princes" literature so criticized by Machiavelli in *The Prince* (1513) proves the contrary.[73] Among others, the following individuals produced treatises on princely rule: Bartolomeo Sacchi (1471), Diomede Carafa (c. 1480), Platina (c. 1481), Giuniano Majo (c. 1492), Francesco Patrizi (c. 1494), Giovanni Pontano (c. 1503), Poggio Bracciolini (1504), Filippo Beroaldo (c. 1509).[74] Quentin Skinner demonstrated long ago the focus of these works on virtue and on a one-to-one relationship between the prince holding to virtue and the welfare of both himself and his state.[75] The virtues most discussed were honour, glory, fame, liberality, magnificence, and clemency. Various virtues were added to these – Patrizi naming a total of forty.[76] That which is most virtuous is by that very fact the most useful. It is precisely this one-to-one relationship between virtuousness and usefulness that Machiavelli attacks. What is virtuous, he demonstrates, is not necessarily useful – and may in fact be very destructive.

Peter Stacey has now shown in his *Roman Monarchy and The Renaissance Prince* that the mirror-for-princes treatises were primarily built from the thinking found in Seneca's *De clementia* and not as had been believed from (other than some secondary points) *De officiis*. While *De clementia*, written in 56 CE, focuses on the virtues needed by a prince, specifically the emperor Nero, *De officiis*, written in 44 BCE, takes into

73 James Hankins may well be thinking of this mirror literature where he states that "all" humanist moral thought before Machiavelli embodies the conviction that there can be no conflict between the moral and the useful. See "Humanism and the Origins of Modern Political Thought," 136.

74 Erasmus was to publish in 1516 a work in this genre, his *Institutio principis christiani*.

75 Skinner, *Foundations*, 1:116–38.

76 See Skinner, *Machiavelli*, 40.

consideration a quite different world and strongly opposes tyranny. Also like *De clementia* the humanist discussions represent Stoic conceptions of fate and providence and the need for constancy, nothing of which is to be found in *De officiis*. The purposes of the two works also differed. Correlating with humanist interest in influencing the Renaissance prince, Seneca's goal, as an advisor to Nero, was to move Nero to practise the ideals of the Stoic wiseman. Employing flattery and persuasion Seneca argues that the emperor relates to god and he is like a father over his children. His behaviour affects for good or ill the entire realm and as a result both his security and his honour (*De clementia* 1.11.4). Again and again he describes what the emperor, as wiseman, will do and what he will not do. The more successful a ruler is at applying Stoic doctrines the happier things will be for himself and his state. Cicero's goal, in contrast, was to show ordinary or at least less-exalted humans – humans lacking the perfection of the Stoic wiseman – how to look at and work out the problems of life.

What most readers, in the fifteenth century as now, have taken away from *De clementia* is one-dimensional – top down – thinking. Doctrines exist that are manifestly true in that they represent reason and being true are entirely applicable in the real world, and the ruler needs to apply these doctrines "as is" to the issues that confront him. Peter Stacey thus sees the thinking imbibed by the humanists as propounding "universal reason" (313), "providential reason" (61), "a monological and univocal conception of *ratio*" (211), and "perfect rationality" (63). In Stacey's view, Seneca's *honestum/utile* formula "demands that you deny that there is, in fact, anything contingent at all about the world."

> Since Seneca's political theory is articulated within a firmly Stoic metaphysics, the question of a conflict between calculations of what is *dignum* [*honestum*] and what is *utile* never arises. To act virtuously is simply to act in accordance with beneficent, providential reason. (14)

The task of rhetoric is to transfer, with exemplifications and the like, these rational truths to the hearts of rulers (199).

In *The Prince* Machiavelli goes all out to show that the mirror-for-princes treatises are wrong, not just conceptually but experientially. As stated in chapter 15, regarding the idea that a prince needs to practice virtue: "some of the things that appear to be virtues will, if he practises them, ruin him, and some of the things that appear to be vices will bring him security and prosperity."[77] In short, Machiavelli dethrones universal reason and the virtues associated with this reason. Rejecting previous humanist discussions of the role of fortune and providence, he shows how the prince needs to act if he is to hold on to his state. He must respond to ever-changing actualities prudently and forcefully, sometimes even impetuously and angrily, in terms of actual self-interest – not theoretical self-interest. What matters is not constancy but the ability to deal with circumstances as they happen. At odds with the virtues described in the mirror-for-princes treatises, virtue is for Machiavelli, in the words of Skinner, "whatever range of qualities the prince may find it necessary to acquire in order to 'maintain his state' and 'achieve great things.'"[78]

What remains to be analysed, however, is the very different mind-sets that frame the contrasting themes of *De clementia* and *De officiis*. Humanists, including Machiavelli, seem to have seen the thinking of *De clementia* in one-dimensional terms, but did they understand the frame of mind worked out in *De officiis* 3? *De clementia* and *De officiis* represent two very different versions of Stoicism. Although *De clementia* was written by a Stoic and *De officiis* by an Academic, note first that *De clementia*, unlike *De officiis*, nowhere describes two very different types of value that unite. Nor are the words *honestum* and *utile*, or *honestum* and *indifferens*, or *katorthoma* and *kathekon* – or the distinctions they represent – referred to.

Above all Seneca wants to instil in the ruler's mind a proper attitude. Health, for example, is in *De clementia* not a preferred indifferent but simply a matter of attitude. "Good health flows to the body from the head" (2.1.1).[79] Compare clemency, the central theme. Clemency "forms its judgements not according to the letter of the law but according to what is right and good" (2.7.3). Clemency is not about excessive harshness nor is it about pity. It is about controlled leniency. The antithesis of clemency is cruelty not strictness (2.4.1). Clemency sides with reason (2.5.1) while pity is "a sickness of the mind" (2.5.4) which does not go to the cause but the situation (2.5.1). While the wiseman ruler will not pity he will offer help and thus benefit the common good (2.6.3). Pointing to the complexity of humans and the difficulty of handling them properly,

77 Machiavelli, *The Prince*, 51.

78 Skinner, *Foundations*, 1:138.

79 Seneca, *De clementia*, ed. and trans. Braund.

Seneca asks the emperor to recognize that humans suffer from diseases of the mind (a core Stoic thesis) and that he should see himself as a doctor (1.17.1–2).[80] While the wiseman does not pardon ("since the person who grants pardon is admitting that he neglected to do something he should have done")[81] he does offer clemency. Depending on the person and circumstances he may issue only a verbal reprimand or even – if, for example, a person has committed a crime when drunk and is sorry – let a person go free (2.72). Even leaders of opposing armies and traitors can on occasion be exempted from punishment. One concrete example given is Augustus' handling of Cinna, a person who had wanted to kill him and take over the government (1.9).[82]

Note that in the above Seneca sees the emperor responding in useful ways to certain variable worldly situations – employing unbending principles. So it is not the case, as Stacey contends, that *De clementia* "demands that you deny that there is, in fact, anything contingent at all about the world" (14). And yet, notwithstanding the referrals to humanity, Susanna Braund believes Seneca's models of rulers "depart from the human measure, either rising to god-like beneficence or descending into beast-like ferocity."[83] What stands out for her, it appears, is a polarity, on one side *honestum* and on the other *inhonestum*, the Stoic virtue/vice dicotomy. Certainly we do not clearly glimpse in *De clementia* a two-dimensional mindset – a mindset comprised of two distinctive types of value that unite.

So why did late fifteenth-century humanists fall, once again, for Stoic abstract principles? One might think they had learned their lessons regarding Stoicism. While fourteenth-century humanists had been impressed by Stoicism, a Stoicism they saw as rejecting all emotion, aloof to worldly affairs and worldly goods, and advocating the contemplative life, fifteenth-century humanists such as Bruni had come to denigrate this unworldly Stoicism. And yet, looking for a way to advise

80 Discussing various Stoic procedures Cicero emphasizes the need "to consider what method of treatment is admissible in each particular case" (*Tusc.* 3.79).

81 Comparing the idea of a moral judge in *De clementia*, *De ira*, and *De beneficiis* Brad Inwood believes *De clementia* 2.7 is arguing that the wiseman "will become wise after having erred, and awareness of that personal history will enter into his subsequent judgments." See "Moral Judgment in Seneca," 80.

82 Unlike any other ancient moral philosophy, in Stoicism narratives and examples play a central role. See Nussbaum, *The Therapy of Desire*, 339.

83 Seneca, *De clementia*, 40.

princes, a great many late fifteenth-century humanists clearly believed that Stoic one-dimensional principles could and should be applied "as is" by real-world princes. They were awaiting, it might seem, a Machiavelli, a person who would clarify their thinking and show them that here too Stoicism is a sham – abstract nonsense.

And yet there was another route humanists could have taken had they grasped the two-dimensional, *katorthoma/kathekon*, nature of Stoicism. Contrast the detailed defining and illustrating of *honestum* on one side and *utile* on the other in *De officiis*. Here we are shown two distinct types of value and the various ways in which they unite. While in *De clementia* rhetoric must make one-dimensional abstractions live, in *De officiis* rhetoric must deal in prescribed ways with the *utile* as well as the *honestum*. Cicero's goal in *De officiis* 3 is not so much to teach readers what to think as how to think, how to work out worldly issues (1.59). Although Cicero well recognizes that the Stoic wiseman, as such, effortlessly ties together the *honestum* and the *utile* (3.13–17), he systematically describes the components of these concepts and illustrates with worldly examples how laymen can apply Stoic two-dimensional but unitary thinking to their own lives.

Considering Machiavelli's argument in *The Prince* and the fact that he was very clearly responding to the one-dimensional views of Stoicism portrayed in the mirror-for-princes literature, there is no reason to believe that he any more than other humanists grasped the two-dimensional thinking found in *De officiis* 3. Cicero would hold, it may be imagined, that Machiavelli's view is simply a sophisticated development of a pervasive assumption, this being, as described in *De officiis*, that acts can be "morally right without being expedient, and expedient without being morally right" (2.9). Even the Peripatetics believe, states Cicero, "that something not expedient may be morally right and that something not morally right may be expedient" – which is why he does not here follow their thinking but the Stoic "system and doctrines" (3.20).[84] Cicero might also criticize modern historians in that they too tend not to see the two-dimensional but unitary Stoic

84 Marcia L. Colish long ago pointed out ties that can be found between *The Prince* and *De officiis* but her claim that Cicero made the *utile* the norm of *honestum* and redefined *honestum* as *medium officium* contradicts what the text explicitly states and shows. See "Cicero's *De officiis* and Machiavelli's *Prince*," 86–7. Michelle Zerba, for one, accepts Colish's contention in relating *De oratore* to *The Prince*, in "The Frauds of Humanism," 219 and n. 14.

mindset. Stacey thus concludes that since the Stoics do not think in terms of a bipartite or tripartite soul (unlike Aristotle or Plato) their thinking relates only to two either/or poles, either virtue or vice, either rational or irrational (72). What is missed here is the distinctive and all-important roles of *kathekon, indifferens,* and *utile*. Seeing *De officiis* in largely fifteenth-century terms, Skinner (1) does not recognize that *De officiis* is a Stoic work, (2) holds that Cicero added *honestum* to the four cardinal virtues (whereas in fact these virtues are parts of *honestum,* as at *Off.* 1.15), and (3) does not differentiate the meaning of *honestum* from the meaning of honesty, which he defines as "a willingness to keep faith and deal honorably with all men at all times" (rather than something that "merits praise even though it be praised by none," *Off.* 1.14).[85]

Even Seneca often works out the two-dimensional frame of Stoic thought, only shadows of which are found in *De clementia*. In *De tranquillitate,* for example, he takes far more account than in *De clementia* of variable real-world situations and how the wiseman can deal with them. *De tranquillitate* shows that the wiseman is in fact an unrivalled expert at coping with evil and change, at recognizing and dealing with the uncertainty of events, the possibilities of error, the obstacles that confront him (14.1; and above, p. 37). The wiseman is an expert because of his incomparable abilities in "selecting" according to nature and in deciding on "appropriate actions" and because of the reservation clauses that he builds into every goal (13.3). If his goals in government or public affairs do not work out, reservation clauses are always present, expressed or unexpressed. Every aim is qualified by an "unless" clause: he will do a particular thing unless for various reasons this turns out to be inadvisable or impossible.[86]

Strikingly, the two-dimensional *katorthoma/kathekon* based reasoning represented by Cicero in *De officiis 3*, and not grasped by humanists, is uniquely set forth by none other than Seneca himself in some of his later letters. Letters 94 and 95 show in detail that the *honestum* and the *utile,* though different words are employed (*decreta* and *praecepta*), do not comprise one type of value but two and the nature of these

85 Skinner, *Machiavelli,* 40–1.

86 Cf. *Ben.* 4.4–5. In consideration of reservation clauses it cannot be assumed that Seneca's long involvement with the nefarious emperor Nero in itself signifies breakdowns of his Stoicism. On reservation clauses, see in particular Inwood, *Ethics and Human Action in Early Stoicism,* 119–26.

values.[87] In Letter 94 we learn that "Virtue is divided into two parts, contemplation of truth and conduct" (In duas partes virtus dividitur, in contemplationem veri et actionem) (45). Letter 95 shows at length that "philosophy is both theoretic and practical; it contemplates at the same time as it acts" (Philosophia autem et contemplative est et activa; spectat simul agitque) (10). Honourable conduct requires, simultaneously, both *praecepta* and *decręta* (6–7). On the former side are "rules regarding what one should do and avoid" (13),[88] on the latter "a fixed and unchanging standard of judgment" (57). *Praecepta* are manifest, *decreta* are concealed (64). *Praecepta* are concerned with the tools of life (8) while *decreta,* though by themselves ineffectual (34), embrace the whole of life (58). *Praecepta* "add new points of view to those which are inborn and correct depraved ideas" (94.30) while *decreta* are "the means of unswerving decision" (95.62). *Precepta* need *decreta,* for "The same act may be either shameful or honorable, the purpose and the manner make all the difference" (43). In short, *praecepta* and *decreta* comprise the inescapable components of all thought (60).[89]

Conclusion

The propositions broached at the beginning of Part I have now been affirmed:

(1) No humanist prior to Erasmus, and not even Machiavelli in 1513, ever truly grasped – or had cause to grasp, considering prevailing social, political, intellectual, and religious factors – the Stoic

87 Dyck finds reason to believe that *De officiis 3* leans in certain passages on the source later used by Seneca in discussing *praecepta* and *decreta.* See *A Commentary on Cicero, De Officiis,* 524. Note that neither *praecepta* nor *utile* are indifferents. I.G. Kidd points out that Cicero ties *praecepta* with *officia* without comment (*Off.* 1.7, 3.121). See "Moral Actions and Rules in Stoic Ethics," 251.

88 Inwood holds that Stoic rules are not fixed but heuristic. See "Rules and Reasoning in Stoic Ethics."

89 "Those who do away with doctrines do not understand that these doctrines are proved by the very arguments through which they seem to disprove them. For what are these men saying? They are saying that precepts are sufficient to develop life, and that the doctrines of wisdom (in other words dogmas) are superfluous. And yet this very utterance of theirs is a doctrine" (95.60). Similarly, "by my very statement that precepts should not be taken seriously, I should be uttering a precept" (95.61). See Phillip Mitsis' discussion, "Seneca on Reason, Rules, and Moral Development."

two-dimensional but unitary (*katorthoma/kathekon, honestum/indifferens, honestum/utile, decreta/praecepta*) mindset. Nor, for greater reason, did anyone apply this mindset to himself or the surrounding world.

(2) Nor have I discovered previous humanists who might be thought to have focused on or employed within this Stoic mindset – or even outside it – Stoic thinking on natural instinct at birth (*oikeiosis*). Far from Stoicism, previous humanists did not think in terms of universal biological instincts. Therewith they did not concern themselves with working out the particular physical and mental nature of these instincts or see a need to think about whether or not instincts can be overcome. Nor did they find reason to be interested in the unique biological makeup of each human being and what this portends. What interested previous humanists, especially in the latter fifteenth century, was abstract thinking on the potentials of humans as humans. Leon Battista Alberti (d. 1472) thus contends that "nature" has created in humans "a great desire for praise and glory."[90] Giovanni Pico della Mirandola (d. 1494) famously argues that unlike other creatures, who cannot change their natures, God ordained that man by free choice can establish the features of his own nature. From the moment of birth it is given to man "to have what he chooses and to be what he wills to be."[91]

Erasmus' outlook cannot be validly opened up and explicated outside of context, one part of which is the fifteenth-century background. Considering this background, what could explain the emergence, and at an early age, of his unparalleled grasp of Stoicism and the deep impression this thinking had on him? What was different about the psychological, social, intellectual, and religious environment – personal or otherwise? In what ways did his life and writings differ, as a consequence, from everything that had preceded?

Part II describes the steps by which Erasmus uncovered the Stoic *katorthoma/kathekon* frame of mind in his edition of *De officiis* (1501) and the ways in which this outlook, and within it natural instinct, afforded a powerful solution to his deep-seated mental and physical problems.

---

90 Quoted by Skinner, *Foundations*, 1:101.
91 *Oration on the Dignity of Man*, 143–4.

Parts III–VI unravel *De taedio Iesu* (1501), working out with regard to Christ the Stoic natural-instinct theme – placed within a Stoic-based unitary worldly/non-worldly, emotion/spirit, setting. Part VII shows that *The Enchiridion* (1503), an advice book for ordinary humans, builds "the philosophy of Christ" for which Erasmus is known directly from the Stoic two-dimensional but unitary *katorthoma/kathekon, honestum/indifferens,* and *honestum/utile* ways of thinking.[92]

---

92 I will demonstrate elsewhere that Erasmus' *Praise of Folly* (1509, pub. 1511) was built from the *honestum/utile* frame but reverts to the *honestum/indifferens* outlook towards the end, where ultimate truth is discussed. Book 2 of Thomas More's *Utopia,* on the other hand, was built exclusively from the *honestum/utile* frame.

PART II Erasmus' Two-Dimensional Stoicism

1 Building Blocks of *De taedio Iesu*, 1499–1501, and the *Enchiridion*, 1503

While fourteenth- and fifteenth-century humanists tended to see only an abstract and one-dimensional Stoicism, Desiderius Erasmus early on grasped the two-dimensional reality of Stoicism. While earlier humanists had relentlessly criticized Stoic coldness and irrelevance to human emotions and human endeavours, with Erasmus it is Stoicism that unfolds human feelings and the uniqueness of one's personality and shows their relationships to higher truth. He saw that Stoicism, unlike Platonism or Aristotelianism, centred on Nature, the nature of oneself and the nature of the universe – and entailed a certain frame of mind. And he used this base to unravel the character and meaning of Christianity.

This Stoic outlook is deeply embedded in one of Erasmus' earliest writings, *Disputatiuncula de taedio, pavore, tristitia Iesu* (*A Short Debate Concerning the Distress, Alarm, and Sorrow of Jesus*).[1] The work builds on a debate with his friend John Colet over the meaning of Christ's agony at Gethsemane and his prayer to God for deliverance. The face-to-face

1 *Disputatiuncula de taedio, pavore, tristitia Jesu, instante supplicio crucis: Deque verbis, quibus visus est mortem deprecari, Pater, si fieri potest, transeat a me calix iste* (Antwerp, Th. Martens, 15 February 1503), LB 5, 1265A–1292A; trans. Michael J. Heath, *A Short Debate Concerning the Distress, Alarm, and Sorrow of Jesus As the Crucifixion Drew Nigh; and Concerning the Words in Which He Seemed to Pray for Deliverance From Death: "Father, If It Be Possible, Let This Cup Pass from Me,"* CWE 70, 13–67. In most cases I will employ the CWE translation. However, for more precision my citations will be to the corresponding LB column and letter.

encounter took place at Oxford in late 1499, during Erasmus' first visit to England. In England from around July to December of 1499, he met not only Colet, soon to be an Oxford doctor, and other leading lights of England, such as William Grocyn and Thomas Linacre, but also Thomas More, the person who became, according to Erasmus in a 1534 comment, "a dearer friend than any other I have ever had."[2] *De taedio Iesu* was published in 1503, in the same volume as his more famous *Enchiridion militis christiani* (*Handbook of the Christian Soldier*), begun in the summer of 1501.

Far from seeing that *De taedio Iesu* is constructed from Stoicism, scholars have hardly mentioned even its explicit referrals to this philosophy.[3] What they comment on is Erasmus' debt to scholastic theologians such as Bonaventure and Aquinas and church fathers such as Jerome, Ambrose, Augustine, and Origen. James D. Tracy thus concludes, in line with Frederic Seebohm a century earlier, that "save for nuances here and there, Erasmus follows rather faithfully in the track of his predecessors."[4] Nor, we are often told, did Erasmus have anything unusual or significant to say vis-à-vis Colet's arguments.[5] The referrals to Stoics and, in passing, to ancients such as Homer, Livy, Quintilian, and Socrates, are considered mere rhetorical additions.[6]

---

2 Erasmus commented thus, in the conclusion to a letter, after hearing that More had been jailed in the Tower of London: "Scitis, opinor, treis viros totius Angliae doctissimos esse in carcere, Episcopum Roffensem, Episcopum Londoniensem et, quo nihil unquam habui amicus, Thomam Morum." *Ep*. 2965. Allen 11, 39/24–7.

3 On *De taedio Iesu*, see Fokke, "An Aspect of the Christology of Erasmus of Rotterdam"; Gleason, *John Colet*, chapter 5; Michael J. Heath, introduction to Erasmus, *A Short Debate*, CWE 70 (1998), 2–8; Lochman, "Colet and Erasmus"; Mara, "Colet et Erasme au sujet de l'exégèse de Mt. 26, 39"; Marc'hadour, "Thomas More on the Agony of Christ"; Santinello, *Studi sull'umanesimo Europeo*, 75–116; and Tracy, "Humanists among the Scholastics."

4 Tracy, "Humanists among the Scholastics," 42, cf. 51. Seebohm states that Erasmus, in *De taedio Iesu*, "followed the common explanation of the schoolmen." See *The Oxford Reformers*, 116–17. The same view is expressed by Allen, 1:245; Fokke, "An Aspect," 182; John O'Malley, CWE 70, xi; Huizinga, *Erasmus and the Age of Reformation*, 31; Gleason, *John Colet*, 103, 105; and Trapp, *Erasmus, Colet and More*, 119.

5 Gleason believes "Erasmus largely confines himself to responding, developing his own view only to the extent necessary to refute Colet's." See *John Colet*, 93. According to Peter Ackroyd, "Colet's dogmatic and insistent arguments vanquished those of his opponent – or perhaps Erasmus was polite, or ironic, enough to retire from the unequal struggle." See *The Life of Thomas More*, 85.

6 Heath holds in his introduction to Erasmus, *A Short Debate* (see n. 3 above) that Erasmus' discussion turns on "rhetorical devices," imitation of Platonic dialogue, and copying of scholastic thought. CWE 70, p. 5.

But before analysing *De taedio Iesu* we need to look closely at the writings that preceded. *De taedio Iesu* represents a radical step in the development of Erasmus' outlook.

A young mind: One-dimensional Christianity

As a youth and young adult Erasmus had seen Christianity in one-dimensional terms. Born in 1466 or 1469 (a subject of debate), he wrote *De contemptu mundi* (*On Contempt of the World*) around 1485–8.[7] As even the title indicates, he at that time saw Christianity as non-worldly and as involving an either/or choice. Leaving aside the final chapter, chapter 12, which was written much later, perhaps around the time the work was published in 1521, chapters 1 through 11 glorify the monastic life. Erasmus belonged to a religious order, the Augustinian, and these chapters are in keeping with that life. Vigils, fasts, labour, solitude, and silence, says Erasmus, allow us to receive the greatest pleasures, ultimately the happiness that is eternal life.[8] The world is evil; we should flee it and seek solitude. True pleasures, as against the false pleasures of the world, are found in carrying out the monastic life and in the contemplation of heaven. Monastic life is in truth not gloomy and harsh but to the contrary represents the highest pleasure. Repeatedly drawing an analogy with Epicureans, based on the account in Cicero's *De finibus*,[9] Christians are advised to pass up small pleasures for greater.[10] Epicurus was right, says Erasmus, in contending that being free from the horrible pain of bad conscience is the ultimate pleasure.[11] Freedom

7 *De contemptu mundi* has been edited and commented on by Sam Dresden, ASD V-1, pp. 40–86, and translated and annotated by Erika Rummel, CWE 66, 135–75. See also Bultot, "Érasme, Épicure et le *De Contemptu Mundi*"; Haverals, "Une première rédaction du *De contemptu mundi* d'Érasme dans un manuscript de Zwolle"; Rummel, "Quoting Poetry instead of Scripture;" Van Eijl, "De interpretatie van Erasmus' *De contemptu mundi*."

8 ASD V-1, 62/612–37, CWE 66, 155. Cf. *City of God*, 14.15: In Paradise, man "did not wish to do anything that he could not do, and therefore he could do all that he wished." Now, however, "who can count the many things a man wishes to do but cannot?"

9 See Erika Rummel, CWE 66, 315 n. 1.

10 ASD V-1, 74/947–9, CWE 66, 166. The analogy with Epicureans was not new. See Delcourt and Derwa, "Trois aspects humanistes de l'épicurisme chrétien," and Timmermans, "Valla et Erasme, defenseurs d'Epicure."

11 ASD V-1, 75/978–80, CWE 66, 166–7.

is found in seclusion, withdrawing from the crowd, giving up our personal wishes.[12] Humans cannot possibly enjoy both physical and spiritual pleasures. It's either/or. "Physical pleasures are false, unreliable, utterly disgusting, vile, deadly, and contain more aloes than honey."[13]

Erasmus brings up Stoicism in *De contemptu mundi* but in monastic, one-dimensional, either/or terms. Thinking of Cicero's *Paradoxa Stoicorum* (5.34), a work that caricatures the Stoic wiseman, Erasmus refers at one point to "Cicero's" definition of freedom as "the ability to live as one pleases."[14] Those who do not know any better imagine, he states, that this definition rules out the monastic life. It is true that rules cover everything in the monastic life, including what one can eat and when one goes to bed, but it is precisely here that true freedom is found. This is the case because "We do not want to do what we are not allowed to do, therefore we are allowed to do whatever we want to do."[15] What Cicero actually says in *Paradoxa Stoicorum* ties in closely with this. The Stoic wiseman "does nothing against his will nor with regret nor by compulsion" because he follows things which are right (*sequitur recta*) and delights in his duty (*gaudet officio*). No one is free who does not have this disposition (5.34–5).[16] Immediately following, Cicero contrasts the slavery and wickedness of the masses, those who are not wise. The first example is a man who thinks he is free but is mercilessly commanded around, due to his sexual desires, by a woman (5.36). Not noted by editors, Erasmus builds on Cicero's illustrations of slavery and vice, as opposed to the freedom of the wiseman, discussing at even greater length the fetters of marriage, domineering mistresses, and "a stinking brothel."[17] The celibate life is a much higher state than married life. Marriage is an affliction. It is not of value in itself but is something that lesser persons submit to. It can be approved only in the sense that it is better than fornication. "I remember him who said: Better to marry than

12 ASD V-1, 68/808f, 82/141–3 passim, CWE 66, 161, 172 passim.

13 ASD V-1, 74/971–2, CWE 66, 166.

14 ASD V-1, 64/669–70, CWE 66, 157.

15 ASD V-1, 64/675–6, CWE 66, 157.

16 Cf. Epictetus' *Discourses*: As epitomized by the Stoic wiseman, that person is free who lives as he wishes subject neither to compulsion or hindrance (Book IV, Ch. 1). In Book I of *De officiis* Cicero contrasts philosophers who have lived "just as they please" with those who apply themselves to statecraft (70–1).

17 ASD V-1, 64/685–98, CWE 66, 157.

to burn" (1 Corinthians 7:9).[18] Worldly and non-worldly are two utterly different things.

Christ as philosopher

An important bridge to *De taedio Iesu* was Erasmus' *Antibarbarorum liber* (*Book against the Barbarians*) composed c. 1489–95.[19] The barbarians are those who do not see that Greek and Roman literature support, rather than distract from, Christianity. Some even think it heresy to know Greek or to speak like Cicero.[20] They scorn things entirely outside their knowledge, things such as Ciceronian eloquence and the acuteness of (the Stoic) Chrysippus.[21] A contrary truth is evident even in St Jerome's writings. "Jerome's 'contempt' for the writings of Cicero and Plato did not debar him from an excellent mastery of them, and he used them continuously."[22] The difficulty of studying ancient culture and literature may frighten some, but without these "there is no approach either to virtue or to learning."[23] Is it actually the case that we cannot be Christian if we are "Ciceronian as speakers, Virgilian or Horatian as poets, or as philosophers Aristotelian, Academic, Stoic, Epicurean?"[24] The barbarians see a clash between Christ's precepts and Plato's Academy, the Stoics, and the Peripatetics, but Christ was like them a philosopher, indeed the very greatest. The apostles followed "not Plato nor Chrysippus or any other philosopher but the very father of philosophy (sed ipsum philosophiae parentem)."[25] Classical culture was a preparation for Christ,

18 ASD V-1, 49–50/264–76, CWE 66, 143–4.

19 *Antibarbarorum liber* has been edited by Kazimierz Kumaniecki, ASD I-1, 7–138, and edited and translated by Margaret Mann Phillips, CWE 23, 16–122. See also Bejczy, "Overcoming the Middle Ages"; Boyle, *Christening Pagan Mysteries*; Kazimierz Kumaniecki, introduction to ASD I-1, 7–32; Margaret Mann Phillips, introduction to CWE 23, 2–15; and Tracy, "Against the 'Barbarians.'"

20 ASD I-1, 56/18–19, CWE 23, 32/21–3.

21 ASD I-1, 76/30–77/2, CWE 23, 51/21–3.

22 ASD I-1, 78/14–16, CWE 23, 55/5–7. Erasmus preferred Jerome to Augustine, he later stated, because Jerome, unlike Augustine, knew Greek and "All philosophy and all theology in those days belonged to the Greeks." *Ep.* 844. Allen 3, 336/216–17, CWE 6, 34/235.

23 ASD I-1, 78/23, CWE 23, 55/16.

24 ASD I-1, 79/11–13, CWE 23, 56/8–10.

25 ASD I-1, 121/31–3, CWE 23, 102/29–31. Erasmus quotes Seneca here (*Ep.* 108.4) on the power of philosophy to benefit even listeners not learned.

the highest good. "None of the liberal disciplines is Christian, because they neither treat of Christ nor were invented by Christians; but they all concern Christ."[26] The task of Christians is "to spoil the Egyptians," "to transfer heathen literature to the adornment and use of our faith."[27]

Later writings were to continue the theme. As the *Enchiridion* (1503) puts it, "The authority of the philosophers would be of little effect if all those same teachings were not contained in the sacred Scriptures, even if not in the same words."[28] According to the *Paraclesis* (Exhortation) which prefaces his Greek *New Testament* (1516), philosophers such as Socrates, Diogenes (the Cynic), and Epictetus (the Stoic), "have presented a good portion of Christ's teaching, but since Christ both taught and presented the same doctrine so much more fully, is it not a monstrous thing that Christians either disregard or neglect or even ridicule it?"[29] While *Antibarbarorum liber* had referred to Christ as the *parentem philosophiae*, the *Paraclesis* refers very directly to the *philosophia Christi*.[30]

Christian "philosophy"?

How seriously should we take this talk about Christ being a philosopher and having a philosophy? Scholars have imagined that Erasmus is speaking figuratively, as a rhetorician. Most commonly Erasmus'

---

26 ASD I-1, 110/14–16, CWE 23, 90/10–12. Not making an issue of the point, Petrarch also held that Cicero never said anything that would conflict with the message of Christ. See *Le Familiari*, ed. V. Rossi and U. Bosco, v. 4 (Florence, 1942), XXI.10 and *Letters on Familiar Matters*, trans. A. Bernardo, v. 3 (Baltimore, 1985), XXI.10. Not once, however, does Petrarch think of Christianity in Stoic both/and terms.

27 ASD I-1, 117/2, 5–6, CWE 23, 97/16–17, 20–1.

28 H 47/26–8, CWE 66, 47. In a colloquy of 1522 Erasmus could even declare: "Perhaps the spirit of Christ is more widespread than we understand, and the company of saints includes many not in our calendar ... Saint Socrates, pray for us." *Convivium religiosum* (*The Godly Feast*). ASD I-3, 251/619–20, 254/710, CWE 39, 192/14–16, 194/34. Although their perspectives differed greatly from Erasmus', late fifteenth-century Italian humanists, such as Pico and Ficino, had also attempted syncretism. Pico ended up by disavowing this approach.

29 LB 5, 137–44 at 142B, trans. Olin 92–106 at 101. Silently recognizing that the goal of the major ancient philosophies was happiness, Erasmus also affirms in his *Paraclesis* that Christ's doctrines "offer the most certain happiness of all." LB 5, 139C, Olin 95.

30 LB 5, 137–44 at 141F passim. The expression next appeared in the Letter to Paul Volz which prefaced the 1518 edition of the *Enchiridion*. *Ep*. 858. Allen 3, 361–77, CWE 6, 72–91.

so-called philosophy is defined as "a combination of good letters and personal piety."[31] Léon-E Halkin considers it, more inclusively,

> a synthesis of theology and spirituality, a synthesis fashioned out of knowledge and love, nourished by meditation, prayer and renunciation, crowned by union with God. The philosophy of Christ demanded a personal approach to the Gospel and increased familiarity with its message. It was a return to the sources.[32]

For John W. O'Malley, the philosophy of Christ (like Erasmus the person) "is dedicated to the *vita contemplativa* of study rather than to the *vita activa* of engagement."[33] Discussing the *Enchiridion*, Christine Christ-Von Wedel sees the *philosophia christiana* as a reconciling "of Christian beliefs and Platonic philosophy."[34] Gary Remer states that the philosophy of Christ, as exemplified in the *Paraclesis* and elsewhere, "asserts the centrality of ethical behavior" and "stands in contrast both to ritual and doctrinal *adiaphora* (indifferent things)."[35] Charles G. Nauert sees three elements in "the philosophy of Christ": "personal spiritual experience," "frank criticism of many clergymen for moral corruption," and "insistence that true religion must be expressed in a morally upright life rather than in punctilious observance of the external trappings of religion."[36] In showing how the *Enchiridion* (1503) originated, James D. Tracy, like others, makes no mention of philosophy:

> [The *Enchiridion* was] a distillation of all of Erasmus's concerns in recent years; his newfound enthusiasm for Greek; his studies in classical

31 Hoffmann, *Rhetoric and Theology*, 29.

32 *Erasmus: A Critical Biography*, 284. Perhaps the broadest defining of the *philosophia Christi* is that of James K. McConica in *English Humanists and Reformation Politics under Henry VIII and Edward VI*, 13–43, and "The Philosophy of Christ."

33 "Grammar and Rhetoric in the *Pietas* of Erasmus," 88 and 97. Elsewhere he contends that the philosophy of Christ is a synonym for "pietas." See *Praise and Blame in Renaissance Rome*, 228–32.

34 See *Erasmus of Rotterdam*, 51. Betty Radice ties the philosophy of Christ to Plato in the introduction to her critical edition of *The Praise of Folly* (*Moriae encomium*) (1511), CWE 27, 81. Discussing the *Adages* Kathy Eden holds that *philosophia Christi* develops the monastic ideal and in so doing conflates pagan thought, building on Pythagoras and Plato, and Christian thought. See *Friends Hold All Things in Common*, 28, 112–14, 139–41.

35 *Humanism and the Rhetoric of Toleration*, 52. Cf. Dodds, *Exploiting Erasmus*, 35.

36 Nauert, "Rethinking 'Christian Humanism,'" 177. He believes Jean Vitrier, who was in contact with Erasmus in 1501 and 1502 and introduced him to Origen, played a crucial role in Erasmus' outlook.

literature; his efforts to revive the "primitive theology (*vetus theologia*)" that was the only viable alternative to scholasticism; and, last but not least, his bitter recollections of life in the cloister.[37]

Most scholars would find the idea that Erasmus might have had a set way of thinking ridiculous. Nor, for even more reason, will they allow that he set forth a philosophy as such.[38] Many have doubted that Erasmus was even a theologian.[39] And if in recent times it is sometimes allowed that he was in some sense a theologian it is not allowed that he was a systematic one.[40] If Erasmus was a philosopher, it was only, it is believed, in the sense that he stood for a certain, very loose, constellation of beliefs and saw Christ in these terms. Erasmus thought like a rhetorician, not a philosopher. He not only thought like a rhetorician he was one of the world's greatest experts on rhetoric, as evidenced by his books on rhetoric (such as *De duplici copia verborum ac rerum*, 1512) and by works such as *The Praise of Folly*. Although he had positive things to say about ancient philosophies, even here he picked and chose, it is believed, for particular literary and religious ends. Philosophy was a tool of rhetoric; rhetoric was not a tool of philosophy. He did not, that is, think in systematic terms or let philosophy govern his essential thought processes. Where philosophy comes into the picture it is always guided by rhetoric. The fact that he made a point of contrasting his way of

37 *Erasmus of the Low Countries*, 32. Pages 104–7 discuss Erasmus' explicit referrals, beginning around 1515, to the philosophy of Christ.

38 Cornelis Augustijn, for example, makes no attempt to explain why Erasmus talks about "the philosophy of Christ" but is certain that this philosophy "is not a matter of a particular doctrine or system." See *Erasmus: His Life, Works, and Influence*, 76.

39 In his immensely learned and influential *Grammaire et rhétorique chez Erasme* Jacques Chomarat contends that Erasmus was not a theologian. According to Chomarat, Erasmus' real achievement lay in rhetoric and grammar. What distinguishes humanity is not reason, as with scholastics, but language, and Erasmus saw things through language. He was particularly influenced by Lorenzo Valla's *Elegantiae linguae Latinate* (1471). As in Cicero's *De oratore*, decorum, accommodation, and aptness are key concepts. Although Erasmus' approach was dualist in that he contrasted spirit and flesh, he was not a theologian. In interpreting sacred scripture he relied on philology and other available testimonies. Nor of course was he a philosopher, notwithstanding that he was ideologically a Platonist. On Chomarat's work, see Mansfield, *Erasmus in the Twentieth Century*, 168–73, and Craig R. Thompson's review in *Renaissance Quarterly* 38 (1985), 113–17.

40 Ernst-Wilhelm Kohls systematized Erasmus' thought, leaning not on rhetoric but scholastic theology, in *Die Theologie Des. Erasmus*. Few scholars have given this study credence.

looking at issues with the logicizing of late scholastic philosophers has buttressed the notion that rhetoric and philosophy were for him conflicting endeavours.

A recurrent theme of his writings, it is widely held, is the struggle between worldly and non-worldly, flesh and spirit, visible and invisible, letter and spirit, temporary and eternal, darkness and light. Noteworthy influences, in this regard, included the Devotio Moderna, St Paul, Origen, and Platonism.[41] Of philosophies, far and away the dominant influence, it has long been held, is Platonism, whether through the church fathers, the Neoplatonists at Florence, or direct reading. Pieces of Stoicism are sometimes perceived, but far in the background – not the ocean but only a few waves. The Stoicism that is seen is one-dimensional and placed within large and vacillating rhetorical schemas.[42]

But are these positions defensible?

2 Distinguishing Stoic Meanings: Erasmus' Edition of *De officiis*, 1501

Immensely significant, for reasons not previously recognized, Erasmus edited and published Cicero's *De officiis* in 1501, his first edition of a classical work.[43] Unlike his Italian humanist predecessors, in his editing and introduction Erasmus shows us that he had comprehended the Stoic unitary both/and way of thinking and not simply in general terms but even in the very technical meanings of keywords. Regarding

41 Cornelis Augustijn reiterates many elements of the accepted view, referring to the *Enchiridion*, in *Erasmus*, 43–55, esp. 47.

42 Starting with the belief that ancient Stoicism was abstract and one-dimensional, book learning, contemptuous of the body, unable to engage and solve practical problems of life, and "hopeless," William J. Bouwsma picks out statements in the *Enchiridion* and other writings which seem to him to support this assumption while attributing to the influence of Augustine statements which he deems not supportive. See "The Two Faces of Humanism," 20, 22, 32–4, and 57.

43 No serious study of Erasmus' edition exists. According to Elaine Fantham, Erasmus "has merely tried to counter scribes' miscopyings and displacement of words, partly by collating editions, partly by informed guesswork based on Cicero's style." See "Erasmus and the Latin Classics," xxxviii. Other comments on the work and its context include those of Béné, *Erasme et Saint Augustine ou influence de Saint Augustin sur l'humanisme d'Erasme*, ch. 3; Margaret Mann Phillips, "Erasmus and the Classics"; and Rüegg, *Cicero und der Humanismus*, 75–8.

his editing, Jill Kraye has noted that he discerned the true meaning of *κατόρθωμα*, *katorthoma*, a word at the very core of Stoic thought, while the Italian Angelo Poliziano (1454–94), who possessed unrivalled philological skills, failed, notwithstanding his efforts.[44] Poliziano failed because he did not grasp that in Stoicism the word did not mean "success" or "victory," as in everyday Greek, but had a specialized definition.[45] In contrast, Erasmus defines in a marginal note to *De officiis* 1.8 the meaning of *κατόρθωμα*. He found the definition, as he points out, in Book 3 of *De finibus*. *Perfectum officium* (absolute duty), which the Greeks call *katorthoma*, referred to in *De officiis* 1.8, is to be interpreted as *recte factum*, a right action (*Fin*. 3.24, 45). He also recognized – the significance of which is not seen by Kraye – that *perfectum officium* is but one of two types of duty defined by the Stoics and supported by Cicero (*Fin*. 3.20). Taking into account *De finibus* as well as *De officiis* he summarizes, intertextually, the difference between the two types as follows:

> Alterum quod perfectum vocant estque cum fine boni coniunctum (*Off.* 1.7), neque in quenquam preterquam in sapientem competit (*Off.* 3.14-5). Alterum medium sive inchoatum quod per se neque bonum sit neque malum sed ad usum aliquem vitae sumitur (*Fin*. 3.58): ut recte depositum reddere, perfecti sit officii; depositum reddere, imperfecti; quum recte nisi sapiens nemo reddat, reddant autem simul et stulti (*Fin*. 3.59).[46]

> The action which they call perfect has as its end the good and is attained by no one other than the wiseman. The action which is called intermediate or imperfect is in itself neither good nor bad but is something provided for the utility of life. Restoring a deposit is an imperfect duty while rightly restoring a deposit is a perfect duty. Although both the wise and the foolish can restore a deposit, only the wiseman can restore a deposit rightly.[47]

44 Kraye, "Cicero, Stoicism and Textual Criticism," 97–8.

45 Francesco Filelfo (1398–1481) also failed to understand the word, Kraye shows, as did contemporary Byzantine critics of Cicero's Greek (86–7). Pietro Marsi, in his widely diffused commentary on *De officiis*, first published in 1481, did not refer to the word *κατόρθωμα*, nor to its location in *De finibus*, but correctly stated the meaning and had consulted *De finibus* 4.15 (96–7).

46 *De officiis Marci Tullii Ciceronis libri tres*, ed. by D. Erasmi Roterodami (Ioannem Kyngstonem, 1574), 6–7. Kraye quotes the same passage, from the first edition: Cicero, *Officia*, ed. Erasmus (Paris, 1501), fol. A iiii v. I have kept her referrals to passages in *De officiis* and *De finibus*.

47 The translation here and the translations in what follows are all mine.

In *De officiis* 1.8, that is, Cicero distinguishes between absolute duty (*perfectum officium*) and mean duty (*medium officium*) and gives the Greek words that had been so relentlessly discussed and differentiated by Stoics. The Greeks call absolute duty *katorthoma* and ordinary duty *kathekon*. *Katorthoma*, or *perfectum officium*, is that which is right (*rectum*) and is attainable only by the wiseman. *Kathekon*, or *medium officium*, "is duty for the performance of which an adequate reason may be rendered" (quod cur factum sit, ratio probabilis reddi possit). *De finibus* 3.58–9 shows that the wiseman, unlike others, combines right actions *(katorthomata)* with appropriate actions *(kathekonta)*.[48] Appropriate actions are choices made between things that are indifferent, neither good nor evil, on the basis of what accords with nature and what is contrary to nature. Both the wise and the unwise make such choices but when the wise selects, this is *perfectum officium*. While restoring a trust on principle exemplifies a right act (*recte factum*) and *perfectum officium*, merely restoring the trust is only an appropriate act (*medium officium*). In other words, *perfectum officium* (*katorthoma*) is both/and, *medium officium* (*kathekon*) by itself is not.

Continuing his comments, Erasmus brings in St Ambrose (d. 397). Ambrose had set forth a Christianized version of Cicero's *De officiis* in his *De officiis ministrorum*:

> Divus autem Ambrosius prioris generis esse putat quae secundum consilia fiunt, posterioris quae secundum precepta; ut bene administrare rem ad inchoatum officium pertineat, erogare in pauperes ad perfectum. (Cf. *De viduis* 12.72–4, *De officiis ministrorum* 1, 2.36–9)

According to Ambrose, that is, merely administering something well is an incomplete duty while perfect duty exists where monetary interests in this administering are lacking.[49]

Clearly, he had closely studied *De officiis*. In addition to the introduction, there are fifteen pages of annotations, as well as intertextual comments or summaries, from one line in length to seventeen, and the margins are stocked with notes.[50] The marginals give equivalents for a

48 The Greek words are not used at *Fin.* 3.58–9. *Kathekon* is referred to at *Fin.* 3.20 and *katorthoma* at 3.24 and 3.45.

49 Erasmus makes no other referrals to Ambrose in his edition.

50 Erasmus criticizes Pietro Marsi and previous versions of *De officiis* in his preface. *Ep.* 152. Allen 1, 356–7/19–32, CWE 2, 30–1/23–39. A study of the differences is needed.

word in the text, restate or add historical information, and emphasize or clarify the philosophical meaning. Not satisfied, for example, that 1.101 notes only that *appetitus* is a translation of the Greek word *ὁρμή* Erasmus points out that the Greek is defined in *De finibus* (3.23) and adds that *πάθη* (*Fin.* 3.35, *Tusc.* 4.10–1, Gellius 19.12.3), *perturbationes* (bad emotions; discussed at 1.102) may arise from *ὁρμή* (p. 51). In another marginal note at 1.101 the reader is in effect referred back to the definition of *kathekon* (*medium officium*, appropriate act) at 1.8. Opposite Cicero's statement that "nec vero agere quicquam, cuius non possit causam probabilem reddere" (neither ought we to do anything for which we cannot assign a reasonable motive), Erasmus refers to the Stoic Cato's discussion of duties in *De finibus*, Book 3, quoting his definition of an appropriate act (3.58): "quod ita factum est ut eius facti probabilis ratio redidi possit" (p. 52).

At 1.14 Cicero states that *honestum*, moral goodness, is in fact the subject of *De officiis*. *Honestum* is "something that, even though it be not generally ennobled, is still worthy of all honour; and by its own nature, we correctly maintain, it merits praise, even though it be praised by none" (quod etiamsi nobilitatum non sit, tamen honestum sit, quodque vere dicimus, etiamsi a nullo laudetur, natura esse laudabile). Erasmus' marginal note demonstrates here too the care with which he was reading and his determination to find the exact meaning. "Ex his honestum, quod est *τέλος*, finis: & *κατόρθωμα*, quod est per se laudabile, etiamsi nemo lauder" (p. 11). Two relationships to *honestum* are here brought in, *τέλος* and *κατόρθωμα*, that are not shown in the accompanying text.

(1) The word *τέλος*, or *telos*, is found nowhere in *De officiis*. His likely source was *De finibus*, 1.42: "That which is not itself a means to anything else, but to which all else is a means, is what the Greeks term the Telos, the highest, ultimate or final good." The Stoic Cato explicitly ties *τέλος* to *honestum* at 3.26. The final aim, *telos*, exemplified by the wiseman, is to live in agreement and harmony with nature. *Honestum* is the only good. "Quod est bonum, omne laudabile est; quod autem laudabile est, omne est honestum; bonum igitur quod est, honestum est" (3.27).

(2) On what basis, however, does Erasmus tie *κατόρθωμα* with *honestum*? *Honestum* is defined at *De finibus* 2.45, as well as at *De officiis* 1.14, but here too the text draws no connection with *κατόρθωμα* or even *recte factum*: "By moral worth, then, we understand that which is of such a nature that, though devoid of all utility, it can justly

> be commended in and for itself, apart from any profit or reward" (Honestum igitur id intellegimus quod tale est ut detracta omni utilitate sine ullis praemiis fructibusve per se ipsum possit iure laudari).[51] Although the text at *De officiis* 1.8 does not connect *recte factum* with *honestum* anymore than does 1.14 connect *κατόρθωμα* with *honestum*, note however Erasmus' marginal: "Cicero tum rectum, tum recte factum interpraetatur: est honestatis actio propter se expetenda." An action carried out in terms of *honestum*, the sole good, that which merits praise even if not praised, is a right action (*recte factum, κατόρθωμα*). Compare *De finibus* 3.58: "Although we say that moral worth (*honestum*) is the sole good, it is still consistent to perform appropriate actions despite the fact that we regard them as neither good nor evil." *Recte factum*, which he knew from *De finibus* 3.24 and 3.45 equates with *κατόρθωμα*, is "an appropriate act perfectly performed" (3.59). In holding to *honestum* the wiseman's actions are all *katorthomata* – perfect appropriate acts.

Where the text begins explication of the four cardinal virtues that inhere in *honestum*, at 1.15, Erasmus writes: "Omnes virtutes una virtus absoluta, iuxta Platonem" (All virtues are one virtue, perfect, as with Plato). Interestingly, Cicero does not state here, or elsewhere in *De officiis*, that Plato considered the four cardinal virtues – wisdom, justice, fortitude, temperance – one virtue (a thesis which does in fact seem to have originated with Socrates, *Protagoras* 328d–34c). What Cicero does here is simply compare the unbending side of *honestum* to Plato's vision of wisdom (*Phaedrus*, 250d), something that were it seen with the eyes would awaken a marvellous love of wisdom. Nor does Cicero use the word *absoluta* in describing the virtue that is *honestum*. Erasmus may have been making a deduction or he may have been thinking of *De officiis* 3.14 and the description there of a type of duty carried out by the Stoic wiseman and the Stoic wiseman alone, in holding to *honestum*, that is "perfectum atque absolutum." Although it is not stated at 1.15 that all the virtues are one, but only that they are "connected and interwoven," at 2.35 it is stated that among the wise "he who has one virtue has them all" – illustrating again the degree of Erasmus' knowledge. He may well have noted the same thesis in Diogenes Laertius: "They [the Stoics] hold

51 The Greek for *honestum, kalon*, is nowhere noted by Erasmus. Nor is the Greek found in either *De officiis* or *De finibus*. On *kalon*, see Dyck, *A Commentary on Cicero, De Officiis*, 97–8.

that the virtues involve one another, and that the possessor of one is the possessor of all" (7.125).[52] Cicero mentions the oneness of the virtues at 2.35 only to point out that his approach in *De officiis* is entirely different; as he is not here writing for philosophers, he will discuss the four virtues separately.

Stoic nature

Erasmus' intertextual recounting of the place and meaning of nature in Stoicism reveals just how deeply he had imbibed the centrality of nature in Stoicism and its various aspects. His encapsulation relies on much more than the accompanying text (1.11–14) or even *De officiis* as a whole:

> The Old Academy[53] and the Stoics hold that the highest good resides in nature. They teach that living in accord with nature, the elements (*semina*) of which are found in each of us, is to live happily (*beate vivere*). Success in life occurs when all our endeavours are related to nature. For in the first place, all living creatures are motivated at birth by a desire for self-preservation. This is a law of nature that humans have in common with animals and is called in Greek *κατὰ φύσιμ πρα τομ*, that is, *secundum naturam primum*. As a consequence all creatures desire what is favourable to their preservation and flee what is harmful. And yet, with humans, nature pertains to the mind as well as the body. So that life can be made whole, humans have been given the power of reasoning, from whence all the disciplines and moral virtues have originated.[54] (8–9, my translation)

---

52 Cf. *Fin.* 5.67. On other sources for the unity of the virtues in Stoicism see LS, 377–9 and 383–4. Plutarch discusses the Stoic view, but Erasmus did not become seriously acquainted with his writings before publication of the Aldine edition in 1509. On relationships to the views of Plato and Socrates, see Cooper, *Reason and Emotion*, ch. 3.

53 Cf. *Fin.* 2.34. The Old Academy was the school of philosophy founded by Plato (d. 347) and carried on by Speusippus, Xenocrates, Polemo, and Crates. The New Academy, which arose c. 266, interpreted true Platonism as scepticism.

54 "Ex veteris Academiae, & Stoicorum sententia, qui summum bonum a natura proficisci putant, & hoc ipsum esse beate vivere, secundam naturam vivere commemorant, docet, quae semina nobis natura inseverit, quaeque adminicula addiderit, quibus accedente industria, ac usu, ad foelicitatem, quo referuntur omnia, proficiamus. Nam primo loco, omni animanti studium tuendi sui indidit, id quod iure naturae est hominum cum pecudibus commune, vocaturque κατὰ φύσιμ πρα τομ, id est, secundum naturam primum: consequens est appetitus eorum, quae incolumitati sunt amica, fuga eorum, quae noxia. Verum homini, quoniam non solum e corpore constat, sed etiam ex animo, ut totus esse possit incolumis, ratiocinandi vim addidit, unde disciplinae omnes, & virtutes illae morales proficiscuntur" (*De officiis*, ed. Erasmus, 8–9).

While Cicero's discussion at 1.11–14 begins with the self-preservation instinct, Erasmus begins by talking about Stoic nature as such. His encapsulation of the Stoic message regarding nature – something not one of his humanist predecessors had been able to do – reveals his sound grasp of the essentials. The broader picture presented, however abridged, did not come from *De officiis* but from *De finibus* and very probably Diogenes Laertius and Aulus Gellius as well. Note the referrals to living in accord with nature, the tie between reason (activated at a certain age) and nature, the relationship of happiness to nature,[55] the fact that nature is found in every human as well as the universe as a whole,[56] and, not least, how everyday affairs are either in accord with nature or not in accord.[57] Although *De officiis* was a work designed to deal with the lives of those not wise, Erasmus saw, unlike all his predecessors, that it was through and through built from Stoic ways of thinking, not only the Stoic both/and but the Stoic view of nature that undergirds and reflects this both/and. In short, he deeply grasped and appreciated the fact that Cicero's worldliness was not something inherently at odds with Stoicism but one with Stoicism.

The referral to the self-preservation instinct that humans share with animals further highlights ways in which Erasmus develops the text. While Cicero merely states that this instinct is a common property of all creatures (1.11), Erasmus refers to it as a law of nature ("id quod iure naturae est hominum cum pecudibus commune"). While neither *De officiis* nor *De finibus* use the words "law of nature" in this context, though the meaning is certainly implied (cf. *Fin.* 3.16f, 4.14f), *Tusculan Disputations* does refer to the self-preservation instinct as a "law of

55 Regarding "*beate vivere*," see *Fin.* 3.29, 3.61 and, less directly, *Off.* 1.13.

56 Regarding "*semina*" (seeds), see *Fin.* 5.43: *semina* are "*prima elementa naturae.*" On conceptualizations of *semina* in history, see Horowitz, *Seeds of Virtue and Knowledge.*

57 Erasmus' statement that for Stoics "the highest good" resides in nature could seem problematic in that for Stoics *honestum* is not the highest good but "the only good" (*Fin.* 3.26) and we know that Antiochus in Book 5 of *De finibus* attempted to redefine *honestum*, influenced by Peripatetic thinking, as "the ultimate good" or "highest good" (*Fin.* 5.26, 40 passim). Since, however, Erasmus is discussing nature as a whole, emphasizing "the primary elements of nature" (*Fin* 3.19 passim) as well as the "reason" found in nature, his statement does not necessarily depend on Antiochus. *De finibus* 3.21 refers to reason as "the *summum bonum*" before pointing out that, in a later development, it is found to be the only good. Erasmus distinguishes between *honestum* as "the only good" and, as Peripatetics would have it, "the highest good," in a comment on *De officiis* 3.20 (p. 133).

nature" (5.38). The Greek words which he gives for this law of nature, *κατὰ φύσιμ πρα τομ*, are also not found in either *De officiis* or *De finibus*. Erasmus almost certainly found these words in Aulus Gellius' *Attic Nights* (c. 180 CE). Drawing on Book 5 (now lost) of Epictetus' *Discourses* Gellius refers to the "first principles of nature" as *τὰ κατὰ φύσιν πρῶτα* (12.5.7), emphasizing that they are inevitable and natural necessities of nature (12.5.10). Erasmus uses these same Greek words in *De taedio Iesu* (1271A-B) in describing, again based on Epictetus, involuntary aspects of human nature (see below, Part III).[58] And yet Erasmus' main source for "first principles of nature" was *De finibus*. Over and over *De finibus* focuses on the primary instincts of nature. Variations of Erasmus' translation, *secundum naturam primum*, the primary thing in accordance with nature, are found in Books 3 (19–21, 30), 4 (16–19, 34, 42, 45) and 5 (17–19, 40, 43–6).

A "formula"

In describing multifarious aspects of *honestum* and *utile* and their oneness, Cicero sets forth the tools for confronting all the variables of life. Similarly, Erasmus' purpose in composing his *Enchiridion*, published two years after *De officiis*, was to show laymen unitary both/and methods for dealing, as Christians, with whatever problems may arise in life (see below, Part VII). Not unrelated to his exemplifications of proper attitudes and behaviour in the *Enchiridion*, in his edition of *De officiis* Erasmus well grasps that a major goal of Cicero in composing the work had been to correct the Stoic Panaetius, who stated but failed to illustrate clashes between what appears to be morally right and what appears to be expedient (3.7, p. 128). An important part of Cicero's discussion is the "formula" he establishes for resolving apparent conflicts between the *honestum* and the *utile*. Based on nature and the fellowship of the human race, the formula disallows depriving others for one's own advantage (3.21). There is nothing wrong with self-interest but not if it is at the expense of society (3.101). Cicero's discussion of the formula at 3.21–7 elicits from Erasmus seven marginal comments (one brings

58 In his edition of *De officiis* Erasmus refers to Gellius' *Attic Nights* at 1.160, p. 80 (5.13) and at annotation 46 (n.p.) on 2.69 (1.4). Commenting on 3.69 (p. 156), Erasmus refers to "*naturae principiis, & veritatis*" where Cicero states that the civil law "is drawn from the excellent models which nature and truth afford (*ex optimis naturae & veritatis exemplis*)."

in St Paul) and three annotations (pp. 134–6). Intertextual comments and notes elsewhere in Book 3 refer a number of times to "the formula" (cf. pp. 133, 144, 147, 156, 165). At one point he alludes to the "formula honesti & utilis" even though the text does not mention the formula as such (3.50, p. 147). His intertextuals on Cicero's discussions of friendship (3.43, p. 144) and affairs of state (3.46, p. 145) hammer home his interest in the differences between apparent expedience and actual expedience. It is expedient to stand by a friend against one's political, social, or economic interests, that which is apparently inexpedient, but it is inexpedient to stand by a friend when it is in one's interest to do so, that which is apparently expedient, if one sits as a judge or the interests of humanity have been violated. In the former instance apparent inexpedience is actually expedient in that it is one with *honestum* and in the latter instance apparent expedience is inexpedient in that it is not one with *honestum*. The issue, Cicero emphasizes, is anything but mere moralizing. Actions that seem expedient but are not in accord with *honestum* cannot actually work in the world of affairs – notwithstanding the perceptions of most mortals, as well as Peripatetics. A person's human nature and the surrounding society is always harmed (2.10–11). Erasmus in the *Enchiridion* works out this thinking within a Christian context (see below, Part VII).

Erasmus took close account also of Cicero's contention that upright men may interpret the formula in different ways, as shown by his intertextual comments regarding the discussion of conflicting views of what can be revealed or not revealed in a commercial transaction (3.50–7, pp. 147–50). Cicero here presents the opposing views not of two philosophers from differing schools but of two Stoics, Diogenes of Babylon (d. c. 152 BCE) and Antipater (late 2nd cent. BCE). Diogenes "asserts that a given act is expedient, without being morally wrong," while Antipater "insists that the act should not be done, because it is morally wrong" (3.53).[59] In his prefatory remarks Erasmus expresses admiration for the fact, as does Cicero, that they are both good men and that they argue openly and sincerely, Antipater seeing the matter in terms of "reason," in Erasmus' interpretation, while Diogenes brings in civil law and, according to Erasmus, "custom." Highlighting again how closely Erasmus was reading the text, Cicero does not mention "reason" and

59 Compare the two types of religious in the Utopian state. See More, *Utopia*, ed. Logan, Adams, and Miller, 228/16–32.

"custom" here, but they are brought in, in a related discussion, at 3.68 and 3.69, respectively. In another intertextual comment, at the end of the debate, he appears to agree with Cicero's position that Antipater had the better argument, albeit "holding one's peace about a thing" does not, Diogenes was here correct, constitute concealment. Concealment would break the formula. What matters, Erasmus – in agreement with Cicero – believes, is that the Stoic principles remain in place, notwithstanding differing arguments. As long as the both/and is in place opposing views are possible.

Consider also Erasmus' intertextual comments preceding Cicero's statement that the general rule or formula he is setting forth, by which the *honestum* is also the *utile* and the *utile* is also the *honestum* (3.20), is "in perfect harmony with the Stoics' system and doctrines."[60] Erasmus supports the Stoic view while allowing a small opening for the Peripatetic contention that *honestum* is not the only good but simply the highest good:

> The formula prescribes that false representations of *utilitas* can never have their own existence separate from the *utilitas* that is one with *honestas*; that justice is either the only good or the highest good and injustice the highest evil; that everything is for the public good and nothing for (untoward) personal advantage.[61] (133, my translation)

In fact, however, this statement is not at odds with Cicero's view. Cicero holds, in the same place, that even if the Peripatetics and older Academics contend that *honestum* is the highest good and not as with the Stoics the only good, it is still the case that expediency cannot conflict with *honestum* (3.20, cf. 3.11). The problem Cicero has with Peripatetics is that they also believe, wrongly, that "something not expedient may

60 Dyck affirms that the *formula* is consistent with Stoic doctrine and shows that Seneca, probably consulting the same source as Cicero, uses the word in the context of his (both/and) discussion of *decreta/praecepta* in *Ep.* 95. See *A Commentary on Cicero, De Officiis*, 520–5. On *Ep.* 95, see above, p. 45. According to Dyck, Cicero makes only limited use of the "formula" as such. Often the rule is simply that *turpe* (vice) must be absent in determining the truly useful (525).

61 "Formula praescripta, ne quando nos falsa utilitatis species ab honestate abducat, ut iustitiam vel solum vel maximum bonum statuamus, iniustitiam malorum maximum: nihil que; ad privatum commodum, sed ad communem societatem referantur omnia."

be morally right and that something not morally right may be expedient." Preceding Cicero's statement in Book 2 that nothing more pernicious can be imposed on human life than this doctrine (nulla pernicies maior hominum vitae potuit afferri) (2.9), Erasmus comments that *utilitas* is not just any type of profit but "quae cum honesto sit coniuncta, & ad vitae societatem pertineat" (p. 84). What is expedient works in the real world; what is only apparently expedient has negative worldly consequences.

In setting forth the formula, Erasmus takes careful account of Stoic advantage/disadvantage thinking and preferred/dispreferred thinking. Here too he finds *De finibus* the best source for theoretical understanding. Where *De officiis* states that it is men that are both most hurtful to men and also most helpful (2.11–12, continued to 2.17), Erasmus' intertextual comment reads: "Quae quaque ex re commoda, aut incommoda capiantur, quae Graeci euchrestemata, & dyschrestemata nominant" (p. 85). Although neither the Latin words nor the Greek are found in *De officiis*, they are found in *De finibus*. At 3.68 we are told that nature requires that humans safeguard and protect each other and this being the case the wiseman should desire to become involved in politics and government, take a wife, have children, and even partake of sexual passion. One aspect of this safeguarding of the tie between humans is the Stoic doctrine of advantages/disadvantages. "Incommoda autem et commoda (ita enim *εὐχρηστήματα* et *δυσχρηστήματα* appello) communia esse voluerunt, paria noluerunt" ("Disadvantages" and "advantages," for so I render *euchrêstêmata* and *duschrêstêmata*, they held to be "common" but not "equal") (3.69). Things that are "equal" do not deal with degree but with good and bad. In response Erasmus notes in his intertextual (p. 85) that "humans are drawn by birth to deal among themselves with advantage and disadvantage."[62]

As the text at *De finibus* 3.69 (which is highly technical) explicitly states, advantages/disadvantages belong to the class of things called preferred/dispreferred (*quae praeposita et reiecta dicimus*). Things preferred and dispreferred are of course indifferents (*Fin.* 3.50 ff.). In a marginal note to 3.14 Erasmus refers to the "mean duties" (*media officia*) of Stoics as "*adiaphora*," the Greek word for indifferents. In *De officiis*

62 "Colligitq́; quicquid est fere in vita commodi, aut incommodi, id homini ab homine nasci."

Cicero uses the word *"indifferens,"* not the Greek word *adiaphoron*. *Adiaphora* are referred to at *De finibus* 3.53 and discussed by Diogenes Laertius at 7.101–7.

In summary, *De officiis* had long been an important text but it had not been important for the reasons Erasmus gives. Erasmus came to see in his editing of *De officiis* what his humanist predecessors had been unable to see, the core way of thinking of Stoics. Never before had readers discerned the Stoic unitary *honestum/utile* frame of thought that is the subject of Book 3 and undergirds the entire work. Indeed, it appears that no author in a thousand years had come near his grasp of Stoicism. He saw, first of all, how *katorthoma* and *kathekon* are defined. While *kathekon* is an appropriate act, *katorthoma* adds to this action action based on principle. A person who acts on principle also acts appropriately ("unitarily both/and" in my wording). The *honestum* (that which is admirable, virtue etc.) and the *utile* (cf. in *De finibus* preferred *indifferentia*) are two sides of one coin. Evident in all this is Nature, the nature of man and the nature of the universe. Here Erasmus highlighted – again going beyond all his humanist predecessors – the self-preservation instinct at birth (*oikeiosis*), discussed at length by Stoics.

3 The Applicability of *De officiis*

Fundamental questions remain. Erasmus claims that no edition is closer to the original than his,[63] but what impelled him to correct and improve this particular text – if he did? Was he merely exhibiting his philological skills with a book that had long been a staple of humanists?[64] He states that the purpose of the large number of brief notes is to "illuminate each obscure passage" but was that all? Did he see himself as simply a scholar and moralist – or was he seeing a direct relevance of Stoicism to contemporary affairs and/or his own life? Equally important, did he see Stoicism as only about ethics or about religion as well?

63 *Ep*. 152. Allen 1, 357/31–2, CWE 2, 31/38–9.

64 Regarding the 1465 printing of *De officiis* (and *Paradoxa Stoicorum*) and the extent to which it was read in the Renaissance, see above, pp. 21–2.

Erasmus' 1501 Preface

In his preface Erasmus states repeatedly that *De officiis* should be carried about as one goes through life.[65] He obviously believes it eminently applicable to present problems, but on what grounds? Unlike his predecessors Erasmus realized that *De officiis* is not fundamentally about Cicero but about Stoicism and that Stoicism is about an *honestum/indifferens* (or *honestum/utile*) methodology, a methodology that is as worldly as it is abstract. His overriding purpose, it is clear, was to set forth the central meaning of the work and to hammer home its relevance to contemporary issues.[66] Virtue (*virtus*), at one with *honestum*, is mankind's "mightiest weapon" and *De officiis* is about this weapon.[67] What needs always to be assessed, Erasmus is saying, is how this unitary *honestum/utile* way of thinking, which Cicero illustrates in the context of Roman life, can be applied to every aspect of a particular Christian life. And this is why *De officiis* is "a pocket handbook" (*enchiridion*)[68] or "tiny dagger" (*pugiunculus*)[69] that needs to be carried about and constantly thought about.[70] The word *enchiridion* is the Greek equivalent of *pugiunculus*, a tiny dagger, but can also mean "pocket handbook." In titling the work that followed *De officiis* by two years "*Enchiridion militis christiani*," Erasmus played on this double meaning of *enchiridion* and, in doing so, pointed to a parallel between the purposes of his work and Cicero's. *De officiis* is a dagger and a handbook because it reveals the formula to be used in all the variables of life – and so too, we will find, is the *Enchiridion*. From *De officiis* those engaged in worldly practices, such

65 *Ep*. 152. Allen 1, 356/16–19, 357/33–50, CWE 2, 30/20–3, 31/40–59.

66 Something of the significance of the choice of this particular work may be indicated by the fact that he was not to edit another classical work until 1514, thirteen years later. See Elaine Fantham, "Erasmus and the Latin Classics," CWE 29, xxxix. *Opuscula aliquot Erasmo roterodamo castigatore* (1514) was a school text, which included excerpts from Aulus Gellius and Seneca the Elder (55 BCE–CE 39) and some excerpts then attributed to Cato the Elder (234–149 BCE) and Seneca the Younger.

67 On the weapon of virtue Erasmus quotes in Greek (a language he was just learning) the dramatist Menander (c. 344–292 BCE). *Ep*. 152. Allen 1, 357/37, CWE 2, 31/44.

68 *Ep*. 152. Allen 1, 356/18.

69 *Ep*. 152. Allen 1, 357/33.

70 Probably responding to the view of his friend Erasmus, whom it appears he had just visited (and refers to as "the very greatest scholar of our age"), Willem Hermans stated in 1494 that *De officiis* should be carried about everywhere and read repeatedly. *Ep*. 38. Allen 1, 138/70–1, 60–4 resp., CWE 1, 74/84–5, 74/72–7 resp.

as the lawyer dedicatee, "will be able to gather herbs, the potent juices whereof may enable you to pass through the midst of monsters and reach the Golden Fleece."[71]

Erasmus' preface to his edition of *Tusculan Disputations*, published in 1523, is not unrelated to the 1501 (and 1519, see below) preface to *De officiis* and is likewise dedicated to a student of law, Johann von Vlatten (1498/9–1562), who was to obtain high political office (on both counts comparing to Thomas More).[72] In thinking about *Tusculan Disputations*, Erasmus marvels at the steady progression of philosophy from mere contemplation of the natural world to the worldly stage. While the progression began with Socrates, and Plato and Aristotle took philosophy into the courts of kings, the legislature, and law-courts (cf. *Tusc.* 5.10), it was only with Cicero that philosophy "has learned to speak in such a fashion that even a miscellaneous audience can applaud."[73] (And of course Erasmus is thinking that his *Enchiridion* had taken philosophy even further into the world of affairs.) Although Cicero wrote so many of his philosophical works when public affairs and the Roman state were in great crisis, he did not use his enforced leisure to escape into mindless pleasures but endeavoured to find a remedy *for these worldly issues* "in the most exalted precepts of philosophy."[74] On two instances Erasmus refers to the "blockheads" who repeatedly imagine that Cicero was only a stylist and do not see the learning, do not see the sifting through the best Greek writers on the good and happy life, do not see the deep understanding of what he was writing.[75] What Cicero says

71 *Ep.* 152. Allen 1, 357/40–2, CWE 2, 31/48–50. On the employment of Erasmus' edition of *De officiis* in English schools, and by the boy who was to become Henry VIII, see Aysha Pollnitz, *Princely Education in Early Modern Britain*, 52–5.

72 *Ep.* 1390. Von Vlatten received a doctorate in civil and canon law in 1526, at Bologna. He became a councillor to the Duke of Cleves in 1524, vice-chancellor of the duchies of Jülich-Cleves-Berg from 1530, and chancellor from 1554. According to the Stoic Cato, involvement in governmental affairs is entirely consistent with being a wiseman (*Fin.* 3.68). Seneca sharply criticized Zeno, Cleanthes, and Chrysippus for not becoming, as their philosophy dictated, involved in politics (cf. *Ot.* 3.2–3, 8.4; *Tr.* 4.1–7, 12.2–3).

73 *Ep.* 1390. Allen 5, 339/41–2, CWE 10, 97/45–6.

74 *Ep.* 1390. Allen 5, 339/48–9, CWE 10, 98/53. Cf. *Off.* 2.2–5, 3.1–4. Incredibly, all his writings on philosophy were written from 46 through 44 BCE. His death, in 43 BCE, was instigated by Octavius and Mark Antony.

75 *Ep.* 1390. Allen 5, 338/24–8, 340/87, CWE 10, 97/27–31, 99/95. What is worth imitating in Cicero, he argues in *Ciceronianus* (1528), is "the most distinctive thing that Cicero offers us, and that lies not in mere words nor in the outer layer of verbal expression but in substance and sentiments, in intellectual ability, in right judgment." ASD I-2, 709, CWE 28, 447–8.

applies to real life, including the contemporary world. The printing press makes it possible for many to converse with Cicero as if they were living with him.[76]

Recalling, it appears, Cicero's exemplifications of the expedience of worldly practices (one type of value) that are congruent with *honestum* (a radically different type of value) and the inexpedience of those that are not congruent, he exclaims: "What power and plenty in the way of sound and truly moral precepts!"[77] In seeing and reflecting on the true happiness of man we can be sure, he adds, that Cicero practised what he preached.[78] But why, we may ask, does Cicero's grasp of "true happiness" entail, in itself, that he practised what he preached? First, actually holding to the *honestum*, Stoics contended, denotes happiness.[79] Second, holding to *honestum* entails working out worldly issues in the best possible ways. Erasmus is saying that since Cicero was so totally focused on and so understanding of the unitary *honestum/indifferens* nature of true happiness, unlike most mortals, there is every reason to believe he practised what he preached.[80]

"Fixed procedures"

But how was it that Erasmus could so easily see the relationship of Cicero's exemplifications of *honestum/utile* in Book 3 of *De officiis* to the realities – 1500 years later – of his own world? And considering that the Stoicism described by Cicero was a product of the social and intellectual world of Greece and Rome, how relevant or applicable, in actuality, was this Stoicism to the world Erasmus knew, or to himself? Note one thing: The purpose of Stoicism and of *De officiis* was not so much to show the solution or solutions to particular social, political, and intellectual problems as to show how to go about solving such problems. There is a

76 *Ep*. 1390. Allen 5, 340/96–101, CWE 10, 99/106–10. Compare Erasmus' dedicatory letter (1516) to his edition of St Jerome (*Ep*. 396): "For such is my opinion: if a man had lived in familiar converse with Cicero (to take him as an example) for several years, he will know less of Cicero than they do who by constant reading of what he wrote converse with his spirit every day." *Ep*. 396. Allen 2, 212/39–43, CWE 3, 256/50–4.

77 *Ep*. 1390. Allen 5, 338/28–9, CWE 10, 97/31.

78 *Ep*. 1390. Allen 5, 338/30–2, CWE 10, 97/33–4.

79 Cf. *Fin*. 3.28, *Tusc*. 5.15–17.

80 Erasmus may also have imagined that the demonstrable actualities of Cicero's life signify this both/and outlook – necessarily entailing happiness.

"method" (*artem*) to the issues of life and those who do not believe this, Cicero contends in *De officiis*, are seriously misguided (2.6). Every situation requires application of the *honestum/utile* "formula" or "rule."[81] The formula is not something abstractly imposed. It must be worked out in every circumstance. To become "good calculators of duty" (ut boni rationcinatores officiorum esse possimus), the relevant questions must be asked over and over (1.59). Experience and constant practice are necessities.

As shown above, Erasmus had carefully studied exemplifications of the formula found in Book 3. And he well recognized, as shown by his intertextual to 1.32–2 (pp. 18–19), that duty to another individual and to society may change with changing circumstances. Again, however, in what ways and to what degree did this way of thinking actually frame his comprehension of contemporary issues and his formal writings?

In a letter to Colet of 1504, around December, Erasmus points to the fact that his concern has been with a set way of addressing issues. After mentioning *De taedio Iesu*, and that Colet may now hardly recognize the arguments set forth, and that the *Enchiridion* is about true goodness as against Jewish formality, he states:

> Conatus autem sum velut artificium quoddam pietatis tradere, more eorum qui de disciplinis certas rationes conscripsere.[82]

> What I have tried to do, in fact, is to teach a method of morals, as it were, in the manner of those who have originated fixed procedures in the various branches of learning.

What was "fixed" (cf. *Fin*. 3.24) was the Stoic *honestum/utile* formula. In fact there is every reason to believe Erasmus was here putting in his own words the "axiom of mathematics" thesis found in *De officiis*. In between pointing out the problematic nature of moral duty, in that it varies with varying circumstances (3.32), and agreement with Panaetius' contention "that no greater curse has ever assailed human life than the doctrine of those who have separated these two conceptions

81 Regarding a second meaning of the formula in *De officiis*, see n. 60 above.
82 *Ep*. 181. Allen 1, 405/50–2, CWE 2, 87/57–60.

[the *utile* and the *honestum*]" (3.34), Cicero compares *honestum* (seen as both/and) to an axiom of mathematics:

> Sed quoniam operi inchoato, prope tamen absoluto tamquam fastigium imponimus, ut geometrae solent non omnia docere, sed postulare, ut quaedam sibi concedantur, quo facilius, quae volunt, explicent, sic ego a te postulo, mi Cicero, ut mihi concedas, si potes, nihil praeter id, quod honestum sit, propter se esse expetendum. (3.33)
>
> We are now putting the capstone, as it were, upon our structure, which is unfinished, to be sure, but still almost completed; and, as mathematicians make a practice of not demonstrating every proposition, but require that certain axioms be assumed as true, in order more easily to explain their meaning, so, my dear [son] Cicero, I ask you to assume with me, if you can, that nothing is worth the seeking for its own sake except what is morally right.

In his edition of *De officiis* Erasmus paraphrases this statement in a marginal note. "Fastigium, id est, summam manum, ab aedificiis translatum: quibus perfectis, conum aliquis imponitur in summo." He then refers, across from *honestum*, to "first principles" (Principia prima per se nota, p. 139). Erasmus understood well that holding to the axiom *honestum* meant holding to that which is truly useful, that *honestum* and *utile* are two words which sound different but have one meaning (3.83) – and that this unitary both/and has to be worked out anew in every circumstance. He also knew that attitude and intent, acting on the basis of principle, have everything to do with the validity of one's decisions.

In the 1504 letter quoted above, Erasmus regrets that he has not heard from Colet for many years, informs him that he has been "wholly absorbed" studying Greek for the past three years, and states that he has learned much about theology from Origen's works.[83] In 1499 Erasmus knew little of either Greek or Origen. But did knowledge of Greek and Origen's works really change the Stoic cast of his mind? The "method of morals" Erasmus here refers to did not come – and this is certain – from Origen but from Cicero.[84]

Erasmus' *Enchiridion* works out at great length, I will demonstrate (Part VII), the ways in which, employing the Stoic formula or rule, ordinary

83 *Ep.* 181. Allen 1, 404/8–9, 404–5/34–6, 405/38–41, CWE 2, 86/10–11, 87/40–1, 87/45–8.

84 On Erasmus' rectifications of Origen in *De taedio Iesu* and the *Enchiridion*, see below, Part III, ch. 2 and Part VII, chs 1 and 2.

humans can be "good calculators of duty." The central difference is the context, Christianity, and that Erasmus goes even lower on the social scale than Cicero in illustrating situations and appropriate calculations.

Cicero's *De officiis* should be seen – as Erasmus saw it – as an end product (albeit modern philosophers often consider it a flawed product) of earlier attempts to relate Stoic *honestum/utile* thinking to real-world situations. Although no surviving Stoic text from the ancient world comes up to the examples found in *De officiis*, it can be noted that Stoics allowed even cannibalism, in certain circumstances (D.L. 7.121), and that from Zeno (c. 300 BCE) onwards the *utile* or *indifferens* side had been relentlessly focused on and conceptually broadened.[85] While the renegade Stoic Aristo (c. 260 BCE) had argued, contrarily, that indifferents are exactly that, entirely lacking in value, since virtue (the *honestum*) is the only good, this was not the position that won out. From the beginning Stoics saw a need to discriminate among indifferents. They determined that some things (indifferents) are preferred and others dispreferred, that some things are in accord with nature and others not, that moral duty can vary with circumstances. Much effort was expended in working out the details and in showing relationships to unbending truth.

Erasmus' *Enchiridion* goes much further than *De officiis* in working out the particulars of one's human nature, life problems, and the surrounding world as one holds at every moment to the central precepts of Christ's teachings. What truly works is inseparable from unbending truth. *De taedio Iesu* works out and expands Stoic discussions of natural instinct within this same unitary *honestum/indifferens* context.

The religiosity of *De officiis*

It is often imagined that what Erasmus appreciated about Cicero's thought was the ethics while Christianity, abetted by Platonism, supplied the spirituality.[86] This is not the case. Stoicism is inseparably spiritual

85 Separation of the two sides of the both/and for purposes of analysis was common. In *De officiis*, Book 1 takes up the *honestum* while Book 2 focuses on the *utile*. Book 3 rectifies apparent conflicts between the *utile* and the *honestum*.

86 Elaine Fantham refers repeatedly to the "moral benefits" Erasmus saw in Cicero and other ancient writers and "the essentially practical motives behind much of his concern with the classics." See "Erasmus and the Latin Classics," CWE 29 xliv and l. Manfred Hoffmann believes *De officiis* is about a "practical philosophy of civic virtues" and contrasts with Erasmus' concern with spirituality as well. *Honestum* is "a civic quality" "sought for mere personal advantage." *Rhetoric and Theology*, 24–7, 148, 205–6, 212. Cf. Rabil, "Cicero and Erasmus' Moral Philosophy," and John W. O'Malley, CWE 66, xxvii passim.

and ethical and Erasmus deeply felt the spirituality. He did not imagine that Cicero's prime concerns in *De officiis* were merely ethical or practical or probabilistic. Nor did he contrast a worldly, one-dimensional Cicero with the spirituality of Christianity. Although Cicero considered himself an Academic and as such a sceptic, he had found nothing more fundamental than Stoic spirituality and Erasmus fully absorbed, it is clear, this pagan religiosity. As he explicitly states in his 1501 preface, *De officiis* is a work about "divine" *honestum* (*fons ille divinus honestatis*).[87] Cicero's worldliness is not one-dimensional but two-dimensional and this being the case ethics is one with spirituality and divinity. Being a "good calculator of duty" requires at each step an uncompromising spiritual commitment. Following Cicero's (*honestum/utile*) method one can become, he concludes, not only eloquent but invulnerable to all the arrows of fortune and in this way immortal.[88]

In his 1519 preface to the second edition of *De officiis,* Erasmus praises Cicero's "rules for living" and the "attitude of mind" he demands of those who govern.[89] The "rules for living" referred to are of course Cicero's exemplifications – located in the social, economic, political, and legal actualities of Roman society – of the *honestum/utile* way of thinking. The "attitude of mind" bespeaks a mindset that, whatever the situation, unflinchingly holds to *honestum*. *De officiis* not only paints a wonderful picture of real-world (*honestum/utile*) virtue, it also reveals, he notes, how virtue in all its manifestations accords with nature.[90] Focusing on the uniqueness and originality of *De officiis* in relating the (*honestum/utile*) way of thinking advocated to the lives of ordinary people, Erasmus marvels that the author was a pagan and layman writing for pagans and laymen.[91] Although others may resist the message of *De officiis,* Erasmus assures the dedicatee that he himself is inflamed with a great zeal for the honour and virtue it teaches.[92] He contrasts the effect on him of the writings of modern scholastic theologians, those who claim to teach Christian philosophy and cover the same topics with great subtlety: "What a disgrace it is that a heart illuminated by the light of the Gospel should not see what was seen clearly by them [pagans] with only nature's candle

87 *Ep*. 152. Allen 1, 357/46.
88 *Ep*. 152. Allen 1, 357/47–50, CWE 2, 31–2/56–9.
89 *Ep*. 1013. Allen 4, 66/44, 46–7.
90 *Ep*. 1013. Allen 4, 66/45, 47–8, CWE 7, 72/51–4.
91 *Ep*. 1013. Allen 4, 66/43, CWE 7, 72/49–50.
92 *Ep*. 1013. Allen 4, 66/36, CWE 7, 72/43–4.

to show them the way; that we, the soldiers of religion under Christ's banner, who look for immortality from him as our reward, do not perform [both/and] what they did."[93] Other late statements also eulogize Cicero's philosophical writings. Consider the comment of Eusebius in the colloquy *The Godly Feast* (1522): "Speaking frankly among friends, I cannot read Cicero's *De senectute, De amicitia, De officiis, De Tusculanis quaestionibus* without sometimes kissing the book and blessing that pure heart, divinely inspired as it was."[94] In his introduction to *Tusculan Disputations* (1523) Erasmus hopes that Cicero lives peacefully in heaven, as he seems to have believed in the immortality of the soul, rewards in a future life, and the confidence brought about by a clear conscience.[95]

In the 1519 preface Erasmus exclaims that Cicero is almost like a deity in the many lessons he teaches![96] These lessons are about actions which reveal contempt for things "the modern public, not merely ordinary Christians but divines and monks as well, will do and suffer anything.[97] Princes and magistrates will find Cicero's (*utile/honestum*) representation of their role in life laughable and "crazy" because their minds and lives are wholly at odds with it. Far from guarding the public interests, even at the cost of their life, they see everything in terms of profit and high position (cf. *Fin.* 3.64, *Off.* 2.75–7).[98] If Cicero's way of thinking is ridiculous, even more so is Christ's.[99]

Could Erasmus' motto have been Stoic inspired?

Compared with the interpretations of Stoicism that preceded and came after Erasmus, in what sense did he think *De officiis'* "rules for living" and "attitude of mind" (1519) could make one "invulnerable" (1501)

93 *Ep.* 1013. Allen 4, 67/65–8, CWE 7, 73/72–6.

94 "Convivium religiosum" (*The Godly Feast*). ASD I-3, 251/620–3, CWE 39, 192/16–18. *De amicitia, De senectute,* and *Paradoxa Stoicorum* were published with the 1520 edition of *De officiis*. Note that he does not refer in the *Godly Feast* quote to *Paradoxa Stoicorum*, which paints a (satirical) one-dimensional picture of the Stoic wiseman.

95 *Ep.* 1390. Allen 5, 339/58–63, CWE 10, 68/64–9. On why the wiseman's conscience is always clear, note Seneca's discussion of reservation clauses (above, p. 44).

96 *Ep.* 1013. Allen 4, 66/48–9, CWE 7, 72/54–5.

97 *Ep.* 1013. Allen 4, 66/50–2, CWE 7, 72/57–9.

98 *Ep.* 1013. Allen 4, 66/55–9, CWE 7, 73/61–6.

99 Thomas More's Utopians illustrate, I will establish elsewhere, this "crazy" *honestum/utile* way of thinking described by Cicero and epitomized by Christ, by laying out the workings of an entire state. Illuminated (as above) by "nature's candle" the Utopians saw more than so-called Christians, those who have (as above) "the light of the Gospel."

to fortune? Was he thinking, like so many fourteenth- and fifteenth-century Italian humanists, of a Stoic wiseman that is oblivious to the trials and tribulations of worldly affairs? Was he thinking like Justus Lipsius and his circle, in the later sixteenth century, that Stoicism was about how to endure worldly affairs without complaint? In *De Constantia* (Antwerp, 1584), inspired by certain treatises of Seneca, Lipsius held that public evils are imposed by God and profitable to us. They are a product of the mind and must be treated as such. Although he sometimes discusses Stoic "indifferents" or related ideas, there was no close relationship with Cato's discussion in Book 3 of *De finibus* of "appropriate actions" (*kathekonta*) and "right actions" (*katorthomata*), much less Book 3 of *De officiis*. He was particularly interested in subjects such as the compatibility of the Stoic idea of fate with Christian belief.[100]

Erasmus' perspective was not only very different from what preceded and what came after, it was closest by far – and this will become ever more evident below, in Parts III–VII – to the ancient meaning of Stoicism. The invulnerability Erasmus thought *De officiis* could teach results from holding unbendingly to a few simple absolute truths (building on the variant ways of describing the *honestum*) at the same time as one works out worldly issues in ways that are inseparable from these truths (the *utile*, that which is truly workable and advantageous in the world of affairs). Being invulnerable in no way meant escapism or detachment from worldly realities – but the contrary. He saw correctly what so many others did not and have not seen, that Cicero's purpose in composing *De officiis* was to demonstrate how the Stoic both/and could be applied and must be applied to the world of affairs. *De officiis* was not about "Cicero's worldliness" but simply a further explication of the Stoic unitary *honestum/indifferens* frame of mind. Christianity is an augmentation, he shows in *De taedio Iesu* and the *Enchiridion*, of the same way of thinking. *Honestum* is simply Christianized. As long as the *utile* can be shown to be at every moment inseparable from the *honestum*, and vice versa, a Christian can be at peace – nothing can compromise his standing with God. The unitary both/and at all times in place he will be "invulnerable" and become "immortal," gaining eternal life.

100 See Brooke, *Philosophic Pride*; Cooper, "Justus Lipsius and the Revival of Stoicism in Late Sixteenth Century Europe"; Gerlo, *Juste Lipse (1547–1606)*; Lagrée, *Juste Lipse et la restauration du stoïcisme*; Long, "Stoicism in the Philosophical Tradition: Spinoza"; Morford, *Stoics and Neostoics*; Papy, "The First Christian Defender of Stoic virtue?"; and Saunders, *Justus Lipsius*.

Is not this Stoic *honestum/utile* invulnerability the hub from which Erasmus developed his much-debated motto?[101] In 1509 he placed on his seal the name "Terminus" and the words "*cedo nulli*," I concede nothing. Terminus was a god who protected boundary markers. Although Jupiter became sovereign god of the Romans, Terminus refused to give way and was left inside the temple when the temple of Jupiter was established on the Capitol.[102] He conceded, that is, nothing. In Erasmus' lifetime as now, Erasmus' meaning has been much debated. Some contemporary critics accused him of arrogance. But what if there is a rather easy explanation for this apparent arrogance? What if Erasmus was seeing Terminus in terms of Stoic *honestum*? Although deeply involved in all worldly issues, the Stoic wiseman holds firm, at every instant, to that which comprises the *honestum*. He is always invulnerable to fortune ("impregnable, fenced, and fortified," completely unafraid, *Tusc.* 5.41), always right, and always happy. There are boundary markers, that is, to all life's activities and here the wiseman concedes absolutely nothing. Compare *Tusculan Disputations* 5.83: "For if the Stoics have rightly fixed the limits of the good [like a boundary stone], the question is settled" (Si enim Stoici fines bonorum recte posiverunt,[103] confecta res est). For Erasmus the boundary markers were precepts at the very core of Christianity.[104] Worldly affairs, however bendable, and even if proper in worldly terms, had to be in accord with the absolute principles. In allowing nothing outside this unitary both/and frame Erasmus could well say "I concede nothing."

101 On Erasmus' motto, see Wind, "*Aenigma Termini*"; McConica, "The Riddle of Terminus"; and Sider, "*Concedo Nulli.*"

102 See the *Oxford Classical Dictionary*, revised edition, ed. S. Hornblower and A. Spawforth (Oxford, 2003), 288, 801, 1485.

103 Note J.E. King's comment in the Loeb edition. "As if it was a boundary stone on which was inscribed 'Finis Posiverunt Vicini' to mark the limits of a field" (511 n. 5). Cf. *Off.* 1.6: "No fixed, invariable, natural rules of duty can be posited except by those who say that moral goodness is worth seeking solely or chiefly for its own sake."

104 In the Colloquy Ἰχθυοφαγία (A Fish Diet) (1526) Terminus is implicitly equated with a proper understanding of divine law. Criticized are those who would make of human law a Terminus, "refusing to defer at all" (ASD I-3, 511/591–2, CWE 40, 693/33–4). "A Fish Diet" is about the correcting of "preposterous judgment" regarding both unbending and bending truth. See ASD I-3, 522/1003–5 passim and CWE 40, 704/26–8 passim.

R.J. Schoeck sees Erasmus' motto as representing Stoic tranquillity amid the tribulations of the world and his own sense of self.[105] In fact, however, this is the Stoicism of modern popular imagination and of the later sixteenth century, not the Stoicism Erasmus represents. J.K. McConica comments that Terminus meant more for Erasmus than Stoic defiance.[106] True, but what if Erasmus saw Stoicism as not one-dimensional and defiant (as in *Paradoxa Stoicorum*) but as two-dimensional and inseparably both/and (represented by *De finibus*, *Tusculan Disputations*, *De officiis*, *De natura deorum*, and *Academica*)? Robert D. Sider finds that Erasmus represents in his *Paraphrases*, contrary to his "I concede nothing" motto, not only an unyielding Paul but a yielding Paul. Sider considers this a "contradiction" and "irony." The yielding is "a purely temporary concession determined by the wiser course of action."[107] But in Stoicism the yielding, providing it does not contradict the unyielding, is neither irony nor a contradiction. And in yielding, some actions are preferred indifferents (the "wiser course") and others dispreferred indifferents.

Reasons for the neglect of *De taedio Iesu*

Oblivious to the Stoicism, scholarly analyses of Erasmus' arguments in *De taedio Iesu* have directed attention to scholasticism, the church fathers, "devotionalists," and rhetoric. The conclusion reached is that Erasmus simply employed his rhetorical skills to restate, with slight variations, accepted opinions. Although such an assessment is based on superficial readings, there are reasons for it. For one thing, Erasmus explicitly states at the end that he shares his view with modern theologians and that his view is not incompatible with writings of the older theologians (1290C). The fact that he pays attention through much of the treatise to statements of the fathers and high-scholastic theologians, in a way not characteristic of any of his later writings, just proves, it is held, that *De taedio Iesu* is immature, lacking in true originality, and little relevant to his later writings. But what did Erasmus mean in stating

105 Schoeck, *Erasmus of Europe: The Making of a Humanist, 1467–1500*, 292–3. Schoeck copies the view of Heckscher, "Reflections on Seeing Holbein's Portrait of Erasmus at Longford Castle," 132 and 144–5.

106 McConica, "The Riddle of Terminus," 3.

107 Sider, "*Concedo Nulli*," 9.

that he shares the views of the moderns? In fact he means little more than that he agrees that Christ had a human nature as well as a divine and that this was evident in Gethsemane. What Erasmus does not state here is that he has throughout unremittingly corrected what he overtly "agrees" with. Also misjudged is Erasmus' adjoining claim that his argument "chimes sweetly with reason and leaves nature unscathed" (pulcre concinere rationi, non pugnare cum natura) (1290C-D). The problem in interpreting this statement, as with the previous statement, is that it does not tell someone who has not analysed his discussion what that discussion was really about, how it recontextualizes, adds to, and changes the traditional arguments. What does he mean by "reason" and what does he mean by "nature"? What he means, worked out in detail, is not what scholastics or the fathers meant.

The fact that Erasmus was a rhetorician and, as such, lacked deep formal training in theology has also given scholars reason to believe that *De taedio Iesu* is of little substance. Being a rhetorician he depended for solutions to complex issues, it is often held, on the thinking of others, and the only viable doctrines around were those set forth in the massive tomes of the scholastics – built from an extreme logicizing of all known sources – or, alternately, the more simple and direct theological theses of the church fathers. Seeing Erasmus' options in this way, his strong disapproval in *De taedio Iesu* of scholastic methodologies has often been made light of on the grounds that there was no other serious source of thought available. This being the case, his opposition to scholastic views had to have been based on method, not doctrine.[108] Scholastic method was logical, humanist method was rhetorical. So from this angle also, it is imagined, the message of *De taedio Iesu* is essentially derivative, that what Erasmus added to traditional thought was little more than a rhetorical format.[109] In fact, I will show, Erasmus rewrites throughout the thinking of scholastics and the fathers – building from Stoicism.

---

108 See, for example, John W. O'Malley, CWE 70, xii. Even John Gleason, who demonstrations that "Colet had nothing to teach Erasmus about scriptural exegesis at any stage," agrees with those who believe (he cites Paul O. Kristeller) humanists had no real alternative to scholastic philosophy and Erasmus believed that the scholastic method was indispensable. See *John Colet*, 233, 143–4 resp. Cf. Ackroyd, *The Life of Thomas More*, 46. Tracy states that the theology of the church fathers "was the only viable alternative to scholasticism." See *Erasmus of the Low Countries*, 32.

109 See above, p. 49.

A further reason for believing that Erasmus' main interest was in opposing a rhetorical style to scholastic methods is that he clearly states that he is opposed to the latter. In his introduction, a letter written in October 1499 in response to a letter from Colet,[110] he agrees with Colet's criticism of the methods and style of modern theologians. Thinking of the influence on theologians of the *"logica moderna,"* methodologies relating to Peter of Spain's widely used textbook *Parva logicalia* (*The Small Logicals*) (c. 1250),[111] theologians are said to "spend their lives in sheer hair-splitting and sophistical quibbling," "a kind of sterile and thorny subtlety." Worst of all is "their stammering, foul, and squalid style of writing."[112] They quarrel over "insignificant trifles," such as "whether God could have taken the form of the devil or an ass."[113] In this regard Erasmus makes a point of showing, in the body of *De taedio Iesu*, that John Duns Scotus (c. 1266–1308) for all his subtlety (he was commonly referred to as "Doctor Subtilis") did not use words carefully (1274A).[114] And we may note here that Erasmus refers elsewhere in the work to such things as the language used by Christ and the role of circumstantial evidence (1267F) – and employs a debate format.[115]

---

110 *Ep.* 108.

111 The logicians had made grammar the servant of logic and had almost entirely ignored rhetoric, the third element in the traditional course of studies known as the *"trivium."* At the centre of this revolutionary, non-Aristotelian, "terminist" thinking was concern with "the properties of terms," analyses of the changes in meaning that can be identified when the positions of terms in a proposition are changed, and rules about "supposition." The "modist" school of logic, influenced in particular by Thomas of Erfurt (c. 1280–c. 1330), went even further from natural language and common sense meanings. Although this type of thinking was in itself "a major achievement: the first systematic syntax developed in Western linguistics," what mattered "was the way reality was described, not reality itself." See Pinborg, "Speculative Grammar," 260 and 261, and Courtenay, *Schools and Scholars in Fourteenth-Century England*, 227. A new edition of Thomas of Erfurt's *Grammatica speculative* was published in London in 1515 and Thomas More was to take on this type of thinking in his *Utopia*.

112 *Ep.* 108. Allen 1, 246/20–1, 247/26–31, CWE 1, 203/24–5, 31–4.

113 *Ep.* 108. Allen 1, 247/37, 43–4, CWE 1, 203/42, 50–1.

114 See below, p. 114. In response to such contentions theologians would mount, a few years later, sustained attacks on Erasmus.

115 Not to be overlooked, Cicero and Aulus Gellius, Erasmus' two prime sources for Stoicism in *De taedio Iesu*, used the debate format (though not obtrusively) in their discussions of Stoic philosophy. The exception, among Cicero's works, is *De officiis*.

In his conclusion he again criticizes scholastics, agreeing with Colet that the modern method of disputation, however precise it may seem to its devotees, is "niggling, nit-picking, threadbare, and thoroughly sophistical" (1290D-E). What Erasmus admires is "the roughhewn style" of the old theologians, such as Origen, Ambrose, Jerome, Augustine, and Chrysostom (1290E). Another problem with scholastic methodology is that, unlike rhetoric, it does not move a larger audience. "It is foolish to perform a play, however brilliantly, if no one is watching" (1290E).[116]

And yet, analysis of the treatise shows that rhetoric is not here a method in its own right. Rhetoric is the handmaiden of a philosophy – and a philosophic methodology. The difference between a philosophic methodology and a rhetorical methodology is huge – as were the consequences.

Natural instinct

The debate with Colet, in late 1499, was anything but a rhetorical debate *in utramque partem*, a setting forth of two more or less equally plausible theses. Erasmus was certain Colet was wrong and was determined to show, building from Stoicism, why. At the time he wrote *De contemptu mundi* (c. 1485–8) he might have found much to agree with in Colet's one-dimensional, non-worldly outlook, but emphatically not now. Whether Erasmus began editing *De officiis* before or after the debate with Colet is unknown.[117] What we do know is that his point of view in the debate, evidenced by letters immediately thereafter, around October 1499, sprang from a mind already deeply affected by Stoicism. Clearly, however, Erasmus worked out his thinking only in the treatise which resulted, probably finished by the summer of 1501 when he began the *Enchiridion*. Since Erasmus had completed work on *De officiis* some time before 5 April 1501,[118] it is clear that he had been working on *De taedio Iesu* at roughly the same time. Although *De taedio Iesu* deals with Christ's Passion and the *Enchiridion* with the meaning of Christianity

116 Cf. *The Praise of Folly* (1509, pub. 1511), ed. and trans. Clarence H. Miller (New Haven, 1979), 43–4, ASD IV-3, 104/591–4, 598–601, 602–3.

117 A statement by Erasmus' friend Willem Hermans in 1494 indicates that Erasmus was even by that date focusing on *De officiis*. See n. 70 above.

118 *Ep*. 151. Allen 1, 355/16, CWE 2, 29/22–3.

for ordinary Christians, the two works are the product of a singular, Stoic mindset. Indeed, the *Enchiridion* should be considered simply a continuation, within a different context, of the way of thinking found in *De taedio Iesu*. Standing out in this regard is the fact that the discussion of Origen near the end of *De taedio Iesu* is taken up again in the *Enchiridion*. Although scholars have unanimously believed that Erasmus' reading of Origen, who is usually considered a biblical theorist and Platonist, had much to do with inspiring the *Enchiridion* (1503), what has never been noticed is that Erasmus radically rewrites Origen in terms of the Stoic *honestum/indifferens* frame, and within this frame works out and expands Stoic natural instinct. This rewriting is found in *De taedio Iesu* as well as the *Enchiridion*.

What Erasmus had learned about Stoicism – from editing *De officiis* and studying, in particular, *De finibus*, *Tusculan Disputations*, and Book 5 (now lost) of Epictetus' *Discourses*, as quoted and discussed by Aulus Gellius in *Attic Nights* – goes far in explaining, even where he finds it necessary to expand or redirect an interpretation of Stoicism, everything deduced and argued about Christ and Christianity. While the *Enchiridion* would systematically apply the Stoic *honestum/indifferens* way of thinking to contemporary issues, both *De taedio Iesu* and the *Enchiridion* work out and expand, at length, Stoic thinking on natural instincts (*oikeiosis*) and character traits.

Of paramount importance, Erasmus is intent on showing in *De taedio Iesu* that Christ himself suffered ineradicable natural instincts – and what this means for our understanding of Christianity. While theologians after the Councils of Chalcedon (451) and Constantinople (681) had attempted to explain *how* it could be that Christ was both divine and human, now a dogma of the faith, and scholastics had subjected the apparent contradiction to masses of distinctions, in *De taedio Iesu* Erasmus assesses the matter from a different standpoint. What he saw was not a logical problem but a human nature problem and a motivation problem – and that Stoicism provided the essential answers. Transfixed by the Stoic doctrine of *oikeiosis* he shows at length that humans are born with natural instincts and character traits that are ineradicable – and that only within this context can one truly see who Christ was and the true nature of Christianity.

Erasmus' all-pervasive and previously unheard of focus on ineradicable character traits and ineradicable natural instincts – found even in Christ himself – leads us to questions regarding the origins of this fixation.

4 What Had Drawn Erasmus to Stoicism? A Resolution of Bodily and Mental Issues

Should we consider Erasmus' attachment to Stoicism merely an intellectual matter? Analysis of *De taedio Iesu* and the *Enchiridion* reveal a preoccupation, building from Stoic *oikeiosis*, with ineradicable natural instincts and character traits – and within this context Christ's human nature. What had inspired this interest? Why did he turn to Stoicism for the basics of his positions, not only the human nature theses but the both/and relationships between worldly variables and absolute principles? Had he merely chanced upon the true nature of Stoicism and being intellectually gifted deduced from this a new understanding of life and Christianity? Or could there be a deeply personal reason that explains his initial interest and all consuming focus on Stoicism? Why had he latched on to this philosophy so early, before even he had a command of Greek, before he had digested Origen – often considered key markers in his intellectual development? Looking ahead, did expertise in the Greek language or Origen and ever-increasing knowledge of ancient literature and other church fathers seriously affect this early mindset?

The secondary literature

The youthful physical and mental sufferings alleged by Erasmus have been examined many times.[119] What should be made, it is asked, of Erasmus' later accounts, particularly in two lengthy letters written in 1514 and 1516 and a short autobiography written in 1524?[120] Scholars have focused not so much on the importance for Erasmus' mental

119 See Brabant, "Érasme, ses maladies et ses médecins," 1:539–68; Charlier, *Erasme et l'amitié d'aprés sa correspondance*; Chomarat, "Pourquoi Erasme s'est-il fait moine?"; Crahay "Recherches sur le *Compendium Vitae* attribué à Erasmé"; DeMolen, "Erasmus as Adolescent"; Godin, "Une biographie en quête d'auteur"; Hyma, *The Youth of Erasmus*; Bruce Mansfield, *Erasmus in the Twentieth Century*, 192–7; Minnich and Meissner, "The Character of Erasmus"; Mestwerdt, *Die Anfänge des Erasmus*; Post, *The Modern Devotion*; Rice "Erasmus and the Religious Tradition"; Schoeck, *Erasmus of Europe I: The Making of a Humanist 1467–1500*; Sowards, "The Youth of Erasmus"; Tracy, *Erasmus of the Low Countries*, 7–32, and *Erasmus: The Growth of a Mind*; and Weiler, "The Dutch Brethren of the Common Life."

120 *Eps*. 296 (Allen 1, 564–73, CWE 2, 294–303) and 447 (Allen 2, 291–312, CWE 4, 6–32), and *Compendium vitae* (Allen 1, 46–52, CWE 4, 403–10).

development of his early sufferings, and their nature, as the accurateness or truthfulness of his later depictions of these sufferings. Looking at the matter in this way, various reasons have been found for questioning, revising, or rejecting Erasmus' descriptions of his youthful sufferings:

- There is a large time lapse between his lengthy autobiographical statements and his youth.
- He is secretive and inconsistent in discussing certain aspects of his youth, most especially relationships with his brother and parents. Particularly problematic here is his illegitimate birth.
- He expresses great bitterness over his monastic upbringing but studies of the schooling carried out by the Brethren of the Common Life at 's-Hertogenbosch and the Augustinian monastery at Steyn (1486–93) have revealed nothing unusual or particularly harsh. In fact Erasmus had some friends and teachers at these schools who recognized his abilities and were not unsympathetic with his goals.
- He wrote chapters 1–11 of *De contemptu mundi* (c. 1485–8), in praise of the monastic life, while at Steyn.
- The 1494 version of the *Antibarbarorum liber* does not contain the statements denigrating monasticism and ignorant monks found in the printed versions, beginning in 1520.
- No evidence from his monastic years proves that he could not at that time endure fasts and vigils.
- The 1516 autobiographical account was part of his request for a papal dispensation from his monastic vows. To this end he may have invented or radically built up the allegation that his original vows were made under constraint.
- When he wrote the autobiographical accounts he was increasingly being attacked for statements and interpretations considered heterodox or anti-monastic found in the *Praise of Folly* (1511)[121] and his Greek *New Testament* (1516).[122] In responding to the attackers, who tended to be scholars of the monastic orders, it is likely, the argument goes, that Erasmus altered the actualities of how he became a monk and his youthful monastic experiences.

121 Note Thomas More's lengthy defence of *The Praise of Folly*, against Martin Dorp, in 1515. CWM 15, 1–127.

122 On the negative reactions, see Rummel, *Erasmus and His Catholic Critics*. Erasmus' *New Testament* included not only the Greek but emendations of the Latin translation and his philological notes. On his annotations, see Rummel, *Erasmus' Annotations on the New Testament*.

In short, what tends to be focused on in explaining Erasmus' mental development is not his youthful sufferings, which tend to be discounted, but a multitude of extraneous factors. Thinking primarily in terms of intellectual development, as distinct from mental and emotional development, scholars have attempted to sort out complex educational and literary influences. They have looked at borrowings from ancient literature, various strands in medieval thought (such as the fathers of the church and late medieval pietism), contemporary intellectual movements, most especially humanism, and his own talent. In particular, they have assessed relationships to the Devotio Moderna environment of his early schooling;[123] pointed to a shift in the themes of his poetry, around 1490–1, from classical and rhetorical to "moral-philosophical and sacred";[124] contended that beginning in 1499 John Colet had an immense influence on his religious development;[125] and agreed that in 1501 he came under the spell (through Jean Vitrier) of the Greek father Origen.[126] The influences of saints Jerome and Augustine and the rhetoric of Cicero, Quintillian, and Lorenzo Valla are also well attended to. Erasmus, everyone agrees, was a many-sided genius.

Questions

Is it the case, however, that Erasmus' repeated complaints about his youth are little relevant to his intellectual development in that they were later in time and reasons have been found for doubting their trustworthiness? Why is it that our understanding of the relationship of Erasmus' youth and early adulthood to his intellectual achievements is so shallow? Have scholars rightly found no serious connections between his complaints and early works such as *De taedio Iesu* and the *Enchiridion*?

Writing before much of the literature doubting the truthfulness of Erasmus' accounts of his youth, James D. Tracy attempted to connect

123 See in particular Hyma, Post, and Weiler.

124 See Harry Vredeveld, ASD I-7, p. 18 and Reedijk, *The Poems of Desiderius Erasmus*.

125 See Duhamel, "The Oxford Lectures of John Colet"; Kaufman, "John Colet and Erasmus' *Enchiridion*"; Lupton, *A Life of John Colet*; Schroeck, *Erasmus of Europe: The Making of a Humanist, 1467–1500*, 226–31; Seebohm, *The Oxford Reformers*; and Trapp, *Erasmus, Colet and More*, 79–141. John Gleason has now shown in *John Colet* that most of Colet's commentaries on scripture postdate Erasmus' 1499 visit.

126 See Godin, *Erasme lecteur d'Origène*.

Erasmus' youth and writings in his influential *Erasmus: The Growth of a Mind* (1972). Using a large amount of secondary and primary material, he brings in family relationships, conflicts with his monastic environment, and a deep need of friendship. In this setting Erasmus' ideas, described (rather unconvincingly) in terms of "*humanitas, libertas,* and *simplicitas,*" are said to have "emerged gradually and from an inner personal logic."[127] What can be made of this explanation? What was the "logic"? Was the inner logic that led to his "ideas" unrelated to any encounter by Erasmus with his emotions and his body? Did Erasmus not understand himself? Is this "inner personal logic" beyond our understanding? If we cannot comprehend the mystery behind the "logic" and do not understand the logic how sure can we be of the meaning of the ideas that allegedly emerged from it?[128]

Illuminated in all this is a major lacuna in current research. What Erasmus learned about himself, his personality, beyond particular societal conflicts, has not been seriously addressed. The questions asked relate to how his intellect developed in confrontation with the world. His suffering, to the extent it existed, ends up as a by-product. Accordingly, his youthful unhappiness is not seen in terms of what he learned from this unhappiness but in terms of perceived intellectual goals. He was on one track, his opponents on another. Against the anti-intellectualism of many monks and the scholastic logical methods of the theologians (both lambasted in *Antibarbarorum liber*), he had early in life devoted himself to classical literature and to writing poetry and prose in a classical style. Like the humanists that had preceded him, his interest was in the *studia humanitatis*, i.e., rhetoric, grammar, poetry, history, and moral philosophy (interpreted in rhetorical terms). In short, the picture that emerges is that of a precocious and sensitive youth whose pain was rooted in the fact that his objectives diverged greatly from those around him. He was blazing new paths and suffering in such cases is more or less the usual result. There was a price to pay for his contempt for "barbarians," those monks and others who

127 Tracy, *Erasmus: The Growth of a Mind*, 19. Writing at about the same time and eschewing psychological interpretations, Albert Rabil attempted to show that Erasmus' intellectual development was "dependent upon some self-conscious resolution of the conflict between a vaguely felt childhood religion and an adolescent love of Latin literature." See *Erasmus and the New Testament*, x.

128 Tracy expands on this outlook in a much later work, *Erasmus of the Low Countries* (1996). See my analysis below, Part VII, pp. 306–16.

spurned learning, opposed Christianity to classical culture, or thought in scholastic terms.[129]

But what if it can be shown that considerable evidence proves Erasmus' central claims regarding his youth and that early writings such as *De taedio Iesu* and the *Enchiridion* are all about the solutions he worked out – building from Stoicism? What if, that is, the "wellsprings" of Erasmus' personality and the effect on his mind and intellect need not be left to psychological speculation but are demonstrable and at the very core of what his life and writings were about?

Revealed below is what Erasmus learned from his youthful and early adult suffering – and the far-reaching effects. Conflict between his goals and his environment was only the larger context. What Erasmus became conscious of through suffering progressed far beyond vexation at insensitive guardians, non-intellectual monks, scholastic theologians, and general societal and religious attitudes. Step by step he came to realize who he was and what the implications were. The way he came to view life and assess issues was rooted in these discoveries of himself. That is to say, there is a direct causal relationship between what he learned about his personality through suffering and how he thought, what he studied, and the content of his writings.

Three steps

Analysis reveals three steps in Erasmus' mental and emotional development that were to forever affect his mindset. The *terminus ante quem* for these three steps is late 1499, the date of Erasmus' debate with Colet – fifteen years before the earliest autobiographical account.

(1) Many years before 1499, it can be shown, Erasmus had distinguished between the variousness of his conflicts with his environment and two base – very personal – causes of his disaccord. One of the causes was mental, the other physical. In short he had come

129 On the divide between scholastics and humanists see, among other works, Rummel, *The Humanist-Scholastic Debate in the Renaissance and Reformation*; Overfield, *Humanism and Scholasticism in Late Medieval Germany*; Kristeller, *Renaissance Thought: The Classic, Scholastic, and Humanist Strains*. More than resulting from different professional goals, the differing methodologies of scholastics and humanists made conflict almost inevitable. See Nauert, "Humanism as Method," 438.

to recognize that the problem was not just with the world around him but with himself, and why this was the case.

(2) Some time after identifying the mental and physical causes of his problem he had arrived, probably by 1495, at a deeply felt explanation, from which he never veered, for these two base causes.
(3) Stoicism was the tool by which he had worked out, beginning at least by 1497, the implications of (1) and (2).

Once it is seen that the two base causes Erasmus sees of his problems, his explanation for them, and the essential solution were arrived at before 1499, and are not in truth contestable, the doubts, revisions, and rejections of Erasmus' accounts of particular sufferings can be recalibrated. Regarding what mattered most for his intellectual development he was quite accurate. His emotional experience was real and had an enduring effect. It was not from reading books or abstract intellectualizing that he ascertained his mental and physical characteristics and came to a conclusion regarding their deeper meaning. On the other hand, grasping these traits and zeroing in on an explanation had a profound effect on what he came to read. There is a reason why he had become so engrossed in Stoicism, why – unlike his predecessors – he was able to see and appreciate Stoic thinking on natural instincts at birth, ineradicable character traits, and the relationship between worldly variables and unbending principles.

The first step: Discovering a mental and a physical cause of his suffering

> I have always regarded as the worst of my misfortunes the fact that I had been forced into the kind of profession which was utterly repugnant to my mind and body alike: (a) to my mind because I disliked ritual and loved freedom, and (b) to my body because, even had I been wholly satisfied to live such a life, my bodily constitution could not tolerate its hardships.[130]

This statement is found in the 1514 autobiographical letter mentioned above, written to Servatius Rogerus, once a fellow monk at Steyn (1486–93) and now head of the house. It encapsulates, I will demonstrate, the nature and actuality of Erasmus' youthful and early adult suffering.

130 *Ep*. 296. Allen 1, 566/28–33, CWE 2, 295/28–34.

There is every reason to believe Erasmus' description of these two root causes and that he had ascertained these causes not later in life but many years before 1499. He had not just suffered in his youth; he had wanted to know what it was about himself that ran so counter to the world that surrounded him – and had found the answers.

(A) A MIND THAT LOVED FREEDOM AND DISLIKED RITUAL

The love of freedom and dislike of ritual Erasmus alleges are buttressed over and over by known actualities.

To begin with, illegitimacy entailed a restriction of his freedom, both mental and physical. Born in Rotterdam, in 1466 or 1469, he was the second of two illegitimate sons. His father was either a priest at the time or later became a priest. Considering that society looked down on illegitimacy and the shifty and obscure manner in which he discusses the issue, particularly in his *Compendium vitae* (1524), we may conclude, as many have, that he felt shame over his illegitimacy throughout his life. However, in assessing this shame we need to think more about the very real curtailment of his mental and physical freedom than the "self-serving" agendas so many see. Even his joining a monastic order can be related to a limitation of choices necessitated by his legal, as well as social, status as an illegitimate.[131] Later in life he had to deal with his illegitimacy in some very consequential situations. A benefice could not be granted to a person of illegitimate birth without papal dispensation, and supplication for a benefice required a statement as to whether one was or was not of legitimate birth.

An even more grievous lack of freedom in his youth resulted from the death of both parents when he was around fourteen. Their deaths left him in limbo, dependent on guardians. He and his brother were first sent to the school of the Brethren of the Common Life at 's-Hertogenbosch. In the 1516 account he states, regarding the Brethren, "Their chief purpose, if they see a boy whose intelligence is better bred and more active than ordinary, as able and gifted boys often are, is to break their spirit and depress them with corporal punishment, threats and recriminations and various other devices – taming them, they call it – until they make him fit for the monastic life."[132] Such practices may have been common but this misses the point. Erasmus was in his youth

131 Chomarat, "*Pourquoi Erasme s'est-il fait moine?*"

132 *Ep.* 447. Allen 2, 295/103–7, CWE 4, 11/109–14.

a very uncommon person, extremely sensitive as well as brilliant. What freedom meant for him was not what it meant for other students. The guardians also mismanaged the estate, according to Erasmus, forcing him and his brother to the brink of starvation. Worst of all they connived, along with others, at getting them into a monastery.

Weak from a recurring sickness, almost destitute, and continually browbeaten from many sides, he eventually joined (his freedom having been curtailed) the Augustinian order at age sixteen.[133] Even if Erasmus somewhat embellished the story, joining a monastic order certainly entailed a limitation of one's freedom. A precocious youth, better fitted for the university, there is no good reason to doubt that this curtailment of his freedom was even at that early age very important to him. In a similar situation many of his contemporaries would not have resisted being nudged or pushed into the monastic life. Nor is it allowable to hold that Erasmus fabricated the story of being "forced" into the monastery to get a dispensation from the pope. The claim that he was pushed into the monastery is found not only in the 1516 account, which accompanied his application for a dispensation, but in the 1514 letter to Servatius.

A letter to an unidentified nun, around 1487, which refers to "all the chaos of my affairs and the miseries of my condition," indicates (there is a dearth of sources) that Erasmus was not in fact having a happy time in the monastery.[134] Over and over the bitterness stands out. His noting that in his probationary year there was pleasant company, singing, games, verse writing competitions, and a non-structured way of life[135] does not support, as often imagined, arguments that his allegations of sufferings are contrived and contradictory.[136] In fact the opposite is proven. In pointing out a happy year and why he was happy he reveals his dislike of ritual and love of freedom. Certainly his poetry writing, letter writing, and other literary endeavours were, among other things, expressions of freedom. Whether his protestations of affection in letters to Servatius Rogerus, a fellow monk, represent exercises in a style of writing or homosexual tendencies or both, they signal at the same time his individuality and freedom from rules. In fact it appears that those

133 *Ep.* 447. Allen 2, 296/136–344, CWE 4, 12–18/146–376.

134 *Ep.* 2. Allen 1, 75/20–1, CWE 1, 3/22–3. Erasmus here quotes Ovid: "shipwrecked am I, and lost, 'mid waters chill.'"

135 *Ep.* 447. Allen 2, 301/351–6, CWE 4, 18/384–9.

136 Sowards represents this view. See "The Youth of Erasmus," 17–18.

in charge did attempt to clamp down on such relationships.[137] While Erasmus' mind and abilities expanded rapidly during this period, even helped along by certain fellow monks, particularly Cornelius Gerard and Willem Hermans, some monks seem to have been jealous of or disapproved of his devotion to poetry and ancient literature and his aloofness from more usual concerns.[138]

He left the monastery at Steyn in 1493 (seeking freedom) after being offered a position as Latin secretary to Hendrik van Bergen, bishop of Cambrai, and then in 1495, thanks to the patronage of Hendrik, made his way (seeking freedom) to the University of Paris to study theology. Although life there, at the Collège de Montaigu, was not that of the monastery, he was distressed by the savage discipline (lack of freedom) and austere living conditions imposed by the headmaster, Jon Standonck. He describes in the colloquy "A Fish Diet" (*Ἰχθυοφαγία*) (1526) not only the harsh and scanty diet and the beatings of students, who were often innocent, but the rotten plaster, lice, and stinking latrines, all of which "caused the deaths of many very capable, gifted, promising youths and brought others (some of whom I myself knew) to blindness, nervous breakdowns, or leprosy. Not a single student in fact was out of danger."[139]

He left the Collège de Montaigu (seeking freedom) within a year, in 1496, taking lodging in a student residence. As a means of supporting himself (seeking freedom) he gave private lessons to young students. In 1496–9 he began creating (as a way of maintaining his freedom) teaching materials, *De ratione studii* (*On the Method of Study*) (1511), *De conscribendis epistolis* (*On the Writing of Letters*) (1521), *De duplici copia rerum ac verborum* (*Foundations of the Abundant Style*) (1512), and *Adagia* (*Adages*) (the short first edition, 1500).

In Paris and especially in his many travels, Erasmus, as a Canon Regular, had trouble with dress codes (ritual, restrictions on his freedom). He later describes at some length these problems.[140] What was proper in one place or country was out of order in another place or country. Even threats of death had resulted. He was "obliged to change his dress as an

137 See Tracy, *Erasmus and the Low Countries*, 22 and 222 n. 31.

138 *Ep*. 22. Allen 1, 103/5–19, CWE 1, 35/5–20.

139 Ἰχθυοφαγία (A Fish Diet). ASD I-3, 495–536/1315–70 at 531/1331–5, CWE 40, 677–762 at 715/33–5.

140 *Ep*. 447. Allen 2, 304–6/464–544, CWE 4, 22–4/507–99.

octopus changes colour."[141] In the company of great persons the dress situation became even more complicated. In 1506, on a trip to Italy, he stopped wearing the dress of a Canon Regular (doing away with this ritual, increasing his freedom).

The need (desiring freedom) for money, resulting from living outside the cloister, was an ever-present source of tension. Over and over his letters come back to his dire straits and the necessity of locating a patron. Among his many attempts to find supporters, two successful examples are Hendrik van Bergen, who made it possible for him to leave the monastery in 1493 and eventually to travel to the University of Paris, and Lord Mountjoy, a former student at Paris, who made it possible for him to make his 1499 trip to England. And yet he never dreamed of giving up his freedom. His contemptuous reaction, in the 1514 letter, to Servatius Rogerus' offer of assistance by placing him in some monastic setting with an ample salary is very much in keeping with what we know of Erasmus' actions and attitude in earlier times. "Perhaps you are going to place me with some nuns, to be a servant to women; I, who have never consented to be a servant, even to archbishops or kings! The amount of my salary has no interest for me, for I do not aim at becoming rich, so long as I possess just enough means to provide for my health and free time for my studies and to ensure that I am a burden to none."[142]

Regarding his illegitimacy and dress he sought dispensations (freedom and release from ritual). In 1506 Pope Julius II gave him a dispensation that allowed him to hold a benefice notwithstanding his illegitimacy,[143] and in 1517 Pope Leo X absolved him of any penalties that might have resulted from abandonment of his monastic dress.[144] Although admitted to the priesthood in 1492, he at no time exercised priestly functions (giving himself freedom and release from ritual).[145]

In short, there is every reason why Erasmus saw his many youthful and young adult problems in terms of a singular desire for freedom and rejection of ritual. This was the case. His path was not a usual path.

---

141 *Ep.* 447. Allen 2, 306/537, CWE 4, 24/592–3.

142 *Ep.* 296. Allen 1, 572/212–18, CWE 2, 302/228–33. The attitude evinced here seems to bespeak a relationship to his motto: "I concede nothing" (*cedo nulli*). See above, pp. 75–8.

143 *Ep.* 187A.

144 *Ep.* 517.

145 No evidence indicates that he did not remain faithful to his priestly vows. See, however, Tracy, *Erasmus of the Low Countries*, 30.

(B) A BODILY CONSTITUTION THAT COULD NOT TOLERATE HARDSHIPS

Erasmus' inability to withstand bodily hardships is also well supported by the evidence.[146]

Even in his 1501 preface to *De officiis* he refers to the walks he often takes after meals, as the dedicatee knows, "because of ill-health."[147] In the second preface to *De officiis*, written in 1519, he again comes back to the need to repair his health.[148] If there is no actual document affirming his contention that at Steyn he could not endure fasts and vigils, there is every reason to believe him.[149] Note, for one thing, that such weaknesses are evident throughout his young adult and adult life and that he emphasizes in a letter of April 1498 that his body is adverse to vigils, fasts, and all hardships. "I am the most sensitive man alive. My health can never, even at its best, tolerate vigils or fasting, or hardships of any kind."[150] This statement cannot be tied to his later controversies with scholars among the various monastic orders. In another letter written about the same time he speaks of a daily recurrent fever, for a month and a half, and that he sees little reason to hope for recovery.[151]

In later discussions he insisted that his body and health had always been very delicate and that the problem persisted. In the year before his entering the monastery he was sick for more than a year with a quartan fever, "contracted from his mean and illiberal schooling."[152] If the latter is perhaps an add-on, it is hard to doubt the sickness itself. In the later accounts he again emphasizes that from a peculiarity of his body he had always found fasting virtually impossible.[153] Most of his health issues, Erasmus here implies, were fully in place during his stay in the monastery

---

146 Scepticism about Erasmus' alleged physical weaknesses and sicknesses reaches a high point in Eugene Rice's contention that Erasmus was here simply making up excuses to support the fact that he was unsuited for monasticism. See "Erasmus and the Religious Tradition, 1495–1499," 396. He accepts that Erasmus had mental issues but defines them, as have many historians, moralistically: a weak will, a weak character, a person given to deceit.

147 *Ep.* 152. Allen 1, 356/12–14, CWE 2, 30/16–18.

148 *Ep.* 1013. Allen 4, 65–6/21–2, CWE 7, 72/27–8.

149 Voicing the prevailing scepticism, Tracy states that there is "no clear indication" that he was unable to endure fasts and vigils in the monastery, "as he later complained." See *Erasmus of the Low Countries*, 22.

150 *Ep.* 75. Allen 1, 202/9–10, CWE 1, 151/11–12.

151 *Ep.* 74. Allen 1, 201/1–4, CWE 1, 150/1–6.

152 *Ep.* 447. Allen 2, 299/240–4, CWE 4, 15/262–6.

153 *Ep.* 296. Allen 1, 564/17–18, CWE 2, 295/18–19.

at Steyn. Because of digestive problems he had to eat small amounts of food, abstain entirely from some types of foods, and eat regularly.[154] Fish he found intolerable. The mere smell gave him a severe headache and even a slight fever. During Lent the problem became acute.[155] In the colloquy "A Fish Diet" he states that a whole array of illnesses come upon him (now as in the past) from eating fish, including fever, headache, vomiting, and kidney stones.[156] "Through some obscure quirk of nature, he has been from very boyhood so averse to eating fish and so incapable of fasting that he has never attempted it without danger to his life."[157] He was also subject to severe sleeping problems, especially when he had no supper or his sleep became interrupted.[158] Climate was also an issue. He mentions in particular heat and the Dutch climate.[159] At the Collège de Montaigu (1495–6) these problems were accentuated, according to his *Compendium vitae*, by the rigid food diets. He became extremely ill from bad eggs and unhealthy living quarters.[160]

In time he obtained a papal dispensation allowing him not to eat fish on Fridays[161] and episcopal and papal dispensations permitting him to eat meat, eggs, and milk on fast days.[162]

It may be debated whether, or in what ways, or why, particular statements in Erasmus' later autobiographical accounts are distorted but what cannot be denied is the reality in his youth and as a young adult of the two root causes he gives for his sufferings – and that these sufferings were very real. The two causes existed even if we do not know exactly when Erasmus first perceived – certainly some years before 1499 – their existence.

The second step: Human nature

In his autobiographical accounts Erasmus attributes, at a deeper level, his youthful problems to human nature. What can be shown here again is that this was not a view later concocted by him but that sometime

154 *Ep.* 447. Allen 2, 302/388–96, CWE 4, 19–20/424–34.
155 *Compendium vitae.* Allen 1, 51/135–7, CWE 4, 409/152–4.
156 Ἰχθυοφαγία (A Fish Diet). ASD I-3, 530/1282–4, CWE 40, 714/17–18.
157 Ἰχθυοφαγία (A Fish Diet). ASD I-3, 529/1250–2, CWE 40, 713/20–3.
158 *Ep.* 447. Allen 2, 302–3/398–406, CWE 4, 20/436–44.
159 *Ep.* 75. Allen 1, 202/17–18, CWE 1, 151/20; *Ep.* 296. Allen 1, 567/65–7, CWE 2, 296/68–9.
160 *Compendium vitae.* Allen 1, 50/103–5, CWE 4, 408/116–18.
161 Ἰχθυοφαγία (A Fish Diet), ASD I-3, 529/1252–3, CWE 40, 713/23–4.
162 *Eps.* 1079 and 1542.

before 1499 he had not only abstracted the two root causes of his sufferings from particular issues but had gone on to account for these causes. Unable or unwilling to give up his persisting longing for freedom and his persisting physical needs – so prone to conflict with societal and religious conventions – he became convinced that these desires and needs had been predetermined. Suffering resulted, that is, in a deep-seated belief that he was not responsible for his mental and physical traits. His particular temperamental characteristics and his particular bodily needs were engrained and no amount of will power could overcome them. It was not merely that he had always sought freedom and had always had special physical needs; there was a deep underlying reason for these traits. They were embedded, he had come to believe, in something that was inherently unchangeable, a human nature that had been imprinted at birth.

He was bitter not only because society did not in many circumstances accept his unusual motivations and unusual physical needs but also, and even more elemental, because society did not want to see that his particular human nature was not a matter of choice. The frustration and anger at those who refused to accept what he could not change is especially pronounced in the 1516 account:

> Who is so barbarous as to blame a man for his lameness, when it was a kick from a mule that broke his leg? Who would hold it against a man that he has only one eye, if the other was removed by the enemy in battle? Who would taunt him with epilepsy or leprosy, if he was by nature born like that? ... The dishonour is not his who has fallen into a pit, but theirs who threw him in. He [Erasmus] laid aside his habit; but it was you who forced him to put it on ... Nothing prevents an institution from being admirable in itself, and yet for this or that individual it may be disastrous.[163]

Jacques Chomarat hypothesizes that statements such as these reflect Erasmus' obsession with his illegitimacy.[164] Where is the evidence? Neither these statements nor the letter as such are about illegitimacy or the legal status engendered by illegitimacy. The subject is genetics, the great variety of mental and physical conditions at birth – and what this entails.[165] "No man can remake his body."[166] At one point Erasmus

163 *Ep.* 447. Allen 2, 311/712–15, 732–5, 741–3, CWE 4, 30–1/787–91, 807–10, 818–19.

164 *"Pourquoi Erasme s'est-il fait moine?"* 242–3.

165 *Ep.* 447. Allen 2, 294/55–7, 309/636, CWE 4, 9/59–61, 28/704.

166 *Ep.* 447. Allen 2, 304/448–9, CWE 4, 21/490–1.

visualizes a situation in his youth where understanding and sympathy replace constraint. He sees a reverend father, sincere and holy, rescuing him from adolescent ignorance and thoughtlessness. "My son, it is foolish to strive in vain; you do not suit this way of life nor does it suit you. While the question is still open, you must choose some other course. Christ dwells in every place."[167] Where nature is contravened there can be no happiness. "Human felicity consists above all in this, that a man should devote himself to what he is fitted for by nature."[168] The unchangeableness of one's human nature needs to be not only seen but accepted, respected, and developed.

A distinction must be made between the reasons Erasmus gives for bitterness regarding his youth and his reasons for denigrating aspects of monasticism and ridiculing the ignorance of monks. Taking into consideration a great amount of secondary literature as well as primary sources, J.K. Sowards is thus at pains to show that no evidence relating to the actualities of Erasmus' youth, including his life in the monastery, ties in with his later autobiographical attacks on monasticism – indicating, that is, fabrications.[169] But in fact Erasmus does not hold in his autobiographical accounts that he opposed monasticism or monastic practices in his youth. What he emphasizes, and repeatedly, is something very different. The problem is not with monasticism but with his unique human nature. "What is life to one man is death to another."[170] The monastic life was, and continues to be, at odds with his temperament and physical makeup. His inability to endure such things as fasts results from a peculiarity of the constitution he was born with.[171] There is nothing wrong with fasting as such. If he states that some of the monks at Steyn were intellectually dull and loved food more than learning, this too was not a rejection of monasticism as such.[172] He had been unhappy because individuals, society, and various church functionaries had used high-handed methods to force him into an avocation utterly opposed to his inborn physical and mental complexion. It was not merely that his desire for freedom and his bodily needs were out of

167 *Ep*. 447. Allen 2, 303/412–25, CWE 4, 20/451–3.

168 E.g., *Ep*. 447. Allen 2, 294/59–61, CWE 4, 9/63–4. What a person does with his constitution is another matter. See my discussion below of the *Enchiridion* (Part VII).

169 "The Youth of Erasmus," 23, 25, 26, passim.

170 *Ep*. 447. Allen 2, 304/458–9, CWE 4, 22/501.

171 *Ep*. 296. Allen 1, 565/17–18, CWE 2, 295/18–19.

172 *Ep*. 447. Allen 2, 302/373–7, 304/451–7, CWE 4, 19/405–10, 21/494–9.

sync with monasticism; the deeper truth, the second step in his thought process, was that nature being what it is he had no ability to change his basic desires and his basic bodily condition.

Clearly, Erasmus' discovery of human nature was subsequent to his distinguishing his core temperamental and physical traits. Why, he had asked, did he have these characteristics in the first place and why did they persist in the face of societal and religious counterforces? Behind the two core traits of his personality that had led to his multifarious sufferings, vis-à-vis his environment, he saw something very powerful and explanatory. If his two core traits were everywhere evident, they were fuelled by something else. While he explained particular issues in terms of the two core traits, the traits themselves were explained by human nature. At root, he came to believe, his problems were caused by a blockage of his particular human nature. And nature cannot be blocked without severe mental and physical repercussions. It was one thing (Step One) to recognize and delineate ever-present desires and needs and to show their conflict with society and the sufferings that resulted. It was something else (Step Two), much more conjectural and interpretive, to conclude that these desires and needs were given at birth and this being the case were inextinguishable.

But when did he arrive at this second step? The dating differs significantly from that of the first step. Regarding Step One it was demonstrated that the actualities of his youth and young adulthood accord well with the two root causes distinguished and delineated in the later accounts – whenever it was, in the years before 1499, that he came to consciously think in this way. The second step, though also prior to 1499, cannot be so easily related to the actualities of his early life and early thought processes. It is certainly not the case that he had serious thoughts about human nature when he entered the monastery at Steyn at age sixteen. Even were we to accept that in some sense he was "forced" into the monastic life, this would not entail that he was thinking in terms of an inborn nature. As illustrated above (p. 96), Erasmus even looked back on himself at sixteen as very immature. Bringing out this immaturity may have served, in 1516, his need for a dispensation, but it is entirely believable. Sixteen-year-olds are almost by definition immature. While it is likely that he felt in some sense a desire for freedom and recognized physical shortcomings at that early age, it is not likely that he had ever thought about human nature as such. More important, the letters and more formal writings of his early life give no hint of concern with nature or a person's particular human nature.

Antibarbaroum liber, reworked in 1494, does not mention human nature as such, much less Stoic nature.[173]

And yet by 1499, probably three or four years before, his mind had focused on the conviction that every person has a unique and inborn nature that is ever-present and unyielding – and must always be studied, understood, and reckoned with. As evidence we have not only a letter immediately after the debate with Colet (dated October 1499) but the major treatise which developed out of this, *De taedio Iesu*. If this evidence – Step Two – depends on Step One, as indicated above, Step One was a conceptualization that preceded – probably long preceded, Step Two. Neither the actuality of his youthful sufferings, seen from the standpoint of the two fundamental causes, nor the deduction he arrived at, sometime before 1499, were fictions Erasmus made up in response to later situations.

The person who came to debate Colet at Oxford in 1499 carried heavy baggage, a deeply held view regarding the causative force behind the particulars of his own nature, and from that the causative force at work in determining the makeup of every human. We can be very sure that it was not Colet who suggested the topic to be debated. If Christ was a human how could he not, Erasmus had already determined, have experienced the ineradicable force of human nature – most particularly natural instincts? The debate was anything but a rhetorical exercise. Although Colet was a devout, learned, and innovative theologian and highly critical of scholasticism,[174] Erasmus found, not surprisingly, they were poles apart regarding the very essence of Christianity. Colet denied not only the importance of human nature as such but, most crucially, its relevance to Christianity.

The third step: Stoicism

By 1499 Erasmus had also come to see a direct tie between the unyieldingness of human nature, as he felt and saw it, and Stoicism. Stoicism had become the tool by which he developed his thinking. An early result

173 Nor does complimenting Robert Gaguin on his "retiring and modest natural disposition," in a 1495 letter, necessarily bespeak a larger philosophic concern with Nature. See *Ep*. 45. Allen 1, 150/58–60, CWE 1, 89/69–70.

174 Referring to Colet's lectures on the Pauline Epistles (which had gained considerable notoriety) in his introduction to *De taedio Iesu*, Erasmus admires, contrasting scholastics, his "combination of learning, eloquence, and moral integrity." *Ep*. 108. Allen 1, 248/71–2, CWE 1, 204/80–1. See also Erasmus' later sketch of Colet, *Ep*. 1211.

was *De taedio Iesu*.[175] *De taedio Iesu*, followed by the *Enchiridion*, reveals just how deeply he had absorbed Stoic thought on natural instinct, the uniqueness of human constitutions, and the unitary *honestum/indifferens* frame of thought.

Had researchers asked different questions regarding Erasmus' youthful and young adult mental and physical sufferings, deeper attention might well have been given to the relationship to *De taedio Iesu* and the *Enchiridion*. Conversely, had the base thinking found in *De taedio Iesu* – a work largely ignored – and the *Enchiridion* been comprehended, different questions might have been posed regarding Erasmus' life experiences before 1499. *De taedio Iesu* and the *Enchiridion* reflect throughout, I will demonstrate, Erasmus' afflictions and experiences of life. Nor is it happenstance that an immediate concern, worked out in *De taedio Iesu*, was Christ's nature. Precocious as he was Erasmus had every reason to want to know whether his particular physical and mental sufferings, so often in conflict with contemporary mores and church rules, were or were not at cross-purposes with Christ's message. First of all, were Christ's physical and mental sufferings unrelated to his own? If Christ was human (as well as divine) and natural instinct is ineradicable how could Christ have overcome – as contemporaries believed – his natural instincts?

Clearly, it is anything but chance that Erasmus alighted on Stoicism and built his way of looking at Christianity from this base. Precocity and general environmental factors did not bring him to this particular interest and these insights, much less the ways he developed his thinking. The fact that he did not come to Stoicism through abstract intellectualizations but from deeply ingrained personal experiences meant that its influence was going to endure.

Parts III–VII below work out the hugely consequential conclusions Erasmus drew from this confluence of Stoicism and youthful mental and physical sufferings. There is for Erasmus a direct relationship

175 Composed even earlier, mainly in 1497 or 1498 (though not printed until 1518), Erasmus' *Encomium matrimonii* (*The Praise of Matrimony*, ASD I-2, 400–29, CWE 25, 129–44) was also heavily influenced by Stoicism. See ASD I-2, 406/3–5, 409/5–7, 414/11–12, 415/44–5, CWE 25, pp. 132, 134, 136. In dating when Erasmus first came to see Stoicism in *honestum/indifferens* terms, note that in 1523 he states that he has never appreciated Cicero more and laments the fact that before age twenty (i.e., around 1486 or 1489) he preferred Seneca and could not bear to read Cicero at length. *Ep*. 1390. Allen 5, 340/103–8, CWE 10, 99/113–17.

between (1) seeing that natural instinct is inherent to Christianity and (2) seeing Christianity in unitary *honestum/indifferens* terms. Changing traditional views in one regard called forth, Erasmus saw, a reexamination of the meaning of Christianity as a whole – and here too Stoicism provided the model. As in Stoicism he worked out the relation of natural instinct to things indifferent and the relation of things indifferent to *honestum* (including *spiritus*). What emerged was "the philosophy of Christ." Although over time he developed "the philosophy of Christ" in various ways, the Stoic platform would remain. *De taedio Iesu* and the *Enchiridion* are his earliest employments of this philosophy.

PART III Stoic Natural Instinct and Christ's Fear of Death, *De taedio Iesu*

Before writing *De taedio Iesu,* before even the late 1499 debate with Colet that inspired it, Erasmus breathed Stoicism. His debate with Colet was anything but a rhetorical game. Youthful mental and physical problems and recognition of the unchangeableness of his own nature had led him to Stoicism and Stoicism had transformed his outlook. He now saw his life and Christianity in two-dimensional terms. Unlike his humanist predecessors he had opened up the true nature of Stoicism, a Stoicism built around Nature, human nature and the nature of the universe, a Stoicism that is unitarily both/and. He was a rhetorician, yes, but beneath that was a mindset formed by philosophy, a particular philosophy. However powerful his rhetorical skills might be, rhetoric was only a tool. Face to face with an issue he considered all important, in *De taedio Iesu* he methodically works out his new-found way of thinking.

The debate with Colet had been over two polar views of the meaning of Christ's sufferings following the Last Supper and including his crucifixion. At stake was nothing less than the nature of Christ and of Christianity. As the title of the resulting work indicates, it was a dispute over Jesus' distress, alarm, and sorrow (*de taedio, pavore, tristitia Iesu*) and his prayer to God for deliverance from death (Matt. 26:39): "If it be possible, let this cup pass from me" (si possible est transeat a me calix iste) (1265E).[1] Colet, contemptuous of the methodologies of

1 Primary sources are shown in Part II, p. 48 n. 1, secondary sources in Part II, p. 49 n. 3. In what follows I will again employ the CWE translation, usually, citing for more precision the corresponding LB column and letter.

modern (scholastic) theologians and dissatisfied with their interpretations (one being their belief that Christ suffered a brief fear of death), had contended that even a momentary fear of death is entirely inconsistent with Christ's character (1269C). In fearing death Christ was not reflecting his own feeling but was hoping that his death would not lead to the death of the Jews, the destruction of Jerusalem, the desertion of his shocked disciples, and the sufferings of martyrs (1269E). Colet had also claimed that hardly anyone has held that Christ truly feared death and its pain (1267B). He allowed that Jesus was alarmed by danger to his body but not that he feared death (1269C). In an October 1499 letter to Erasmus, shortly after the debate, he declared that his opinion resulted from having thoroughly absorbed Jerome. Erasmus' intellect, says Colet, is worthy of "a philosopher," and he brilliantly argues his case, the only thing missing being the truth.[2]

Erasmus begins his response by emphasizing the often conflicting plurality of opinions set forth by the church fathers (1267C–1269B).[3] The fathers are more unclear about Christ's fear of death than any other issue, often contradicting themselves. The Councils of Chalcedon (451) and Constantinople (681) established that Christ was human as well as divine, against the contention of many that he was only divine, but great confusion and controversy still exists. Well-known authorities, among them Augustine (c. 354–430) and Hilary of Poitiers (c. 315–67), have set forth conflicting statements regarding whether Christ feared or did not fear death. Origen (185–255) deliberately represented opposing views, as was his custom, and Jerome (c. 342–420) and Ambrose (c. 339–97) followed his method with regard to Christ's fear. The idea that Christ feared death and was therefore truly a man has been denied many times by many persons.[4] The theologians can see that Christ died a painful death on the cross but have trouble allowing that he feared it.

Late medieval theologians had attempted to resolve the conflicting and contradictory opinions of the church fathers by working out, in

2 *Ep*. 110. Allen 1, 253–4/1–20, CWE 1, 211–12/1–22. The fact that Colet refers to Erasmus as "a philosopher" in this late 1499 letter clearly indicates that Erasmus had pointed to the Stoic basis of his arguments in their debate.

3 The diversity of positions on Christ's divinity and humanity in the early Christian era has been explored by Grillmeier, *Christ in Christian Tradition*, and Ehrman, *Lost Christianities*.

4 See also an October 1499 letter to Colet, *Ep*. 109. Allen 1, 252/106–7, CWE 1, 209/117–18.

scholastic fashion, multitudes of logic-framed distinctions.[5] They built their arguments from the patristic *sententiae* selected and commented on by Peter Lombard (c. 1100–60).[6] Very much aware of scholastic thinking, Erasmus mentions in particular, regarding Christ's Passion, Bonaventure's *Commentary on the Sentences of Peter Lombard*, Book Three, Distinction Fifteen (1270B).[7]

Perhaps it is not too far-fetched to see the problem faced by the theologians vis-à-vis Christ's humanity as analogous with the problem central to contemporary Ptolemaic astronomers. Before Copernicus, Galileo, and Kepler, astronomers were intent on "saving the appearances." They sought, that is, mathematical relationships (making use of epicycles) that could account for their conviction that they were observing a rotating and circular heaven. What the theologians "saw" as an absolute of faith after the Council of Constantinople (681) was that Christ was both human and divine, and they sought to discover logical distinctions that could account for this unquestionable dogma. That Christ, although one person, was human as well as divine might seem contradictory but this could not be. A linchpin of many complex and brilliant scholastic distinctions was the contention of John of Damascus (d. 749) that there was no redundancy from superior (Christ's divinity) to inferior (Christ's humanness). "He permitted each of his powers to act according to its own laws."[8] And yet Christ's humanity, as Aquinas puts it following John of Damascus, was "a kind of instrument of his divinity."[9] In high scholasticism, reason, not nature, always had the upper hand.

Erasmus began from a very different standpoint, unrelated to scholastic methodologies. What deeply interested him were particularities of human nature and relationships of these realities to highest truth. Fifteenth-century humanists were interested in human nature but looked at it in terms of rhetoric and communication skills. As demonstrated in Part I, they failed to see the human nature side of Stoicism, much less

---

5 Kevin Madigan shows that through their methodology the scholastics subtly unitized the diversity of opinion found in the fathers of the church. See "Ancient and High-Medieval Interpretations of Jesus in Gethsemane." On popular representations of the Passion in the later Middle Ages, see below, Part VI.

6 Lombard, *Sententiae in IV libris distinctae*, 2 vols (Rome, Collegii S. Bonaventurae, 1971–81).

7 Bonaventure, *Opera omnia*, 3:327–42.

8 Aquinas, ST III, q. 46, a. 6, resp. 3.

9 Aquinas, ST I-II, q. 112, a. 1, ad. 1; III, q. 18, a. 1, ad. 2.

the unitary both/and way of thinking. What had so indelibly impressed Erasmus were the "laws of nature" delineated by Stoicism, comprising most importantly natural instincts and character traits, as rendered or developed in particular by Cicero in *De finibus*, *De officiis*, and *Tusculan Disputations* and by Epictetus in Book 5 (now lost) of his *Discourses*, as quoted and paraphrased by Aulus Gellius in *Attic Nights* (c. 180 CE). He was determined to show that Christ's nature – and ultimately Christianity – had to be seen in terms of these laws of nature and the accompanying unitary both/and outlook. Although at one point he refers to the "no redundancy" thesis (1284F), unlike the medieval theologians he interpreted it in terms of the two types of value (unbending/bending) that comprise, in Stoicism, a unitary both/and way of looking at existence.

Far from being an unoriginal work, *De taedio Iesu* radicalizes virtually every subject it takes up. Readers have been thrown off course because other than Bernard and Jerome, especially Colet's interpretation of Jerome, the author does not talk negatively about the theses and authors he discusses. This being the case, scholars have simply assumed, without a close reading, that he agrees with these theses and authors and has little or nothing new to say. Analysis reveals the complete opposite. What will be shown below and in later parts is that Erasmus' view of Christ's Passion is unprecedented. He has a viewpoint built from Stoicism and his own youthful sufferings, and he works out this viewpoint in detail. In the process he reveals a deep understanding of Stoic doctrines and ways of thinking. He knows a great deal about the thinking of Zeno and Chrysippus and recognizes ways in which the thinking of later Stoics, such as Panaetius, Seneca, and Epictetus, differ. In line with all these Stoics, he holds throughout to two inseparable types of value. And yet in one way Erasmus' Stoicism goes far beyond even late classical Stoicism. While early Stoics considered emotion false reasoning and later Stoics tended to see emotion as something that needs to be subordinated to reason, Erasmus makes emotion a natural and ineradicable natural instinct and places it among things that are in Stoicism "indifferent." Hunger and fear come from the same source (1282E). The ways in which he works this out will be unravelled further below. Considered in historical terms this change should be seen as Erasmus saw it, not as a rejection of Stoicism but a working out of the implications of Stoicism.

1 *Oikeiosis*, Inborn Character Traits, and True Bravery

Christ feared death: Stoic proofs

The author wastes little time in going to the core of his thesis. "Philosophically" considered it is evident that fear of death is inherent in human nature and thus existed even in the state of innocence before Adam's fall. Since Christ assumed the state of being that existed before Adam's sin, why do we not want to ascribe to him fear of death?

> In fact, if you will allow me to address you a little more philosophically, I shall venture to say – possibly with the approval of some theologians, and leaving to one side the issue of sin – that it is only human nature to fear death, and that, such is the human condition, there would have been a place for it even in the state of innocence (*etiam in statu innocentiae*). (1270F)

Since fear of death is inseparable from the original human condition, there is no reason to believe that attributing this fear to Christ involves him in even a touch of sin. And this is all the more certain in that Christ "was both a perfect man and, as far as was possible, a party to our afflictions" (1270F).

But Erasmus is begging the question! Everything depends on acceptance of his assertion that fear of death is inherent in human nature and that Christ embodied this particular view of human nature. The problem is that, as he well knew but tries to slide around, his contention contradicts a tenet that had been very much a part of the Christian world view. Like other emotions considered detrimental, fear of death, like death itself, came about *as a result*, it had always been held, of Adam's fall. Christ could not, that is, have feared death. "Some theologians" certainly allowed that fear of death is human nature,[10] but what theologian would have agreed that fear of death was found even in the state of innocence, much less that Christ embodied this fear? Augustine explicitly denies that fear of death, something connected with sin, could have been found in the state of innocence (*City of God* 14.10). Aquinas allows joy in the state of innocence but not fear (ST I, q. 95, a. 2).

10 Cf. Aquinas, ST III, q. 46, a. 6, resp. 1.

In support of his contention that fear of death is not hostile to nature but in entire accord, Erasmus places Stoicism at centre court:

> Proinde Stoici, qui sapienti suo plusculum etiam tribuunt, quam humanae conditionis imbecillitas recipiat, tamen hanc reformidationem non solum concedunt, sed eam inter τὰ κατὰ φύσιν πρῶτα, id est, inter naturae prima, primo loco constituunt. Nihil enim nos prius docet natura, quam ut primum sensibus, deinde & animi judicio refugiamus ea, quae naturae lenitatem offendunt, multo magis quae totam perimunt, ac modis omnibus, id quod sumus, tueamur perficiamusque. (1271A–B)
>
> Therefore the Stoics, who generally expect rather more of their wiseman than human frailty can bear, not only will allow him this fear of death, but even give it the leading place among the "first principles of nature." For the earliest lesson that nature teaches us is to avoid, at first instinctively but later by reasoning too, anything that threatens her gentle rule, and still more anything that may destroy it entirely, and in every way to protect and cherish our existence.

These statements are at the very base, it will become evident, of Erasmus' entire discussion. Disentangling the threads that went into their composition will allow us to discern just how deeply he had gone into Stoic and Stoic-based sources, the significance of what he is saying, and, most important, how he understands and develops Stoic thinking. Analysis reveals the following:

(1) He takes note of the unbending side of Stoicism – "more than human frailty can bear" – seen by previous humanists, fathers of the church, and medieval theologians, at the same time as he makes Stoic human nature and Stoic fear of death the centre of interest and discussion. He is not discounting the hard side but intends to show in what follows that there is another, all important, side to Stoicism.

(2) The statements build from a centrepiece of Stoic philosophy, the doctrine of *oikeiosis*. At birth humans are governed by a self-preservation instinct. Immediately upon birth, states Cato in *De finibus*, "a living creature feels an attachment for itself, and an impulse to preserve itself and to feel affection for its own constitution and for those things which tend to preserve that constitution; while on the other hand it conceives an antipathy to destruction and to those things which appear to threaten destruction" (3.16). Diogenes Laertius, in his *Lives of the*

Philosophers, a work well known in the Renaissance, states the matter similarly, directly quoting at one point Chrysippus (7.85). Seneca begins a lengthy treatment of the self-preservation instinct with the assertion that animals "are born fully-trained." Immediately at birth, without the effect of experience, without learning from pain, every animal knows instinctively how to use its body (*Ep*. 121.7; cf. *ND* 2.128–9). "Nature is easier to understand than to explain; hence, the child of whom we were speaking does not understand what 'constitution' is, but understands *its own* constitution" (*Ep*. 121.11). "Even young animals, on issuing from the mother's womb or from the egg, know at once of their own accord what is harmful for them, and avoid death-dealing things. They even shrink when they notice the shadow of birds of prey which flit overhead" (*Ep*. 121.18).

A little later Erasmus again encapsulates the doctrine. "Nature implanted in us an affection for the essentials of life, teaching us to pursue whatever is conducive to survival and to recoil from whatever harms us" (1272A). In his edition of *De officiis* (published 1501) Erasmus develops at even greater length his portrayal of the self-preservation instinct (see above, pp. 61–3).

(3) *De finibus* focuses on "the first principles of nature." Variations of Erasmus' "*naturae prima*" are found in Books 3 (17, 19–21, 30), 4 (16–19, 34, 42, 45), and 5 (17–19, 40, 43–6). Without question, however, Erasmus took the Greek, *τὰ κατὰ φύσιν πρῶτα*, not given by Cicero, from Gellius' *Attic Nights*, 12.5.7 – just as he does in his edition of *De officiis*. Gellius attributes the theory of first principles of nature not simply to Epictetus but to the founders of Stoicism, Zeno and Chrysippus (19.1.14). In his referral to the "gentle rule" of nature (*naturae lenitatem*) Erasmus again depends not on *De finibus* but on Gellius, who pictures the "*mansuetudinem lenitatemque*" of nature (12.5.10). In Part IV below it will be shown that Erasmus makes major use of Epictetus' *Discourses*, as copied by Gellius from the fifth book (now lost).

(4) Consider also "at first instinctively but later by reasoning too." Ability to understand, to see the order in things, is not present at birth, Cato states, but comes into being later (*Fin*. 3.21). As Diogenes Laertius words it, "reason supervenes to shape impulse scientifically" (7.86). After gradually gathering "preconceptions" a child begins to reason around age seven and reaches mental maturity at age 14.[11] With the

---

11 See Dyck, *A Commentary on Cicero, De officiis*, 291.

advent of reason we "select" things that are "indifferent" (everything not virtue or vice) depending on whether they are in accord or not with "nature's starting points" (*Fin. 3.22*). Epictetus describes the starting points with which reason deals as follows: "Who has come into being without an innate concept of what is good and evil, honorable and base, appropriate and inappropriate, and happiness, and of what is proper and falls to our lot, and what we ought to do and what we ought not to do?" (*Disc.* 2.10.11). Some things are thus "preferred" by reason and others "dispreferred." Diogenes Laertius reports that using reason we select, according to Stoics, life over death, health over disease, pleasure over pain, beauty over ugliness, strength over weakness, wealth over poverty, and the like (7.102). Regarding the material from which reason selects the Stoic Cato goes even farther at the conclusion to his discussion in Book 3 of *De finibus*, holding that the feelings which humans have for other individuals, for society, for their state, for all mankind, and for the universe are rooted in the self-preservation instinct humans are born with (*Fin.* 3.62–71).[12]

But is Erasmus' rendering of the Stoic view entirely valid?

How true is Erasmus' claim that Stoics consider fear of death a natural instinct and even give it "the leading place" among the first principles of nature?

(1) Certainly Stoics, including their wiseman, show that the infant, through natural instinct, rejects things that lead to its destruction, including death. But does the infant "fear" death? Seneca states, rather uniquely it seems, that "No animal when it enters upon life is free from fear of death (*metu mortis*)" (*Ep.* 121.18). We need to recognize, however, that the infant's "fear" is instinctive and not at this time a product of reason. Nor do the Stoic sources make a point, as such, of the newborn's "fear of death." Cato's explication of Stoicism in *De finibus* 3 does not show that the newborn "fears" poor health or "fears" death. The newborn instinctively chooses life – the example given at 3.16 is health – over destruction and threats to destruction. Even should one think that

12 Malcolm Schofield argues that in Stoicism an individual develops ethical standpoints by means of social *oikeiosis*, as evidenced by *De finibus* 3.62f, and that this upward movement must precede the downward movement of first principles. See "Two Stoic Approaches to Justice."

fear of death is implicit, there is all the difference between self-love, the desire to perpetuate oneself, not to die, and fear of death as an emotion. In Stoicism emotion is not a natural instinct but represents false reasoning.

Although Cato emphatically denies, as does Cicero, that the self-preservation instinct includes pleasure (*voluptas*) (*Fin.* 3.17, cf. 2.33), and Diogenes Laertius attributes this denial to all Stoics (7.85), Gellius, following Epictetus, considers the "sensation" of pleasure as well as pain one of the first principles of nature (12.5.8). It would appear, therefore, that Gellius' conceptualization of self-preservation was even more remote from concern with "fear of death" than was common among Stoics. Nor does Gellius, in his rendering of Epictetus, say anything about fear of death being part of the self-preservation instinct. Although Erasmus employs Gellius' Greek in translating "first principles of nature," he did not get the idea of fear of death as a first principle from Gellius.

(2) The real problem with Erasmus' view arises only with regard to his interpretation of the Stoic contention that nature teaches us to avoid "later by reasoning too" anything that threatens our existence. The Stoic indeed uses reason to choose, when considering things indifferent, life over death (usually), and this is considered an extension of the child's self-preservation instinct. But there is all the difference between choosing things like health over ill health and choosing fear of death over death. Even if it should be allowed that the newborn suffers from fear of death, that is not the case with the Stoic wiseman, a person imbued with *honestum*. From the standpoint of *honestum*, death is something that needs to be accepted as an inevitable and inherent aspect of nature. For the Stoic wiseman it is death that is natural and fear of death that is unnatural. All of which is directly at odds with Erasmus' argument. Immediately preceding the above referral to the Stoics, Erasmus comments that death is the offspring of sin and that it is fear of death that resists this evil. "Nothing is more hostile to nature than death, whose role is to bring extinction, from which every living being shrinks" (1271A).

Since death is for the wiseman not an evil (*turpe*, the opposite of *honestum*) it is unworthy of fear. As stated in Epictetus' *Handbook*, what is terrible is not death but only the notion that death is terrible (theme 5). His *Discourses* criticize at length those who have not formed a judgment on death and consequently fear and flee death (2.1.14). The Stoic Cato develops the point in *De finibus* 3. The wiseman is at all times steadfast, firm, high-minded, and happy. He does not fear death but is superior to and despises death and other vicissitudes of life (3.25). Only those who think death an evil necessarily fear death (3.29). Fear is an emotion and as such is not a part of nature (3.35). In disdaining emotion the wiseman disdains fear of death. Fear of death, like other emotions, is simply a false judgment of reason (*Tusc.* 3.24).

Although Erasmus' argument was clearly built from Stoicism, and with considerable justification, it is ultimately out of sync with orthodox Stoicism. Orthodox Stoics would emphatically not agree with either his implying that "fear of death" is felt by the wiseman or his claim that "nothing is more hostile to nature than death."

Was Erasmus an Antiochean?

(1) In fact Erasmus' claim that fear of death is preeminent not only at birth but after the input of reason and is experienced even by the Stoic wiseman has an almost certain heritage. In Cicero's *De finibus* 4 and 5, inspired by Antiochus (who formed the "Old Academy" in 87 BCE) attempts are made to broaden Stoicism. Here it is argued not only that every living creature loves itself (5.27–34) but that the newborn's self-preservation instinct is lifelong (5.24). Fear of death (*metus mortis*) is found in all humans and, indeed, even in lesser forms of life. Wild animals are horrified by the prospect of death. Where fear of death is found excessive this only helps to show that the reaction itself, in its moderate form, is entirely natural (5.31). What cannot be doubted, moreover, is that even the wiseman feels, from natural impulse, fear of death (5.32).[13]

Antiochus' belief that fear of death is lifelong is embedded in the contention that natural instinct progresses linearly to the highest good. Following Antiochus' line of reasoning in Book 4 of *De finibus,* Cicero contends that in differentiating between the primary impulses of nature (*principia naturae*) and the *honestum* Zeno made a fundamental mistake. He went along with those who did not allow that the chief good, the *honestum,* is based on natural instinct. All sorts of controversy have come about, unnecessarily, because he did not employ the arguments and doctrines of those who grasped that natural instinct leads to the good. The chief good is built on natural instinct (4.45). Nothing could be more contradictory

13 On the differences between the "self-realizationist" views set forth in Books 4 and 5 of *De finibus* and the Stoic Cato's account in Book 3, see in particular White, "The Basis of Stoic Ethics."

than to hold that *honestum* is the sole good and yet hold "that we have a natural instinct to seek the things conducive to life" (4.78).

(2) Modern scholars have pointed out that Antiochus' thinking is at root muddled in that the Stoics did not contradict themselves in holding at one and the same time to two types of value.[14] In this regard it needs to be emphasized that Erasmus at all times holds, unlike Antiochus, to the Stoic two-dimensional – two types of value – outlook. He believed – and works out his reasoning in detail (see below) – natural instincts as such last throughout life and yet are not to be confused with *honestum*. Natural instincts are on one side of the both/and coin, *honestum* on the other.

Points that stand out in the above are the following:

(1) Erasmus was greatly impressed by the Stoic focus, unlike anything argued by Peripatetics and Platonists, on natural instincts at birth (*oikeiosis*).
(2) The statements quoted, however succinct, reveal a deep acquaintance with Stoicism and the varied discussions of Stoicism available, particularly Cicero's rendering of the views of Cato and Antiochus and Gellius' rendering of Epictetus.
(3) He ties with some justification fear of death to the inborn self-preservation instincts described by Stoics (*oikeiosis*).
(4) He recognizes that a person who reaches the age of reason, and the ability to choose between preferred and dispreferred indifferents, considers natural instincts "first principles of nature."
(5) The revisionist Antiochus helped solidify his belief that fear of death is a natural instinct and that natural instincts last throughout life (although unlike Antiochus he did not see them as linear stepping stones to *honestum*).
(6) Although he recognizes that Stoics do not consider emotion (fear of death being an emotion) a natural instinct but an exemplification

14 See Gisela Striker on Antipater above, p. 6 n. 4. Antiochus' conceptualizations, most particularly his grasp of Stoicism and his attempt to combine Peripatetic thought, have often been discussed and criticized by modern philosophers. See Annas, *The Morality of Happiness*, 180–7, 277–9, and "Aristotelian Political Theory in the Hellenistic Period," esp. 81–3; Barnes, "Antiochus of Ascalon"; Brennan, *The Stoic Life*, 123–31; Gill, *The Structured Self*, 166–73; Glucker, *Antiochus and the Late Academy*; and Striker, *Essays on Hellenistic Epistemology and Ethics*, 262, 269–70.

of false reasoning, he shows that the Stoic self-preservation instinct (*oikeiosis*) in fact includes emotion, most particularly fear of death.

Notwithstanding his transferring of emotion to Stoic *oikeiosis*, Erasmus retains, of utmost importance, the larger Stoic frame of thought. As will become evident below and in later parts, he shows that emotion is firmly embedded in a fundamental Stoic category, that being *indifferentia*. And he sees *indifferentia* as comprising, as in Stoicism, one side of a unitary both/and frame of thought (*katorthoma/kathekon, honestum/indifferens, honestum/utile*).

The Stoic Panaetius lends support

Recognizing that his belief that emotion is a natural instinct is at odds with orthodox Stoic thinking, Erasmus brings in the Stoic Panaetius – who succeeded Antipater as head of the school in 129 BCE – in support of the view that *apatheia*, freedom from emotion, a concept central to orthodox Stoicism, is unacceptable, "incompatible with being human":

> At istud est non fortem, sed *ἀνάλγητον, ἀναίσθητον, ἀῶαθέα* hominem constituere, id est, indolentem, hebetem ac stupidam. *Ἀναλγησίαν* autem *καὶ* ἀῶάθειαν adeo Panaetius Stoicorum doctissimus non requirit a sapiente, ut eam ne homini quidem tribuat. (1273F)
>
> The person you [Colet] are imagining is not brave, but insensible, insensate, and unfeeling; otherwise stated, free of pain, sluggish, and stupid. Panaetius, the most learned of the Stoics, does not insist that his wiseman should practise insensibility and lack of feeling, and indeed considers them incompatible with being human.[15]

The Greek words and the referral therewith to Panaetius tie this statement to Gellius' rendering of Epictetus. At one point a Stoic assures Gellius that the wiseman can endure (*tolerare*) such things as groaning, panting, and sighing in sickness, things not evil, "but he cannot exclude them altogether from his consciousness; for *ἀναλγησία*, or 'insensibility,' and *ἀπάθεια*, or 'lack of feeling,' not only in my judgment," said he, "but also in that of some of the wise men of that same school (such

15 The translation here is mine.

as Panaetius, a serious and learned man) are disproved and rejected" (12.5.10). According to Diogenes Laertius, Panaetius and Posidonius, at odds with Zeno and Chrysippus, "deny that virtue is self-sufficing; on the contrary, health is necessary, and some means of living and strength" (7.128). According to Cicero, in *Prior Academics* 2.135, the Old Academy held "that in all emotion there was a certain measure that was natural" and that in support of this position the Stoic Panaetius advised studying word for word the *On Grief* of the Academic Crantor (c. 335–275).[16] Regarding Crantor, Cicero states in *Tusculan Disputations* (3.12) that "we are not sprung from rock" and expresses sympathy for Crantor in his disagreement with those who advised insensibility (*indolentia*), something that involves brutishness and callousness. Compare Erasmus: Anyone insensible to danger or pain, even when it starts, is "like a block of wood," less than human, brutish and stupid (1272C). Infants, drunks, and madmen, not understanding their situation, sometimes laugh in the face of danger but they are to be pitied, not applauded. Sometimes even Roman soldiers, mindless and brutish, laughed when subjected to extreme torture (1273D, cf. Gellius 12.5.13). In truth, however, those incapable of being terrified by anything are "mindless, brutish, and stupid" (amentes potius, feros, ac stupidos) (1273F).

De finibus 4.23 refers to Panaetius as a Stoic "with no superior in intellect or high-mindedness." Cicero points out in *De officiis* that he is following Panaetius, "although not slavishly," in Books 1 and 2, and that Panaetius was one of the greatest (*doctissimi*) philosophers (2.60, cf. 3.7). Many times elsewhere in the volume he comments on Panaetius, comments Erasmus would have been quite familiar with, considering his editing at about this time of the work.[17] "When it comes to those emotions with which nature has endowed us," states Erasmus, "the philosophers (Panaetius and those who followed in his wake) expect even the wisest to practise *μετριότης*, moderation, and not *δέρησις*, abstinence" (1274A).[18]

---

16 Taurus, a Platonist who flourished c. CE 145, states that Panaetius adhered to the view that Stoics may accept moderate emotions. See Knuuttila, *Emotions in Ancient and Medieval Philosophy*, 66. Sorabji believes that Panaetius most likely did not consider *apatheia* a freedom from emotion but a moderating of emotion by reason. See *Emotion and Peace of Mind*, 106.

17 On the large role played by Panaetius in the production of Books I and II of *De officiis*, see Dyck's introduction and textual explication, *A Commentary on Cicero, De Officiis*.

18 On the attempts of Seneca and Epictetus to cope with fear and other emotions see, as a beginning, Sherman, *Stoic Warriors*.

What Erasmus added to Panaetius' rejection (as reported by Gellius) of "insensibility" (*ἀναλγησία*) and "lack of feeling" (*ἀπάθεια*) was the need not to be "insensate" (*ἀναίσθητο*). Being a rhetorician as well as a philosopher, he wanted to think out the meaning of words and to focus on the locations of feeling. He contends that insensibility and lack of feeling relate mostly to mental shortcomings while insensate (ἀναίσθητο) relates mostly to physical shortcomings (1274A), at which point he criticizes the subtlety of the scholastic John Duns Scotus (d. 1308). Scotus "says that only physical pain should, strictly speaking, be called *dolor*, pain."[19] In fact, "pain (*dolor*) is an affliction found in *both* mind and body, while sorrow (*tristitia*) exists only in the mind." Not using words carefully, Scotus just made up meanings unconnected with common usage. Erasmus brings in the word *insensate* to distinguish physical pain from mental pain. He was determined to build up and show the reality of mental suffering for humans, most particularly Christ. Pain and sorrow, *dolor* and *tristitia*, are both found in the mind. Mental pain is very real.

"Bravery is not insensitivity to these provocations of nature" (1272B)

Fear is natural, not, as orthodoxy would have it, a false judgment of reason. "It is no sign of bravery to take arms against nature, like the Giants" (1272A).[20] What is cowardly is refusing to face up to involuntary mental and physical reactions to danger. Natural instincts are not evil but things to be endured. There is a kind of fright that arises "not from cowardice but from nature, and found of necessity in the very bravest of us" (1272E). The truly brave person recognizes and accepts the reality of these fears arising from natural instincts while the coward tries to ignore them. In illustration of the point Erasmus describes, openly paraphrasing a story set forth by Gellius (19.1.1–9), the differing

19 Scotus, *Commentary on the Sentences of Peter Lombard*, 3.15.

20 In Cicero's *De senectute* (*On Old Age*), the Stoic Cato asks: "To rebel against nature – is not that to fight like the giants with the gods?" (2.5). It is likely that Erasmus was looking at Gellius' similar Stoic comment on the giants at 12.5.13. See also the *Enchiridion* (below, p. 276). Hesiod's *Theogony* (c. 700 BCE) seems to have been the inspiration behind many ancient versions of the myth. See Price, *Religions of the Ancient Greeks*, 13. Jenny Strauss Clay argues that the Giants were "the ancestors of the human race." See *Hesiod's Cosmos*, 154.

reactions to a life-threatening typhoon of a rich Asiatic and of a Stoic philosopher (1272F–1273A). Utterly insensitive to the realities of what was taking place, the Asiatic was not frightened. The philosopher, on the other hand, was extremely sensitive and thus had all sorts of physical and mental reactions. He could not escape "nature's command." And yet throughout the ordeal the philosopher held firmly to his precepts (*honestum*). In another illustration of that which is tolerable for a Stoic, Gellius describes the reactions of a sick and dying Stoic to extreme pain. The Stoic struggled against the pain, sighing, panting, and groaning, but his outlook, his reason, his virtue, and his spiritual nature, remained firm (12.5.1–3).[21]

Turning to warfare, Erasmus judges that the bravery of soldiers, where it exists, is not that of persons who feel nothing. There is no bravery lacking feeling and recognition of danger (1273B). And he relates in this regard many of the heroes of ancient history (all those named are found in Cicero's philosophical works). The brave are brave not only because of a noble undertaking but "all the braver since they have had to overcome a natural desire to flee" (1272B). "Someone is not lacking in bravery if, when danger approaches, he shudders inwardly, his face turns pale, his heart beats faster, his blood ebbs away, and his suffering wrings from him a groan" (1272B; cf. *Tusc.* 2.55–6, 3.83, *De ira*, 2.3.3). Such reactions are involuntary, inherent in a person's human nature. It is natural to be afraid and natural also to feel pain. Some persons are so afraid they cannot even control their bodily functions (1273C). And yet a brave person "will say," with all truth, that "my physical and mental agitation was not the result of any vice or virtue, but of nature and necessity" (neque vitii erat, neque virtutis, sed naturae, and necessitatis) (1273C). After illustrating involuntary factors in life, Gellius' Stoic states, similarly, "These and many other things are not under the control of the will, the judgment, or the reason, but are decrees of nature and of necessity (set naturae necessitatisque decreta sunt)" (12.5.12).

And yet there is a fundamental difference between Gellius' view and Erasmus'. Gellius simply assumes, following Epictetus and other Stoics, that true emotions as distinct from involuntary reactions are neither natural nor necessary but false judgments (cf. *Tusc.* 4.60, *Fin.* 3.35). Erasmus will demonstrate (Part IV below) that Gellius' assumption is false.

---

21 Gellius' story compares to what is said in *Tusculan Disputations* about the reactions to pain of the Stoic Posidonius (2.61).

Bravery and unique natural traits: Socrates was not necessarily brave in taking the hemlock

Where Erasmus' mind was headed and what he had set out to demonstrate have much to do with his contention – on the surface shocking – that Socrates was not necessarily brave in the manner in which he died. Revealed here is not only a close analysis and development of Stoic sources but an original, as worked out, and enormously consequential deduction. It is impossible to tell from observing a person's physical and emotional reactions to events anything about that person's bravery or moral character.

According to Erasmus, Socrates' famous death scene (399 BCE) as well as that of Phocion (318 BCE), "the most principled of Athenian commanders," reveals nothing about their moral character (1274C–E).[22] It cannot be doubted that Socrates was saintly, blameless, brave, his spirit unconquered, but this is not evidenced by the fact that his habitual expression changed not at all when condemned to death; that he slept peacefully as the final day approached; that he behaved on his final day as on any other day, interspersing serious topics with jokes; that he drank the hemlock as if it were wine. Such outward expressions by these and other such persons tell us nothing about their moral integrity.

> Verum non patiar te ex iis rebus fortitudinis magnitudinem metiri, quae non tam virtute, quam naturae proprietate, non tam mentis, quam corporis habitu accidunt. Non ideo fortis Socrates, quia cicutam hausturus, non mutarit vultum, aut ea gratia non fortis fuerat futurus, si exalbuisset. (1274F)

> I will not allow you [Colet] to measure bravery by these examples [Socrates and Phocion], which owe more to their natural inclinations than to moral principles, to their physical and not their mental make-up. Socrates was not necessarily brave because his expression did not change as he took the hemlock; nor would he have been a coward if in the same circumstances he had happened to turn pale.

Socrates' peacefulness in the face of death was possible because of his innate physical constitution and had nothing necessarily to do with his

22 On Phocion's death, see Plutarch, *Life of Phocion*, 36. Plutarch's *Lives* (written 75 CE), translated from Greek into Latin in 1470, was much read in the fifteenth century.

moral convictions. Had he not had this constitution and had reacted differently, becoming pale and perhaps reclusive, there would be no more reason to downgrade his moral character than there is to upgrade it on the basis of his imperturbability and good spirits. We have differing biological make-ups and thus respond to danger in all sorts of ways. What matters is not the way we react to danger but what underlies the reaction.

Observable reactions to danger show nothing about bravery

Humans tend to mistake surface reactions for reality, tying pallor with anger, blushing with shame, laughter with joy, tears with sorrow, and the like, just as Colet ties extreme joy (*alacritas*) with love, but such expressions are only "outward signs, not causes, and are extrinsic to the emotions they indicate. Not everyone who turns pale, for example, is necessarily angry, and anger does not turn everyone pale" (1281F–1282A).[23] Often, in fact, there is an inverse relationship between moral character and what we observe. When the trumpets of war sound, "usually the braver the soldier the paler he becomes, and the brasher the noise a man made as the battle began the quicker he is to flee the field" (1275A). The braver soldier may become pale because he is sensitive to the reality of what is to come. The brasher soldier may act fearlessly because he is insensitive to reality. On the other hand, it can be that the brave soldier does not become pale or fearful and it can be the case that the coward does become pale and fearful. Whether a person fears or lacks fear throws no light, in itself, on moral character – or judgments about moral character. (The numbering is mine.)

> (1) The signs of fear and fearlessness are found alike in the brave and the coward, the wiseman and the inane half-wit. If nature has endowed me with more hot blood or thicker spirits than others, does that make me braver? Conversely, if she has given me colder blood, and less of it, together with thinner spirits, does that necessarily make me less bold? I cannot change nature and stop myself blenching if I suddenly come upon some horrifying sight (2) but I can exercise self-control and stop even

23 Compare (and contrast) *Tusc.* 4.27: "Not all men who are at times anxious are of an anxious temper, nor are all those who have an anxious temper always feeling anxious."

death deflecting me from the straight path. (3) Thus fearlessness, since it depends on one's physical constitution or some other natural cause, should not be required of the wise, nor mistaken for bravery in those who are merely *ἀνάλγητος* or *ἀναίσθητος*, insensible or insensate. (1274F–1275A)

(1) Inborn character traits, however variable, are what the brave and the coward, the wiseman and the fool have in common. A brave person can fear and a coward can fear. A brave person can be fearless and a coward can be fearless. A wiseman can fear and a fool can fear. A wiseman can be fearless and a fool can be fearless. Medical doctrine (worked out in particular by Hippocrates and Galen and current in the Middle Ages and Renaissance) also shows the uniqueness and intractableness of character traits. The four humours (blood, phlegm, black bile, yellow bile) account in complex ways for the particulars of a person's physical and mental state, including his basic temperament, and Erasmus sees this too as proof that a person "cannot change nature," cannot, that is, override inborn physical or emotional impulses. On these matters, reason goes nowhere.
(2) Nature, with all its variables, from one person to another, cannot be changed and yet we can still hold to a straight path. There is no contradiction. Truth is unitarily both/and. Natural instincts and character traits are tolerable, not evil. What is intolerable is deviation from moral principles. The lives of Socrates and Phocion, not the manner of their deaths, "prove that, especially among the wise and the good, the human spirit may remain unconquered" (1274E). Socrates was saintly and blameless, Phocion absolutely incorruptible. And yet, at the same time, neither exhibited torpor or insensibility.
(3) Contrary to orthodox Stoicism and in accord with the Stoic Panaetius, lack of emotion (*apatheia*), most particularly lack of fear, should not be required of the wiseman. The wiseman has no control over his inborn ways of reacting to danger. And those who lack fear may not be wise at all, but "merely *ἀνάλγητος* or *ἀναίσθητος*, insensible or insensate."

The bottom line is that there is no way to distinguish from particular reactions to danger those who are brave and those who are not, those who live by the highest moral standards and those who lack such, those who are insensible or insensate and those who are sensitive.

In itself Christ's fear tells us nothing

What Erasmus is intent on showing is that Christ, in his Passion, feared death but that this fear in itself reveals only natural instinct. Colet had contended that Christ could not have feared death because, for one thing, brave persons overcome human nature and worldliness and in the process experience extreme joy, *alacritas*. Christ was super brave, a martyr of martyrs. But Erasmus has now shown that there is no necessity, faced with danger, that brave persons exhibit fearlessness (much less *alacritas*), or any other particular emotion or reaction. In fact, and this point needs to be emphasized: It is impossible to discover from outward reactions whether or not a person is brave. It is not possible, apparently, to say whether martyrs were brave or not. Socrates was condemned to death and yet was at peace and fearless to the very end, but this behaviour does not tell us whether he was brave or not – though we know from other evidence that he was brave. Christ knew from foreknowledge that he was going to be crucified and therewith suffered unsurpassed fear – but this fear does not tell us in itself any more than Socrates' lack of fear. His incomparable bravery is demonstrated not by an ability to overcome human nature but by the fact that he could not overcome human nature, fear of death particularly – and yet endured, both/and, demonstrating the deepest love (see below, Part IV.3). Fear can mean cowardice but with him it meant exactly the opposite.

So too, Erasmus' temperament tells nothing

Clearly, Erasmus' depiction of Christ as suffering from an ineradicable natural instinct relates directly to his own youthful sufferings and the conclusions he had drawn from them. He had long before arrived at the belief that no amount of effort could overcome his physical and mental character traits. Against the assumptions and expectations of those around him and society at large he had come to see himself, with the help of Stoicism, as a brave Christian dealing, inescapably, with natural instincts and inborn and ineradicable character traits. Others, he was convinced, were simply passing over, refusing to acknowledge and come to grips with, these unyielding aspects of their natures, a thesis that was to be elaborated in the *Enchiridion*. He had come to see Christianity as two-dimensional, on the one side ineradicable natural instincts and particular character traits and on the other unbending principles.

All this at odds with the modern belief that Erasmus' youthful struggles were fabrications or of little substance (Part II.4 above).

Natural disabilities increase opportunities for virtue

A core component of Erasmus' assessment of the human situation and, most particularly, his analysis of Christ's Passion is that natural disabilities – contrary to Colet and contemporary opinion – do not diminish opportunities for virtue but greatly expand them.

Consider the fear and trembling of great orators. Quintilian, Demosthenes, and Cicero were all fearful when getting up to speak but this fear simply highlights their bravery (1275B). They carried on, notwithstanding. In his handling of a great number of important legal cases no one was braver than Cicero. Cicero did not just exemplify bravery, he believed that bravery is defined by the ability to overcome fears. Most significantly, attests Erasmus, he believed that the greater the natural shortcomings the greater the opportunities for bravery:

> If on these grounds [extreme nervousness in public speaking] you charge Cicero with cowardice, he will instantly (being a ready speech-maker) countercharge you with ignorance and say you know nothing of the nature and meaning of bravery. The greater a person's natural fear, he will say, the more his bravery is to be honored and applauded, since natural disabilities which come about through no fault of our own increase our opportunities to cultivate virtue (augent materiam segetemque virtutis).[24] (1275B)

Would Cicero have actually said this? Clearly Erasmus is not referring here to a specific passage or argument in Cicero's writings but simply imagining what Cicero would say. The fear experienced by orators is not something that results from lack of character, or poor training, or little effort – ingredients of cowardice. It comes about involuntarily from natural instinct or inborn character traits. Three principles come into view:

(1) Bravery cannot be measured outside the instincts and traits a person is born with.

24 I have changed Heath's translation from "greater his natural dread" to "greater a person's natural fear."

(2) Natural disabilities increase our opportunities to cultivate virtue: "augent materiam segetemque virtutis" (enlarge the material and soil of virtue).[25] The greater the natural handicaps, mental or physical, the greater the opportunities for virtue.

(3) Those lacking natural handicaps have less opportunities for virtue.

> Anything you cannot attribute to natural gifts may be added to the total of your virtuous deeds. Take a pair of brave men; if one of them was born with less and colder blood but simply ignores this natural disability, he deserves greater credit for bravery than the other, who is well provided with the hottest of hot blood, when in a similar crisis he too makes light of some dreadful danger. In the latter nature claims some of the credit for his conduct, while in the former everything results from his own virtue. Despite your efforts, you will diminish the glory attaching to bravery, not increase it, if you allow bravery itself fewer chances to shine. (1275C)

In short, the greater the natural handicap the greater the opportunity for virtue. Those born with attributes that make it easy to respond to a dangerous situation have actually been given something unhelpful, since an appropriate temperament allows less opportunity for virtue than an inappropriate. Such persons can be brave but the scope of their bravery will always be limited in comparison with what is possible for the person born with natural disabilities. In ignoring his disability the soldier with colder blood is not eradicating his disability but simply rising above it, faced with the need to respond to a particular, unpalatable, situation. And we, as onlookers, must recognize that bravery is diminished where the disability is not taken into account.[26]

---

25 In a long and important letter to William Croy in 1519, criticizing Croy's one-dimensional view of Stoicism, Erasmus states that worldly goods and benefits "must be turned into opportunities and materials for virtue" (*in materiam organumque virtutis*). See *Ep.* 959. Allen 3, 569/28–30, CWE 6, 345/36–8. Chrysippus believed, according to Plutarch, that getting the "things selected," i.e., the primary things according to nature, is not the end but rather "virtues matter" (*C.N.* 1071A,B, 1069E). Cf. Epictetus, *Disc.* 2.51. As *De finibus* words it, for Stoics the primary things of nature "form so to speak the subject-matter, the given material with which wisdom deals (*quasi materia sapientiae*)" (3.61).

26 Elsewhere in *De taedio Iesu* the relationships of natural instincts and character traits to highest bravery are worked out in very different and deeply philosophical contexts. See below, chapter 2, and Part IV.

Going beyond Panaetius/Cicero's four *personae* theory

Again, is it actually the case that Cicero's outlook corresponds with what can be called Erasmus' "greater handicap" thesis? For orthodox Stoics bravery means holding fast through all the happenings of life to an unbending standard, the *honestum*.[27] They do not measure bravery in terms of inborn character traits and natural instincts. Nor, for greater reason, do they come up with the idea that negative inborn traits or instincts augment opportunities for bravery. But what about later Stoics, such as Panaetius? A partial basis for Erasmus' thinking may be found in Cicero's discussion of his four *personae* theory, in *De officiis* 1.93–121[28] – edited by Erasmus at about this time. Reflecting Panaetius, Cicero here focuses on the differences between individuals and emphasizes the need for humans to develop their own particular natures. Humans have both a universal and a particular character (1.107). While the first *persona*, the universal, consists of reason and, derived from this, that which is honourable and decorous, the second *persona* constitutes our unique characters as individuals.[29] The second *persona* is all about the extreme variety of traits found naturally among humans. Although there are enormous physical differences, such as strength or beauty, diversities of character are even greater.

Erasmus' distinguishing between innate polar temperaments, cold and hot, and the relationship of these temperaments to bravery can be compared in some ways with Cicero's contrasting of opposite types of temperaments. Some humans are crafty by nature (Themistocles and Solon) while others are straightforward and hate fraud (Ajax, with his fabled temper). Some humans are gracious and some not, some clever and some simple-minded, some exhibit unusual seriousness (*severitas*)

---

27 On orthodox views of bravery as related to warfare and attempts by later Stoics to soften this thinking, see Sherman, *Stoic Warriors*.

28 On the background and meaning of the four *personae* theory, see Gill, "Peace of Mind and Being Yourself." Gill sees Panaetius as here modifying Stoicism by employing Democritean and Epicurean thought and, in return, influencing Seneca and Plutarch. Dyck subjects *De officiis* 1.107–14 to detailed textual analysis in *A Commentary on Cicero, De Officiis*, 269–85.

29 Commenting in his edition of *De officiis* (1501) on 1.107 and the difference between the universal and particular characters, Erasmus sees highest decorum as that which is proper to a unique individual considering, successively, the nature allotted to that individual at birth, events imposed by fortune, and mental outlook. See *De officiis Marci Tullii Ciceronis libri tres* (Ioannem Kyngstonem, 1574), p. 54. Cf. also D.L. 7.87–8 with 1.107.

(Cato), while others exhibit unbounded jollity or wit (*hilaritas*) (Socrates). *Tusculan Disputations* shows, with many complex distinctions, that individuals have a "proclivity" to one or another failing (including the emotion of fear), similar to proneness to a physical sickness, while others have a proneness, or "facility," to what is good (4.27–8).[30]

Whatever the innate traits, these must not be criticized (*Off.* 1.109) – a proposition Erasmus would have immediately agreed with. Although diverse inborn features are everywhere evident, this does not mean that we should choose between them, disvaluing some and valuing others. It is pointless to war with nature (1.110) and thus it is pointless and even harmful to criticize the character traits of any individual. There is a place in the world, here again exemplified with historical examples, for all types of character traits.[31] What works for one person does not work for another. Even where external circumstances are the same, different natures justify different decisions. Suicide, for example, can be a duty for one person and a crime for another. It was right that a stern and consistent person such as Cato chose death but such a decision might be very wrong for a different personality facing the same situation (1.112).

While the third *persona* relates to our social position, seen as largely related to chance, the fourth *persona* emphasizes that choosing a career is something we ourselves decide on (1.115). Here as elsewhere – and directly connecting with Erasmus' deepest feelings, stemming from his belief that others had choosen a career for him – we must "follow the bent of our own particular nature; and even if other careers should be better and nobler, we may still regulate our own pursuits by the standard of our own nature. For it is of no avail to fight against one's nature or to aim at what is impossible of attainment" (1.110).[32] The task for each human is to "make a proper estimate of his own natural ability and show himself a critical judge of his own merits and defects" (1.114). A similar thesis is set forth in Books 4 and 5 of *De finibus*, influenced by Antiochus: "We must study what we ourselves are, in order to keep

30 On *Tusculan Disputations* 4.23–33 and the complexities of Stoic discussions of character, see Graver, *Cicero and the Emotions*, 148–60.

31 Among all the ancient philosophies, Gretchen Reydams-Schils notes, "Stoic theory has the strongest sense of selfhood." See *The Roman* Stoics, 17. See also Long, "Representation and the Self in Stoicism," and Sherman, "The Look and Feel of Virtue."

32 Commenting on 1.110, Dyck states that *nostra natura* has replaced the good man as the standard. See *A Commentary on Cicero, De officiis*, 279.

ourselves true to our proper character" (4.25).[33] Starting with our own particular personality at birth (5.33) we must gradually gain knowledge of ourselves (5.41)[34] and follow the path of life that fully employs our powers of body and mind (5.44). In being a critical judge of our own merits and defects and developing at the same time our individual natures, we integrate, *De officiis* shows, the four *personae*, achieving harmony and peace of mind.[35] That is, if a person's individual capacities and inclinations are developed in a fitting or appropriate way they will accord with our universal character, as well as the other two *personae*. Humans should see development of their unique natures as something like a work of art.[36]

And yet Erasmus' argument differs in one crucial aspect from the second *persona* described by Panaetius/Cicero. He limits the contention of Panaetius/Cicero that any type of temperament can work in worldly affairs and that society has appreciated every type of temperament. In my quote above of 1275C (121) Erasmus pictures two brave persons faced with a similar battlefield situation. The one has an inborn trait, "hottest of hot blood," that allows him to easily respond; the other has an inborn trait, "less and colder blood," that makes it very difficult to respond; but the opportunities for virtue are greater for the latter person than the former. The differences with Panaetius/Cicero stand out in three ways:

(1) Contrasting with Panaetius/Cicero, some inborn traits are positive and others are negative. Assessments of who is brave and to what degree depend on these differentiations between positive and negative inborn traits.
(2) Contrasting with Panaetius/Cicero, there is great value in negative handicaps. The arena or scope for bravery is much greater for the negative than the positive.

33 As will become evident below, Part VII, the *Enchiridion* is built around this thesis – developed within a Christian context.

34 Cf. *Tusc.* 3.2: "Seeds (*semina*) of the virtues are inborn in our characters, and if they were allowed to mature, nature itself would lead us to perfect happiness. But as it is ..." (trans. Graver). The Stoic Cato develops this thinking in *De finibus*, 3.16–23.

35 Elizabeth Asmis shows that Seneca's referral to "one's own" happy life in *De vita beata* 3.3 may have been influenced by Panaetius' second *persona*. See "Seneca's *On the Happy Life* and Stoic Individualism," 224–8.

36 See Gill's discussion, "Peace of Mind and Being Yourself," 4606–7. "The 'essential' self," Gill concludes, "is conceived as the expression in each of us, of the deepest principles of our shared humanity" (4635).

(3) Contrasting with Panaetius/Cicero, handicaps are natural instincts or character traits that society looks down on or that do not easily work in worldly affairs.

In summary, *honestum* is only one aspect of bravery. Bravery, or lack of bravery, or degree of bravery, cannot be known without an assessment of character traits and natural instincts. Panaetius/Cicero occupy an in-between position here. They describe various and opposite traits but show that one temperament can be as successful, in its own way, as another. For Erasmus, in contrast, there is all the difference between positive and negative innate traits, traits that are out of sync with the surrounding world, and it is the negative innate traits – not the positive innate traits – that allow highest virtue and bravery.

Erasmus' prime exemplar in all this, and what his discussion leads up to, is Christ. While Colet had imagined that Christ escaped from his human feelings and other natural weaknesses, triumphantly exhibiting a martyr's *alacritas*, Erasmus argues that such an outlook grossly diminishes Christ's achievement. His Passion was all about the fact that he could not put aside his natural instincts, could not escape from his human feelings. Further below it will be shown that his natural disabilities were greater than ever experienced by a human, which gave him opportunities for virtue that exceeded that of any human. My quote above of 1275C ends with a statement that is in fact aimed directly at Colet: "Despite your efforts, you [Colet] will diminish the glory attaching to bravery, not increase it, if you allow bravery itself fewer chances to shine." Bravery cannot be described by abstract theses, particular behaviours, or the outcome of events. It occurs only in the context of natural instincts and particular character traits. Near the conclusion of *De taedio Iesu* we read:

> You [Colet] set out, when our debate began, to add something to the Redeemer's love, but have diminished it, whereas I have enlarged and not decreased it, contrary to your expectations. I have thrown into the scale a weighty argument which you wished to see removed. Perhaps you think that virtue does not increase when there are more opportunities [from natural disabilities] to do good? (1285B–C)

If the contention that natural disabilities increase opportunities for virtue was not taken from Stoic, or Stoic-based, sources, how did it come about? Here again we must return to Erasmus' youthful sufferings, sufferings that differed markedly from that of any Stoic, as far as we know, and Cicero.[37] He had seen himself as being seriously and unusually handicapped by a body that could not tolerate hardships, including certain foods and fasts, and by a mind that could not tolerate lack of freedom, in first place being the monastic life. Many personal acquaintances, various church functionaries, and the ethos of the society that surrounded him ignored, resisted, or rejected his physical and mental makeup but he had found this makeup inexpungeable. He had been attracted to Stoicism precisely because it helped him come to grips with the fact that his physical and mental traits were inborn and, as such, unyielding – and had to be dealt with on their own terms. But he had found that the Stoic insights did not here go far enough. Indelibly imprinted on his mind, from bitter and prolonged experience, was the certainty that it takes much more courage to deal with innate traits that are objected to on religious and social grounds than with innate traits that are common, socially accepted, or commended and which have immediate personal and social benefits. He came to see that his troublesome physical and mental drives, more than coming about through no fault of his own and being ineradicable, provided opportunities for virtue not found among more common and easily adaptable character traits.[38]

Colet no more grasped the irrevocableness of Erasmus' natural disabilities and the possibilities for virtue they allowed than he grasped the irrevocableness of Christ's incomparable natural disabilities and the incomparable possibilities these handicaps allowed.

2 Versus Origen: The Soul Is Neither Flesh Nor Spirit

Near the end of *De taedio Iesu* we are shown in detail that natural instinct (including emotion) has a unique location within Christianity. Natural instinct is not, as theologians have imagined, something located in or related to "flesh." It is one of the things that are indifferent (as this word

37 Cicero was overcome by grief at the death of his only daughter, Tullia (*Att* 12.15, *Tusc.* 3.76, 4.63), and Seneca lapsed into grief at the death of his friend Serenus (*Ep.* 63.14), but their interest in Stoicism did not begin with problems with their own natural instincts or character traits.

38 In the gulf which in Erasmus' mind separated his struggles from the more adaptable traits of most humans we may well be seeing another aspect of his motto, "I concede nothing."

is defined by Stoics) and it is located between spirit (*honestum*) and flesh (*turpia*). Another word for things that are indifferent, he shows, is "soul." Christian spirituality is not about a one-dimensional climb to spirit but about the working out of both "soul" and "spirit." Natural instinct is ineradicable, not something Christians can escape or should want to escape. In criticizing the accepted views, Erasmus focuses directly on Origen (c. 185–c. 255).

It is well known that Erasmus had become interested in the writings of Origen at the time his *Enchiridion* was taking shape, beginning in the summer of 1501, but what is not seen is that Origen impacted *De taedio Iesu* also.[39] In neither case, and this too is not recognized, does Erasmus accept, as is, Origen's main theses. In fact he radically alters or rejects these theses. Although Origen was acquainted with Stoicism, the influence was peripheral and tacked on to larger – Platonist and biblical – theses.[40] For Erasmus, in contrast, Stoic or Stoic-based thinking was at the very core of thought. And he corrects Origen by way of Stoicism. The fact that Origen's thought is considered and then rejected in detail only near the conclusion of *De taedio Iesu* probably indicates that the work, begun in late 1499, had been essentially completed, as would be expected, by the time he read Origen in late 1501. However much he admired some aspects of Origen's writings, he immediately saw, it appears, that Origen's outlook pivoted on a thesis entirely at odds with his own thinking.[41]

39 On Origen, see Chadwick, *Early Christian Thought and the Classical Tradition*; idem, "Origen, Celsus, and the Stoa"; Clark, *The Origenist Controversy*; Crouzel, *Origen*; Mark Julian Edwards, *Origen Against Plato*; Fairweather, *Origen and Greek Patristic Theology*; Heither, *Translatio Religionis*; Scheck, *Origen and the History of Justification*; Smith, *The Ancient Wisdom of Origen*; Trigg, *Origen*; Tripolitis, *The Doctrine of the Soul in the Thought of Plotinus and Origen*; McGuckin, *The Westminster Handbook of Origen*.

40 Although Origen had first-hand knowledge of Chrysippus, Henry Chadwick concludes that "the main structure of Origen's system does not seem to have been deeply affected by Stoic thought, except in its emphasis on providence." See "Origen, Celsus, and the Stoa," 40. M.J. Edwards argues that "the Bible, rather than Plato, is Origen's manual, and the Bible, rather than Plato, must be our guide to the interpretation of his vocabulary." See *Origen against Plato*, 114 passim.

41 André Godin sees only one-to-one relationships between Erasmus and Origen in his *Érasme lecteur d'Origène*. See, for example, pp. 39 and 467. On Origen in the fifteenth and sixteenth centuries, see Schär, *Das Nachleben des Origenes im Zeitalter des Humanismus*; Scheck, "Erasmus's Reception of Origen's Exegesis of Romans," 158–68; and Walker, "Origène en France au début du XVIe siècle." Humanists who had been interested in Origen before Erasmus include Cristoforo Persona (who had published a translation of *Contra Celsum* in 1481), Marsilio Ficino, Pico della Mirandola, and Aldus Manutius.

In considering the differences between spirit and flesh, the endless strife between them, and the many arguments as to whether there are three wills, two wills, or one will (1286C–F), Erasmus arrives at the view that the will is like an iron bar pulled between two opposed magnets (1287A). One magnet pulls it towards good (*ad honesta*), the other towards evil (*ad turpia*). Using a different metaphor, he compares the will to a palm tree in that a branch can be pulled down but as soon as one lets go the branch springs back. In this scenario there are not three wills or two wills but one will, a will pulled at every moment in opposite directions.

> The will, like an iron bar between two magnets, is attracted towards both sides at once: towards good by the power of our original state of innocence, which, though corrupted by sin, was not destroyed by it; towards evil by vice, or rather by the vestiges of original sin. It is like bending down a branch of a palm tree, which is naturally springy; it is still the same branch, and keeps its natural resilience, which is merely in abeyance. As soon as you let go, the branch will spring back into place. (1287A)

What Erasmus is doing here is simply restating a major theme in Origen's writings: the soul and its will inevitably attaches to either flesh or spirit. Origen concisely words the theme near the beginning of his *Commentary on The Epistle to the Romans*, in explaining why Paul "does not explicitly designate the soul."

> It is my belief that the Apostle (Paul) is using the customary habit in this passage [Ps 16:10, Acts 2:27], knowing that the soul (anima) is always midway between the spirit (spiritus) and the flesh (caro) and that it joins itself either to the flesh, thus becoming one with the flesh, or it associates itself with the spirit and becomes one with the spirit. Consequently if it is joined with the flesh men become fleshly; but if it unites with the spirit they become spiritual. For that reason he does not explicitly designate the soul but only the flesh and the spirit. For he knows that the soul inevitably attaches itself to one of these two aspects, as in those to whom he writes, "But you are not in the flesh but in the spirit" [Rom 8:9], and, "Whoever unites himself with a prostitute is one body" [1 Cor 6:16], here calling "prostitute" the flesh or body. "But whoever unites himself with the Lord is one Spirit" [1 Cor 6:17]. (1.5.3)[42]

---

42 *Commentaria in Epistolam B. Pauli ad Romanos* 1.5.3. PG 14, 850 (cf. 1.18.5–9, PG 14, 866–7), *Commentary on the Epistle to the Romans Books 1–5*, 71. See also *Origenes Vier Bücher Von Den Prinzipien*, 3.4.2–4, and *Origen, On First Principles*, 3.4.2–4.

Origen continues with an even more important reason why Paul "does not explicitly designate the soul." He did not want to "break apart the unity of Jesus" by distinguishing his soul from spirit. Jesus did not exemplify two separate things, soul and spirit, but a soul that is inseparably attached to spirit. For other humans the soul plays an either/or role. Although located between flesh and spirit it inevitably – comparing to Erasmus' metaphors of iron between magnets and a springing palm branch – attaches to either flesh or spirit.

The fact that Christ had a soul attached to spirit and was not just spirit shows that he was human as well as divine but what did this humanity actually consist of? If there is in Christ a soul intermediate between flesh and spirit that holds to spirit in its entirety, what is distinctive about the soul? With ordinary humans the soul can attach to flesh as well as spirit but here too the soul has no true autonomy, no independent existence, as it always bonds with one or the other. It is also incorporeal, though always joined to the body, as distinct from "flesh."[43] Although a person's soul needs to acquire self-knowledge regarding its origin, identity, and disposition,[44] the soul's will has to make an either/or, flesh or spirit, choice with regard to any particular issue. Indeed, it would be better for the will of the soul "to be mastered by the flesh than to remain within the sphere of its own will." Better because staying in between flesh and spirit would be "to occupy the position of an irrational animal" (*Princ.* 3.4.3).

Origen's assessments of the soul's functioning in various contexts are quite consistent. Questioning in *De Principiis* whether there are one or two or three souls, he concludes that there are only two in that the intermediate soul must serve either flesh or spirit (3.4.1–4). The intermediate soul has no true existence. Those Greek philosophers who say that the soul consists of three parts are wrong (3.4.1). Even in the few places where influenced by the Stoics he discusses things that are indifferent as well as good and bad, he sees the issue in either/or terms (3.2.7). Indifferent things – contrary to Stoicism, though not pointed out – have no independent existence. Indifferent

43 On the incorporeality of the soul, see Crouzel, *Origen*, 90, and Tripolitis, *The Doctrine of the Soul in the Thought of Plotinus and Origen*, 106.

44 See Riemer Roukema, in McGuckin, *The Westminster Handbook of Origen*, 202. On souls in a pre-existent state, see below, pp. 283–5.

and neutral things are called such, according to his *Commentary on Romans*, "because when attached to evil works they can be called evil and when joined to good works they can be designated as good" (4.9.6). "And so the affliction of the righteous cannot be called indifferent but is clearly good, by which the good of virtue is fulfilled. The unrighteous, however, even if they suffer affliction, which we have already said are called by Scripture scourges, do nothing in these scourges and corrections according to the spirit's virtue" (4.9.9). Righteous affliction, the "narrow and constricted road," is found among the saints and with Christ, as well as the generality of righteous persons (4.9.8). The affliction of a righteous person exists "when he is hungry and when he is well-fed, and when he endures persecutions and when he has rest" (4.9.10). In short, indifferent things have no more substance or autonomy than the soul and appear to be just another way of talking about soul. Indeed he sometimes refers, as in his *Commentary on John*, to the soul as "indifferent" and receptive to either virtue or vice (32.18). Having no unattached existence or corporeality, "indifferent things" and "soul" are words that have little tangible meaning other than that they relate to the path, either/or, the soul's will has chosen. "The will of this soul is something intermediate between the flesh and the spirit, undoubtedly serving and obeying one of the two, whichever it has chosen to obey" (*Princ.* 3.4.2).

Although Erasmus asserts, reminiscent of Origen's speculative frame of mind, that he is "leaving these questions [of will and soul] undecided" (1287A),[45] the discussion that follows amounts to an all-out rejection of Origen's outlook.[46] What exists between spirit and flesh is something in its own right. The soul is an independent and substantive entity, not something that simply attaches to either spirit or flesh. There are not just two factors in play, spirit and flesh, but three. The third is natural instinct. More than this, natural instinct is soul (1288A). Soul is

45 Origen's approach in *De principiis*, as in many of his writings, is questioning and tentative, as he himself many times points out. At 2.8.4, for example, he states that "we must not be supposed to put these (statements) forward as settled doctrines, but as subjects for inquiry and discussion."

46 Commenting in his *Annotations on Romans* (1516) on Origen's distinction between flesh, soul, and spirit, in interpreting Romans 1:4, Erasmus finds his argument "rather foreign and forced." With regard to Romans 13:1 he finds Origen's interpretation of the soul "more clever than true." See CWE 56, 18 and 346.

not incorporeal and not one with free-will. Soul is something that comes about naturally, without any free-will:

> Verum ut rem expediamus, ego mihi videor triplicem quendam nisum animi deprehendere in homine. Unum qui spiritus est, & non nisi ad invisibilia, ad honesta, ad aeterna nititur; Alterum huic diversum, qui carnis est, & ad turpia sollicitat, quatenus turpia sunt ... Tertium, inter hos duos medium, qui neque ad honesta, tamquam honesta, neque ad turpia, tamquam ad turpia, sed ad ea fertur, quae naturae sunt amica, ab iis resilit, quae laedunt incolumitatem, aut etiam tranquillitatem. Primus ille judicio constat & gratia, secundus depravatione, tertius naturali affectu. (1287C)
>
> However, to pass rapidly on, it seems to me that three different kinds of impulse can be detected in the human psyche. The first belongs to the spirit and impels us purely towards the invisible, the good, and the eternal; the second belongs to the flesh and does the opposite, tempting us towards evil simply because it is evil ... The third kind of impulse is midway between these two, attracted neither towards good for its own sake, nor towards evil for its own sake, but instead towards anything that is favourable to nature; and it recoils from anything that threatens our survival, or even our peace of mind. The first of these impulses derives from judgment and grace, the second from corruption, the third from natual instinct.

Let's look carefully at the three components of this statement.

Note, first, the tie of *spiritus* to *honesta*, a Stoic word (the good, virtue, the honourable, unbending truth), used three more times at 1287C and at 1286E, 1286F, and 1287A.[47] The description here of spirit is a correcting or refining of previously mentioned views. Whereas earlier divinity and reason reflect separate wills (1286C) they have now become components of one thing, spirit – comparing with Stoic *honestum*. Differing from flesh and soul, spirit "is pure and simple, and is called 'reason' by the (Stoic) philosophers." Paul calls spirit "law of the mind" (1286E). As stated in the quotation, not out of line with Origen, spirit consists of grace and judgment.[48] It is also an impulse that "impels us purely

47 On *honestum, honestas,* and *honestus* as Stoic words in Rome, see above, p. 6 n. 5.

48 Crouzel shows that for Origen spirit consists of two elements. It "represents the active aspect of grace, it is a divine gift, while the intellect is the passive and receptive aspect, the one that receives and accepts this gift." See *Origen*, 89.

towards the invisible, the good, and the eternal" (ad invisibilia, ad honesta, ad aeterna). Stoics, it may be remembered, connected *honesta* with the invisible and the eternal as well as with reason and virtue.

Spirit and flesh are opposites in Stoicism. On the spirit side is Stoic *honesta* and on the flesh side is Stoic *turpia* (evil). The one impulse is attracted "towards good for its own sake" (ad honesta, tamquam honesta), the other impulse is attracted "towards evil for its own sake" (ad turpia, tamquam ad turpia). As Cicero shows in so many instances, the Stoics hold (unlike Epicurus) that "nothing is good but what is honorable, nothing is evil but what is base" (Nihil bonum nisis quod honestum, nihil malum nisi quod turpe) (*Tusc.* 2.30). Or, even closer to Erasmus' conceptualization, "Nothing is less open to doubt than that what is morally good is to be desired for its own sake, and similarly what is morally bad is to be avoided for its own sake" (Nihil est enim de quo minus dubitari possit quam et honesta expetenda per se et eodem modo turpia per se esse fugienda) (*Fin.* 3.38).

Between *honesta* and *turpia* are found, in Stoicism, things indifferent (*indifferentia,* Greek *adiaphora*) and it is here that Erasmus places the impulse from natural instinct (*naturali affectu*). Natural instinct is attracted – *independent* of spirit or flesh – "towards anything that is favourable to nature" and recoils "from anything that threatens our survival." A little farther on natural instinct is described as both an inclination to want things such as food and water and an inclination to recoil from things such as death (1287D).

Although Origen would likely have accepted Erasmus' Stoic-based way of wording spirit and Stoic-based contraposing of flesh, he would not have made sense of Erasmus' talk about something that is *not* attracted towards good for its own sake and *not* attracted towards evil for its own sake – natural instinct. He would have found his placement of natural instinct in between spirit and flesh and his equating of natural instinct with soul (1288A) radical, incomprehensible, and heretical.

What Erasmus' focus on natural instinct and placing of natural instinct build on, as brought out in his edition of *De officiis* (published April 1501) and near the beginning of *De taedio Iesu* (1271A–B, above pp. 106–8), is the concept, unique to Stoicism, of *oikeiosis*. Although they lack reason, newborn humans have at birth a self-preservation instinct. It is self love, states Cicero's Cato, that impels the newborn to seek, without ever having experienced pleasure or pain, things that preserve his constitution and reject things that threaten its destruction. Concern for his own constitution impels the human infant to promote health and reject the contrary and to take action (*Fin*. 3.16, cf. D.L. 7.85). Animals, Seneca holds, "are born fully-trained." Immediately at birth, without the effect of experience, without learning from pain, every animal knows instinctively how to use its body (*Ep*. 121.7). Every animal avoids automatically things that can lead to death. No animal, humans included, is at birth free from the fear of death (*Ep*. 121.18).

Although Origen was undoubtedly acquainted with the Stoic concept of *oikeiosis*, he opted not to see a relevance to Christianity. He allows in *De principiis* that there are bodily necessities, such as emitting semen or feeling hunger, and that the devil is not the original cause, but immediately states: "we derive the beginnings and what we may call the seeds of sin from those desires which are given to us naturally for our use." Then, when "first movements towards intemperance" occur, "hostile powers," most notably "daemons," spread these sins (3.2.2, cf. 3.4.4).[49] Noting Paul's statement that "The flesh lusteth against the spirit, and the spirit against the flesh" (Gal. 5:17), he states that some sins *begin* in natural instincts (3.2.3).[50] Natural instincts do not, it is clear, have a life of their own, something that impels a human at birth to seek out anything that is favourable to one's nature and to reject anything that is hostile.[51] Nor would Origen have ever dreamed of connecting natural instincts with soul. In fact, he explicitly denies that flesh, however natural, has a soul (3.4.1).

In his criticism and rewriting of Origen it is evident that for Erasmus, here again, the natural instincts we are born with are lifelong and not, as in orthodoxy, overtaken by reason as one becomes older. However, the quote above brings out one additional point: natural instinct recoils not only from anything that may threaten our survival but from anything that may threaten "even our peace of mind." By natural instinct we desire, for example, health and recoil from ill health. More broadly we desire life and recoil from death. Therewith we recoil, according

49 The referral to "first movements," which include "evil thoughts" (3.2.4), is Stoic inspired. See below, Part V.

50 "Quod autem sint quaedam peccata, quae non contrariis virtutibus veniant, sed ex naturalibus corporis motibus initium sumant, manifestissime declarat apostolus Paulus in eo cum dicit ..."

51 Not only is self-preservation a concept not found in Origen's writings, he almost never, states Riemer Roukema, refers to law of nature in its physical sense, "according to which, for example, a human being is bound to die." See McGuckin, *The Westminster Handbook of Origen*, 140.

to Erasmus, not only from that which would threaten our body but from that which would threaten our mind – the very thought of death. Fear, for example, is an ineradicable natural instinct that arises where death is a physical possibility and this possibility also affects "our peace of mind." In short, more that just reacting to a physical event fear responds, as a natural instinct, to a mental event.

But in orthodox Stoicism, peace of mind comes not from dealing directly with natural instinct but from the wisdom found in a correct philosophical outlook. With the advent of reason it becomes possible for young persons to realize that death is not an evil and thus death, like pain, is not to be feared (*Fin.* 3.29). Death is an indifferent and fear, including fear of death, represents false reasoning. Unlike those who think death an evil the Stoic wiseman is always tranquil and happy. Philosophy banishes fears (*Tusc.* 2.11). In a paen to (Stoic) philosophy in the last book of *Tusculan Disputations*, Cicero refers to philosophy as "thou that hast freely granted us peacefulness of life and destroyed the dread of death (terrorem mortis)" (5.5). Humans do not have control over the universe but what they can control is attitude. Death is inevitable, nature's law, and must be accepted with equanimity. Life has been granted like a loan (*Tusc.* 1.91, 93). Warriors with Stoic mindsets prefer death in battle rather than to part with their principles (*Tusc.* 2.59). What is terrible, avers Epictetus, is not death but the judgment that death is terrible (*Handbook*, 5). Regarding the death of loved ones, we need to always be prepared and to know when to stop grieving. To hang on to such grief is to fight against god (*Disc.* 3.24.85, 3, 21–4).

And yet, what needs to be understood is that Erasmus sees natural instinct, as evident in the quotation, as a thing indifferent (as defined by Stoics) – not as something competing with *honestum*. That is to say, natural instinct (and with it emotion) is located by him within the second side of the Stoic unitary both/and frame of thought. As an indifferent (ineradicable) natural instinct needs to be dealt with, it will become clear, like any indifferent, as either "preferred" or "dispreferred." What can also be seen in the above, not of little consequence, is that Erasmus has made Christian spirituality consist not just of one thing but two; not just spirit but *indifferentia*.

Natural instinct is not "flesh" but "soul"

Acknowledging that "some theologians call flesh (carnem) what I here call soul (animam)" (1288A), Erasmus insists, nonetheless, on the difference. Natural instinct is not flesh but soul. Nor is soul something that merely latches on, as Origen would have it, to one of two poles, one evil the other good (spirit). Soul is autonomous and as such does not depend on either evil or good. It is not evil, as such, and it is not good, as such. And it is not incorporeal but profoundly substantive.

From cover to cover *De taedio Iesu* is an attempt to delineate what others had not seen, the inseparability from Christian spirituality of natural instinct. All humans are subject to natural instinct and Christ was no exception. Being a Christian is not about negating or bypassing natural instincts but in seeing their importance and learning to live with them.

> Now, just as any inclination towards something is to some extent an act of the will, so disinclination and fear seem to be acts of refusal. In this sense hunger and thirst are partly acts of will, the will of nature, not of the spirit or the flesh. But if such feelings of inclination or fear (disinclinations), being natural and not intrinsically connected with the spirit or the flesh, are simply natural, there is nothing to prevent them existing even in the best of us, and ultimately even in Christ.[52] (1287D)

Here yet again Erasmus is thinking in terms of *oikeiosis*, an innate impulse to seek what is favourable to nature and recoil from what threatens our survival. We desire food and water but we fear, rather than desire, death. But whether such desires are inclinations or disinclinations they are natural.[53] They are not spirit and they are not flesh. Christ experienced to the full these natural instincts. Contrary to Origen, soul and spirit are very different things. Origen had claimed that Paul did not want to "break apart the unity of Christ" by distinguishing soul from spirit, but Erasmus emphatically rejects this outlook. It was right and meet that soul be separate from spirit and that soul not be incorporeal but profoundly substantive. There were two radically different sides to Christ's being.

Erasmus arrives at "the will of nature" as distinct from a will of spirit and a will of flesh by first setting forth alternative views. Earlier he had mentioned various opinions regarding will and soul, whether there are one, two, or three, and how they function. Some had seen a triad

52 I have revised Heath's translation.

53 The Stoic wiseman distinguishes between "preferred" and "dispreferred" indifferents. The former (things such as life, health, pleasure) can excite "inclination" and the latter (things such as death, disease, pain) can excite "aversion." See D.L. 7.102–5.

comprising a will related to divine wisdom, a will related to reason, and a will related to flesh (1286C). It is in this setting that he brings in, here too not indicating sources, Origen's very different view. Origen sees a will of spirit, a will of flesh, and a "will of soul," a will of soul that is incorporeal and inevitably ties to either flesh or spirit. But all this is only background. Erasmus is not jumping "rhetorically" from one view to another but bringing in previous and alternate positions as a way to contextualize and pinpoint what is different about his own conceptualizations. What he leads up to is independent of any of the positions he describes, carefully thought out, and unprecedented. "Will of soul" is replaced with a "will of nature" that is at one and the same time soul. Soul is natural instinct and natural instinct is "the will of nature," something autonomous and substantive.

Whereas in his earlier rendering of existent non-Stoic triads, "*infirmitas*" was shown to be another word for *caro* and its evils (1286D), now *infirmitas* is said to be from natural instinct (*naturali affectu*) and unconnected with evil and corruption (1287F, 1288A). Earlier, opposite the reason and highest good of "the philosophers," things of the flesh were placed "under the general heading of (Stoic) *πάθη*, that is passions [i.e., emotions], or disorders, or appetites (affectus seu perturbationes sive appetites)" (1286F). Compare *Tusculan Disputations* 3.7: Emotions (*perturbationes animi*) such as terror, lust, and fits of anger, "belong, generally speaking, to the class of emotions which the Greeks term *πάθη*." Erasmus often uses the word *affectus* for *πάθη*, though note his referral to "*turpibus instinctibus*" (1287B).[54] Immediately following the referral to *πάθη*, Erasmus shows that St Paul calls such feelings variously "the law of sin," "the law of the members," "the flesh" (*carnem*), and "the body" (*corpus*)" (cf. Rom 7:23–5) (1286F). Earlier, that is, he shows that even Paul did not distinguish between "flesh" and "body." Both represent *πάθη*. Now, however, he makes a distinction. Natural instincts, fear of death being one, are not "flesh" (1287F, 1288A).

It is evident that taking the infirmities of natural instinct away from flesh lessens the place and role of flesh (*caro*). On the other hand, a sizable part of what had been flesh has now had a huge increase in status. Humans are responsible for evils of the flesh but they are not

54 On the use of *perturbatio*, *turbatio*, and *adfectus* by Cicero and later authors, see Graver, *Cicero on the Emotions*, 80. She translates *perturbatio animi* as "emotion" rather than "passion" or "disturbance" (xxxviii–ix).

responsible for natural instincts. Natural instincts simply exist. "Soul," unlike "flesh," is about that which in human nature is unalterable.

Attempting to find authority for his walling off of natural instinct from sin and the flesh, Erasmus brings in Augustine (1287B), but the connection is forced. "When Augustine remarks that there is some degree of sin whenever the flesh desires something against the spirit, either he means by 'sin' the corruption of the will that attracts it to evil, or else he is discussing not mere instincts (non de nisu simplici loquitur) but desires that involve some measure of approval and pleasure." Some confirmation for this statement can be found in Augustine's *De natura et gratia*,[55] but the context and point being made is very different. Augustine separates sin and human nature but the distinction is moralistic. His discussion is about sin and that which is blameable whereas Erasmus is focusing on natural instinct and that which is not blameable. What Erasmus leads up to is almost the opposite: natural instincts frame human life and are essential components of spirituality and Christianity. Augustine is combating Pelagius, claiming that Pelagius allows humans to find a defence for their sins by holding that the will is helpless where there are necessities of nature, such as hearing, seeing, and smelling, whereas Erasmus is showing – more related to Pelagius' alleged argument than Augustine's – that natural instincts are not only unrelated to sin but all important. Far from Augustine's outlook, Erasmus' purpose, central to his entire discussion, is to show that natural instinct, something humans are not responsible for, is central to one of three categories that define the human condition. Nor would Augustine have imagined that soul could in any way be equated with natural instinct.

Colet may find his argument unfamiliar and indeed he would not blame (theologian) Colet for scorning his thesis as "some mere fancy of mine" "were it not," Erasmus insists yet again, "that St. Augustine supports me" (1287E). The correlation with Augustine's view is evident, Erasmus believes, in Augustine's interpretation of Jesus' statement to John, John 21:18.[56] "When you were young, you girded yourself and walked where you wished; but when you are old, you will hold out your hands, and another will gird you, and will take you where you do not

55 Augustine, *De natura et gratia* 54.62–3, PL 44, 277–8, also *Sermones* 128.5–6, PL 38, 716–17.

56 Augustine, *In Ioannis evangelium tractatus* 123.5, PL 35, 1969.

wish to go." According to Augustine, the passage shows that Peter faced martyrdom unwillingly and that "feelings of frailty (affectum infirmitatis) that make us unwilling to die" are "so natural that not even old age had set Peter free of them" (1287E-F). To which Erasmus responds:

> You will notice that the feeling is called frailty (*infirmitas*), not an inclination towards evil; it is a fear, deeply implanted in us by natural instinct, of anything inimical to nature (sed penitus naturalibus insitam affectibus reformidationem eorum, quae naturae sunt insensa). (1287F)

The fact that with regard to Peter's fear Augustine separates human nature from sin allowed Erasmus to infer that Augustine recognized that natural instinct is not flesh (*caro*) and not evil. Here again, however, Erasmus' larger meaning is far from Augustine's. Augustine is merely employing a Bible passage to show what had to be shown, that Peter's unwillingness to die was not evil or even a shortcoming. Fear of death when one is old is natural and thus Peter's fear of death, his *infirmitas*, was natural. Augustine is not approaching the issue philosophically. He is not setting forth a thesis regarding the functioning of natural instincts, much less their importance in life. He is not imagining that natural instincts have an indispensable role to play in the practice of Christianity. And he is far from recognizing a self-preservation impulse, something that is "deeply implanted in us by natural instinct, of anything inimical to nature," or, as stated earlier, an impulse which is attracted "towards anything that is favourable to nature" and "recoils from anything that threatens our survival, or even our peace of mind" (1287C).

Erasmus continues:

> Now if you ask me what kind of will it was in Christ that made him unwilling to die, I shall reply that it was the same as that he foresaw in Peter, simply a natural fear of death (mere naturalem mortis reformidationem), which in the best of us, and especially in Christ, is not opposed to the spirit, nor connected with the flesh. (1287F–1288A)
>
> That he shrank from death was a sign of weakness (infirmitatis), natural but not sinful. (1288B)
>
> (When he asked,) "Father if it be possible, let this cup pass from me," (Matt. 26:39,) (he was reacting to) natural instinct (naturalem affectum). (1288C)
>
> The promptings of nature (affectus naturae) (had overwhelmed him). (1288C)

> (It was as if he had said:) My human senses make me reluctant to die, because death is inimical to nature. (Non vult mori sensus humanus, quia mors insensa naturae.) (1288D)
>
> This natural weakness, so deeply implanted in human nature that it can be conquered but never eradicated (ut vinci quidem queat, revelli prorsus nequeat), is the surest evidence of humanity, and the Redeemer not only took it upon himself, but did so in a remarkable way. (1288B)

Here too Erasmus' thesis goes far beyond Augustine's interpretation of John 21:18. The following differences stand out: (1) Augustine refers only to fear of death as being natural whereas Erasmus is seeing fear of death as just one (though the most abiding and powerful) of many natural instincts and that natural instincts occupy a central place within Christianity. (2) Augustine did not make natural instinct, including fear of death, one of three basic impulses, one of three categories which at all times define the human condition. (3) He did not describe human nature, much less natural instinct, as something between spirit and flesh, "not opposed to the spirit, nor connected with the flesh." (4) He did not contend (and would have been horrified by the thought) that "natural instinct," or "the will of nature" (1287D), defines the meaning of soul. (5) He was not arguing that natural instincts as such "can never be eradicated." (6) He was not imagining that Christ's Passion was about an uncontrollable and overwhelming fear of death. (7) Augustine considers Peter, in the same place, a martyr (implied by Erasmus, 1287F) but Erasmus has argued at length that Christ was not a martyr in that he lacked *alacritas*.

The thesis is "not invented"

Erasmus knows that his interpretation of soul as natural instinct – and therewith placing soul within a Stoic-inspired triad – is not found in any of the sources he uses, but he also wants the reader to believe that his analysis does not contradict any of these sources, that he merely explicates and details what others have passed over. The reality is something else. His interpretation is unprecedented. Two paragraphs after contending against Colet that his argument is not built on "some mere fancy of mine" he insists yet again that he has "not invented." His denial proves, even more decisively, the opposite:

> Do not protest, my dear Colet, that I have invented this division of humanity into three parts, spirit, flesh, and soul (spiritum, carnem, & animam); I

> am following Jerome's lead. Jerome followed Origen, and Origen Paul. Paul of course followed the Holy Spirit. But in using this division I am giving Christ only spirit and soul, with no part that is flesh. Some theologians call flesh what I here call soul, the part in which we must assume Christ feared death, as did Peter, the closest and thus the most similar to the head. I shall not take issue with them over the words, since we are agreed on the facts (equidem nihil contendo de verbis, quandoquidem convenit de re). (1288A)

What could be farther from the truth than the claim that in dividing humanity into three parts – spirit, flesh, and soul – he has followed Jerome who in turn followed Origen who followed St Paul?[57] If Jerome followed Origen's exposition of a threefold division this proves only that he made the same errors as Origen!

Equally at odds with the truth is the claim that his differences here with "some theologians" do not extend to "the facts." The facts agreed on are only that Christ had a human nature as well as a divine. What theologians – certainly none of those used or mentioned by him – would have agreed with his transforming of a significant part of what had been flesh into a soul consisting of natural instinct? Scholastics, as Erasmus well knew, tended to see the human soul in rational terms.[58] Making much of Aristotle's descriptions of soul as the form or essence of any living thing, in his *Commentary on De anima* (412a1–415a14), Aquinas shows that the soul, though sensitive and nutritive, is in humans fundamentally "rational." Theologians of a Platonist or Neoplatonist bent considered soul something separate from the body. Marsilio Ficino (1433–99), who published translations of all Plato's dialogues in 1484, had gone all out to demonstrate the ascent of the soul to God and its immortality.[59] Indeed, Colet was a great admirer of Ficino and envisioned the soul in like manner.[60]

---

57 Jerome was saturated with Origen's thought and translated many of his works. See Schatkin, "The Influence of Origen upon St. Jerome's Commentary on Galatians," and Heine, *The Commentaries of Origen and Jerome on St. Paul's Epistle to the Ephesians*.

58 Erasmus brings in the scholastic view of the soul as both rational and sensible at 1289A. On scholastic views of the soul, see below, Part V.

59 Ficino's long commentary on Plato's *Philebus* was written between 1464 and 1469 and comprises the first of his many systematic interpretations of the spiritual ascent of the soul to God. See Ficino, *Marsilio Ficino: The Philebus Commentary*, 43. Ficino composed his *Platonic Theology: On the Immortality of Souls*, consisting of 18 books, around 1469–74.

60 See Jayne, *John Colet and Marsilio Ficino*.

Nor did Erasmus think that he was setting forth his thesis in a loose manner. In his conclusion he states that he has attempted to persuade not by mere entreaty but by strict reasoning (1289B).[61] Most certainly he does not jump rhetorically from one idea to another but develops his argument methodically. In Part V I will describe Erasmus' detailed criticism of Jerome's claim, so influential over the centuries, that Christ in his Passion did not suffer true emotion but only "pre-emotion." Jerome had been much influenced by Origen, some works of which he had translated, and in Erasmus' mind his denial that Christ suffered true emotion in his Passion ties in directly to Origen's refusal to believe that Christ had a soul and intractable natural instincts separate from spirit.

Stepping back we can see from the above that Erasmus was determined to show that Christian spirituality embodies – at odds with Origen's one-dimensional spirit/flesh (either/or) outlook – both sides of the Stoic unitary *honestum/indifferens* frame of thought. What differs from orthodox Stoicism is not the frame but only the content of the frame, the fact that Erasmus moves emotion from the cognitive realm to the realm of natural instinct, character traits, and things indifferent.

3 Unbending Principles, but Not "*Alacritas*"

In developing the unbending side Erasmus sets forth the Stoic distinction between things that can be "endured" and things that are "unendurable."

> Nam fortitudo est scientia rerum tolerandarum, aut non tolerandarum, definitore Socrate. Aut si mavis, honestorum laborum constans susceptio. (1272A)

> For "bravery is the knowledge of what is endurable or unendurable," according to Socrates' definition. Or, if you prefer, "the steadfast performance of honorable endeavours."

61 In a letter to Colet in 1504 Erasmus states that what he has tried to do in *De taedio Iesu* and (most especially) the *Enchiridion* is "is to teach a method of morals, as it were, in the manner of those who have originated fixed procedures in the various branches of learning." *Ep.* 181. Allen 1, 405/50–2, CWE 2, 87/57–60. See above, pp. 71–2 and below, pp. 327–9.

The sources he is looking at and the conceptualizations he is thinking of, leaving aside the referral to Socrates, are through and through Stoic. The words used relate directly to Gellius' rendering of Stoicism in *Attic Nights* and Cicero's *Tusculan Disputations*. One of Gellius' two important accounts of Stoicism concludes with the assertion that true and noble bravery, as contrasted with struggles against nature, is what our forefathers – Zeno and Chrysippus – called "scientiam rerum tolerandarum et non tolerandarum" (12.5.13). Pain can be tolerated but what cannot be tolerated is deviation from principles (*honestum*). Erasmus states that "fortitudo est scientia rerum tolerandarum, aut non tolerandarum, definitore Socrate," the difference being only that Erasmus wants to include Socrates in this type of thinking.

Erasmus' follow-up statement, "Or if you prefer, 'the steadfast performance of honorable endeavors'" (honestorum laborum constans susceptio), also represents core Stoic doctrine. Contradicting the Peripatetic argument that anger is a useful tool for the brave person and wondering if Stoics are not "the only true philosophers," Cicero gives the following Stoic definitions of bravery:

> Courage is "a condition of mind which is obedient to the highest law as concerns things to be endured," or "the preservation of a stable judgment in meeting and overcoming what seems alarming," or "the knowledge of things which are either alarming or the reverse, or which are to be ignored altogether, and the preservation of a stable judgment concerning these things." Chrysippus' definition is shorter – for the previous definitions are those of Sphaerus, whom the Stoics consider particularly adept at definition. All the definitions are pretty similar, but some go further than others in clarifying ordinary notions. Anyway, what is Chrysippus' definition? "Courage," he says, "is knowledge as concerns things to be endured" or "a condition of mind which is obedient without fear to the highest law with respect to suffering and endurance." Criticize them [Stoics] we may, just as Carneades used to do, and yet I suspect they are the only real philosophers.[62] (*Tusc.* 4.53)

The brave person steadfastly (cf. 1273C) endures everything except lack of virtue and principles. In holding to principles he needs and allows no props.

62 The translation is that of Graver, *Cicero and the Emotions*. For Aristotle, in contrast, bravery is the mean between foolhardiness and cowardice (*Eudemian Ethics* 1220b 35–9).

But why does Erasmus claim, against the sources he was actually looking at, that the first statement is "Socrates' definition"? Very likely he was seeing Socrates' famous death scene, to which he refers a little later (1274E), as definitively showing that what is intolerable is only the rejection of virtue and principles. Regarding what is tolerable, in *Tusculan Disputations* Cicero recounts an anecdote about Socrates. Witnessing Euripides' play *Orestes*, Socrates asked for a repetition of the first three lines:

> No speech so terrible in utterance,
> No chance, no ill imposed by wrath of heaven,
> Which human nature cannot bear and suffer. (4.63)

In never allowing principles to be compromised, no matter the worldly happenings that may come along, Socrates' outlook was one with the Stoic wiseman.[63] What was not Socratic, Erasmus well understood, was the Stoic's larger two-dimensional, *honestum/indifferens*, mindset. Here as elsewhere (see the summary below, p. 305), that is, Erasmus places Socrates within a Stoic frame – on the unbending side. Clearly, this was his answer to the Platonism streaming out from Florence.

Christ was not a martyr

Late in the treatise Erasmus notes that "our whole debate" arises from the fact that Colet wants to see Christ's Passion in terms of *alacritas*, a word which had often come up, whereas Erasmus denies that Christ had *alacritas* (1286B). Over and over Erasmus had been at pains to show what was wrong with associating *alacritas* with Christ. First and foremost, *alacritas* contradicts natural instinct. *Alacritas* manifests what natural instinct is not. Martyrs may have overcome natural instinct and in so doing exhibited *alacritas*, but Christ did not. His Passion, however unique, can only be understood from the vantage point of natural instinct. He was filled with an uncontrollable and incomparable fear of death resulting from natural instinct.

---

63 Cicero recognized that the Stoic tie of virtue and happiness owed much to Socrates (*Par.* 4). The Stoics (as also their Cynic precursors) often praised Socrates, but not Plato. See Brennan, *The Stoic Life*, 22–5; Long, "Socrates in Hellenistic Philosophy"; and Striker, "Plato's Socrates and the Stoics."

What is the precise meaning of the word *alacritas* and what is the significance of the author's contrasting it with Christ's fear? The word *alacritas* is not, to my knowledge, a word used by any of the fathers of the church or any of the medieval theologians, such as Bonaventure or Aquinas, in their discussions of the Passion. Nor, as Germain Marc'hadour has ascertained, does "*alacer* and family" occur in the New Testament.[64] Scholars have found the exact meaning problematic. After puzzling over possible meanings, Michael J. Heath, in his translation of the treatise, settles on "eagerness" as a best guess.[65] James D. Tracy believes Erasmus' use of the word relates to Plato's concept of the spirited part of man and contrasts with St Bernard's concept of Christ humbling himself.[66] In fact, as I will demonstrate below, the word has a very definite provenance: Stoicism.

What needs to be remembered here is that it was Erasmus, not Colet, who developed and wrote up the debate and that it is he who used the word "*alacritas*" to pinpoint Colet's argument. The word may well capture the essence of Colet's depiction of the Passion, but the choice of the word and the context within which it is placed belong to Erasmus. In a 1504 letter to Colet, Erasmus states, regarding the end product, that Colet may now hardly recognize the arguments set forth.[67] This statement is certainly true. There is no reason to believe that Colet ever used the word "*alacritas*."[68]

Colet's position

As Erasmus describes his position, Colet considered Christ a super martyr – the unequalled example of *alacritas*. Overcoming nature, Christ, Colet argues, went to death with great eagerness. The idea that Christ could have dreaded death was for him inconceivable. Christian martyrs had accepted the most inhuman tortures with eager joy (*alacribus*), exalting, taking pleasure in pain – all because of love. Christ,

64 "Thomas More on the Agony of Christ," 497.

65 Introduction to Erasmus, *A Short Debate*, 7.

66 "Humanists among the Scholastics," 40–2. For other guesses as to the translation of *alacritas*, see Marc'hadour, "Thomas More on the Agony of Christ," 497.

67 *Ep*. 181. Allen 1, 405/42–5, CWE 2, 87/49–52. *De taedio Iesu* was published in February 1503.

68 On Erasmus' rewriting of Colet's views in terms of his own conceptualizations, see below, pp. 152–7.

who is love and charity and who came to give us eternal life, could not have dreaded death, could not have taken on suffering with a fear that martyrs did not have (1266A). Martyrs such as St Andrew, St Martin of Tours, and St Paul wished, with eager joy, for death (1269D):

> It cannot but seem to be a slight on Jesus' perfect charity if you suggest for any reason that he feared his own death. I grant you that it is natural to fear death, more natural even than to desire food. I grant you that it is unconnected with original sin. But the role of charity is to surmount nature and bring it to perfection. Hunger is one of nature's sternest tests, but exceptional love can shrug off its pangs. Death is a powerful opponent, but love is stronger and can make death itself desirable and even pleasant. (1278B–C)

Christ was fired with charity and love for others and to this end he wished "to surmount (vincere) nature." Love can overcome even the need for food and make death "desirable and even pleasant." The abject terror Erasmus imagines is "not the effect of nature pure and simple, but of nature corrupted and damned" (1278E). Erasmus would see Christ as wallowing in human nature and even sin (1276B–C). Charity eliminates natural frailties (1278E). As demonstrated so often by martyrs, not least Peter, fear of death disappears as love grows. Christ was all about perfecting nature. It is natural to fear evil but this belongs to our fallen state. Erasmus' depiction of Christ mixes incompatible elements. Christ had a human nature but his charity, obedience, and bravery testify to a readiness to suffer and overcome nature with *alacritas* (eager joy) (1271F).

We may add that Colet's argument relates to the fascination of late medieval Christians with martyrdom. Discussion of what it means to be a Christian and of sainthood had much to do with martyrdom, and Christ was the ultimate model for martyrdom. A central component of martyrdom, admired by ordinary folks, was willingness to engage in patient suffering in the face of adversity. Medieval writers tended to underpin this emphasis on patient suffering with the Stoic doctrine, as they understood it, of *apatheia* (freedom from emotion) and indifference to worldly things,[69] all of which allows us to believe that late medieval Christians would have agreed wholeheartedly with the contention that

69 See Kieckhefer, *Unquiet Souls*, 66, 68, 78 passim and below, Part VI.

Christ supremely represented *alacritas*, that the martyrs imperfectly exhibited the *alacritas* that with Christ was perfect.

The Stoic meaning of "*alacritas*"

In fact, there is a clear explanation for Erasmus' use of the word "*alacritas*." Here again he is building on Stoicism. In *Tusculan Disputations* Cicero brings in this word to represent Stoic *laetitia*, one of the four false types of emotion. Cicero ties his use of *alacritas* to the Roman poet Trabea (c. 200 BCE): "And if the mind has secured the object of its desire it will be transported with eagerness (*alacritate*), 'so that there is no rule' in what it does, as says the poet who thinks that 'excessive pleasure of the soul is utter folly'" (4.35).[70] The Stoics reject *alacritas* and Cicero agrees with them.

"Empty eagerness, that is, exuberant delight" (inanis alacritas, id est laetitia gestiens) differs little from a mental abberration (*Tusc*. 4.36). Like the other false emotions, *alacritas* is alien to right reason and nature (4.11). The person who exhibits *alacritas* has lost his sanity (4.37). "When a man is frivolously excited, and in a transport of empty delight (laetitia) and reckless extravagance, is he not all the more wretched, the happier his life appears in his own eyes?" (5.16). In *De finibus* Cato refers to "that emotional disturbance which the Stoics call by a name that also denotes a bodily feeling, *hēdonē*, 'pleasure,' but which I prefer to style 'delight' (laetitiam) meaning the sensuous elation of the mind when in a state of exultation" (3.35). Having nothing to do with nature, *alacritas*, like the other disturbances, consists of mere fancy and frivolous opinion. In the words of Diogenes Laertius, "To be in transports of delight is the melting away of virtue" (7.114).

That Erasmus was thinking about the concept of *alacritas*, as defined by the Stoics, even before writing *De taedio Iesu* (and most likely before the debate itself) is evident in a letter to Colet immediately after the debate, dated October 1499. Even at that early date he uses the word at least twelve times and denies, against Colet's contention, that Christ overcame his feelings in this way. Christ's purpose was not that of his martyrs.[71]

70 That the "poet" referred to is Trabea is made clear by *De finibus* 2.13. See also Graver, *Cicero on the Emotions*, 162.

71 *Ep*. 109. Allen 1, 249–53.

To illustrate *alacritas* and Colet's depiction of Christ, Erasmus brings in the philosopher Epicurus' outlook, as represented in *Tusculan Disputations* (2.17–18), though no mention is made of his source. Colet holds that love is stronger than death and can make death itself desirable and even pleasant, and this correlates with Epicurus' claim that an Epicurean tortured and roasted alive in the brazen bull of the tyrant Phalaris (6th cent. BCE) will find the experience pleasant – because clear conscience has immense power:

> Epicurus claims that even inside Phalaris' bull, the wiseman will cry, "I feel no pain; it's very pleasant." If the mere semblance of virtue has such effect on a philosopher [argues "Colet"], will true and perfect charity have less effect on Christ? Granted, [argues "Colet,"] it is not a dereliction of duty to accept death with sorrow instead of willingly, eagerly (alacriter), and joyfully (exsultanter), but it argues a lesser love. (1278C)

In other words, Christ is for Colet a super Epicurean and a super martyr. Christ showed his true love for humans in eagerly and joyfully seeking death and martyrdom.[72]

In context, Cicero is contrasting Epicurus' position with that of the Stoics. He ridicules Epicurus for imagining that the Epicurean being burned and tortured in Phalaris' bull will say: "How sweet; how indifferent I am to this!" The Stoic wiseman rightly thinks that wisdom does not have such power against pain. What is required of the brave man is only endurance, not rejoicing or asking for more (*Tusc.* 2.17–18, 53). Unlike Epicurus the Stoic does not consider such pain an evil, however unpleasant, difficult, hateful, contrary to nature. Later in the same work Cicero comes back to Phalaris' bull. Epicurus merely puts on "the mask of a philosopher." In counting being burned, placed on the rack, and cut to pieces as nothing, Epicurus "restricts evil to pain and good to pleasure, and makes a mock of this 'right (honesta) and base (turpia)' of ours" (5.73, 75). Christ, Erasmus wants to show, was not a super Epicurean but a super Stoic.

In Christ's *entire life*, not just his Passion, there was nothing of the martyrs' eagerness, their *alacritas*. *Alacritas* goes beyond human nature,

72 Like *alacritas*, the bull of Phalaris illustration relates to Erasmus' original thoughts. The 1499 letter to Colet refers to the bull of Phalaris discussed "by a philosopher" and here too the contrast is with Christ. *Ep.* 109. Allen 1, 252/90–4, CWE 1, 209/100–4.

beyond natural and ineradicable instincts. As a human Christ had no way of escaping these instincts. Had he faced death with exaltation (*exsultanter*), as did martyrs, he would not have been able to truly demonstrate (versus what Colet imagines) his love (1289E). "A show of eagerness (alacritatis ostentatio) would have done us little service, but his dismay (moestitia) brought us gain" (1289F, cf. 1290B). He knew that humans would not respond to eagerness for death and the ostentatious display and dramatic speeches that could accompany such. "It is for the proud and haughty to face torture with a dauntless heart and to make some fine brave speech upon the very rack" (1290A).

Incomparable joy / incomparable fear: Inseparable opposites

And yet, if Christ did not respond to his suffering with *alacritas*, if he was not fearless and eager for death, if he did not overcome his human instincts, how precisely did he respond? Here too the base model is that of the Stoic wiseman. On the unbending side of his soul Christ "endured," "consistently" and "constantly" (1268A, B, 1278C, 1288B, 1289E–1290A). "He endured the ordeal with constancy, but found no pleasure in it" (Constanter pertulit cruciatum, at non delectatus) (1280F). He was steadfast (*constans*) in his obedience to the father (1268A, B).

Constancy is at all times a characteristic of the Stoic wiseman. In holding to unbending truths the wiseman is unwavering and lacks, through all the ups and downs of life, eagerness (*sine alacritate ulla*) (*Tusc.* 5.48):

> That person, then, whoever it may be, whose mind is quiet through consistency and self-control (moderatione et constantia), who finds contentment in himself, and neither breaks down under adversity nor crumbles with fright nor burns with any thirsty need nor dissolves into wild and futile excitement (nec alacritate futili gestiens deliquescat), that person is the wise one we are seeking, and that person is happy. Nothing in human life is so difficult for him to bear that he must be downcast, nothing so excessively delightful that he must be carried away by it. For what in human life would seem great to one who has grasped the magnitude of eternity and of the entire universe? (*Tusc.* 4.37)

In his steadfastness Christ experienced joy, but it was not the eager exaltation, *alacritas*, of the martyr. It was a contemplative joy, located in his inner soul. "Though we deny Christ the outward signs of eager joy (alacritas), which are in your [Colet's] view inseparable from charity, yet we must allow to him, and to him alone, an inward joy unmatched by all the martyrs" (1270A). The applicable word here, Erasmus finds, is not *alacritas* but "*gaudium*" – here again a Stoic word, the meaning of which Erasmus transfers from the Stoic wiseman to Christ.

> In that very hour [when he began to feel distress and dismay], I repeat, he rejoiced inwardly with inexpressible gladness (idem intus ineffabili gaudio gestiebat) because at last the time ordained by his Father was coming, when by his death he would reconcile humankind to himself as God. (1286B)

In Stoicism there are three good emotions, one of which is *gaudium* (*Tusc.* 4.12–4).[73] *Gaudium* is a joy, a rational elation, that is the counterpart of *alacritas* (alternately *laetitia*), a false emotion (*Tusc.* 4.36, 67, D.L. 7.116). Only the wiseman experiences *gaudium*, something, Seneca emphasizes, that is not external but internal (*Ep.* 23.4–6). Consider here too the discussion in *Tusculan Disputations*:

> Where we are satisfied that we are in possession of some good, this comes about in two ways: for when the soul has this satisfaction rationally and in a tranquil and equable (constanter) way, then the term *joy* (gaudium) is employed; when on the other hand the soul is in a transport of meaningless extravagance, then the satisfaction can be termed *exuberant* or *excessive delight* (laetitia gestiens vel nimia) and this they define as unreasoning excitement of the soul. (4.13)

The joy in Christ's soul (*gaudium animae*) in endless contemplation of the divine and in the prospect of humanity's salvation was not dimmed notwithstanding that he, unlike those experiencing *alacritas*, was completely affected, in the lower part of his soul, by natural instincts (1284A, C).

> To the extent that Jesus' soul was in touch with bodily emotions (corporis affectibus), he was afflicted by horrible suffering; to the extent that it was in touch with his divine nature, he was filled with triumph and boundless joy (gaudium) by precisely the same thing, his death. (1289B)

---

73 Besides *gaudium*, the wiseman has the good emotions of precaution (*cautio*), a rational avoidance instead of fear (*metus*), and wish (*voluntas*), a rational appetency instead of desire (*cupiditas, libido*). On the good emotions (*eupatheiai*), see Reydams-Shils, *Roman Stoics*, 49–52, 134–41, and comments by Graver, *Stoicism and Emotion*.

Combined in him were "complete fear and perfect eagerness, sublime joy and intense pain, supreme bliss and extreme suffering" (summam reformidationem, cum summa mentis alacritate [unlike the *alacritas* of martyrs], summum gaudium, cum extremo dolore, summam felicitatem cum summis cruciatibus) (1284A, cf. 1286B, C).

Evident here, as in all the above, is the Stoic unitary both/and mindset, as worked out by Erasmus and applied in unique ways to Christ. As in Stoicism there are, simultaneously, two types of value at play, one unbending and the other bending. On the one side Christ's mind was constant, enduring, contemplative, and filled with joy (*gaudium*); on the other side his mind was overwhelmed by the emotions of fear, terror, and anxiety (*timor, reformidatio, pavor*) (1284A). The central difference between Erasmus' conceptualizations and orthodox Stoicism is that, for all the reasons given earlier, he deliberately transferred emotion from the unbending side of the both/and to the bending. That is, he placed emotion, as such, among the things Stoics considered "indifferent," preferred or dispreferred things such as health or poverty or pain, everything neither *honesta* nor *turpia* (*Fin*. 3.25). Christ's uncontrollable fear, terror, and anxiety, was a unique response (see below, Part IV.3) within this radicalized indifferent setting.

PART IV Larger Philosophical Issues

Far from bypassing inconvenient philosophical issues, and showing us yet again how closely he had studied Stoic thought, Erasmus describes at considerable length Stoic doctrines that might seem to throw into question his contention that emotion, most particularly fear, is an ineradicable natural instinct. In Stoicism emotion had always been considered, in one way or another, a failure of reason. After criticizing his own views from the standpoint of orthodox Stoicism (chapter 1 below) Erasmus gives us a deeply thought out analysis and criticism of Gellius' real world illustration of Epictetus' thinking in *Attic Nights* (c. 180 CE) (chapter 2 below). The illustration – which describes and explains the reactions of a Stoic in a typhoon, as observed by Gellius – does not prove what Gellius thinks it proves but something very different.[1] It does not show that emotion is a false judgment – as Epictetus and other Stoics hold – but an ineradicable necessity of nature. The Stoic experienced actual emotion, emotion that did not originate in assent to an external impulse but in the mind itself – as that mind contemplated a fearful outcome. And the emotion experienced was not a pre-emotion, something that the wiseman overcomes almost immediately. Demonstratively, it lasted as long as what instigated it.

And yet Gellius' error does nothing, Erasmus believes, to the essential Stoic, unitary both/and, way of thinking – the mindset of "my Stoics." The problem is that orthodox Stoics have simply misplaced, in terms of their own schema, emotion. Emotion originates, as was shown

1 Assuming that Erasmus is a rhetorician and not a philosopher, Heath concludes that Erasmus finds "stylish inspiration in Gellius' description of the storm at sea." See CWE 70, p. 5.

in Part III, in Stoic *oikeiosis* (although he does not use the word). That is, it is one of the instincts humans are born with. Emotion does not relate to the unbending side of truth but to the bending side – the location of *indifferentia*. It is within this original, thought out, and credible correction of Stoicism that Erasmus places (chapter 3 below) Christ's fear of death in Gethsemane – the issue that had brought about the debate with Colet and the central focus of *De taedio Iesu*.

1 Objections of Orthodox Stoics: Colet becomes "Colet"

It is "Colet" that Erasmus charges with representing orthodox Stoicism against his own analyses and corrections of Stoicism. Not noted by scholars, however, "Colet's" erudite and lengthy summaries of many basic Stoic doctrines had nothing to do with Colet the person. Erasmus delineates here and in much of the treatise what Colet *could* have said in the debate, considering his basic outlook, rather than what he had actually said. In *De taedio Iesu* 1266E Erasmus informs the reader that what has been shown up to this point, 1265E–1266E, faithfully describes Colet's argument in the debate, though with a little more precision, but much of what we learn about Colet's thinking from that point onward is extrapolation and conjecture. Near the beginning of the work he states that in preparing to write he had looked at the issues "in a harder and more concentrated way." "I put together and weighed the arguments on both sides; indeed I altered things round so as to adopt your arguments exactly as if they were my own and to criticize my own no less severely than if they had been yours" (1265C). Over and over he begins discussion with statements such as, "If you are also arguing here that ..." (1269C) or, most often, "'But,' you will say ..." (1269C; cf. 1267E, 1270A, 1271E, 1272F, 1275D, 1276C, E, 1277E, 1278D). At 1271E the text states: "At this point, Colet, I can easily guess what you are murmuring in reply as you read on." In 1272F he informs Colet of Gellius' story of the Stoic in the typhoon, with no thought that Colet knows anything about the story, and then wonders what Colet would say in response. All of which explains how "Colet" ends up giving the reader lengthy and learned disquisitions on basic parameters of Stoic thought. The point "Colet" drives home, in his rendering of orthodox Stoicism, is that the Stoic wiseman would never allow Erasmus' all-consuming focus on natural instinct and inborn character traits, as described in Part III above.

Many additional factors confirm that Colet did not set forth any Stoic thesis in the actual debate:

(a) In his one existing letter to Erasmus immediately after the debate, dated October 1499,[2] he does not mention anything even remotely related to Stoicism and Erasmus' lengthy letters at that time also do not in any way connect Colet to Stoicism.[3]
(b) His October 1499 letter shows animosity towards philosophy and connects Erasmus, as distinct from himself, with philosophy. He prides himself on the fact that his view results from having "thoroughly absorbed Jerome," while Erasmus' argument, however brilliant, is "worthy of a philosopher," clever but untrue.
(c) Encapsulating in *De taedio Iesu* Colet's argument (1265E–1266E) – his denial that Christ's agony in Gethsemane was from fear of his own death – Erasmus mentions nothing about any Stoic, much less philosophic, buttressing of this argument by Colet.
(d) Nowhere in his many later writings does Colet show the slightest interest in Stoics or Stoicism.
(e) Colet was a theologian by training, soon to become a doctor of divinity. His goal was to interpret scripture directly, especially St Paul, without regard to the logical intricacies of scholastic theologians or the philosophical systems of antiquity. Indeed, he loved to ridicule scholastic philosophy and theology and does so in an October 1499 letter to Erasmus, which no longer exists, to which Erasmus responded.[4] His interest in philosophy was restricted to the Neoplatonist ideologies, heavily influenced by Plotinus, radiating from Florence.
(f) He was not interested in serious or detailed analysis. Exasperated with Colet's short and dismissive response to a long letter written immediately after the debate, Erasmus points out that Colet merely daydreams and has failed to even consider his arguments.[5] After writing *De taedio Iesu* Erasmus did not bother for more than a year and a half to even send a copy to Colet, much less discuss the work with him. Nor had Colet, Erasmus' letter makes clear, written to him.

---

2 *Ep*. 110. Allen 1, 253–4, CWE 1, 211–12.
3 *Ep*. 108. Allen 1, 245–9, CWE 1, 202–6; *Ep*. 109. Allen 1, 249–53, CWE 1, 206–11; *Ep*. 111. Allen 1, 254–60, CWE 1, 212–19.
4 *Ep*. 108. Allen 1, 246–7/19–73, CWE 1, 203–4/22–82.
5 *Ep*. 111. Allen 1, 259–60/212–19, CWE 1, 219/255–63.

I know of no instance in which Colet mentions the work in later letters or publications.

(g) In his *John Colet* John Gleason has shown that Colet was a dogmatic thinker, settling on opinions early and never retreating, essentially immune to reason.[6]

(h) Below I will demonstrate that the Stoic theses "Colet" so brilliantly sets forth were worked out primarily from Gellius' quotations, in his *Attic Nights*, from the Stoic Epictetus' *Discourses*. Nothing in his writings shows that Colet was in any way acquainted with Gellius' *Attic Nights*.

(i) On the other hand, consider what we now know about Erasmus' mental and emotional state before even the debate took place (above, Part II.4). He was a person consumed by Stoicism and determined to think out all the relationships and implications for Christianity. Indeed, we can be quite sure that it was Erasmus, not Colet, who initiated the original debate. Contrary to what has been supposed, Erasmus was not merely reacting to Colet's outlook[7] and not, as everywhere held, doing little more than countering Colet's views with common, especially scholastic, theses.[8] The debate was anything but something that just happened, anything but a light-hearted rhetorical dispute *in utramque partem*, a drawing out of inconclusive polar views. Erasmus was an inspired person and that inspiration had not originated in either rhetoric or scholastic thinking. *De taedio Iesu* is all about Stoicism and the learned discussions attributed to Colet are a piece of this.

Analysis shows something more. In his exposition of Stoic "pre-emotion," Greek *propatheia* (1271E), "Colet" silently and unwittingly contradicts the actual thesis of Colet in the debate, vociferously contended, that Christ could not have feared his own death for even a moment.

6 See Gleason, *John Colet*, 185. There is, however, a major contradiction in Gleasons's work. Had Gleason pointed out Colet's erudite rendering of Stoicism, in his lengthy summary of *De taedio Iesu*, he would have had to recognize that a central thesis of his book is untenable, that Colet was not after all a person incapable and uninterested in analytic or higher level thinking. Of course, once one sees that Erasmus was making up arguments for Colet, Gleason's thesis is confirmed.

7 Although Gleason shows that Colet comes off second best in the debate, he still believes, pointing out his agreement with J.H. Lupton, that *De taedio Iesu* is about Colet's view and that Erasmus merely responds. See his *John Colet*, 93, and Colet, *An Exposition of St. Paul's First Epistle to the Corinthians*, xvi.

8 See above, p. 49.

Recognizing, it appears, that Colet's argument was not truly sustainable – in that it comes close to denying that Christ was human as well as divine, a fundamental teaching of the church – Erasmus has "Colet" argue the pre-emotion thesis that had dominated the thinking of the fathers and the modern scholastic theologians with regard to Christ's Passion. Christ feared but only momentarily. In the actual debate Colet had emphatically rejected this view, "disseminated by modern theologians" (1265E) and, not grasping Erasmus' argument, had tied Erasmus' view to it.

Martyrs, Colet had argued, have overcome extreme torture with joy in their hearts so it is absurd to imagine that Christ himself feared death. Love and charity were in his heart (1266A). Jerome was "the only one to have glimpsed the truth" in that he commented that Christ did not actually feel alarm and dismay because of fear of dying but because he was concerned about the fate of the Jews (1266E–F).[9] Although Colet attributes his thesis to Jerome it was in fact not too far from that of Hilary of Poitiers (d. 367) (mentioned at 1267D and 1268B), whose thinking, often referred to over the centuries, had verged on heresy. The accepted view was that Christ's prayer for deliverance from death, "If it be possible, let this cup pass from me" (Matt 26:39), means that in being a human as well as divine Christ was "temporarily deprived of the protection of his divinity" and feared the ordeal that was about to come. However, he mastered his emotions "at once," responding: "Nevertheless, not as I will, Father, but as you will" (Matt 26:39). It is not Colet's view but this standard view – that Christ feared death but overcame this fear almost immediately – that "Colet" argues against Erasmus in the treatise.

Although Colet had taken pride in resting his argument entirely on Jerome, Erasmus shows in his treatise that Jerome also sets forth, most of the time and with great force, what became – though formulated in multiple ways – the standard position. Here Jerome does not contend that Christ in Gethsemane had no fear of death but that he had suffered only beginning emotion, "*propassio*," rather than true emotion or full-blown emotion, "*passio*." Colet has latched on to a mere comment while the thesis Jerome truly represented is passed over (1267B–C). More than this, the modern theologians Colet had taken so much pleasure in despising had spent by far the greatest amount of time and effort working out the propassion thesis (cf. 1270B). But, again, Erasmus has "Colet" represent this thesis, the very position Colet had rejected.

9 Jerome, *Commentary on Matthew* 4:26. PL 26, col. 197.

And yet, the sources used by "Colet" in representing the pre-emotion thesis are radical – not recognized by theologians in more than a thousand years. What Erasmus saw that theologians had not seen is that the concept of propassion had originated in Stoicism. Over the centuries theological thought on Christ's experience in Gethsemane had pivoted on Jerome's discussions but no theologian had seen, it appears, that Jerome's thinking had been built from Stoic thinking, that there is a direct tie between a fundamental of Stoicism and a fundamental of theological conceptions regarding Christ's fear of death (see below, Part V.1). Colet the person had denied pre-emotion as set forth by the medieval theologians while "Colet" describes with precision and at some length pre-emotion as set forth by the Stoics.

Probably, we may think, Erasmus was not trying to be ironic in tying "Colet" to Stoic discussions of pre-emotion. Since Erasmus found Colet's claim that Christ lacked all fear of death unjustifiable and not backed up by theological or rational argument, he simply took the liberty, we may imagine, of forcing Colet into a philosophical debate. Theologians had shown ad infinitum that Christ had suffered pre-emotion and it is this argument that he has "Colet" silently defend by means of Stoicism.

As will be seen below, however, Erasmus no more accepted with regard to Christ the position of the modern theologians, opposed by Colet, than he did the Stoic position that had originally brought it into being, detailed by "Colet." Different conclusions can be and must be drawn, he shows, from Stoic thought. The message of *De taedio Iesu* is that Christ did not suffer pre-emotion ("propassion") but full-blown emotion ("passion"), extreme fear – a position that was for Colet beyond comprehension, a sign that Christ was weak and involved with evil.

In short, nothing could be truer than Erasmus' statement in the letter by which he transmits *De taedio Iesu* to Colet a year and a half after publication, that the work is so beyond arguments actually put forth in the debate that Colet will hardly recognize what he will read.

> I am sending you a small literary gift, consisting of a few of my minor works, including that same debate on the fear of Christ in which we once confronted each other in England, though it is so much altered that you would hardly recognize it.[10]

10 *Ep.* 181. Allen 1, 405/42–5, CWE 2, 87/49–52. *De taedio Iesu* was published in February 1503. Allen dates the letter around December 1504.

While the debate itself was extemporaneous, the writing of *De taedio Iesu* had allowed Erasmus the time, as he notes (1265D), to work out and further develop his arguments. In 1499 Erasmus had not even read Origen, whom he criticizes late in *De taedio Iesu* for seeing Christ and Christianity in either/or, spirit/flesh, terms rather than (Stoic) both/and, spirit/*indifferentia*, terms – with natural instinct and "soul" on the indifferent side (see above, Part III.2). Nor had he thought out in detail his criticism of Jerome's propassion (pre-emotion) thesis, which had been the platform for medieval thought on Christ's Passion, or worked out his criticisms of Bonaventure's high scholastic reshaping of that thesis (see below, Part V). And he had certainly not worked out and criticized in detail Stoic thinking on "*phantasiai*," focusing particularly on the thought of Epictetus and Gellius' illustrations – which I will now turn to.

"Colet" on Stoic *φαντασία*

Erasmus has "Colet" lead into his rendering of Stoicism by contending that Stoic thinking on natural instinct is irrelevant to discussions of Christ. Erasmus rejoins, in "spoiling the Egyptians" fashion, that Stoic thought that approaches the truth should be respected:

> I can see Colet that you have been shaking your head for some time and that so far you remain unconvinced. But patience: I shall not rest until I have answered every point. "What are the Stoics to me," you say, "when I am discussing Christ?" And yet when we talk about Christ, who is the truth [cf. John 14:6], if the Stoics have said something that is not too far from the truth, it does not seem incongruous to be able to cite it. (1275D)

But "Colet" is not satisfied. He is intent on showing that Erasmus has left out of his discussion core Stoic doctrines. The fundamental principles by which the Stoic wiseman lives contradict Erasmus' claims. The evidence he brings forth leans heavily – not pointed out by "Colet" – on statements excerpted by Gellius from Book 5 of Epictetus' *Discourses* (now lost) and translated from the Greek into Latin in his *Attic Nights*. Epictetus' focus here on involuntary aspects of life is very different in tone and way of stating issues from anything found in Cicero's philosophical works. And yet there is reason to believe Gellius' assurances that the views here represented by Epictetus are in accord with the thinking of Zeno and Chrysippus, the founders of Stoicism.[11] (The numbering as elsewhere is mine.)

> "I do not care," you say, "however truly they (Stoics) spoke. But you (Erasmus) have not even dealt fully with their views on the ideal wiseman. (1) Not one of the Stoics would allow the wiseman *συγκατάθεσις*, or 'assent'; (2) nor do all of them allow *φαντασία* (phantasia), meaning terror brought about by a sudden view of evil. Horace saw well that a Stoic wiseman is oblivious to all the evils that befall him, even the end of the world. (3) Even those who admit this kind of terror (from *phantasiai*) do not allow that it is an opportunity to act well (non eam virtutis materiam esse dicunt) but merely a pardonable fault, to be ignored not commended, because such *phantasiai* usurp (if 'assent' occurs) rational thought and are thus beyond human control. Moreover, they do not allow their sage excessive or lasting terror, and allow it at all only when some sudden vision of great evil assaults the senses and stirs up disorder in the mind before its ruler, reason, can pass judgment on it. But as soon as reason perceives that this false vision of evil, which has terrorized the senses, is not in fact evil, then at once, wielding its sceptre, it soothes the feelings and calms the mind. (4) Finally, did any Stoic ever allow his wiseman to do what you say Christ did, to refuse to face death and to fear death? They will not allow him *συγκατάθεσις*, or 'assent,' but you foist it on Christ. Are not refusal to accept death and fear of death 'assents' (to that which is not rational)?"[12] (1275D–F)

(1) "Colet" is correct. A major theme of Stoicism, not found in the thought of Aristotle or Plato, is that the wiseman never allows assent (*συγκατάθεσις*; the Greek is used by Gellius, 19.1.16) to emotions (leaving aside *eupatheiai*). Accordingly, orthodox Stoics would never allow that fear of death is a natural and unyielding instinct.

(2) *Phantasiai*, or impressions (other translations are appearances, representations, presentations), were fundamental to Stoic thought.[13]

---

11 See Graver, *Stoicism and Emotion*, 85–8, and Abel, "Das *Propatheia*-Theorem." I discuss Seneca's extensive thought on pre-emotion below, at pp. 189–91.

12 I have altered the translation. Note in particular Heath's translation of the last sentence, "At non est asentiri, nolle mortem, & mortem meturere?" as "Are not refusal and fear of death 'assents to reality'?" The wiseman does not oppose "reality" but represents it.

13 *Phantasiai* were of many varieties, sensory and non-sensory, rational and non-rational, false and true (cf. D.L. 7.45–54). Long states that the task for a Stoic, and Epictetus insists on this, is to make correct or proper use of representations. See "Representation and the Self in Stoicism," 111. On the complexities of *phantasia* and assent, see Brennan, *The Stoic Life*, 49–114.

"Colet" is talking about an external *phantasia* (*φαντασία;* the Greek is used by Gellius, 19.1.15), such as a sudden and unexpected sound, that involuntarily affects one's physical and mental state.

Regarding *repente mali speciem* (this "sudden view of evil") it may be noted that Gellius refers to *visa animi terrificà* (19.1.18) and "Colet" a little further along refers to *visis illis terrificis* (1277F). Consider also Gellius' illustrations of these involuntary reactions: "Inquire also, if you please, why a man involuntarily winks when someone's hand is suddenly directed against his eyes, why when the sky is lit up by a flash of lightning he involuntarily drops his head and closes his eyes, why as the thunder grows louder he gradually becomes terrified, why he is shaken by sneezing, why he sweats in the heat of the sun or grows cold amid severe frosts (12.5.11, cf. 19.1.15–17)." A Stoic cannot resist the immediate affect but he refuses "assent" (*συγκατάθεσις*). The *phantasia* is involuntary but assent is voluntary.

In stating that not all Stoics allow even *phantasiai,* "Colet" may be referring to the rigid Stoicism described in Cicero's *Paradoxa Stoicorum.* The wiseman presented here has a "heaven-sent firmness of mind" (29) and nothing influences him other than "his own will and judgment" (34). No mention is made of the effects of any involuntary responses to outside stimuli. This picture of the Stoic ties in with the claim of Horace (65–8 BCE), referred to by "Colet," that the Stoic wiseman is oblivious to "all the evils that befall him, even the end of the world."[14]

Whether the Stoic wiseman allows *phantasiai* or does not allow *phantasiai,* he never allows assent to emotion.

(3) Erasmus has insisted that the greater the handicap a human suffers, from things such as natural instincts or character traits, the greater the opportunity for virtue (above, pp. 120–6), but Stoic teachings in fact, "Colet" shows, directly contradict him. Fear of death, for example, is not something that can add to "the opportunity to act well" (*virtutis materiam*)[15] but is positively detrimental. The wiseman rejects such fear for good cause. Reason recognizes that the *phantasia* that precedes it is not in fact an evil "but merely a pardonable fault, to be ignored not commended." "Assent" would be here a false judgment, lack of virtue, and would signify mental and emotional disturbance. The wiseman

14 *Odes* 3.3.7.

15 On "*materiam virtutis,*" see above, pp. 120 (on 1275B) and 121 n. 25, and below, p. 293 n. 41. It appears that this wording is not found in Gellius. *De finibus* refers to "*materia sapientiae*" (3.61).

never fears because he never assents to fear, even if, on occasion, his senses are momentarily assaulted by an external *phantasia*, "some sudden vision of great evil."

(4) In Stoicism death is not an evil but an indifferent and this being the case Stoics do not assent to "unwillingness to accept death," much less fear death. But Erasmus, in contrast, has shown that Christ considered death an evil (1276D) and that he assented to fear of death. In fact, contends "Colet," Christ no more feared death than did the Stoic wiseman. He never "assented."

In short, it is "Colet" who speaks up for the Stoic positions, not Erasmus. Christ was a super Stoic and super martyr, a person who never assented to human emotions. In holding unbendingly to virtue and truth the Stoic is always happy (cf. *Fin.* 3.75) and Christ, "Colet" has emphasized, went to his death with extreme joy, *alacritas*.

"Colet" continues as follows (here again my numbering):

> (1) Terror and fear are not the same thing. The (Stoic) wiseman may sometimes be terrified, but he fears nothing, since he believes that nothing need be feared except evil, and considers nothing evil except moral turpitude; that therefore is the one thing he fears, but it does not terrify him. Why should it terrify him, when it lies in his own power to avoid it? (2) Death, they say, is as natural as birth; it carries no moral taint and is thus to be feared only by fools. For what could be more foolish than to dread, as though it were the worst of all evils, an event that is by no means evil and is even a natural necessity? They also believe that the wiseman will never fear the rest of nature's enemies, such as disease, hunger, thirst, and pain. If they are inevitable, say the Stoics, and if they really are evils, then why double the evil [by fearing them]? If they are not evils [which is the case], then fear of them is an evil in itself. If what you fear is not inevitable, then why draw down evil on yourself with your vain fears? In every one of these cases it is wrong to be afraid. (3) Either one mistakenly takes for an evil something that is not, or one knows that something is not evil but none the less fears it, which is both foolish and illogical. But the Stoics' wiseman is never mistaken or illogical. (1275F–1276A)

(1) Terror (*expavescere*) from a *phantasia* is one thing, fear (*metuere*) another.[16] Terror is something that relates to the senses and is involuntary

16 Cf. Gellius, 19.1.18.

while fear is a judgment of reason and is voluntary. Ordinary humans experience terror from a *phantasia* and so too does the wiseman but the wiseman does not fear a *phantasia*. He recognizes this terror for what it is and does not assent. He knows that the only thing that needs to be feared is moral turpitude (*turpe*, the opposite of *honestum*). But since he knows how to recognize and avoid moral turpitude he is never terrorized by moral turpitude. Stated otherwise, a *phantasia* that results in "terror" is not an emotion (*pathos*) but merely a "pre-emotion" (*propatheia*, 1271E). It follows that terror is entirely separate from the emotion of fear. Fear occurs only if a person assents to the terror.

(2) At this point "Colet" switches the discussion from *phantasiai* to "the rest of nature's enemies," things like death, disease, hunger, thirst, and pain (i.e., dispreferred indifferents). Since they are natural necessities and as such not evil there is no reason to fear them. "Death, they say, is as natural as birth."[17] Fear of physical harm is based on a false belief, the belief that physical harm is a real evil. Emotion results from assent to such false beliefs. The wiseman no more assents to these beliefs than he does, after being momentarily affected, to *phantasiai*. Again, the only thing that is evil is vice, moral shortcomings, that which is contrary to *honestum*.

(3) The wiseman is "never mistaken" (cf. *Fin*. 3.75) because he never mistakenly judges as evil either a *phantasia* or things such as disease, hunger, thirst, pain, and death (*phantasiai* passively imputed). Nor, Seneca emphasizes in *On Benefits*, does the wiseman change his mind, "as long as all the circumstances remain the same as when he made it up. He is never filled with regret because at the time nothing better could have been done than was done, no better decision could have been made than was made" (4.34, cf. *Tusc*. 5.54).[18]

The person not wise, states "Colet," either mistakenly takes for an evil something that is not (things indifferent) or "knows that something

17 Although death seems terrible to others, *Tusculan Disputations* emphasizes, we should "count nothing as an evil which is due to the appointment of the immortal gods or of nature, the mother of all things" (1.118). James Jaquette relates ancient views of death as an indifferent to St Paul, in "Life and Death, 'Adiaphora,' and Paul's Rhetorical Strategies" (see his note 6 for an extensive listing of relevant Stoic sources).

18 On the reservation clauses by which the wiseman protects himself from error, see above, p. 44.

is not evil but none the less fears it, which is both foolish and illogical." And misery is the result. Cicero describes Stoic methods by which these two types of failures can be corrected at length. The safest approach is to concentrate on the emotion itself, leaving for later discussion the reasons why that which the emotion derives from is not an evil (*Tusc.* 4.58–62f).

In short, against Erasmus' locating fear of death in natural instinct, something unyielding and central to the human condition, based on Stoic sources, "Colet" shows that things such as disease, hunger, thirst, pain, and death are indifferent, that death is natural and fear of death is a false judgment. And yet Erasmus has the nerve to claim that he is thinking like the Stoics!

The Stoic wiseman is oblivious to fear of death and so too was Christ, the fount of wisdom – and yet, exclaims "Colet," Erasmus argues the opposite and attributes his thinking to Stoicism:

> (1) First, how could he (Christ) be terrified, when nothing unexpected could assail his senses, as he had complete foreknowledge of everything?
>
> (2) How truly wicked to allege that some terrifying visions of evil could have seized Christ's reason and stunned or overthrown it, so that vain terrors and phantoms overwhelmed the composure of his senses, and overwhelmed him so completely that he oozed bloody drops from every pore, and so long that his distress persisted unto death! For I think that that is Jerome's reading of "My soul is sorrowful unto death": he suggests that death was not the cause of Christ's sorrow, but its end.[19] "But surely," you [Erasmus, in accord with scholastics] will say, "for a while Christ's reason was benumbed?" Not at all ...
>
> (3) And finally, even though a while ago you yourself removed from Christ any propensity to sin, you now give him the sort of emotions that most persistently tempt us to sin. Although you have just distanced him from any reluctance to act aright, you now foist on him a fear of death, even though that death was a work more pleasing to God and more meritorious than any other. (1276B–C)

(1) With regard to Christ's foreknowledge "Colet" augments Stoic thought. The wiseman does not have foreknowledge but he is never

19 Jerome, *Commentary on Matthew* 4:26. PL 26, col. 197.

mistaken in that he rehearses in advance, Erasmus surely recognized, every possible outcome to an action and knows how to deal with whatever comes his way. As *Tusculan Disputations* words it: "What could disturb such dignity and consistency? A sudden or unforeseen event. But what could be unforeseen by one who has rehearsed in advance every one of the things that can happen to a person?" (4.57).[20] "This anticipation therefore of the future mitigates the approach of evils whose coming one has long foreseen" (3.29). But Christ took this one step further. "Nothing unexpected" could have assaulted Christ's senses in Gethsemane as he had, the Bible shows, "complete foreknowledge of everything" – which would include *phantasiai*.

(2) "Colet" assumes that in Erasmus' view, which is "wicked," Christ's reason was temporarily "stunned or overthrown" in Gethsemane by a *phantasia* and that Erasmus' position is that of the Stoics on pre-emotion (which, developed by medieval theologians as "propassion," became the standard position). Against Erasmus' alleged position and the standard view, "Colet" brings in, as had the person Colet in the actual debate, the statement Colet had picked out from Jerome's writings: "Death was not the cause of Christ's sorrow but its end." He did not suffer pre-emotion. What Erasmus had actually argued in the debate and develops in *De taedio Iesu* is the radical contention – entirely outside Colet the person's comprehension – that Christ suffered not pre-emotion but full-blown emotion.

(3) Referring to emotions that do not arise from external shocks but internally, as natural instincts, "Colet" believes Erasmus also associates Christ, notwithstanding what he claims, with "the sort of emotions that most persistently tempt us to sin." Here again "Colet" shows that the Stoics are on his side, not Erasmus', in that emotions are false judgments. Far from fearing death Christ desired death because this was more meritorious and pleasing to God than anything.

To sum up, what can be seen in the above is not Colet the person criticizing Erasmus' views but something much more significant, Erasmus criticizing his own employment of Stoicism from the standpoint of orthodox Stoicism.

---

20 Graver translation, *Cicero and the Emotions*, 60. This work fully translates Tusc. 3 and 4.

2 "My Stoics": Terror from *Phantasiai* or Natural Instinct?

Erasmus was impressed by Epictetus' focus, differing from Cicero's, on natural necessity but what Epictetus failed to understand, Erasmus will demonstrate, is that emotion is itself a natural necessity – not, as such, something under the control of judgment or will. He does not reject "Colet's" differentiations between allowance of external *phantasiai* and denial of assent, but thinks his discussion is limited and distorts Stoicism in that he fails to bring into view and explicate another and more important type of terror, terror that does not result from *phantasiai*. He is troubled by the fact that "Colet," like Gellius, makes no distinction between reflexive reactions to a *phantasia* and affective reactions to the everyday issues of life, things like hunger, disease, poverty, death, and pain.[21] "Colet," like Gellius, sees no essential difference between the situation of a Stoic responding to a *phantasia* and a Stoic responding to pain from extreme sickness in that in neither case does the Stoic assent. The real problem Erasmus finds here is not, however, with "Colet" and Gellius but with Stoicism itself. He contends that it is wrong to believe that denial of assent is as possible and necessary with emotion deriving from everyday issues as from *phantasiai*. There is all the difference between the cure of pre-emotions from *phantasiai* and the cure of affects arising from common happenings. Pain resulting from extreme sickness cannot be overcome in the same way as a reflexive shock from thunder or lightening. Stoics have here incorrectly developed their arguments. His proof, we will see, is worked out in terms of Gellius' real life illustrations of orthodox Stoic thought. These illustrations do not prove, he shows, what Gellius thinks they prove. In his typhoon story Gellius sees the Stoic's mental and physical reactions as resulting from *phantasiai* but this is clearly not the case. Standing out, these reactions were demonstratively not brief and not overcome by reason. And the Stoic's fear did not relate to something that had already happened or even the present but to concern about the future. He feared death and this fear did not come from a *phantasia* but from natural instinct. Although concise, Erasmus' criticism of Gellius' story is detailed, carefully thought out, and entirely original.

21 Bodily and mental reactions to *phantasiai* had been an important issue only because Stoics needed to explain how their wiseman could be affected by such if emotions are erroneous judgments.

Erasmus begins by summarizing "Colet's" argument that there is no place in Stoicism, notwithstanding Erasmus' claims, for emotion as a natural instinct, much less for "assent" to an emotion such as fear of death. "Colet" has shown (1) that terror is something very momentary for the wiseman, (2) that reason is dormant only briefly, and (3) that fleeting alarm (pre-emotion) is allowed only when a *phantasia*, "suddenly bursts upon the senses." That is, the Stoics not only disallow emotion, they do not allow even pre-emotion lacking a *phantasia*.

> Now, you ["Colet"] say that my Stoics (meos Stoicos) allow their wiseman only a moment of terror, such as may disturb the mind briefly until reason reasserts itself, and that they will permit him such fleeting alarm only if a *phantasia*, a terrible vision, has suddenly burst upon his senses. Be that as it may, what exactly do you mean by terror? (1277E)

"Be that as it may," responds Erasmus, the problem is that "Colet" has not adequately thought out the meaning of terror. "My Stoics" indeed say what "Colet" alleges but there is more to the issue than that of reflexive reactions to *phantasiai*. Entirely outside "Colet's" purview there is another far more important type of terror.

Externally induced terror, lacking Stoic tools

Before taking up terror from natural instinct Erasmus refocuses externally induced terror, showing the situation that exists where no wiseman is present to counter by reason a *phantasia*. The masses allow an involuntary reaction to a *phantasia*, pre-emotion, to develop into full-blown emotion, emotion that is at odds with reason and truth.

> Is it (terror) a massive shock, an attack of panic as it were (quasi πανιχὸν animi tumultum), which completely unhinges my reason and drives me out of my mind? Far be it from me to attribute anything so monstrous to Christ. (1277E)

If not halted, the "massive shock" from a *phantasia* completely unhinges a person's reason and even drives him out of his mind. "Colet" had held similarly that *phantasiai* that are assented to, "usurp rational thought and are thus beyond human control." Gellius refers to attacks among those not wise ("the foolish"), "which forestall the power of the mind and of reason." The unwise believe that such visions are as terrifying as they appear and rightly feared (19.1.17–19). Erasmus does not allow that Christ's reason, anymore than that of the wiseman, could have been overcome by shock (pre-emotion) from a *phantasia*. "Far be it from me to attribute anything so monstrous to Christ."

Internally induced terror

What Erasmus really wants to describe is a very different type of terror, terror that comes about internally, created in the mind of the Stoic. But what is his meaning? How does he arrive at this thesis? The wording may seem problematic:

> Sin expavescentiam dicis, molestam ac cruciabilem reformidationem imminentis mali, quae sensum quidem acerbum incutiat affectibus animi, neque tamen eum loco dimoveat, haec neque semper exoritur ex visis illis terrificis, imo vero ex animo demanat in corpus. Et adeo non excludit rationis usum, ut ex ipsa ratione nascatur, videlicet, imminentis mali vim perpendente. (1277F)

> Or do you mean by "terror" a vexing, painful dread of impending evil, which certainly deals a hard blow to the emotions, but does not unbalance the mind, and is not necessarily produced by one of those terrible visions we spoke of, but instead is transmitted from the mind to the body? In fact, far from cutting reason off, it is actually produced by our reason as it weighs the gravity of the approaching evil.

"Colet's" discussions of terror from *phantasiai* seem precise and orthodox, and they should be since they are based on Epictetus, but how precise and thought out is the exposition of internal emotion now before us – which appears to be Erasmus' own making? Ostensibly he is still supporting "my Stoics," against "Colet's" rendering of Stoicism, but, again, how does he envision or define Stoicism?

If Erasmus is here thinking in Stoic terms, how can reason not be negatively affected, "unbalanced," by emotion? How can reason, as such, "produce" emotion if in Stoicism emotion amounts to erroneous reasoning? And how in the process can reason remain fully intact? In Stoicism, fear comes about where reason is misfocused or lacking. According to Hecato and Zeno, as reported by Diogenes Laertius, falsehood leads to perversion of the mind, "and from this perversion arise many passions or emotions, which are causes of instability" (7.110). According to *Tusculan Disputations*, "Every emotion is a movement of the mind either destitute of reason, or contemptuous of reason, or disobedient to reason" (3.24). "In all cases where the mind recoils from reason there is always some such overhanging terror" (omnibus enim, quorum mens abhorret a ratione, semper aliqui talis terror impendet) (4.35). Not only does Erasmus hold, in the above, that emotion is born from reason, he gives no indication that notwithstanding their impact the emotions referred to are necessarily base or evil. At this point it could be thought that Erasmus is setting forth an anti-Stoic thesis.

Let us begin analysis by looking at the statements regarding internal terror in their own terms, irrespective of whether or not there is agreement with standard Stoic theses.

(1) The second type of terror is "produced" internally, in the mind itself. It is "not produced by one of those terrible visions (*phantasiai*) we spoke of."
(2) The "far from cutting off reason" is a contrast with the momentary numbing of reason by a *phantasia*. Emotion that comes about internally does not in the process harm reason. Indeed this emotion is triggered by reason.
(3) "Colet" does not take into account an emotion such as fear of the future. Fear of the future cannot be described in terms of an external *phantasia*. Such emotions do not come from the outside. The assaults on the emotions described by "Colet" are instigated by present happenings whereas the emotion Erasmus is focusing on is built from something that has not yet happened, recognition of an "impending evil." As Cicero states, in *Tusculan Disputations*, fear (one of the four false emotions) is "a belief that some great evil is impending" (3.25).
(4) Nor, unlike shock from a *phantasia*, are these emotions necessarily sudden. Most important, it would appear that by their very nature they are not quickly overcome and thus not short in duration.
(5) Reason brings the fear into being in that it is reason that recognizes that there is something to fear. Reason "weighs the gravity of the approaching evil."
(6) The terror is real and worthy of fear, not something that reason discovers is unreal and not to be feared, as with the terror produced by a *phantasia*.
(7) While pre-emotion can be halted by a voluntary decision not to "assent," the second type of terror appears to be involuntary, an

automatic response to reason, "as it weighs the gravity of the approaching evil." And since the fear is triggered by reason it cannot be imagined that reason can or would want to cut it off. Emotions such as fear of the future are just as involuntary as pre-emotions, arising from *phantasiai*, but unlike the latter cannot be voluntarily halted by reason.

(8) Reason recognizes the danger, that there is something to fear, and this results in "a hard blow to the emotions" – emotions that are natural instincts.

(9) Clearly, Erasmus' description of the second type of terror is his attempt to relate his discussions of natural instinct to larger Stoic ways of thinking. He recognizes, unlike Gellius and "Colet," that pre-emotion is in Stoicism only a subtopic. And yet he emphatically disagrees with orthodox Stoic thinking on the place and nature of emotion with regard to the common happenings of life. So how can he see himself as representing, versus "Colet," Stoicism – "my Stoics" – at the same time as he moves emotion from the cognitive realm to the realm of natural instinct?

The first question is this: Does Erasmus have a deeper rationale for the above theses or is he simply making an argument?

Correcting Gellius' typhoon story

Further analysis reveals that the true meanings of Erasmus' description of the second type of terror cannot be grasped without seeing that he is refuting and correcting Gellius' story of the Stoic in the typhoon. He had paraphrased this story earlier (1272F–1273A) and immediately following his description of the second type of terror explicitly refers to Gellius' story, "which I told earlier" (1278A). As with his silent but radical rewriting of Origen (and of Bonaventure: see below, Part V), he does not state that he is criticizing or rectifying Gellius' illustration; he simply shows us, with considerable precision and without a touch of rhetorical license, how the story should be interpreted.

Gellius had recounted the story of the Stoic in the typhoon to illustrate the mindset of Stoics not just in theory but in practice. Indeed, he claims that it was the experiences of this Stoic that had led to his quoting Epictetus. Rather than explain his physical and mental reactions to the typhoon in personal terms, the Stoic had advised Gellius to read the discussion of Stoic reactions found in Epictetus' *Discourses*, Book

5. Gellius had found it obvious, as did of course the Stoic himself, that there is an exact correlation between Epictetus' concisely worded statements, which he translates from the Greek, and the actualities of the Stoic's response to the typhoon.

Erasmus disagrees. Gellius' story does not prove what he thinks it proves. What actually occurred in the typhoon does not correlate with Epictetus' discussion of *phantasiai* and their effects. The Stoic imagined that his experience in the typhoon reflects Epictetus' thinking but it does not, and Gellius makes the same mistake. Epictetus' theory is at odds with not only the type of situation but, crucially, the actual workings of the Stoic's emotions and reason. All of which indicates that there is a problem, since it does not apply to actuality, with Epictetus' philosophy. And Erasmus is determined to show how the typhoon event should be interpreted and how, as a consequence, Stoic philosophy should be understood.

Gellius' story is as follows. In a voyage across the Ionian Sea, Gellius had himself undergone a life-threatening event. Almost the whole night a fierce side wind blew and filled the ship with water, and everyone was working hard at the pumps. When day dawned the situation became even more dire, with "more frequent whirlwinds, a black sky, masses of fog; and a type of fearful cloud-forms, which they call 'typhoons,' seemed to hang over and threaten us, ready to overwhelm the ship" (19.1.3). On board was an eminent Stoic philosopher. Gellius expected to find him unterrified and courageous but to his surprise discovered that he was "frightened and ghastly pale, not indeed uttering any lamentations, as all the rest were doing, nor any outcries of that kind, but in his loss of colour and distracted expression not differing much from the others" (19.1.6).[22] Observing this, a rich Greek from Asia ridiculed the Stoic and his philosophy, claiming that he himself, in contrast, was unafraid and did not change colour. To which the Stoic responded that the Asiatic was too worthless to understand. Later, when the sea calmed and they were approaching their destination Gellius asked the philosopher what the reason for his fear was. At this point the Stoic quietly and courteously replied:

> "Since you are desirous of knowing, hear what our forefathers, the founders of the Stoic sect, thought about that brief but inevitable and natural

22 Epictetus holds similarly that a wiseman experiencing a *phantasia* may be affected "slightly in his colour and expression" (Gellius 19.1.20).

> fear, or rather," said he, "read it, for if you read it, you will be the more ready to believe it and you will remember it better." Thereupon before my eyes he drew from his little bag the fifth book of the *Discourses* of the philosopher Epictetus, which, as arranged by Arrian, undoubtedly agree with the writings of Zeno and Chrysippus. (19.1.13–14)

Clearly, the Stoic who experienced the typhoon believed that what he had experienced was a *phantasia* and that he had suffered in his physical and mental reactions "that brief but inevitable and natural fear" described, as recorded by Gellius, in the *Discourses*. In reading Epictetus Gellius had accepted without question the Stoic's belief that Epictetus' discussions fully explain what happened in the typhoon, that there is a one-to-one relationship between the real-world event and Stoic doctrine. He sees no differences between the reactions of the Stoic in the typhoon and the reactions of a Stoic involuntarily terrified, momentarily, by, for example, some unexpected and sudden sound. He assumes that all terror is for a Stoic the same and thinks his story very obviously proves the point. The Stoic simply refuses "assent" no matter what ill fortune may befall him.

While Erasmus' earlier paraphrase of Gellius' story (1272F–1273A) had been set forth to show that true bravery does not escape "nature's command" (above, p. 115), the discussion at 1277E–78A carefully works out the larger meaning he finds in the story – as distinct from what the Stoic and Gellius imagine the meaning to be. The Stoic did not in actuality experience the type of terror described by Epictetus, Gellius, and "Colet." Epictetus, Gellius, and "Colet" see the first type of terror but interpretation of the typhoon story in terms of this type of terror is flawed through and through and reveals a problem with Stoic thinking itself.

Let us now look again at Erasmus' account of the second type of terror and then compare his statements with the typhoon story, showing how he reconceptualizes, point by point, what actually happened in the typhoon – how the Stoic and Gellius should have interpreted the typhoon event, but did not. Erasmus not only rewrites in all originality the story in terms of natural instinct he shows, we will find, that in some regards Gellius' description of the event directly contradicts Gellius' interpretation.

> Or do you mean by "terror" a burdensome, torturous dread of impending evil, which certainly deals a hard blow to the emotions, but does not unbalance the mind, and is not necessarily produced by one of those terrible visions we spoke of, but instead is transmitted from the mind to the

body? In fact, far from cutting reason off, it is actually produced by our reason as it weighs the gravity of the approaching evil. (1277F)

(1) While Gellius' purpose in bringing in the illustration of the Stoic in the typhoon (and of the sick and dying Stoic, 12.5) was to illustrate the effect of *phantasiai*, Erasmus states that the reactions of a Stoic are "not necessarily produced by one of those terrible visions we spoke of." Terror does not have just one type of source but two.
(2) Gellius and "Colet" also talk about "a hard blow to the emotions," and the Stoic in the typhoon obviously received such a blow, but what is the cause of the blow? Erasmus sees the hard blow as triggered internally, not externally.
(3) In accord with orthodox Stoicism the Stoic in the typhoon, Epictetus, Gelius, and "Colet" all show the need for reason to deny assent to emotion. Erasmus rejects this view with regard to the emotion embodied in the second type of terror. The second type is not something outside reason that can be rejected by reason for it is "produced by reason." It is produced by reason in that here emotion comes about as we contemplate, employing reason, the possibility that something calamitous may in the future happen to us.
(4) Erasmus believes the Stoic in the typhoon is experiencing true emotion, not pre-emotion. Pre-emotion results from a reflexive reaction to a *phantasia* but Erasmus denies that this is what occurred. Fear of an impending evil, "is not produced by one of those terrible visions we spoke of." And "far from cutting reason off," as does a pre-emotion allowed to develop, this fear of an impending evil "is actually produced by our reason." If the emotion is triggered by reason it is obviously, he believes, not a pre-emotion but true emotion.
(5) The Stoic had reckoned that he was responding to an event that had happened and continued to occur, not an event that might happen. Erasmus thinks Gellius was here wrong about the facts. The terror Erasmus sees is "a burdensome, torturous dread of impending evil." He refers twice to an "impending evil." The Stoic's fear was not, essentially, about what was presently occurring but what might well be a consequence, what might happen in the future, that he might drown. A *phantasia* is something that is already here, while fear of dying concerns something that is yet to come. Earlier Erasmus had stated: "It is more natural to dread some evil that is yet to come than to be troubled by one that is already here" (1274B).

(6) It could be imagined that the typhoon began as a *phantasia*, i.e., with extra large waves, wind, and thunder, and then developed into an internal second type of terror, but since Erasmus clearly distinguishes the typhoon story from *phantasiai* we know that he did not see the event in this way. The fear that Erasmus sees – unlike what Gellius sees – came about not because the Stoic's senses were suddenly and unexpectedly shocked by a *phantasia*, something quickly controlled by reason, but by thoughts about the possible outcome – fear of the future.

(7) Earlier Erasmus had stated that "the effect of feeling pain in the present or fearing it in the future is the same, though in the one case the pain begins in the body and spreads to the mind, while in the other suffering starts in the mind and overflows into the body" (1272B). While Erasmus sees *phantasiai* as first affecting the body and then, if not controlled, mind and reason, the fear he now describes originates not externally but internally, in the mind, and is therefore "transmitted from the mind to the body." In either case there may be involuntary trembling, sweating, whiteness, and the like, but the original source is entirely different. On the involuntary movement of fear from mind to body among Roman heroes preceding battle and in battle, fighting to the death, see 1272C–E and 1273A–B (all those named are found in *De finibus*, *De officiis*, or *Tusculan Disputations*).[23]

(8) The Stoic who experiences the typhoon believes that having fear would be unnatural and irrational whereas Erasmus believes that he actually had fear and that this was entirely natural and rational. The Stoic holds with Epictetus that his reaction had come about because of a "brief natural impulse" and "human weakness" (19.1.21) rather than because of any reality, that the terror is only a false appearance and a vain alarm and that there is nothing to excite fear (*metus*) (19.1.18). Such things are not what they seem. For Erasmus, in contrast, it is the Stoic's reason that makes clear the reality of the approaching evil, the fact that the ship could go down and that death would result. This type of fear is "produced by our reason as it weighs the gravity of the approaching evil." What the Stoic's reason recognizes and what his emotions respond to is not, contrary to what this Stoic wants to believe, a false appearance but something very real. Accordingly, he actually experienced not a pre-emotion but true emotion, true fear.

23 Cf. Seneca, *De ira* 2.3.3.

(9) The Stoic's terror was a natural instinct. Reason triggered the fear in that it was reason that recognized a real and imminent danger, but the emotion that resulted, in line with a central theme of *De taedio Iesu*, was an ineradicable natural instinct.

(10) The Stoic who experienced the typhoon believes that what is "natural" is pre-emotion but Erasmus shows something far more extensively natural, emotion that originates internally.

(11) What the Stoic fears is that the ship may go down, "an imminent evil," but the fear itself, the emotion, is not – at odds with orthodox Stoicism – something that is in itself base or evil.

(12) Neither Gellius nor Erasmus believes that the typhoon destroyed or "unbalanced" the Stoic's mind, but the contexts are entirely different. Gellius imagines that the Stoic's mind holds firm in the face of an unprovoked attack on his senses from the typhoon (and rejects the pre-emotion) while Erasmus contends that his mind holds firm in the face of a fear that arises within himself – from natural instinct (which cannot be rejected).

(13) According to Stoic doctrine, emotion is voluntary, a failure of reason. The Stoic who experienced the typhoon believes that he did not give "assent" to the *phantasia* so he did not experience true emotion and his reason remained intact. Erasmus holds, to the contrary, that he experienced true emotion, not voluntarily but involuntarily, and that notwithstanding there was, as it turned out (see below), no failure – though unable to affect natural instinct – of reason.

Emotion lasted as long as what instigated it: Reason was active but could do nothing

A particular understanding of emotion and a particular understanding of reason frame Erasmus' reconceptualization of the typhoon story, but the meaning of neither can be fully grasped outside the time factor. And no factor in Erasmus' argument is more empirically based. Demonstratively, the affective reactions of the Stoic in the typhoon were not – as imagined by that Stoic and Gellius, in accord with Epictetus' thesis (19.1.21) – "fleeting," "brief," or "momentary," overcome almost immediately by reason.

> I can see nothing to prevent either of these types of terrors lasting for some time. For the first kind (which Christ does not share with us) often damages people's mental faculties so badly that they never return to their senses. The second must necessarily last for as long as the impending evil hangs over us. The Stoic in Gellius' story, which I told earlier [1272F–1273A], was

alarmed for as long as the storm raged, and never regained his accustomed composure until the sea subsided and the skies cleared. All that time his mind (animus) was far from untroubled, and yet reason (ratio) was not inactive within him. The philosopher was battling against his thoughts, and could hardly be called brave had he not done so. (1277F–1278A)

Analysis reveals the following:

(1) While the first type of terror can last "for some time" among non-Stoics but not Stoics, the second type can last "for some time" *among Stoics*. The first type can be halted, the second type cannot. The first type may continue only because, unlike the Stoic, ordinary humans do not have the ability to halt it. With the second type it is the Stoic himself who has in fact – Erasmus contends – no ability to halt it.
(2) The second type "must necessarily last for as long as the impending evil hangs over us." Against what Gellius wants to believe, Gellius' own illustration proves the point. The Stoic's fear in the typhoon was not something that affected him only "briefly" (19.1.13), "a short time and slightly" (19.1.20).[24] The typhoon lasted a night and a day and the Stoic was fearful as long as the typhoon lasted. He did not and could not have vanquished his fear shortly after the first great waves hit or even a little later. If the typhoon had lasted a week his fear would have lasted a week.
(3) Emotions that come about internally are as such ineradicable natural instincts (explicitly stated at 1277B and 1288B) and this is why fear must "necessarily last for as long as the impending evil hangs over us."
(4) The first type of terror is about something that has unexpectedly happened while the second type is about a threat, something that may happen. In Gellius' example, the ship may go down.
(5) Gellius saw the terror of the Stoic in presentist terms, as an involuntary response to a *phantasia*, while Erasmus saw this terror as an involuntary internal response to concern about the future – a fear of death.
(6) Nor in actuality did the Stoic come to see, as with a *phantasia*, that what he feared was only a mirage, a reflexive reaction. The fear was about a reality and in consequence the fear continued as long as the reality that caused it.

24 Gellius ends Book 19 as follows: "In that brief (*brevi*) but natural impulse we yield rather to human weakness than because we believe that those things are what they seem" (19.1.21).

(7) The Stoic's terror was triggered by reason but his reason was unable to affect the emotion that resulted. His reason had no ability to overcome his fear before the cause of the fear ended. Far from his reason overcoming the emotion almost immediately, in accord with Epictetus' theory, the Stoic "was alarmed [mentally] for as long as the storm raged."

(8) Erasmus notes that the Stoic's reason was "not inactive," even if it could not overcome the emotion. Throughout the ordeal the philosopher "battled his thoughts," his fear of drowning and dying, "and never regained his accustomed composure until the sea subsided and the skies cleared." His reason was not overcome by emotion but, on the other hand, his emotion (fear) – not pre-emotion but full-fledged emotion – was not affected by reason.

(9) In battling against his thoughts the Stoic was "brave" in that unlike the rich and overbearing Asiatic, who was insensible and insensitive to the very real danger and the actuality of dying, he completely grasped and felt the situation – with emotion, not pre-emotion – and yet did not allow his reason to give in. In short, he exhibited Stoic "constancy" (see above, p. 148).

(10) Nor, related to the issue of bravery, was the Stoic's attitude that of a martyr. Colet the person, we remember, had contended that martyrs, Christ being the most important, overcome all pain and fear. "Colet" emphasized Christ's sense of joy, *alacritas*, in martyrdom. Building directly on *Tusculan Disputations* and Gellius, Erasmus had corrected "Colet" by showing that the Stoic wiseman faced with harsh realities does not overcome pain but simply endures. Similarly, the mind of the Stoic in the typhoon was troubled, unable to overcome emotion, but his reason held firm. He was constant and lacked *alacritas* while the Asiatic was not constant but variable and foolish. The Asiatic took pride in his *alacritas*, being unaffected by danger.

(11) Fear is as much a natural instinct as hunger (1277C–D, 1282C–E, 1287D). Hunger cannot cease before it is satisfied and the Stoic's fear in the typhoon did not cease before the cause of this fear no longer existed. A 1499 letter to Colet emphasizes this commonality, distinguishing between a natural inclination and a natural disinclination. By nature we desire food when hungry and when faced with death we fear it.[25]

25 *Ep.* 109. Allen 1, 250–1/41–52, CWE 1, 208/49–60.

In seeing emotion as a natural instinct, rather than as in orthodox Stoicism something cognitive (a rational but wrong impulse), Erasmus was clearly impressed by late Stoic emphasis on the force of nature. Particularly influential here were not only Gellius' quotes of Epictetus on the effects of *phantasiai*, in *Attic Nights* 19.1, but even more his discussion of Stoicism in 12.5, which seems also to have been built from Epictetus. The reach of reason, the latter account emphasizes, has limits. The self-preservation instinct, and "the first principles of nature" that accompany it, is given to humans at birth and this develops into a deep concern with making choices among "things indifferent," everything between virtue and vice, but there are limits to what reason can accomplish. "Reason, which is given to him later, is hardly able to uproot and destroy those inclinations which were originally and deeply implanted in him" (12.5.8). While in orthodox Stoicism "reason supervenes [around age 14] to shape impulse scientifically" (D.L. 7.86) the Stoicism represented by Gellius places limits on the degree to which impulse can be shaped scientifically. "It is true that no compulsion can be exerted upon a wiseman when he has the opportunity of using his reason, but when nature compels, then reason also, the gift of nature, is compelled (cum vero natura cogit, ratio quoque a natura data cogitur)" (12.5.11).

In emphasizing things which reason cannot control, Gellius brings in not only the force of the self preservation instinct (and of our natural attractions and repulsions towards things indifferent) and *phantasiai* (why a person involuntarily winks, or is terrified by thunder, or sweats from heat) but points out, not of little significance, that "many other things are not under the control of the will, the judgment, or the reason, but are decrees of nature and of necessity (set naturae necessitatisque decreta sunt)" (12.5.12). Regarding the latter Gellius relates at some length an encounter (which Erasmus had surely read) with a Stoic extremely sick and suffering chronic and excruciating pain, seemingly dying. Significantly Gellius sees no difference in the mindset of this Stoic and the mindset of Stoics reacting to *phantasiai* – notwithstanding that in the one case there was long-term endurance of pain and in the other case an impulse that was immediately overcome. In neither case does the Stoic "assent" to what is happening.

Erasmus' analyses exhibit an even greater emphasis on the "decrees of nature and necessity," focusing not just on decrees brought about by *phantasiai* and long-term physical pain but the decree of emotion – true emotion. Emotion is for him a natural instinct, something that is for humans not external but internal and innate. Fear of something that may happen, a future event, such as the ship sinking, or dying, is as much a decree of nature and necessity as a *phantasia* or the pain from an incurable sickness. Unlike the pre-emotion that results from a *phantasia*, true emotion lasts as long as that which instigated it. And unlike long-term physical pain from sickness true emotion is not necessarily accompanied by any physical pain. Gellius shows that the Stoic experiencing extreme pain held on to his reason throughout while Erasmus demonstrates and proves that fear – something that is mental, not physical – lasts as long as what instigates it and that during this time reason is not overcome but is simply powerless (however much reason struggles).

Looking at the larger picture, a core tenet of orthodox Stoicism had been that emotion is a false judgment of reason. Later Stoics had gradually whittled this thesis down, Panaetius (d. 110 BCE), as mentioned earlier (112–14), being one. In *De officiis* (44 BCE) reason simply attempts to control emotion.[26] Epictetus (d. 135 CE) and his spokesman Gellius (c. 180 CE) go much further, pointing to the many areas in which reason has no power. It was only Erasmus, however, who directly rejected the Stoic tie of emotion to reason. Fear is as much a decree of nature and necessity as the external phenomena discussed by Epictetus and Gellius. Emotion, as such, is innate and as such has no relationship at all to reason. Emotion, as such, cannot be controlled by reason. Emotion, as such, is as inherent to the human makeup as reason. The human psyche is by its very nature two-dimensional and the emotion side is just as integral and important as the reason side.

3 Christ in Gethsemane and the Stoic in the Typhoon

Erasmus' depiction of Christ's fear in Gethsemane is a development of everything he has unravelled and corrected regarding the Stoic's experience and response in the typhoon. Stoicism cannot be understood lacking a grasp of natural instinct and neither can Christ and Christianity. "Colet's" argument fails utterly because he imagines that Christ's fear was merely a Stoic pre-emotion, brought about by an external *phantasia* – seen as foreknowledge that he was going to die and concern for the Jews – and that he was a martyr that refused "assent" to the pre-emotion. Like the Stoic in the typhoon, as correctly interpreted, Christ

26 See Dyck's comment on *De officiis* 1.100–3 in *A Commentary on Cicero, De officiis*, 259.

was overwhelmed by ineradicable natural instinct, one aspect being full-fledged emotion, and one component of the latter being fear of death. Although hunger is something physical and fear is located in the lower part of the mind, both are inherent parts of natural instinct. Colet, like others, accepts the former but takes offence at the latter (1282C–E). "Either you [Colet] must allow Christ these feelings [of fear], or else you must argue that throughout his life he suffered none of the handicaps of our human condition" (1289B). Christ's humanity is proven by the fact that he did not overcome and could not have overcome his human nature. Colet's claim that Christ surmounted his human nature is an affront to his humanity. Like the Stoic in the typhoon there was no way Christ could have eliminated his fear. Fear "left him only with life itself" (1286A). It was a natural instinct and natural instincts are felt as long as what prompts them. Epicureans and Christian martyrs may overcome their fear and their humanity, but not Christ.

With regard to the time factor and the way Erasmus' mind was working, note one additional point. The Stoic's travail in the typhoon lasted a night and a day and so, too, Erasmus surely recognized, did Christ's Passion last a night and a day.

Christ's emotion and reason compare with that of the Stoic and yet there was a unique augmentation of each. By various routes we are shown that "he possessed the same emotions (and same reason), but not in the same way or with the same effects" (Res easdem in illo constituo, at non eodem modo, neque idem efficientes) (1277A). Erasmus describes Christ's expansion of the Stoic mindset at the conclusion of his rewritings of the typhoon story:

> Christ was not alarmed, as the (Stoic) philosopher was, by an inescapable consequence of his human nature, and he did not possess a mind, unlike the Stoic, that could (potentially) be unhinged.[27] (1278A)

Two factors, which I will expand on, stand out here: (a) Like the Stoic, Christ's emotions were ineradicable and lasted as long as their cause *but* unlike the Stoic he was not disturbed by the fact that his emotions ran riot. (b) Like the Stoic, his reason held firm throughout the event *but* unlike the Stoic he did not have to work at keeping his reason from giving in to his emotions.

---

27 The translation is mine.

(a) Christ had the same emotions but differing effects

Christ's agony in Gethsemane arose internally as he contemplated what from foreknowledge he knew was going to happen. It did not result from a sudden assault on his senses from an external *phantasia* any-more than it resulted, as with the story of the sick and dying Stoic told by Gellius, from physical pain. There is also the difference between a future possibility and a future certainty. The Stoic in the typhoon feared because he saw that it was possible that the ship would go down and that he would die whereas Christ's fear was based on the certainty that crucifixion awaited him.

Earlier Erasmus had established that bravery – even that of a Socrates – can be evaluated only in terms of a person's particular bodily and mental makeup. As a corollary he held that the greater the handicap from natural instincts, or from the particular bodily and mental makeup one is born with, or from adverse worldly situations, the greater the opportunity for virtue (120–6). It may be nice to have only small and few handicaps but this means that there is little room for virtue to develop. Humans with large handicaps have an advantage in that they can work out virtue, if they are brave, on a large stage. Christ's handicaps were incomparable and so too was the bravery that matched them. The following handicaps stand out:

- Unlike others Christ chose – increasing the effect exponentially – to be bound by natural instincts and other human disabilities. He chose this path notwithstanding spotless innocence, plenitude of grace, and enjoyment of divinity (1283F, 1285B, 1289B).
- The force of his emotions – standing out being his fear of death – was incomparably greater than ever experienced by a human. This was the case, for one thing, because the greater the nobility of body and soul the greater the impact of pain (1271D). There has never been a body and soul less tolerant of pain (1284E).[28]
- He assumed the disabilities imposed on humans as punishment for the fall (1270B). Suffering many of the ills arising from original sin, but not sin itself, "added to the total of his virtue and merit" (1277C).

---

28 On contrasts between Erasmus' outlook on Christ's nobility and pain and late medieval devotionalist thought, see below, pp. 252–4.

- The fact that his handicaps did not result from sin meant, believes Erasmus, that he had no tools to mitigate them. His emotions could not be in any way curbed. Unlike the ancient pagans, he did not and could not have dealt with his fear by strength of character, or by diverting his thoughts to things more pleasant, or by contemplating the rewards of suffering (1284D). He could only endure.

Through unparalleled emotional suffering, inseparable from his unparalleled emotional handicaps, Christ allowed humans to feel and not just acknowledge his identity with them. Had he been a martyr people might have admired his achievement but they would have felt nothing. There is all the difference between love and admiration. At the close of his treatise, answering yet again why Christ showed outward signs of fear rather than, as with the martyrs, outward signs of eager joy (*alacritas*), we read:

> On display were the lineaments of humanity not the trappings of divinity. He was setting an example for us to love and to emulate, not merely to admire. (1289E)

"A powerful example was being given, which would inspire even the coldest of hearts towards love, and encourage the most sluggish to emulate it for the health of their souls" (1285D). The greater the vulnerability and despair the greater the love revealed. Had he set himself up as mere divinity, "with eager joy on his face and in his words, like a man practically devoid of feeling," he would have done us little service (1289F).

And if Christ could suffer from natural instinct, ordinary humans can take courage in that they can recognize and accept their own natural instincts (as well as character traits and life situations) and learn how to deal, as Christians, with them. Christ's ideal Christian was not a martyr.

> Perhaps it was because he does not expect us to go against nature and show eager joy amid great torments that he did not choose to exhibit it in himself. Instead, he set us an example of charity and gentleness, the gentleness he had earlier told us to learn from him, saying, "learn from me, for I am gentle and humble in heart." And even in the hour of his death he continued to commend love to us." (1290B–C)

Failing to grasp the force and irrevocableness of natural instinct humans have imagined that they can and should override nature, substituting eager joy (*alacritas*) for the harsh and inextinguishable realities of existence. But this is impossible, and Christ tried to show us the correct path. As the concluding sentence of a 1499 letter to Colet puts it, quoting Horace (*Ep.* 1.10.24), "Though ye pitchfork Nature out, sure she will run back again."[29]

But why does Erasmus tie in Christ's "charity and gentleness" and his being "humble in heart" with "nature" – and here too contrast eager joy (*alacritas*) and martyrdom? And what is he thinking of when he insists that ordinary humans should follow this example and be charitable, gentle, and humble? Readers have imagined in finding such statements in Erasmus' writings that he is conceptualizing something conventional; that Christ, the embodiment of perfection, felt from high above compassion, pity, tolerance, leniency, and magnanimity. Emphatically, this is not here the meaning. In advising gentleness and humbleness Christ was not, in Erasmus' view, thinking of mushy abstract ideals but something close to the opposite. Erasmus sees Christ's gentleness and charity as residing in his ineradicable natural instincts, "this natural weakness (infirmitas), so deeply implanted in human nature that it can be conquered but never eradicated," which is "the surest evidence of humanity" – and which the Redeemer took on "in a remarkable way" (1288A). Others should deeply imbibe this "natural weakness," which is on full display. Acceptance of weakness, gentleness, and humbleness is one with accepting the ineradicable nature of one's constition, body and mind – as well as the constitutions of others. Acceptance, however, is only the starting point. It takes great courage and determination to positively develop the "weaknesses" of natural instinct, particular character traits, and particular situations – as was to be demonstrated in detail in the *Enchiridion*.

What also needs to be recognized is that in advising "weakness" Erasmus was speaking of himself as well as others. In his youth he himself had tried, unsuccessfully, to override his natural instincts, character traits, and environment; he had not always felt gentle, humble, and charitable towards himself or others.

(b) Christ had the same reason but differing effects

While the Stoic in the typhoon never allowed his reason to be harmed by emotion and his reason fought against his fear although it was unable to subdue it, Christ went beyond this in that "he did not possess

29 *Ep.* 109. Allen 1, 253/154–5, CWE 1, 211/168–9. On Stoicism in Horace's writings, see Colish, *The Stoic Tradition from Antiquity to the Early Middle Ages*, 1:160–94.

a mind, unlike the Stoic, that could (potentially) be unhinged" (1278A, above, p. 178). The Stoic had to work at holding onto reason, had to fight against moral breakdown, but Christ did not. His mind, the upper side, was not touched by, disturbed by, affected by, or concerned about the turmoil going on within his emotions. It remained intact, unchallenged, and tranquil, "not alarmed by a necessary consequence of his human nature."

> He was afraid, not because his emotions seized and overwhelmed his reason as ours do [lacking the type of wisdom practised by the Stoic wiseman], but in untroubled serenity of mind. (1283F)
>
> (Fear, dread, and alarm) did not dictate to his reason or in any way disturb his composure. (1284A)

Discussing not just Christ's fear of death but various emotions he experienced, Erasmus exclaims:

> Why should I not affirm that Christ knew anger, if his anger was no more than a detestation of evil that in no way challenged or disturbed his use of reason nor hindered his unbroken and serene contemplation of heaven. (1277D)

The mind of the orthodox Stoic wiseman, as distinct from the Stoic in the typhoon, was likewise serene and untroubled, his reason at one with the universe and god, and yet there is a fundamental difference. The wiseman considers emotion a false judgment whereas with Christ, according to Erasmus, reason was separate from emotion (just as emotion was separate from reason).

In summary, lacking knowledge of where Erasmus was headed with his two-pronged corrections of the typhoon story it could be imagined that he wanted to show that Christ's reason was struggling throughout his Passion, though unable to control his fear, and returned to its normal state only when his fear disappeared with his death on the cross. But this was not how Erasmus saw it. Although Christ felt the most extreme emotion rather than mere pre-emotion and not momentarily but for a day and a half, his reason was not, Erasmus argues, put on hold as events transpired. Throughout the ordeal his reason was totally unaffected, oblivious to what was going on with his emotions. The Stoic's situation was problematic because compromise with emotions was always possible, even if in the typhoon case this did not occur, but with Christ there was not even a possibility that reason might be dishonoured. Undoubtedly Erasmus saw the storm experienced by the Stoic as a stand-in for the storm raging in the lower part of Christ's soul, but in the one case reason struggled while in the other reason took no notice. Fear, a natural instinct, overwhelmed one side of his soul while the other side remained aloof and serene, at one with reason and the contemplation of heaven.

Clearly, Erasmus' way of thinking about Christ and Christianity was radical – and carefully and consistently worked out. In Parts V–VII below I will further develop his thought showing in the process that it was no more derived from scholastic insights or methodologies than from Platonist or Peripatetic philosophies. Nor are there parallels in the fathers of the church or the devotionalist literature of the late Middle Ages or previous humanists. *De taedio Iesu* describes a debate but unlike humanist debates it is not rhetorical but philosophical. The author's thesis is elaborated in detail and set forth without qualification. He had no interest in decking out opposed positions with fine words and then asking readers to reflect at their leisure on which path might be more supportable or appropriate for an occasion.

His working out of Stoicism conflicts with the orthodox Stoic contention that emotion is simply faulty reason, something opposed to nature, and also goes far beyond the focus of late classical Stoics on subordinating emotions to reason and (especially with Epictetus) interest in the force of nature. Radically developing late Stoicism, *De taedio Iesu* transfers emotion to the heart of nature. Now emotion becomes one with things that are in Stoicism "indifferent," something between flesh and spirit (between Stoic *turpe* and *honestum*). The Christian journey is not – contrary to the prevailing view among Erasmian scholars – about a flesh/spirit either/or. It is about a both/and consisting inseparably of natural instinct, character traits, and situations on one side and spirit/reason on the other. Although emotion is not in itself an evil, and as such reason has no power over it, humans, ever so fallible, often turn emotion as well as other things belonging to the indifferent category into evil. The *Enchiridion*, written immediately after *De taedio Iesu*, illustrates at length unitary both/and ways of dealing with all the issues of life – the mindset of "my Stoics."

Devoid of all evil, though a complete human being, Christ took this both/and way of thinking, Erasmus shows, to its ultimate: his emotions (most important his fear of death) were entirely uncontrolled, and his reason was remote, serene, and one with heaven. Emotion was no longer in conflict with reason. Reason was no longer in conflict with emotion. Stoicism had always been about two radically different types of value, neither contradicting the other, and Christ's mindset was here, as in Stoicism, unitarily both/and, the crucial difference being that emotion had moved from the cognitive realm to the realm of natural instinct and things indifferent.

PART V Correcting a Thousand Years of Christology

Early on in *De taedio Iesu* Erasmus takes note of "propassion," commenting that the Greeks call this *προπάθεια*, meaning "a sort of beginning of passion," and he ties the concept to Jerome (d. 420): "Qua de causa Hieronymus, quam & Graeci *προπάθεια*, propassionem nominat, quasi passionis initium" (1271E).[1] The context is a discussion of the terror that must have gripped Christ as he contemplated, through foreknowledge, his coming crucifixion. Now, much later, at 1285E–F, we can see that Erasmus has been throughout leading up to a very major thesis regarding propassion. Christ did not suffer propassion (pre-emotion), as Jerome and other theologians have held, but full-fledged passion (emotion). His mind was "violently disturbed" (vehementissime perturbarit). Following comments that point to Christ's mental sufferings, as shown in scripture and in the writings of "learned theologians," unnamed, we find a concise rendering (the numbering here and elsewhere is mine) of the thesis rejected and the counterthesis:

> (1) That [the evidence of Christ's emotional suffering] is why Jerome's interpretation holds no great attraction for me. He calls the Redeemer's suffering "propassion," rather than passion, (2) something that, to use St Bernard's distinction, disturbed (turbarit) but did not overwhelm (perturbarit) him. (3) If they [theologians] define "passion" (passio) as something

1 On "propassion," see Graver, *Stoicism and Emotion*, 85–108, and "Philo of Alexandria and the Origins of the Stoic *Propatheiai*"; Inwood, *Ethics and Human Action in Early Stoicism*, 175–81, and "Seneca and Psychological Dualism"; Abel, "Das Propatheia-Theorem"; Sorabji, *Emotion and Peace of Mind*, esp. 66–75; and Knuuttila, *Emotions in Ancient and Medieval Philosophy*.

> that dethrones reason and "overwhelm" (perturbatio) as being driven out of one's mind, I do not object [to the distinguishing of *propassio* and *turbatio* from *passio* and *perturbatio*]. (4) But I should not hesitate also to call "passion" these feelings which not only disturbed Jesus' mind (or at least the lower part of it), but most violently overwhelmed it (non turbarit solum, sed vehementissime perturbarit). (1285E–F)

Scholars have imagined, unanimously, that Erasmus' discussions of Christology in *De taedio Iesu* merely repeat the common views of scholastics and others, adding little more than rhetorical florishes.[2] In what follows I will demonstrate in detail the exact opposite. Erasmus sets forth a thesis that contradicts a thousand years of theological thought on Christ's Passion – a thesis built directly from his own youthful existential problems and the life-changing impact of Stoic *oikeiosis*.

Influenced particularly by Jerome's statements, the concept of propassion was present throughout the early medieval period[3] and then later became a fixture of discussion among scholastics. Peter Lombard (d. 1160), Alexander of Hales (d. 1245), Albert the Great (d. 1280), Bonaventure (d. 1274), and Aquinas (d. 1274), among others, all accept Jerome's distinction – although the ways they frame and develop the issue are quite different. In short, many church fathers and all the major scholastics had built their conceptions of Christ's emotional state before his crucifixion around the concept of propassion, the purpose being to deny that Christ suffered true emotion, much less extreme emotion. Erasmus' central goal in *De taedio Iesu* was to demonstrate the contrary.

In a 1499 letter to Erasmus, shortly after their debate, Colet smugly brushes aside a lengthy letter from Erasmus with the assertion that his own opinion results from "having thoroughly absorbed Jerome."[4] Erasmus comments that the whole debate had arisen because Colet wanted to see, ostensibly following Jerome, Christ's Passion in terms of extreme joy, *alacritas* (1286B, and above, III.3), resulting from the overcoming of worldliness. As Colet saw it, Christ was a supermartyr, a person whose reason was not benumbed by emotion for even a moment (1276B–C). And if, in accord with Jerome, he suffered any fear of death it was not for himself but for the Jews and others who would be left behind. Ordinary

2 See above, pp. 49, 78–81.

3 See Knuuttila, *Emotions in Ancient and Medieval Philosophy*, 180 n. 5.

4 *Ep*. 110. Allen 1, 254/10–11, CWE 1, 211/12–13.

humans may fear death but Christ did not. All of this is against the very core of Erasmus' argument.

Actually, as Erasmus points out, Colet had not brought up Jerome's pre-emotion thesis but only an odd statement that could indicate a view that Christ did not suffer any emotion (1267B–C), not even pre-emotion. Since this outlook verges on heresy in that it comes close to denying that Christ was human as well as divine, a dogma of the faith following the Councils of Chalcedon (451) and Constantinople (681), it had been supported by few previous theologians. Throughout the Middle Ages the considerable writings of Hilary of Poitiers (d. 367) had been found problematic precisely because for one thing he argued that Christ had felt neither pain nor fear, which seemed to deny that he was human. On the other side of the spectrum there was no theologian, to my knowledge, who ever held that Christ was overcome by fear of death. Erasmus was on his own. Those who followed in the wake of Jerome were consumed by the need to show that Christ did not experience any true fear of death but only propassion. *De taedio Iesu* hinges on the denial of propassion, in all its varieties, as applied to Christ. Throughout, Erasmus' purpose is to show that Christ suffered full-fledged emotion and why this was the case.

Although Origen (d. 255) and Didymus (d. 398) built their discussions of the Passion on Stoic pre-emotion and influenced Jerome (see below, chapter 1) the degree to which Jerome saw the Stoic background to propassion is unclear.[5] Those theologians who discussed propassion in the ensuing centuries certainly did not see that it was a Stoic doctrine, much less a central Stoic doctrine. Where theologians consciously recognized Stoic thinking it usually had to do with the doctrine of *apatheia*, freedom from the emotions – which was often seen as an ideal. Christ had overcome his emotions and ordinary humans – as exemplified by martyrs – should attempt the same, all of which is not out of sync with discussions of propassion or even Colet's more extreme view.

What is so striking is that unlike any of his Christian predecessors Erasmus deeply understood Stoic thinking on pre-emotion and yet used other aspects of Stoic thought and his own analyses to show the limitations of the concept and to demonstrate that it in no way applies to

5 Colish concludes that Jerome's writings reveal few gleanings from Stoicism and that his uses were tendentious and superficial. See *The Stoic Tradition from Antiquity to the Early Middle Ages*, 2:70–91 at 90.

Christ's Passion. And he shows himself to be as cognizant of scholastic thought on propassion as of Jerome's. At one point he explicitly refers to Bonaventure and advises those interested to examine the relevant part of his massive *Commentary on the Sentences of Peter Lombard* (1270B). Readers have assumed that he is simply agreeing with Bonaventure, in essentials at least, but nothing could be further from the truth. Just as he radically rewrites Origen (above, III.2) and Gellius (above, IV.1–2) without telling us, so too, it will become clear, does he refer the reader to Bonaventure without pointing out that his own views diverge radically from those of Bonaventure and other scholastics. Nor does he rewrite any of these authors from a "rhetorical" standpoint, "stylistically" restating positions or setting forth for the reader's consideration multiple possible viewpoints. He thinks about the issues philosophically and argues a singular thesis.

Part IV.1–2 uncovered the philosophic ways in which Erasmus demonstrated what was wrong with Gellius' illustration of the Stoic in the storm – and what the illustration really tells us. What this painstaking analysis and rewriting of Stoic arguments on pre-emotion lead up to (IV.3) is a retelling of Christ's Passion in terms of a two-dimensional Stoic mindset – on one side of which (transforming late Stoicism) was an unrestrained and unrestrainable fear of death. What remains to be unravelled is how Erasmus deals with the contrary arguments of the theologians.

1 Pre-Emotion versus Emotion: From Seneca, Origen, and Jerome to Peter Lombard, Bonaventure, and Aquinas

Before Erasmus' criticisms and rewritings of particular theological theses regarding Christ's Passion can be unfolded, the subject of chapter 2, we need to better understand the thousand-year-old thesis he was opposing and the various ways it had been worked out. In "A" below I will describe the Stoic sources of Jerome's thinking, taking account particularly of Seneca (d. 65 CE), Origen (d. 254/5), and Didymus (d. 398), followed in "B" by an analysis of the way Jerome (d. 420) defines and illustrates propassion with regard to Christ. In "C" I will then work out the ways scholastics – not the least being Bonaventure, singled out by Erasmus – developed or radicalized Jerome's conception of propassion.

The word "passion" (*passio*), it should be noted, has in English a dramatic connotation at odds with Hellenistic and medieval sources. In what follows I will use the word "pre-emotion" interchangeably with "propassion" (*propassio*) and the word "emotion" interchangeably with "passion" (*passio*).[6]

A Stoic origins

While aspects of the theory of pre-emotion were set forth by Zeno (c. 335–262 BCE) and Chrysippus (c. 280–208 BCE),[7] the examples and explications of Seneca (4 BCE–65 CE), which relate closely to the discussions of Epictetus (c. 50–120 CE) preserved by Gellius, are the most detailed in existence.[8] Although Origen had at hand works of Zeno and Chrysippus, he could have been influenced by Seneca as well.

Seneca

The question Seneca asks at the beginning of *De ira* (*On Anger*) is whether anger, an emotion, originates from choice (*iudicio*) or from impulse (*impetus*) (2.1.1). He then describes a great variety of affective reactions (i.e., feelings) that are not preventable by reason and therefore, he argues, are not emotion. Although the emphasis seems to be on involuntary physical reactions, many involuntary reactions are mental and some seem to have shadings of both. Examples given are shivering when sprinkled with cold water; hair standing on end from bad news; blushing from an improper use of words; vertigo when we look at a steep drop (2.2.1); the first shock (*ictus*) of the mind following a perceived injustice (2.2.2); viewing happenings in a theatrical production or listening to the recital of ancient deeds, such as the killing of Cicero

6 Graver believes "emotion" is for English speakers a better word than "passion" for rendering Stoic thought (*Stoicism and Emotion*, 3) and Sorabji sees the issue similarly (*Emotion and Peace of Mind*, 7). Knuuttila uses the words "passion" and "emotion" interchangeably, as do I (*Emotions in Ancient and Medieval Philosophy*, 3).

7 According to Seneca (*De ira* 1.16.7), Zeno stated that even the wiseman will carry a scar from the experience of wrongful deeds, and Epictetus, as reported by Gellius, attributes pre-emotion views to Zeno and Chrysippus (19.1.14). Although early Stoics employed the concept, they did not use the word *propassion* (*προπάθεια*). See LS, 2:417 and Abel, "Das Propatheia-Theorem."

8 Whether Erasmus was acquainted with Seneca's thinking on pre-emotion as well as Epictetus' is not known.

by Antony (2.2.3); singing and quick rythums or the martial sound of trumpets; a grim painting; viewing the meting out of punishment, no matter how just (2.2.4); laughing when other people laugh; feeling sadness in the presence of mourners; being excited in observing contests (2.2.6); being affected by another person's yawn or our eyes blinking when fingers are suddenly poked towards us (2.4.2); the excitement of a retired military man at hearing the sound of the trumpet (2.2.6); paleness, tears, sexual arousal, deep sighs, flashing eyes (2.3.2); paleness which creeps over even the bravest man when he puts on his armour; the trembling knees of a hardened soldier when the signal for battle is given; the jumping heart of a great commander; the stiffening extremities of a most eloquent speaker when he gets ready to speak (2.2.2); and "that first agitation of the mind which the presentation of injustice (*species iniuriae*) inflicts" (2.3.5).[9]

Neither sadness nor fear nor anger nor any other emotion is found in such examples. "All of these things are movements of minds unwilling to be moved, and not emotions but preliminary preludes to emotions" (2.2.5). If not halted, however, a "first agitation of the mind" (prima agitatio animi) (2.3.5) or "first movement" (primus motus) (2.4.1) can lead to emotion, that which is entirely voluntary and blameable. There is a time gap and this time gap needs to be quickly closed. Once a first movement is assented to it becomes an emotion and is irreversible. For emotion to occur a second and a third movement of the mind takes place. In the second movement there is assent to the presentation (Latin *species, visio*; Greek *phantasia*) of having been injured (where anger is the issue) and to the presentation that it is appropriate to react. In the third movement there is vengeance, come what may, and reason is utterly vanquished (2.4.1, 2.3.4). Once emotion has been let in its force cannot be checked (1.7.4). Reason has rejected right reason (1.7.2–3). This outcome can be prevented only if assent is not given to the presentation, the second movement (1.8.2). Born of judgment, the second movement is removed by judgment (2.4.2).

Stoics were concerned about involuntary reactions because their monistic psychology depended on such things not being emotions. They recognized that their wiseman is as subject to these involuntary affects as anyone else (1.16.7) but were these affects emotions, it would not be possible to hold that emotion is simply defective reasoning and that the

9 On Seneca and pre-emotion, see in particular Knuuttila, *Emotions in Ancient and Medieval Philosophy*, 63–7, and Sorabji, *Emotion and Peace of Mind*, 55–75.

soul is unitary. So the challenge was to show that their unitary way of thinking could embrace such phenomena, that the wiseman is susceptible to *propatheiai* but that this does not entail a dualistic psychology. Since *propatheiai* are not caused by reason, the wiseman can deal with them – unlike those not wise, "fools." Plato and Aristotle, in contrast, held in their different ways that emotion can reflect non-rational powers and that some of these emotions are appropriate and not blameworthy.

There has been much debate as to whether Seneca's discussions of pre-emotion were swayed by the Stoic Posidonius' Platonist-tinged view or whether he was deliberately rejecting Posidonius' view in favour of Chrysippus.'[10] The question underlying this debate is whether Seneca's thinking was entirely monistic. Although Posidonius (135–51 BCE) insists on the necessity of reason's assent (unlike Plato), he considers non-rational affective movements, such as wordless music and tears, genuine emotions. Whether we lead a virtuous and happy life is not, this being the case, entirely up to us.[11] Richard Sorabji has argued that in fact Seneca rejected Posidonius' view and considered, in line with Chrysippus' thought, wordless music and tears not passions but merely presentations and first movements.[12]

Emotion and reason do not have distinct and separate locations; "they are just the transformation of the mind into a better or a worse condition" (*De ira*, 1.8.3) and Seneca emphasizes the complexity (2.1.5). In line with Stoics generally, emotions are processes of thought, products of reason and subject to control by reason. For Chrysippus and other Stoics, states John Cooper, "human emotions, and indeed all other species of 'impulse' in mature human beings, are functions of our mind, of our power to reason about and decide for ourselves what to do."[13]

10 See Cooper, "Posidonius on Emotions"; Fillion-Lahille, *Le "De Ira" de Sénèque et la philosophie stoïcienne des passions*, 163–9; Holler, *Seneca und die Seelenteilungslehre und Affektpsychologie der Mittelstoa*; Knuuttila, *Emotions in Ancient and Medieval Philosophy*, 53–63; and Sorabji, *Emotion and Peace of Mind*. In his *Ethics and Human Action in Early Stoicism*, Inwood argued that Seneca's thinking in *De ira* is dualistic (180) but later rejected this view in "Seneca and Psychological Dualism."

11 Cooper, "Posidonius on Emotions," 482.

12 Sorabji, *Emotion and Peace of Mind*, 72.

13 Cooper, "Posidonius on Emotions," 455. Cf. Inwood, "Seneca and Psychological Dualism," 43 and Sorabji's discussion of the difference between Stoic capacities of the soul and Platonist parts of the soul, *Emotion and Peace of Mind*, 313–15. The aim of the founders of Stoicism, states Graver, "was not to eliminate feelings as such from human life, but to understand what sorts of affective responses a person would have who was free of false belief" (*Stoicism and Emotion*, 2).

What Origen and Didymus handed to Jerome

Origen had first-hand knowledge of Chrysippus' writings and was significantly influenced by Stoicism, not least being Stoic thinking on pre-emotion.[14] His application of pre-emotion thinking to Christianity then influenced Didymus the Blind and Jerome.[15] Unlike Seneca and other Stoics, Origen, Didymus, and Jerome employed Stoicism not to solve complex and abstract philosophical issues but to help them explain biblical texts and to better understand Christian doctrines.

In accord with Stoics, Origen believed that pre-emotion is something experienced by everyone, including even those "perfect."[16] Only genuine anger is sinful. Anger occurs when thoughts stemming from a pre-emotion are allowed and rational assent is given to the desire to exact punishment. Commenting on Psalms 4:5 and the counsel to "Be angry and do not sin," Origen wonders why the Psalmist would say this if anger is an emotion and thus wrong. He judges that "anger" can designate something voluntary or something involuntary. In the former instance it denotes a desire to take vengeance where injustice is perceived. In the latter instance we find, he states, what some call a *propatheia* (pre-emotion). Origen then paraphrases the meaning of Psalms 4:5: "Inasmuch as you grow angry, and this occurs to you without having thoughts with regard to anger and you do not add to what issues from these things, let not something blameworthy follow upon what has occurred that is not blameworthy."[17]

The concept is evident in his detailed study of Matthew 26:37, where it is stated – with regard to Christ's reaction in the garden of Gethsemane to the prospect of dying – that he "began to be grieved and distressed."

> And consider that Scripture did not say "he was grieved and distressed," but *he began to be* grieved and distressed (sed coepit tristari et taediari). For there is a great difference between "to be grieved" and "to begin to

14 In *Contra Celsum* Origen mentions having read Chrysippus, at 1.40, 2.12, and 5.57, and quotes him elsewhere in that work. See Chadwick, "Origen, Celsus, and the Stoa," 34.

15 See, in particular, Layton, "*Propatheia*," and Sorabji, *Emotion and Peace of Mind*, 346–52.

16 See Layton, "*Propatheia*," 267 n. 18.

17 Origen, *Commentary on the Psalms* 4:5. PG 12, col. 1144A.

> be grieved." Therefore, if someone who defends human passions should bring it up to us that Jesus himself was grieved, let him hear that [he was] "the one who was tested in every respect as we are, yet without sin" (Heb. 4:15). This man was not grieved by grief for his own suffering. This happened instead with respect to the human nature only to the extent of the very beginning of grief and trembling, so that by these very things he might show to his disciples who were present (especially Peter, who thought great things of himself) – what he also later said to them – that "the spirit is willing, but the flesh is weak" (Matt. 26:41), that at no time should confidence be placed in the flesh, but the flesh must always be feared. Unwary confidence leads to boasting, but fear of weakness encourages one to take refuge in the help of God, just as the Lord himself advanced a short way and fell to the ground and prayed (Matt. 26:38–40). Therefore, he indeed "began to be grieved and distressed" according to human nature, which is subject to such passions, not however, according to the divine power, which is quite distant from passion of this kind.[18]

Christ only "began" to grieve and did not pass beyond this. This ideal, limiting emotion to pre-emotion, is what all believers should aim for. Regarding Christ's suffering being not for himself but for others, we may note that Colet would have agreed. Also comparing to Colet's thesis is emphasis on the need to fear the flesh and his sharp separation of human nature, including even pre-emotion, from divinity.

In many places, however, Origen is unclear regarding the relationship of involuntary reactions to emotions or, alternatively, redefines first movements. Notably, Origen turns Stoic first movements in *On First Principles* into bad thoughts.[19] The problem here, from a Stoic standpoint, is not that there are bad thoughts but that they are incorporated into pre-emotions. For Seneca and other Stoics pre-emotions do not involve thought. What are for Seneca preliminaries (*principia*) of emotion are for Origen beginnings and seeds of sin.[20] Sometimes these bad thoughts come from the devil, demons, or bad angels; other times from our natural constitution.

Richard Layton points out that the boundary between passive receptivity to an "impression" (*phantasia*) and "an image internal to the mind

18 Origen, *Commentarius in Matthaeum*, in Rufinus' Latin translation, GCS 38, 205f, trans. Layton, "*Propatheia*," 268.

19 Sorabji, *Emotion and Peace of Mind*, 346–51.

20 Origen, *On First Principles* 3.2.2.

in anticipation of approaching events" starts to blur when applied to Christ's agony. Origen sees *propatheia* in Christ's sorrow in the garden of Gethsemane whereas the more apt location would be the confusion that erupted when Christ was arrested.[21]

Didymus the Blind, deeply influenced by Origen, shows us just how problematic parts of Origen's thought were and the extent to which these inconsistencies could be developed by others.[22] Didymus treats *propatheiai*, according to Layton, "as features of regular and predictable psychological processes, rather than sudden or unforeseeable occurrences."[23] Nor are these processes value-neutral. Even "ideas" are for him a source of *propatheiai*.[24] The emotion of fear voiced by the Psalmist was only a *propatheia*. All this comes out in Didymus' discussion of the very text that motivated Origen: Christ "began to be astonished and dismayed."[25] In short, Didymus depicts an agent who suffers shocks to his psyche but also one who produces these disturbances. As a consequence a *propatheia* was potentially sinful and the difference between voluntary and involuntary became blurred.[26]

B Jerome

Jerome's statements on propassion require careful analysis, not only for what they tell us about his thinking but because they provide a yardstick by which we may discern and assess the changes made by scholastics.[27] He too is not, it will be found, entirely consistent.

Eight themes can be found in Jerome's thinking on propassion. The first three relate to his interpretation of Mathew 26:37: "He took Peter

21 Layton, "*Propatheia*," 270. I demonstrated in Part IV.3 that Erasmus did not find pre-emotion either in Gethsemane or in later events.

22 Knuuttila believes "Jerome may have been influenced by Didymus in using the Greek term *propatheia* and its Latin form *propassio* in his Commentary on Matthew." See *Emotions in Ancient and Medieval Philosophy*, 143.

23 Layton, "*Propatheia*," 272.

24 Layton, "*Propatheia*," 274.

25 Layton, "*Propatheia*," 280–1.

26 Layton, "*Propatheia*," 282.

27 On Jerome and propassion, see Sorabji, *Emotion and Peace of Mind*, 352–5; Madigan, "Ancient and High-Medieval Interpretations of Jesus in Gethsemane," esp. 163–5; Knuuttila, *Emotions in Ancient and Medieval Philosophy*, 193–4; Grillmeier, *Christ in Christian Tradition*, 363–402; and Gondreau, *The Passions of Christ's Soul in the Theology of St. Thomas Aquinas*, esp. 66–9 and 367–70.

and the two sons of Zebedee and began to be sad and sorrowful" (coepit contristari et maestus esse).

> What we said above about passion and propassion is shown also in the present chapter, namely that the Lord was indeed truly saddened, in order that he might display the truth of the humanity he had assumed. But so that emotion should not dominate in his mind, he began to be sad by way of propassion. For it is one thing to be sad and another to begin to be sad.[28]

(1) Christ only "began" to be sad. He suffered, that is, not passion but only "propassion." This is how in fact the words of scripture should be read. Being sad and beginning to be sad are two different things (aliud est enim contristari, et aliud incipere contristari).

(2) He suffered only propassion so that emotion would not dominate (ne dominaretur) his mind. He believed, that is, that there is a quid-pro-quo relationship between emotion and harm to the mind and this being the case, Christ could not have suffered passion.

(3) Yet, as a propassion, he was "truly sad" (vere contristatus). This was necessarily the case because he had become human to take on the burdens of humanity. Jerome appears to be diverging from Stoicism here in that Stoics did not allow that an involuntary reaction could be, as such, an emotion.

(4) Immediately following the above statements Jerome shows that the sadness (propassion) Christ suffered was not from fear of physical pain, much less fear of death, but from sorrow for others:

> The Lord sorrowed not from fear of suffering. He had come that he should suffer for the wretched Judas, for the offences of the rest of the apostles, for the rejection and reprobation of the Jewish nation, and the overthrow of unhappy Jerusalem – and had rebuked Peter for his fearfulness.[29]

(5) All humans are subject to propassions – as well as passion.

> It is difficult, or rather impossible, for anyone to be free of the beginnings of passion (perturbationum initia), which the Greeks with much significance call *propatheiai*, and we, translating word for word, call *antepassiones*. For

28 Jerome, *Commentary on Matthew* 26:37. PL 26, col. 205, my translation.
29 Jerome, *Commentary on Matthew* 26:37. PL 26, col. 205, my translation.

> incentives to sin tickle our minds, and our judgment has the task of accepting or rejecting what is thought. Hence the Lord spoke in the gospel and said (Matt 15:19), "Out of the heart come bad thoughts, murder, adultery, fornication, theft, false witness, blasphemy."[30]

Like many others after Origen, Jerome here equates "bad thoughts" with propassion.[31] "Bad thoughts" are suggestive of sin. Having "bad thoughts" seems to take away from the idea that propassion is always an involuntary reaction. Although humans bear some responsibility for propassions, Jerome believes that all humans have the task of accepting or rejecting these beginnings of emotion. With Christ, however, it was different as he and he alone suffered only propassion – with no propensity to evil (theme 2 above).

(6) Propassion is a sudden and involuntary movement. Commenting on Matthew 5:22, the *Glossa ordinaria* (compiled in the twelfth century) refers to the view of Jerome that "propassion is a sudden movement that is not consented to" (Subitus motus cui non consentitur, propassio est; accedente autem consensus, passio est, et tunc mors in domo).[32] The idea of suddenness is, of course, central to the Stoic view of propassion. A propassion arrives without consent. Passion occurs when consent occurs.

(7) Two ways of understanding anger – and other emotions.

> The word "anger" is understood in two ways, not only among ourselves but also among philosophers. For either when we are provoked by an injustice and stirred up by natural stimuli or when the provocation has quietened

30 Jerome, *Letter* 79.9 to Salvina. PL 22, col. 731, my translation.

31 Sorabji, *Emotion and Peace of Mind*, 346 and 352–5. On "bad thoughts," see also Jerome, *Commentary on Matthew* 5:28–9 (PL 26, cols 38–9), and *Commentary on Ezechiel* 18:1–2 (PL 25, cols 168–9).

32 See *Glossa ordinaria*, 4:20. The subject of Matthew 5:22 and the context of the quote is anger. Actually, Jerome's *Commentary on Matthew* 5:22 does not make this statement. There is every reason, however, to believe Jerome is the author. Who else, in the first place, could have made a statement so close to Stoicism? Alexander of Hales repeatedly ties this statement, which he found in the *Glossa ordinaria*, to Jerome (see below, pp. 205–6). Bonaventure also quotes and attributes this statement to Jerome (see below, p. 208). In a commentary on Matthew, Geoffrey Babion (early twelfth century) states that *propassio*, as contrasted with *passio*, is "a sudden movement which does not involve deliberation about good and evil and which is a venial sin." He also makes Jerome's distinction between propassion as a non-deliberated reaction and passion as consent (*consensus*) (PL 162, col. 1294). On Babion, see Knuuttila, *Emotions in Ancient and Medieval Philosophy*, 179–80.

and fury has been quenched, our mind can make a judgment and still desire revenge just as much on the person who is thought to have harmed us. I think the present saying concerns the former case. It is allowed to us as humans that we should be moved in the face of anything undeserved, and that like a light breeze it should disturb the tranquility of our mind. But in no way is it allowed that we should be worked up into swollen whirpools.[33]

Let us apply what is said about one emotion (*perturbatio*) to the others. Just as it is human to get angry, and Christian not to bring one's anger to completion, so all flesh desires the things of the flesh and draws the soul by various enticements (*inlecebrae*) to deadly pleasures.[34]

(8) Lust for a woman exemplifies the difference between propassion and passion.

There is this difference between *pathos* and *propatheia*, that is, between passion and propassion: passion is counted as a sin (*vitium*); pre-passion, though it involves the fault (*culpa*) of something beginning, is not treated as a matter for accusation (*in crimine*). So someone who on looking at a woman has his soul titillated (*titillata*) is struck (*percussus*) by pre-passion. But if he once assents, and makes a thought (*cogitatio*) into an emotion (*affectus*), as is written in [the Psalms of] David, "They have passed to an emotion (*affectus*) of the heart," he has passed from pre-passion to passion. And what he lacks is not the will (*voluntas*) to sin, but the opportunity. So whoever looks at a woman to lust after her, that is, if he has looked at her in order that he may feel lust, and in order to dispose himself to act, he is rightly said to commit adultery with her in his heart.[35]

---

33 Jerome, *Commentary on Ephesians* 4:26. PL 26, col. 543, trans. Sorabji, *Emotion and Peace of Mind*, without his Latin inserts, 355.

34 Jerome, *Letter* 79.9 to Salvina. PL 22, col. 731, trans. Sorabji, *Emotion and Peace of Mind*, 355.

35 Jerome, *Commentary on Matthew* 5:28–9. PL 26, col. 39, trans. Sorabji, *Emotion and Peace of Mind*, 354. Regarding Matthew 5:28, the interlinear gloss quotes Jerome (without naming him): "Et anima eius titillata fuerit quod propassio dicitur que est culpam habet non tamen crimen. Concupiscentia est mater adulterii." The marginal note on concupiscience, only part of which is verifiably Jerome's words, reads: "ubi non deest voluntas sed occasio quod passio dicitur que est mors in domo. Propassio est animi subitus affectus vel ire vel amoris. Passio quaedam animi forma vel deliberatio ex consensus unde dicitur aliquis ira cundus vel amator. Propassio est subitus motus sine deliberatione boni vel mali operis. Passio est affectio deliberati animi si sit locus perficiendi." See *Glossa ordinaria*, 4:21.

Although the titillation is a fault (*culpa*), the sin (*vitium*) comes only if one assents to the propassion, turning a thought into a passion. In the latter situation adultery has been commited with one's heart. There is the desire to act on the lustful desire. Making propassion a fault (*culpa*) seems to tie in with his (and Origen's) talk about "bad thoughts."

C Scholastics

Although Stoicism was a considerable force in the early Middle Ages, its impact was uneven and often seriously skewed.[36] The doctrine of *apatheia*, freedom from emotion, had the greatest effect. Most often patristic authors saw *apatheia* as supporting Christianity.[37] It was commonly believed that Christ overcame his emotions and that humans – as exemplified by martyrs – should attempt the same. Extraordinarily influential in this regard were the views of Hilary of Poitiers (d. 368), set forth in his *De Trinitate*.[38] Hilary was determined to refute those who believed Christ suffered pain or had actual fear. "I would ask those who think this way if it stands to reason that the one who, in casting out all fear of death from the apostles and in exhorting them to the glory of martyrdom, should himself fear death."[39] Against the Arian view that the Son of God was inferior to the Father and had experienced in his Passion such things as pain, sorrow, and fear, Hilary contended not only that Christ had no fear but that his flesh was not susceptible to physical pain. Pain was for him like water to a knife. The reason was that he was born of a virgin. In the garden of Gethsemane he was not

36 On the impact of Stoicism from the third to the sixth century, see Colish, *The Stoic Tradition from Antiquity to the Early Middle Ages*, vol. 2. Augustine's writings on theodicy, natural law, epistemology, rhetoric, logic, and physics were all affected in some way by Stoic thought. However, the main point of contact, as in the later Middle Ages, was ethical. See also Lapidge, "Stoic Inheritance."

37 Gerard Verbeke lists patristic authors who appropriated Stoic impassibility (*apatheia*). See *The Presence of Stoicism in Medieval Thought*, 48. Sorabji discusses *apatheia* in the thinking of Evagrius of Pontus (d. 399) and a number of other patristic authors in *Emotion and Peace of Mind*, 357–71 and 385–99. John Cassian (d. c. 435) "impressed the ideal of *apatheia* on the monastic tradition" (397). Gondreau gives two examples from the twelfth century in *The Passions of Christ's Soul*, 284.

38 See Gondreau, *The Passions of Christ's Soul*, 48–51, 404 passim, and Madigan, "On the High-Medieval Reception of Hilary of Poitiers's Anti-'Arian' Opinion."

39 *De Trinitate*, vol. 62A, 10.10.

sad for himself but for the disciples. He had no fear of death because he died willingly, knew his death would be for only three days, and that he would rise again.[40]

Augustine was an exception, albeit an important one, to the tendency to pass over or deny Jesus' human emotions. Far from seeing that Stoics had anything significant to add to discussions of emotion, he argued against Stoics, in *The City of God*, that Christ had true emotion and so do we.[41] He considered *apatheia*, or *impassibilitas*, an invalid concept. Emotions are real and have an important role, albeit they sometimes lead to sin.[42] His criticism of Stoicism was, however, built on false premises. He did not see Stoicism in terms of a unitary soul but in terms of a Platonist distinction between irrational parts and reason[43] and believed the differences between Stoics and Platonists and Peripatetics was merely a matter of words, citing at one point *De finibus* – thinking of Antiochus' criticisms of Stoicism in Books 4 and 5.[44] Although he takes up at some length Gellius' discussion of Stoic thinking on emotion, he was unimpressed and had little grasp of the context or meaning. He concludes that involuntary affects are actually passions (*passiones*) and that even the Stoic wiseman is in reality subject to them.[45]

And yet Jerome's conceptualizations of propassion continued to be quoted or referred to in earlier medieval times,[46] and in the twelfth century, with the establishment of the University of Paris and the rise of scholastic ways of thinking, propassion came to play a pivotal role in analyses of Christ's Passion. At this time propassion was subjected to much more technical and systematized analyses. As it turned out, however, scholastics took the term further and further away from the descriptions established by Jerome – not to mention the Stoic roots.

---

40 *De Trinitate*, 10.23, 37, 12 resp.

41 *The City of God*, 14.9.

42 *The City of God*, 9.5, 14.9. On anger and lust, see 14.15 and 14.19.

43 Cf. *The City of God*, 14.19.

44 *The City of God*, 9.4. See also 14.9.

45 *The City of God*, 9.4. Sorabji argues that Gellius' use of the word *pavescere*, "to grow jittery" (instead of *pallescere*, "to grow pale"), was ambiguous and contributed to Augustine's misunderstanding of first movements. See *Emotion and Peace of Mind*, 375–84.

46 See Knuuttila, *Emotions in Ancient and Medieval Philosophy*, 180 n. 5.

Peter Lombard

Peter Lombard's *Book of Sentences* (c. 1150), a work which became a textbook for later scholastics, played a central role in the development of the meaning of propassion as applied to Christ's Passion.[47] Adapting the approach of Peter Abelard in his *Sic et Non* (*Yes and No*) (1120), Lombard put together glosses on particular biblical texts used by earlier masters in their lectures on the Bible. The glosses came from a variety of sources, including especially fathers of the church such as Augustine and Jerome, and represented vastly differing opinions, sometimes registered by the same author. Lombard's own conclusions (usually but not always set forth) resulted from a complicated process that began with deciding on which glosses to include, working out the meanings of quotations, distinguishing between these meanings, and then arriving at an interpretation that best accounted for and resolved, in his view, apparent disagreements or contradictions. Later scholastics were to further develop Lombard's methodology, beginning each problem area with a list of disputed statements, followed by the author's reply, followed by answers to the beginning list of disputed statements.[48] The methodology had a great deal to do with the particular conclusions reached. It provided a logical framework by which differing opinions and a variety of texts could be brought together, categorized, analysed, and then subjected to criticism. On the negative side, pitting one statement against another made it easy to pass over context and to miss larger philosophical issues. It is not accidental that scholastics never realized that propassion was a concept that had originated in Stoicism.

Regarding Christ's Passion, discussed in Book III, Distinction 15 of the *Sentences*, Lombard focuses mainly on comments of Augustine, Jerome, Ambrose, and Hilary of Poitiers. The biblical statements brought to the fore by these authors include "Coepit Iesus pavere et taedere" (Jesus began to quake with fear and to be weary) (Mark 14:33), "Coepit

47 Lombard, *Sententiae in IV libris distinctae*. Secondary works on Lombard's thought, though they hardly mention propassion, include Colish, *Peter Lombard*; Rosemann, *Peter Lombard*; Evans, *Medieval Commentaries on the Sentences of Peter Lombard*; Ghellinck, *Le mouvement theologique du XIIe siècle*; Landgraf, *Einführung in die Geschichte der theologischen Literatur der Frühscholastik unter dem Gesichtspunkte der Schulenbildung*; and Nielsen, "Peter Lombard and His School."

48 On the evolution of commentaries on the *Sentences*, up to the time of Luther, see Rosemann, *The Story of a Great Book*.

contristari et moestus esse" (He began to be sorrowful and anguished) (Matt. 26:37), "Tristis est anima mea usque ad mortem" (My soul is sorrowful unto death) (Matt. 26:38), "Pater, si possible est, transeat a me calix iste" (Father, if it is possible, take this cup from me) (Matt. 26:39).

Distinction 15 comprises four chapters. Chapter 1 takes up the human nature Christ assumed and the relationship to his sadness and fear; Chapter 2 shows how the concept of propassion resolves the lingering issues; Chapters 3 and 4 quote at some length Hilary. Hilary's views, we learn in the first sentence of Chapter 3, are "extremely obscure" and contrary to common opinion.[49] Although Lombard was opposed to Hilary's basic outlook, the very fact that he devotes this much space to Hilary tells us much about the sway of Hilary's views over the centuries.

Chapter 1 attempts to answer Ambrose's question as to how it could be that Christ feared death while his disciple Peter did not. Peter was willing to lay down his life for Christ (John 13:37) while Christ stated that his soul was in turmoil (*turbatur*; John 12:27). What needs to be understood, Ambrose shows, is that Christ' soul was not in turmoil because of his virtue or divinity but because of the fragility of the human nature he had assumed. "Non turbatur eius virtus, non turbatur eius divinitas, sed turbatur anima: secundum humanae fragilitatis assumptionem turbatur."[50] Other authorities affirm that Christ's body was not *impassibilem* but *vere passibilem*. A difference between our passibility (ability to feel or suffer) and Christ's passibility is that Christ took on the human condition and its suffering not from necessity but from will.[51]

The question still remains, however, as to why Christ expressed fear of death while Peter was without fear. Ambrose and Augustine have the answer. Properly understood Peter was not braver than Christ, the soldier was not stronger than the emperor. Christ was not truly sad and did not truly fear his own death. His fear was about our infirmities and the negative consequences his death might entail.[52] Nor does Lombard correct on this score Hilary's contention, in Chapter 4, that "death is not the cause of [Christ's] sadness but the end" and that "he was not sad for himself" but for others, such as the apostles and the Jews.[53] This view – expressed also, we showed earlier, by Jerome – was clearly standard.

49 Lombard, *Sent.* III, d. 15, Ch. 3.1.
50 Lombard, *Sent.* III, d. 15, Ch. 1.11.
51 Lombard, *Sent.* III, d. 15, Ch. 1.12; also Ch. 2.4.
52 Lombard, *Sent.* III, d. 15, Ch. 1.11 and 1.13.
53 Lombard, *Sent.* III, d. 15, Ch. 4.

Colet's representation of this outlook against Erasmus was anything but radical.

Of considerable significance, Chapter 2 subjects propassion to analysis *before* a relationship is drawn to Jerome's view. The reason, investigation reveals, is that Peter Lombard saw the issue quite differently from Jerome. Not out of sync with Jerome, he begins by asserting, without reference to sources, (a) that Christ had as propassion true fear and sadness, in accord with his human nature but not ours; (b) that because of our defects, brought about by sin, we are subject to both propassion and passion while Christ was subject only to propassion;[54] and (c) that propassion and passion are with ordinary humans degrees of sin.[55] What is missing is the frame of thought that had, with Jerome, brought these statements into existence. There is not even a hint of involuntary reactions in the discussion. Nothing is brought out about the difference between responses over which one has no control and the point at which true responsibility and culpability begin.

What separates Lombard from Jerome is not only what Lombard does not say but also what he does say. He defines propassion/passion not in terms of involuntary reactions on one side and assent or dissent on the other but of movement or non-movement of the mind.

> Afficitur enim quis interdum timore vel tristitia, ita ut mentis intellectus non inde moveatur a rectitudine vel Dei contemplatione, et tunc propassio est. Aliquando vero movetur et turbatur, et tunc passio est.[56]
>
> Propassion is when there is fear and sadness and the understanding of the mind is not moved from rectitude and contemplation of God. Passion is when (there is fear and sadness and) the mind is truly moved and disturbed.

---

54 Lombard, *Sent.* III, d. 15, Ch. 2.1. Marcia Colish's interpretation is in no way supported by the text. "While men undergo temptation (*passio*) and contemplation of the temptation (*propassio*) prior to the consent (*consensus*) which is the essence in their moral decisions, Christ only experienced the *propassio* and the *consensus*" (*Peter Lombard*, 1:444). In fact, Peter never talks here about temptation and *passio* is not temptation but actual sin. Nor is the word *consensus* used. Peter does not say or infer that either humans or Christ "consent" to anything. Philipp Rosemann has also noted Colish's erroneous referral to the word *consensus*. See his *Peter Lombard*, 239 n. 48.

55 Note Jerome's statement that propassion is with us the beginning of blame even if not a crime (see above, pp. 197–8, theme 8).

56 Lombard, *Sent.* III, d. 15, Ch. 2.2, my translation.

There is fear and sadness with propassion and there is fear and sadness with passion. The difference is that with propassion the mind is not moved "from rectitude and contemplation of God" while with passion it is moved.

Questions come to mind: (a) Are propassions and passions distinguished only by the fact that they represent opposite mental states? (b) What instigates the emotions found in propassion and passion? Lombard refers only to occasions where emotions already exist. (c) What is the substantive difference between the two types of fear or two types of sadness? If the defining issue is only whether the mind is moved or not by these emotions, are the emotions as such all the same? (d) By what logic can it be said here that Christ suffered fear and sadness? If fear and sadness occur when the mind is moved, why would an unmoved mind suffer fear and sadness – even as propassion?

When Lombard finally brings in Jerome it is only to quote a part of his discussion of Matthew 26:37. What can be seen here again is how and to what degree he has silently changed the focus and meaning:

> He [Christ] was truly saddened in order to display the truth of the humanity he had assumed. But so that emotion should not dominate in his mind he began to be sad by way of propassion. For it is one thing to be sad and another to begin to be sad.[57]

Left out is what leads Jerome to this statement, what it means to be struck by something that precedes emotion (things such as being "titillated" by a woman) and that emotion occurs only where there is assent.

Acccording to Lombard, Jerome believes that Christ could not have suffered passion since passion entails movement and therefore harm to the mind. Propassion is lack of movement in the mind. "Pre-emotion" does not, in effect, result from an external *phantasia* but has to do with the functioning of the mind. Passion is about harm to the mind while propassion is about lack of harm. In other words, propassion is not a "pre-emotion" resulting from a shock of some sort but a state of mind that has not been dominated or harmed by passion. While Jerome is thinking of propassion in terms of involuntary first movements, Lombard finds propassion where the mind lacks movement. That Christ only began to be sad reflects the fact that sadness did not move his

57 Lombard, *Sent.* III, d. 15, Ch. 2.3, my translation.

mind. Lombard is not imagining that "beginning to be sad" has anything to do with involuntary reactions.

Lombard's scholastic methodology greatly affects the way he looks at the issue and here too he is far from Jerome. What especially interests him is showing how two seemingly contradictory statements can both be true. From one point of view Christ did suffer fear and sadness. From another point of view he did not suffer fear and sadness. A statement following Lombard's quotation from Jerome shows how this is the case – and that Jerome's meaning must be understood in this bifocal way:

> According to this distinction (of Jerome) it is sometimes said that Christ did not truly fear while at other times it is said that he truly feared, in that he had true fear and sadness – but not as passions and not from a condition of necessity.[58]

There are two ways of talking about Christ's fear and sadness. Christ both feared and did not fear, was sad and not sad. He had true fear and sadness if we are talking about propassion but he did not have true fear and sadness if we are talking about passion. In such manner does Lombard neatly resolve contradictory viewpoints, as designed by his methodology.

Radically different also is the distinction Lombard makes at the end of my last quotation between emotions that result from a condition of necessity and those taken on voluntarily (further supported in a paragraph that follows, quoting Augustine).[59] Christ suffered propassion voluntarily. Far from encasing propassion in that which is involuntary, propassion now represents the opposite. Again, questions come to mind. (a) We have been told that propassion reflects, as with Christ, an unmoved mind and, now, that Christ took on propassion voluntarily, but what does this tell us about the nature of propassion as such? If propassion is for Christ voluntary what is its nature? Christ took on sadness and fear voluntarily but what is the difference between the sadness and fear suffered by Christ and that of other humans? What is the difference between the sadness and fear found in propassion and that found in passion? In the one case there is destruction of the mind and in the other not, but how can sadness and fear have a harmful effect in the one case and not in the other? (b) In seeing propassion as

58 Lombard, *Sent.* III, d. 15, Ch. 2.3, my translation.

59 Lombard, *Sent.* III, d. 15, Ch. 2.4. See also Ch. 1.12.

voluntary is Lombard imagining that it has something to do with the activity of the mind? Propassion does not, unlike passion, harm the mind but is the mind somehow deeply related to the very nature of propassion? If propassion is found with a mind that is unmoved, as Lombard infers (wrongly) from Jerome, and if propassion is voluntarily arrived at, could it be that propassion now has something to do with reason – perhaps created by reason?

Lombard does mention that all humans suffer propassion and passion, but without explanation. Nowhere does he show how it is possible for ordinary humans to experience propassion. Nothing indicates that he found propassion important or relevant to our understanding of the situations of ordinary humans. Nothing indicates that it is a common experience of mankind. No mention is made of propassions originating from sudden movements. Nothing is said about ticklings of our senses or minds; nothing about "bad thoughts." He is silent about positive and negative ways of dealing with affects such as anger. Passed by also is how lust for a woman exemplifies these two approaches, how a natural reaction can slide into sin.

How could it be that Lombard's methodology was all about coming to grips with divergent or contradictory views and yet no place was found for Jerome's true thinking on propassion? The omission was surely not by chance. It was not only that scholastic methodology (built on Abelard's *Sic et Non*) did not lend itself to contextual or historical thinking. More important, note the tools used: abstract reason and logic. Jerome, in the footprint of the Stoics, had pointed to events and reactions outside of reason and logic.

Alexander of Hales

Peter Lombard's decisive shift away from Jerome's understanding of propassion was to be built upon by Bonaventure, Aquinas, and many other scholastics. Not everyone, however, was immediately convinced. Alexander of Hales takes note in Distinction 15 of his *Commentary on the Sentences* of Lombard's views but what really interests him and what guides his discussion is Jerome's actual thinking on propassion. He wrote his *Commentary* between 1220 and 1227, some twenty-five years before Bonaventure's *Commentary* and around thirty years before Aquinas' *Commentary*. In discussions of Christ's sadness and distress (*coepit tristari et maestus esse*), Alexander brings in from the *Glossa ordinaria*, in four locations, Jerome's statement that "subitus motus cui non consentitur est propassio."[60] Christ's sadness and distress are explained by a propassion and propassion is "a sudden movement that is not consented to." He saw not only that propassions come about suddenly and are involuntary but that reason and emotion are something else. In one instance he points to an interpretation that considers propassions neither good nor bad.[61] And he recognizes throughout that propassions are common human experiences. Distinguishing like other scholastics the intellective and sensitive appetites, he concludes that a sudden movement occurred in Christ's sensitive part but was not consented to by his intellect. His sadness and fear, his propassions, are found in the sensitive part – not in the intellective. Christ experienced an involuntary reaction and this pre-emotion was not – as could be inferred from Lombard – something originating in the mind. Following his final reference to Jerome's definition, Alexander quotes Jerome's illustration (above, pp. 197–8, theme 8) of the meaning of propassion for ordinary Christians:

> Passio reputatur in vitio, et propassio, licet initii culpam habeat, tamen non tenetur in crimine. Unde anima videntis mulierem est titillata et propassione percussa; si vero consentit et de cogitatione affectum fecerit, de propassione passionem fecit.[62]

There is a beginning of culpability involved in a propassion but propassion is not a crime. The sensual tickling in looking at a woman is not a passion but a propassion, as long as one does not give in to these feelings.

Like others, of course, Alexander of Hales had no idea that these views were originally derived from Stoicism. He believes they somehow relate to Aristotle's *Ethics*.[63]

Bonaventure: The setting for Erasmus' radical rewrite

Early on in his treatise Erasmus states that Bonaventure "skilfully explains in Book III, Distinction 15, of his *Commentary on the Sentences of Peter Lombard*" what Augustine and others confirm, that Jesus not

60 Alexander of Hales, *Commentary on the Sentences* III, d. 15, Nos. 54e, 5, 9, and 31b.

61 Alexander of of Hales, *Sent.* III, d. 15, No. 5.

62 Alexander of Hales, *Sent.* III, d. 15, No. 54e.

63 Cf. Alexander of Hales, *Sent.* III, d. 15, Nos. 27, 32, 54e and Aristotle, *Nicomachean Ethics*, Ch. 5. Seneca is brought into the discussion five times regarding the wiseman's unbending virtue and lack of emotion.

only took on a human nature but was subject to many of our afflictions (1270B).[64] But why does he bring in Bonaventure and even advise readers to take note of his "skilfully" argued account? Distinction 15 is all about Christ's propassion and Bonaventure appears to have gone further than any scholastic prior to Aquinas in radicalizing Jerome's propassion thesis. In the process he does not take the discussion closer to what was to be Erasmus' argument but even further away – which might seem impossible. He argues at length that Christ's propassion was such because it was thoroughly infused by reason. Propassion is no longer something that resulted from some type of mental or physical shock, prior to any possible rational and emotional response, but something that with Christ was brought about by reason. Contrast Erasmus' thinking, extrapolated from a knowledge of Stoic *oikeiosis* not found in more than a thousand years:[65] (a) Christ did not suffer propassion – not Jerome's Stoic-rooted propassion nor Bonaventure's scholastic-rooted rational propassion – but passion (see below, chapter 2). Full-fledged emotion "not only disturbed his mind (or at least the lower part of it), but most violently overwhelmed it (non turbarit solum, sed vehementissime perturbarit)" (1285F). (b) Christ's emotion had nothing to do with reason but arose involuntarily, from natural instinct.

The fundamental reason Erasmus brought in Bonaventure was the same as that which led him to bring in Origen and Gellius. He was setting the stage. He was bringing attention to a prestigious view in order to (silently) rewrite it. Although his ultimate goal remained the same – to demonstrate that Christ suffered emotional breakdown from natural instinct – each of these authors allowed him to explore and develop surrounding issues from a different angle.

Objections to Christ's propassion

Citing Jerome's and Lombard's distinguishing Christ's propassion from passion (without noting the gulf separating their thinking), Bonaventure begins by referring to the contrary views held by some unnamed

64 On the structure and particular nature of Bonaventure's *Commentary on the Sentences*, see Rosemann, *The Story of a Great Book*, 70–80. On Franciscan education and the context of Bonaventure's *Commentary*, see Roest, *A History of Franciscan Education*, esp. 123–33.

65 A comparison of Erasmus' knowledge and employment of Stoicism with that of Ambrose (d. 397) in works such as *De officiis ministrorum*, modeled on Cicero's *De officiis*, would be of interest.

persons.[66] What they object to is the claim, found in the *Glossa ordinaria* on Matthew 5:22, that with Christ "propassion is a sudden movement which has not been consented to by reason" (propassio est subitus motus, cui ex ratione non consentitur).[67] Their argument, as described by Bonaventure (my translation), is as follows:

(1) Propassion is defined as a venial (minor or pardonable) sin in addition to being a sudden movement not consented to[68] but Christ could not have experienced a venial sin.
(2) It could not be that Christ suffered even a sudden movement not consented to for with him reason preceded everything.
(3) What Christ experienced, deduced from (1) and (2), is not propassion but passion. If Christ could not have suffered a propassion in that a propassion is venial, his suffering had to have been passion rather than propassion and since with Christ reason preceded everything his passion had to have come into being by means of reason.

In holding that propassion is a venial sin the objectors are clearly considering the *Gloss* on Matthew 5:28 (not 5:22), which quotes Jerome. The problem seen – very legitimately – is that Jerome does not explain how propassion can relate to Christ if propassion is a venial sin (above, pp. 197–8, theme 8) and Christ was without sin. What is denied here is not propassion (as described by Jerome) but only the applicability to Christ.

The second criticism, however, makes an assumption that had the potential of destroying the very foundation of Jerome's thought. While the first criticism shows that one aspect of propassion does not apply to Christ, the second criticism rejects, with regard to Christ, the very pins on which propassion had been built. The whole purpose had been to separate reason from pre-emotion, to show that pre-emotion precedes the action of reason. Now, however, it is held that with Christ reason

66 Bonaventure, *Sent.* III, d. 15, dub. 4 (*Opera*, ed. Quaracchi, 3:342). Nowhere does Bonaventure, unlike Erasmus (1271E), give the Greek for propassion – for the reason, most importantly, that he did not see the Greek heritage.
67 Quotes from the entire discussion in the *Glossa ordinaria*, actually of Matthew 5:28, are found in n. 35 above.
68 On medieval debates as to whether first movements are venial sins (most often concluded in the affirmative), see Knuuttila, *Emotions in Ancient and Medieval Philosophy*, 178–93. An indispensable source here, and for many related issues, is Lottin, *Psychologie et morale aux XIIe et XIIIe siècles*.

had to have preceded propassion but since this was impossible, considering Jerome's definition of propassion, Christ did not experience propassion but passion. While Alexander of Hales (one of Bonaventure's teachers) had made a major issue only twenty-five years earlier of propassion as a sudden and unforeseen movement and had found the concept extremely relevant to Christ's experience, something radically different has now emerged. Lombard had broached the idea that reason had something important to do with pre-emotion but the critics referred to by Bonaventure simply assume that reason has to have preceded anything that applies to Christ. The contention that propassion can be with Christ a movement not consented to by reason is rejected out of hand. While the first objection appears well taken, the second may seem inexplicable, unjustifiable, unprecedented, and utterly transforming.

Why are these objectors so certain that Christ's reason had to precede everything and that this being the case his reason had to have preceded propassion? The thesis, as reported by Bonaventure, is set forth as though it were self-evident. The answer may well have something significant to do with scholastic methodology, a methodology that was built on "reason," seen as the ability to solve problems by making multitudes of logical distinctions. Whatever the links that we are missing may be, if lack of reason makes propassion inapplicable to Christ and complete reason makes passion entirely applicable, how long would it be before the entire propassion argument collapsed – even with regard to ordinary mortals?

Bonaventure redefines Christ's propassion

While Peter Lombard had implied that reason is somehow involved in Christ's propassion, Bonaventure shows how. While the unnamed critics discussed above explain why propassion is not applicable to Christ, Bonaventure shows that it is applicable. Propassion is not, with Christ, something that precedes reason or is a venial sin. With Christ reason precedes propassion. It is not necessarily the case that propassion, defined as a sudden movement, "contradicts" reason.[69] It is the case with us in that our senses move contrary to reason, but it is not the case with Christ. Christ's fear of death, even if a sudden movement, was in complete accord with reason. Propassions were with him not

69 Bonaventure, *Sent.* III, d. 15, dub. 4 (ed. Quaracchi, p. 342).

involuntary reactions which reason reacted to but affections voluntarily put into place and circumscribed by reason.[70] Propassions are with us negative in that they are antagonistic to reason while with Christ they were preceded by and governed by reason. While with Jerome propassion is "a sudden movement not consented to by reason," most certainly not Christ's reason, now a situation is described which is exactly the reverse: reason precedes propassion. Unacknowledged is the fact that this move reverses what had been the entire raison d' être of the concept, not only with Stoicism – Bonaventure like other theologians had no idea that pre-emotion had been a fundamental of Stoic thinking – but with Jerome, in the wake of Stoicism, and those who had followed.[71]

And yet, though reason is responsible for propassion, reason and propassion are also described in terms of the distinction of Aristotle and Augustine between the sensitive and the intellective parts of the soul.[72] Propassion is "a passion of the sensual parts or of the natural virtues" (propassio dicit passionem partis sensualis, vel virtutis naturalis) existing below reason.[73] With Christ, unlike with us, there was a perfect obedience (*obedientia perfecta*) of the inferior to the superior, of the senses to reason. Since his fear of death was in the senses, it is with all justification referred to as a propassion. This is what, according to Bonaventure, Peter Lombard and Jerome mean where they say the passions were in Christ.

But how, we may wonder, can pre-emotion, something that comes as a shock to mind or body, exist in the sensitive part of the soul – and be

---

70 Thomas Aquinas' view closely relates. "In Christ, however, his movements of sorrow arose only according to the dictates of higher reason, inasmuch as his reason decreed the appropriate manner by which his sensuality could undergo sorrow" (*Sent.* III, d. 15, q. 2, a. 2, sol. 1). Aquinas began his *Commentary on the Sentences* (*Scriptum super Sententiis*) about the time Bonaventure finished his, in 1252. Jill Kraye holds, at odds with the evidence, that Thomas Aquinas' rationalistic interpretation of Christ's propassion – in line, allegedly, with the views of Thomas Wright (d. 1623) and Edward Reynolds (d. 1676) – was that of Jerome. See "Ἀπάθεια and Προπάθειαι in Early Modern Discussions of the Passions," 247, 248, and 251.

71 Nowhere does Aquinas mention, much less discuss, any aspect of Jerome's actual argument – other than the distinction between beginning to be sad and being sad. Considering his encyclopedic knowledge we can be sure this was not an oversight. He saw that Jerome's thinking was fundamentally at odds with his scholastic way of addressing issues as well as, in particular, Aristotle. Propassion with Aquinas (see the notes below) is (a) not a sudden jolt to the senses, (b) not involuntary, (c) not separate from reason, and (d) not experienced by all people but only one. Reason at all times precedes, activates, infuses, and governs propassion.

72 Following the lead of Aristotle and Augustine, Aquinas likewise accepts that humans have a sensitive appetite as well as an intellective (ST I, q. 80).

73 Bonaventure, *Sent.* III, d. 15, dub. 4 (ed. Quaracchi, p. 342), my translation.

already an emotion? Analysis shows that Bonaventure redefines even the word "propassion." Propassion is now not a "pre-emotion" but a "small emotion," a *passio diminuta.* "Small emotion," we can see, is something that is in existence, an actual emotion – not, like pre-emotion, something that comes before emotion, a "first movement" that is involuntary. The concept of pre-emotion had originated in the desire to separate emotion and reason from what was not emotion and not reason. Pre-passion was not a product of reason but something that reason deals with after the fact. Defining propassion as "a small passion," rather than something that comes before passion, pre-passion, allowed Bonaventure to more convincingly show that Christ's reason preceded "propassion."[74] But again, how had this new understanding of propassion evolved? Bonaventure states that his description is "according to accepted understanding."[75]

This redefinition of propassion was bound to affect the way propassion was conceptualized even for ordinary humans – notwithstanding that Bonaventure has little to say in any of his writings about the emotions of ordinary humans.[76] And while Bonaventure holds with the *Gloss* that venial sin is with us found in propassion, a theme that accords with Jerome, he says nothing about any need for ordinary humans to assent or not assent to a pre-emotion. Indeed, pre-emotion for ordinary humans seems to immediately equate with both unreason and "small emotion."

---

74 Where Jerome states that Christ "began" to be sad, distinguished from actually being sad, he was not imagining that Christ had suffered a part of real passion. Madigan certainly errs in translating propassions, as defined by Jerome, as "half-passions." See "Ancient and High-Medieval Interpretations of Jesus in Gethsemane," 165 and 166.

75 Bonaventure, *Sent.* III, d. 15, dub. 4 (ed. Quaracchi, p. 342). Aquinas explains Jerome's distinction between beginning to be sad and being sad (Matt: 26, 37) in various ways. Christ did not experience the "perfect" passion of sorrow but the (imperfect) "initial" stage (ST III, q. 15, a. 6, ad. 1). Passion is an alteration of reason whereas propassion is not. A passion transforms one (*immutatur*), and is "complete," whereas a propassion does not transform one (*non immutatur*) and, by implication, is not complete. Since Christ's emotions were in no way transformed he suffered only propassion. Propassion "begins in the sense appetite but does not go any farther" (ST III, q. 15, a. 4, resp.). In short, a propassion is a passion that is "unaltered" or "incomplete" or "not transformed" or "imperfect" – and yet reason inheres in propassion but not passion. Since Christ's reason was in no way moved, unlike that of other humans, only he suffered propassion.

76 See Gondreau, *The Passions of Christ's Soul*, 132. Aquinas discusses human emotions in *Summa Theologiae* I-II, Questions 22–48; however, their interactions with reason, which is supposed to govern them (ST I, q. 81, a. 3; ST I–II, q. 38, ad. 1), are ultimately obscure. See King, "Aquinas on the Passions," 131. See also Robert Pasnau's extensive commentary and translation of Aquinas' *The Treatise on Human Nature: Summa Theologiae, Ia 75–89.*

Not only does reason govern Christ's propassion, true emotion is found in his propassions. How could something preceded by reason not, he imagines, be perfect? While holding firm in denying full-fledged passion to Christ, Bonaventure filled propassion, *passio diminuta*, with highest emotion.[77] He emphasizes, that is, the deep reality of Christ's emotions even if only propassions. Consider first of all, he tells us, Christ's physical pain. As the Gospels testify and as the Catholic faith holds, Christ experienced, without any doubt, the true passion of pain. "Dicendum quod absque dubio, sicut Evangellium dicit, et fides catholica sentit, vera doloris passio fuit in Christo."[78] And this pain was extreme ("fuit acerbissimus et acutissimus").[79] It was of two types, physical pain and perception of physical pain:

> As his flesh was passible and was pierced by nails, and as he possessed the ability to perceive the pain, his soul suffered with his bodily injury. Since, therefore, there were two kinds of pain in Christ, namely true injury and the true perception of the injury, there can be no doubt that Christ experienced the true passion (*vera passio*) of pain.[80]

Erasmus was to bring up and focus on a third and, to his mind, infinitely more important type of suffering – deriving from the mind alone.

In showing that Christ suffered pain, as propassion, Bonaventure, like Peter Lombard and other scholastics, was intent on showing that Hilary of Poitiers did not mean what it may appear that he meant.[81] Hilary holds that Christ did not feel pain, although he suffered, which may seem "false, doubtful and erroneous" but properly understood this is not the

---

77 Aquinas also finds that Christ suffered deepest emotion notwithstanding that it was only a propassion. Versus the Stoics, some sadness, as Augustine proves (*City of God*, 14, ch. 8f), is praiseworthy and useful: "In order to atone for the sins of all men, Christ suffered the most profound sadness, absolutely speaking, but not so great that it exceeded the rule of reason" (ST III, q. 46, a. 6, ad. 2. Cf. I-II, q. 64, a. 2, ad. 2). Reason dictated every aspect of Christ's senses and yet he suffered "maximum" emotion. When all the distinctions are in place it can be seen that he suffered true sadness (*vera tristitia*) (ST III, q. 15, a. 6, resp.), even true fear (ST III, q. 15, a. 7, ad. 2; *Sent.* III, d. 15, q. 2, a. 2, qc. 3), and true anger (ST III, q. 15, a. 9, ad. 1).

78 Bonaventure, *Sent.* III, d. 16, a. 1, q. 1 (ed. Quaracchi, p. 346).

79 Bonaventure, *Sent.* III, d. 16, a. 1, q. 2 (ed. Quaracchi, p. 349).

80 Bonaventure, *Sent.* III, d. 16, a. 1, q. 1 (ed. Quaracchi, p. 346), my translation.

81 "Despite vividly registering their initial impressions of unorthodoxy, Bonaventure and virtually all of his high-scholastic contemporaries strove to interpret and revise Hilary so as to retrieve him from suspicion of error." See Madigan, "On the High-Medieval Reception of Hilary of Poitiers's Anti-'Arian' Opinion," 216.

case. What Hilary means is that Christ did not give in to the passions.[82] He felt pain but as a propassion, a *passio diminuta*, governed by reason.

Even allowing for the saturation of propassion by reason, against everything propassion had once stood for, there are questions of logic: (1) If propassion is a small passion, a *passio diminuta* (leaving aside pre-passion or beginning of passion), how can it be that Christ suffered "true passion"? (2) Even more troubling, how can it be that he suffered the most extreme pain and yet that this was only a small or incomplete passion (*passio diminuta*)? (3) How can "true passion" be found in both passion as such, the evil emotion of ordinary humans, and propassion, the reason-based good emotion of Christ?[83]

Bonaventure's *turbatio* – and Erasmus' referral

Erasmus makes a point of the fact that *turbatio* has been used as a synonym for *propassio*. Why does he find it important to bring out this alleged tie? And why does he attribute the view to St Bernard? As quoted earlier (p. 185, thesis 2):

> [Jerome wrongly calls the Redeemer's suffering *propassio*, rather than *passio*,] something that, to use St. Bernard's distinction, disturbed (turbarit) [Christ] but did not overwhelm (perturbarit) him. (1285E–F)

Analysis reveals something strange. In making this statement Erasmus was not looking at St Bernard's writings but directly at Bonaventure's

82 "Non enim vult negare sensum et experimentum passionis, sed vim et dominium passionis." See Bonaventure, *Sent.* III, d. 16, dub. 1 (ed. Quaracchi, p. 359). Elsewhere: Hilary "non excludit sensum doloris a Christo secundum humanam naturam, sed secundum divinam." "Hilarius non vult ostendere, Christum non habuisse verum dolorem, sed non habuisse causam doloris." See Bonaventure, *Sent.* III, d. 16, a. 1, q. 1 (ed. Quaracchi, p. 347).

83 Turning to Aquinas, if propassion thoroughly represents reason how can it "begin" to represent something (sadness) that is not reason, something that is imperfect? If sadness writ large alters reason why does sadness writ small not alter reason – to a small degree? Christ distinctively represented the sadness found in propassion, something imperfect, and yet, contrary to Jerome's thinking, this was not something that needed to be dealt with or curtailed, since it was infused with reason. Looked at from one angle, Christ's emotions, his propassions, were extremely limited in that they had nothing to do with the full-blown emotions allowed by passion (unreason or anti-reason). Looked at from another angle, he suffered emotion to the highest degree possible because his reason dictated every aspect of his emotion. Propassion and passion both represented highest emotion.

extensive discussions in Distinction 15. Bonaventure here details the differences between *turbatio* and *perturbatio*, their relationships to *propassio* and *passio* respectively, and explains why and how Christ applied reason to *turbatio* but not *perturbatio*. In chapter 2 below and Part VI I will work out the ways in which Erasmus rejects the claim of theologians, Bonaventure being one, that Christ did not suffer *perturbatio* or *passio* as well as the claim that reason had something to do with Christ's emotion – whether reason is said to have halted his *propassio/turbatio* or, with the likes of Bonaventure, created it. Christ's emotion in the Passion was as strong at the beginning of his ordeal as at the end and entirely brought about by natural instinct. Not least, I will explain why, in response to Colet and the devotionalist impulses of his time, Erasmus refers to Bernard rather than Bonaventure, the source he was actually looking at.

Bonaventure's lengthy explications of the differences between a *turbatio* (and not just a *propassio*) built from reason, as against a *perturbatio* (and not just a *passio*) opposed to reason, appear to be uncommon or unique among scholastic discussions.[84] No such distinction is made by Peter Lombard or Alexander of Hales.[85] Albert the Great and Thomas Aquinas, who wrote his *Commentary on the Sentences* a few years after Bonaventure's work, mention the distinction but make little of it.[86] The issue was about more than words. Bonaventure's purpose was to build up and refocus *propassio/passio* issues by means of *turbatio/perturbatio*.

Bonaventure gives many scholastic-framed reasons as to why Christ did not, unlike ordinary humans, suffer *perturbatio* and why, against Hilary, Christ did suffer sadness but as *turbatio* and not *perturbatio*. With *turbatio* as well as *propassio* the discussion centres on Christ's sadness.[87] Against (*sed contra*) the idea that

---

84 P. Augustin Sépinski does not show that Bonaventure makes this *turbatio/perturbatio* distinction, much less draws out its importance. See his *La psychologie du Christ chez Saint Bonaventure*.

85 Lombard here brings in the word *turbatio* in quotes of Jesus from Matthew, Mark, Luke, and John but never contrasts *turbatio* with *perturbatio*, or even uses the latter word. Also at odds with Bonaventure, *turbatio* is connected not with propassion but with passion. "Aliquando vero movetur et turbatur, et tunc passio est." See *Sent.* III, d. 15, ch. 1.11, 2.2, 2.3. Alexander Hales gives a quote of Gregory the Great (540–604 CE) that uses the two words. See *Sent.* III, d. 15.6 (ed. Quarracchi [1954], v. 3, p. 152).

86 See below, n. 91.

87 Bonaventure, *Sent.* III, d. 15, a. 2, q. 2 (ed. Quaracchi, p. 338). The translations that follow are mine.

Christ did not experience sadness he cites Isaiah, Proverbs, Seneca, and Augustine:

(1) Isaiah 42:4 states: "Non erit tristis neque turbulentus" (Never will the servant of God be sad and never will he break down).
(2) According to Proverbs 12:21, "Non contristabit iustum" (no sadness will befall the just). Christ represented highest justice; therefore, he could not have been sad.
(3) Seneca proves in many ways that "tristitia non cadit in sapientem" (sadness is not found in wisdom) because "virtutem nihil potest laedere" (nothing can damage virtue).[88] If Christ was truly wise, it is clear that his virtue could not have been compromised by sadness.
(4) According to Augustine, nothing is sad except what is against our will.[89] Nothing can have been against Christ's will so he could not have been sad.

In response Bonaventure contends that Christ did suffer sadness.[90] John states (11:33) that "Iesu autem infremuit spiritu et turbavit se ipsum" (Jesus groaned in spirit and was troubled), "which shows that *turbatio* and *tristitia* did not precede reason but were subject to reason." We can see that Christ was sad here, but note how easily and certainly Bonaventure assumes that the passage indicates that reason had to have governed Christ's sadness. Nothing in the text itself indicates (for us) that this is the meaning. Considered in context, Jesus groaned in spirit and was troubled because he saw Martha, and the Jews with her, weeping because her brother Lazarus had died. On hearing two days earlier that Lazarus was ill, Jesus stated (not pointed out by Bonaventure): "This illness will not end in death; it has come for the glory of God, to bring glory to the Son of God" (John 11:4). Most probably Bonaventure was imagining that Christ had foreknowledge of the event that brought about his sadness just as he had foreknowledge of what would happen to Lazarus, that he would rise from the dead, and from this found cause to deduce that Christ's reason preceded and governed his *turbatio* and sadness. And since John 11:33 makes no mention of *perturbatio*, Bonaventure was free to theorize that other humans suffer *perturbatio* as well as *turbatio* but not Christ.

88 For the former quote, see *De clementia* (*On Mercy*) 2.5.
89 *City of God*, 14.15.
90 Bonaventure, *Sent.* III, d. 15, a. 2, q. 2, concl. (ed. Quaracchi, pp. 338–9).

Bonaventure then replies to each of the four statements or arguments (see above) that seem to deny that Christ suffered sadness:

(1) What is said in Isaiah does not exclude all types of sadness but only *"tristitiam perturbantem."* The problem for us, as not apparently for Bonaventure, is that the passage in Isaiah referred to, 42:4 (in the Vulgate), is not supportive: "Non erit tristis neque turbulentus." The sadness excluded here is not that of *perturbatio* but *turbatio*. *Perturbatio* is not mentioned.
(2) The denial in Proverbs that sadness is found with the just ("Non contristabit iustum"), and that Christ was obviously just, must be understood as referring only, argues Bonaventure, to that sadness, *tristitiam perturbantem*, which overturns the state of mind "quae statum mentis evertit" of the just.
(3) Seneca must be interpreted in similar fashion. "Seneca was not attempting to prove that *tristitia turbans* is not in wisdom but that wisdom is not in *tristitia perturbans*."[91] The wiseman may be sad and disturbed where a *turbatio* exists but he does not allow a *perturbatio*, so here he is not sad and not overwhelmed (nec tristatur nec perturbatur). Only *perturbatio* is a deflection of reason from justice.
(4) And regarding Augustine's assertion that nothing can go against Christ's will, what he was stating is that nothing can go against the will of absolute reason (de voluntate rationis absoluta). He was not talking about the will that handles the senses and takes account of circumstances. A problem here of course is that Bonaventure has contended that Christ's sadness was preceded and governed by reason and was taken on voluntarily. What can "true sadness" mean within this context?

---

91 Bonaventure, *Sent.* III, d. 15, a. 2, q. 2, concl. 3 (ed. Quaracchi, pp. 338–9). "Seneca enim non vult probare quod tristitia turbans non sit in sapiente, sed quod non est in sapiente tristitia perturbans." In fact, of course, Seneca demonstrates that a pre-emotion (or *propassio*, which Bonaventure ties in with *turbatio*) can develop into sadness if wisdom does not reject it. Wisdom is not here "in sadness" but the contrary. Aquinas' understanding of Seneca compares with Bonaventure's. See *Sent.* III, d. 15, q. 2, a. 2, sol. 1 ad 2: "Perturbari dicitur ex toto turbari, et hoc est quando turbatio inferioris partis ad superiorem pervenit, ut eius ordo turbetur. Et hoc non est in aliquo sapiente nec in Christo fuit; et sic concludunt rationes Senecae." Albert the Great states, *Sent.* III, d. 15, a. 8 ad 1: "tristitia turbatio sit in viro sapiente, tamen non est perturbatio: Christus enim non est minus sapiens quam philosophi."

A number of reasons can be adduced as to why Bonaventure wanted to make the *turbatio/perturbatio* distinction in addition to the *propassio/passio* distinction and that unlike Peter Lombard and previous theologians he does not deign to even mention, much less quote, Jerome's statement on the difference between Christ's "beginning" to be sad and actually being sad:

(a) *Turbatio*, as I have already shown, allowed Bonaventure to redefine propassion. "Propassions" were not now pre-passions, affects prior to the consent of reason, affects that needed to be halted by reason. Now "propassions" were, with Christ at least, feelings preceded and governed by reason.
(b) *Turbatio* is focused on because *turbatio*, unlike *propassio* and the use of *propassio* from Jerome onwards, does not in any way connote a "pre-emotion." *Turbatio* is simply a disturbance.
(c) *Turbatio* allowed Bonaventure to talk about a "small emotion" as distinct from a pre-emotion.
(d) *Turbatio* tied more directly than *propassio* (as exemplified by Bonaventure's referral above to John 11:33) to words found in the Bible.
(e) Allowing Christ *turbatio* did not necessarily conflict (unlike propassion defined as something prior to reason) with the idea that reason created it.
(f) Unlike pre-passion *turbatio* did not call into question the contention that Christ's emotions were entirely voluntary.
(g) As exemplified by sadness, *turbatio* is an emotion, not something that precedes an emotion.
(h) Where Hilary comes into the picture, *turbatio* better shows that Christ does have true emotions.
(i) The contrast of *turbatio* and *perturbatio* builds up the contrast between the sadness of ordinary humans and that of Christ. Ordinary humans suffer not only *passio* (full-fledged emotion) but *perturbatio* (extreme disturbance). On the one hand Christ's reason was not destroyed by a *perturbatio* and on the other his reason created and governed every *turbatio*.

Types of sadness, anger, and fear

Bonaventure distinguishes three types of sadness that humans can experience, only one of which relates to Christ. Although Christ experienced true sadness (among other emotions) he did not experience every type of true sadness. Humans can experience sadness that is "beyond the imperium of reason" or "contrary to the judgement of reason" or, opposite both these types, "subject to the imperium and judgement of reason." Christ experienced only the latter type.

> (1) That sadness is beyond the imperium of reason which arises from necessity and surreptitiously, as a first movement (motus primi). This movement is common to both the wise and the unwise, and to the good and the evil. (2) That is true sadness which is contrary to the right judgement of reason, when reason is subjected to the senses and is not only disturbed but even overwhelmed (nec tantum turbatur sed etiam perturbatur). (3) On the other hand, that sadness is according to the imperium and judgement of reason when someone is made sad by the dictate and sway of reason (ratione dictante et suadente). In such a case a person is bound to be sad. I say therefore that with Christ sadness was only of this third type, in which there was no sadness unless dictated by reason (quia de nullo tristatus fuit, nisi secundum quod dictabat ei ratio).[92]

(1) The referral to a "first movement" that arises from necessity and is unforeseen and is common to the wise and unwise, the good person and the evil, accords with not only Jerome but – though little seen by Bonaventure – Origen and Stoics such as Seneca, not to mention what was to be Erasmus' understanding of Stoicism (above, Part IV). What does not agree with Jerome is the contention (a) that a first movement is "true sadness" (i.e., true emotion) rather than something that precedes true sadness and (b) that this sadness is not a false judgment of reason but irrelevant to reason (whereas ideally it would be comprised of reason).

(2) The second type of "true sadness" is found where reason is not only disturbed but overwhelmed by (the emotion of) sadness (nec tantum turbatur sed etiam perturbatur). Here there is a one-to-one relationship between "true sadness" and opposition to the right judgment of reason. Presumably, the greater the sadness the greater the opposition to reason. It is not merely that reason is one thing and the senses another; the senses bring down reason. Here again Bonaventure is referring to the sadness experienced by ordinary humans. Ordinary humans can experience *perturbatio* as well as *turbatio* but Christ experienced only the latter.

92 *Sent.* III, d. 15, a. 2, q. 2 (ed. Quaracchi, p. 338), my translation.

Erasmus' thesis, as it relates to Christ, directly contradicts the implications of this type of sadness: (a) Jesus suffered *perturbatio* and not simply *turbatio* – his mind was not only disturbed but most violently overwhelmed (non turbarit solum, sed vehementissime perturbarit)" (1285E–F) – and yet (b) his reason was entirely unaffected (see below, chapter 2).

(3) The third type of "true sadness" is the opposite of both 1 and 2 in that here sadness is dictated by reason, "the imperium of reason and the judgement of reason." One could imagine that there would be no sadness where reason has not been harmed, but this is not the argument. Sadness is spawned by reason. There is no sadness *unless* brought about by "the dictate and sway of reason" (ratione dictante et suadente). It is not merely that sadness is not in opposition to reason, reason subjects propassions such as sadness to its absolute rule and even seems to decide on the content. Reason, that is, does not take action after the arrival of a propassion but precedes propassion and "dictates" the sadness propassion embodies.[93] Christ, and seemingly only Christ, exemplified this type of sadness. Contrast again the entire purpose and meaning of the propassion concept with Origen and Jerome, not to mention Seneca and the Stoics.

Although Bonaventure is primarily interested in Christ's sadness, he follows up with discussions of anger and fear.[94] It is possible to be angry in a number of ways, but with Christ anger did not touch the eye of the mind (*oculum mentis*) and, more than this, was set in place and governed by reason – all of which compares with his sadness.[95] Although it has been held (*sed contra* 3) that Christ's perfect humility, perfect gentleness, and lack of pride (Matthew 11:29) entailed that he never had anger, this is not the case. There is no necessary conflict between his humility, gentleness, and lack of pride, and his anger. Anger (unlike with Stoics) can represent virtue as well as vice. And with regard to Aristotle's view

93 Compare Aquinas: "Sed in Christo nunquam surgebat motus tristitiae nisi secundum dictamen superioris rationis, quando scilicet dictabat ratio quod sensualitas tristaretur secundum convenientiam naturae suae; et ideo non fuit in eo tristitia rationem pervertens, nec fuit necessaria, sed voluntaria quodammodo" (*Sent.* III, d. 15, q. 2, a. 2, sol. 1). "In the man Jesus Christ there was no movement of the sensitive parts that was not arranged by reason" (ST III, q. 19, a. 2, resp.). His reason preceded, activated, infused, and governed his emotions at every step.

94 While Lombard discussed sorrow, fear, and sensible pain, Bonaventure added anger and Aquinas wonder.

95 Bonaventure, *Sent.* III, d. 15, a. 2, q. 3 (ed. Quaracchi, pp. 339–40).

that anger is the boiling of blood around the heart[96] and the contention of John of Damascus (d. 749) that it causes an evaporating of the gall bladder[97] and the conclusion from this that anger is a perturbatio that Christ could not have had (*sed contra* 4), the truth is that it was very suitable for him to have this anger, but moderately (as a propassion).[98]

Regarding fear,[99] John 4:18 states that perfect charity casts out fear and Augustine writes that not fearing is a sign of perfection. Christ was highest perfection and therefore, it is argued, it was not possible that he feared.[100] In response Bonaventure differentiates various types of fear. As with sadness, however, those who deny fear in Christ do not deny, he believes, all fear in him but only fear that would precede or disturb (*perturbaret*) his reason. In taking on the defect of "passibility" (ability to feel or suffer), Christ did not take on the defects of disorder or of corruption. The final sentence of Distinction 15 tells us that Christ's fear of death was in the sensual part of his soul (like sadness), as Jerome (allegedly) and Lombard hold, and ought to be considered a propassion,[101] but the problem here, from a conceptual standpoint, is that his fear of death, like all his propassions, had been brought into being and was governed by the intellective part of his soul.

For Erasmus, of course, Christ's fear of death was not voluntary and not produced by abstract reason but was an intractable natural instinct, something that arises internally, a full-blown emotion – entirely separate from intellect. And he does not tack on referral to Christ's fear of death at the end of the discussion but places it at the very centre of thought.

The fact that Erasmus gives a specific location for Bonaventure's thought allows us to see very clearly what Bonaventure's thinking was – and that Erasmus' thinking radically differed. Erasmus may have appreciated Bonaventure's discussion more than that of some other scholastics, such as Aquinas (who was even more the logician), but his

96 Aristotle, *De anima*, 403a31.

97 John of Damascus, *De fide orthodoxa* I, c. 16.

98 Bonaventure, *Sent.* III, d. 15, a. 2, q. 3, sol. 4 (ed. Quaracchi, p. 340).

99 Bonaventure, *Sent.* III, d. 15, dub. 3 (ed. Quaracchi, pp. 341–2).

100 Augustine, *De diversis questionibus octaginta tribus*, 36.1.

101 Bonaventure, *Sent.* III, d. 15, a. 2, q. 3, dub. 4 (ed. Quaracchi, p. 342). Here again Bonaventure reinterprets Hilary, contending that he did not mean to remove fear from Christ, against scripture and the saints, but was talking about heretics. See *Sent.* III, d. 16, dub. 2 (ed. Quaracchi, p. 360).

purpose in referring to Bonaventure's discussion was only to provide – as was so often his procedure – background and a starting point.

2 Emotion versus Pre-Emotion: Correcting Bonaventure

While Part IV.1–2 above has detailed Erasmus' rationale for rewriting on both empirical and theoretical grounds the Stoic pre-emotion thesis – as set forth by Epictetus and described and illustrated by Gellius and "Colet" – the task at hand is to show how Erasmus criticizes and radically transforms the theological arguments so laboriously worked out (as described above) by Jerome and then scholastics such as Bonaventure.

First, consider again the statements quoted at the beginning of Part V (185–6), especially the reasoning found (the numbering is mine) in (3) and (4):

> Unde non ita nimis me delectat illa Hieronymi interpretatio, qua dicit, hanc in Redemtore molestitiam, propassionem fuisse, non passionem, quae illum, juxta divi Bernardi distinctionem, turbarit modo, non etiam perturbarit. Si passionem appellant eam, quae rationem a statu suo dimoveat, si perturbari vocant a statu mentis dimoveri, non reclamo. At ego non dubitem, & passionem nominare, quae mentem Jesu, saltem secundum inferiorem partem, non turbarit solum, sed vehementissime perturbarit. (1285E–F)
>
> (1) That [the evidence of Christ's emotional suffering] is why Jerome's interpretation holds no great attraction for me. He calls the Redeemer's suffering "propassion," rather than passion, (2) something that, to use St Bernard's distinction, disturbed (turbarit) but did not overwhelm (perturbarit) him. (3) If they [theologians] define "passion" (passio) as something that dethrones reason and "overwhelm" (perturbatio) as being driven out of one's mind, I do not object [to the distinguishing of *propassio* and *turbatio* from *passio* and *perturbatio*]. (4) But I should not hesitate also to call "passion" these feelings which not only disturbed Jesus' mind (or at least the lower part of it), but most violently overwhelmed it (non turbarit solum, sed vehementissime perturbarit).

Immediately following (4), the contention that emotion "not only disturbed" (non turbarit solum) Christ's mind "but most violently overwhelmed it" (sed vehementissime perturbarit), Erasmus summarizes and critiques the theological arguments that had been used to deny that Christ suffered true emotion and *perturbatio*. Each of these statements deserves careful attention. What we need to understand here as elsewhere is not simply Erasmus' conclusions but the way, from a philosophical standpoint, he reaches these conclusions – i.e., the workings of his mind.

(4a)

> Similarly, when the evangelist (Paul) says, "He began to be distressed and dismayed" [Matt. 26:37], does this really mean that distress and dismay merely touched (alligerit) his mind and did not take it over? Even though he cries out that his soul is brimming with troubles ...? (1285F)

We need to rethink, that is, the meaning of "He began to be distressed and dismayed." Is Jerome's interpretation really correct? Jerome states that "it is one thing to be sad and another to *begin* to be sad." Is there really a difference here between *being* sad and *beginning* to be sad? In fact, argues Erasmus, there is no reason to conclude that "began" means that Christ's emotions were tiny or undeveloped. "Began" does not entail a limitation of distress and dismay. "Began" should be taken at face value. It was simply the starting point. In addition, Matthew 26:37 reports that Jesus cried out in anguish. This clearly indicates that his soul was "taken over" and not merely "touched." Jerome and all those who have followed him are very mistaken. Consider also the following:

(1) In this instance Erasmus clearly employs his rhetorical and humanist (in the Renaissance meaning) outlook and skills. What matters is the actual meaning of the word "began" and the context. Jerome's usage, in contrast, was based on an inference. Scholastics amplified the error with their logic-based "distinctions."

(2) The referral to Christ's "distress and dismay" (taedium & moeror), rather than "sadness" (tristitia), is significant. One can be sad without being distressed and dismayed. Distress and dismay seem to denote a higher emotional involvement and can lead to fear of the future. The theological works as well as the devotional literature (discussed below, Part VI) focus on Christ's "sadness." And so often Christ's sadness is not related to himself but to the fate of the Jews or "the wicked." This is the sadness referred to by Jerome, the *Glossa ordinaria*, and the scholastic theologians – and in their wake Colet.

(3) Part III.2 above shows that Erasmus explicitly ties Jerome to Origen's spirit/flesh dichotomy and the effectual denial of natural instinct. He now criticizes, it is clear, Jerome's pre-emotion thesis from the same standpoint. Christianity is not about simply the opposition of spirit and flesh. As in Stoicism, there is a third factor located between these opposities. That factor, for Erasmus, includes natural instinct. Emotion is not an evil or false judgment but a natural instinct located among things indifferent. Christ "cries out" from natural instinct. Emotion and spirit (reason) are not opposites but two sides of one coin.

(4b)

> And [are we to believe] that [his mind was not overwhelmed] even though he cries out that his soul is brimming with troubles, and that he is sorrowful unto death [Matt 26:38]? And while I believe that his death was more painful than any other, I also think that his sorrow, the first stage (initium), as it were, of his death, was as deep as could be (puto fuisse gravissimam) and left him only along with life itself. (1285F–1286A)

Christ's sadness at the beginning, in the garden, was extreme, not a propassion but a passion, not a *turbatio* but a *perturbatio*. And it left him only at the Crucifixion. He did not have the choice of assenting or not assenting to a *phantasia*. What he experienced was internal and fully formed at the very outset – and lasted from that moment until his death. Consider also the following:

(1) Christ's physical death brought extreme pain but his sorrow was also extreme – and more important. The devotionalists (see below, Part VI) and the theologians, followed by Colet, emphasized the pain rather than the sorrow. Erasmus agrees that Christ's physical suffering at his crucifixion was more painful than that suffered by any other human but contends that this misses what matters most, his emotional suffering. This suffering, and no suffering could ever be greater, lasted from Gethsemane through the crucifixion. His physical suffering, which may have been less, demonstrably lasted for a much shorter period.

(2) His sorrow was the "first stage," the beginning (*initium*), of his death. His death began, that is, not with physical pain, the crucifixion, but with sorrow. His death was first and foremost about his mental pain. And in referring here to Christ's "sorrow" (in accordance with Matthew 26:38), Erasmus is clearly thinking of his fear of death. This

sorrow, this fear, was "as deep as could be." It was not something that came before emotion. Nor was it a small emotion. It was true emotion. Full-fledged emotion was apparent from the first moment.

(3) In emphasizing the extreme suffering from the very beginning of the Passion, Erasmus is not just imagining that there is with Christ pre-emotion as well as emotion; pre-emotion simply does not exist. Much earlier in his treatise, at 1271E, he had made this explicit, without explaining why. In that location, bringing up "propassion" for the first time and giving even the Greek, he had connected the meaning with Jerome. But what he states about propassion at 1271E does not fit with either propassion or Jerome's interpretation of propassion, for it does not allow that propassion is for Christ something mild. The context is Christ's foreknowledge of his death and the great impact on him since his body and soul were more noble than anyone's. Regarding fear of death, Erasmus makes a point of asserting that, "the first onslaughts of dreadful experiences are the most painful" (Sunt autem formidabilium rerum primi incursus acerbissimi) (1271E). The problem is that Jerome and those who see Christ's passion in terms of pre-emotion say exactly the opposite.

(4) What this earlier reference to propassion and the novel and unexplained interpretation given there shows is just how crucial Erasmus saw the issue and the degree to which his treatise has been systematically building up to the overt claim that Christ suffered true passion and not propassion. Now, at 1286A, we are told that fear of death not only was full blown in the garden of Gethsemane but "left him only along with life itself." More than "the most painful" of experiences (1271E), his sadness and fear lasted until he was dead on the cross. As with the Stoic in the typhoon (above, Part IV.3), neither the issue that caused the fear nor the fear itself was quickly overcome. Nor could it have been. His involuntary reaction was extreme and it was caused by an extreme situation. His fear lasted as long as its cause. It lasted till the last breath had gone out of him at his crucifixion. The fear could not have been gotten rid of before the disappearance of what instigated it. No amount of will power can overcome these involuntary reactions. Again, propassion is for Christ a misnomer.

(5) There is a correlation between the time the Stoic spent in the typhoon, as described by Gellius, and the length of Christ's passion. The Stoic suffered mentally almost the whole night and through much of the next day (19.1–12) while Christ suffered mentally beginning in the evening, in the garden of Gethsemane, and lasting through his crucifixion,

on the hill called Golgotha, mid-afternoon of the next day (Matthew 26, Mark 14, Luke 22, and John 12). In both cases, that is, the time period was approximately twenty hours – and Erasmus undoubtedly recognized the relationship.

(4c)

> It will not do, either, to suggest that the word "began" (*coepit*) implies that he felt the beginnings of an emotion (*affectum*) that could not be allowed to develop fully within him. (1286A)

Here Erasmus objects to the idea that "began to be sad and distressed" refers to a small emotion (as distinct from a pre-emotion) that should not be allowed further development. As shown in 4b the beginning of Christ's death was severe. Here again the word "began" does not in fact imply a limitation. It is simply the point at which something starts. Ordinary humans may experience a pre-emotion and may sometimes need to deny assent but pre-emotion (or small emotion, as Bonaventure and scholastics would have it) is not something relevant to Christ's situation. Ordinary humans may also experience full-blown emotions, originating internally, and it was the latter that Christ experienced. As Erasmus shows us in so many ways, Christ had the same emotions as other humans but with him they were not worked out in the same way. "Res easdem in illo constituo, at non eodem modo, neque idem efficientes." (1277A)

(4d)

> Compare the theory that our first impulses (primi motus), as they are called, cannot be considered culpable so long as we reject them at once. (1286A)

Here Erasmus is referring directly to Stoic thought. Seneca refers to "first movements" (or "first impulses") in his discussion of involuntary reactions in *De ira*. "Est primus motus non voluntarius, quasi praeparatio adfectus et quaedam comminatio" (the first prompting is involuntary, a preparation for emotion, as it were, and a sort of menace) (2.4.1). Although Erasmus states in a 1523 letter that up to age twenty he was much more impressed by Seneca than Cicero,[102] there is no clear

102 *Ep*. 1390. Allen 5, 340/103–8, CWE 10, 99/113–17.

evidence that he had read *De ira* before writing *De taedio Iesu*. However this may be, he was certainly holding in mind Epictetus' contrast, as reported by Gellius, of the wiseman with the fool. After a short time the wiseman "denies assent" to such impulses while the unwise allows these impulses free reign. "In that brief but natural impulse (In eo tamen brevi motu naturali) we [wise persons] yield to human weakness but we do not believe those things are what they seem" (19.25–6).

Having very carefully studied Bonaventure's *Commentary on the Sentences*, Distinction 15, Erasmus was undoubtedly aware of the referral there also to "first movements" – although Bonaventure, unlike Erasmus, did not of course recognize the connection to Stoicism. Clearly influenced by Jerome and the *Glossa ordinaria*, Bonaventure refers to these impulses in his listing of the first of three types of sadness. "That sadness is beyond the imperium of reason which arises from necessity and surreptitiously, as a first movement (motus primi). This movement is common to both the wise and the unwise, and to the good and the evil."[103] Bonaventure does not accept, as applied to Christ, this type of sadness because it is *not* dictated by reason. Although Erasmus, unlike Bonaventure, recognizes pre-emotion he finds no relevance to the issue at hand. What he is set on demonstrating is that Christ experienced true emotion, *passio*, and this emotion was not a *propassio* governed by reason, as Bonaventure and Aquinas would have it, but a natural instinct that was as such uncontrollable.

(4e)

> Or perhaps the idea is that he took to himself feelings that could not be allowed to develop in his followers, feelings of sorrow and distress. I prefer to think that the phrase "He began to be distressed" applies to his feeling of dread, which he took on for a limited time, whereas his grief over the destruction of the wicked was always with him. It [his fear] is nature's way, too (Et enim natura quoque sit): everyone knows for certain that they will die some day, but they do not worry about it until death seems to be imminent. (1286A)

The question is this: Were Christ's feelings an exception to the rule that emotion – considered a false judgment or evil – must not be allowed

103 Bonaventure, *Sent*. III, d. 15, a. 2, q. 2 (ed. Quaracchi, p. 338), quoted above, p. 218.

to develop? While Christ's followers were not allowed, as good Stoics, "assent" to emotions such as sadness and distress (affectum tristitiae ac taedio), could it be that Christ was doing the very opposite – assenting to them? If Christ suffered the most extreme emotion ever known, as argued by Erasmus, was he not taking a path not allowed for his followers? His followers were taught to struggle against such emotions. Was it the case, notwithstanding, that Christ did not struggle and even allowed these feelings to develop? Colet had found such a view, which he attributes to Erasmus, abominable in that it would associate Christ with sin. Erasmus' answer is that everyone will have such feelings, including fear of death, when death seems imminent. Although Christ responded in unique ways the fear itself was not unique. Natural instinct guarantees that his feelings were not unique and not sinful. Consider also the following:

(1) Grief over the destruction of the wicked, the accepted view, was one thing, his emotion in the garden another. And the time factors were also very different. The grief (*dolor*) over the fate of the wicked "was always with him." His fear of death, on the other hand, was not always with him. It was a "beginning" in the sense that he had not had it before and this is how we should understand Matthew's statement that "He began to be distressed" (*coepit taedere*). While his grief over the wicked (most especially the Jews) was long term, his fear of death was for only a limited period. His emotion here was not a pre-emotion, not momentary, and not small, but neither was it unlimited in time. Compare again what he has shown about the Stoic wiseman in the typhoon. He began to suffer at Gethsemane, of course, but this in no way entails that the suffering was only momentary. He suffered sadness and distress and fear not before Gethsemane but from Gethsemane through his crucifixion.

(2) Erasmus ends by tying Christ's fear and suffering, for a period of time, to "nature's way." What he wants to discuss and investigate are Christ's natural instincts, not his long-term concerns about the effect on the wicked. Christ's fear came about naturally, as with ordinary humans, only when the reality of imminent death presented itself. The fear here did not result from an involuntary reaction to an external *phantasia* but from a natural instinct which "everyone" has when face to face with the fact that death (or some other potentially catastrophic future happening) is not far off.

All the above was of course contrary to Colet's view. Ironically, Colet was an admirer of Neoplatonists such as Ficino, disdainful of scholastics, well known for his direct study of the Bible, and soon received an Oxford doctorate in theology, and yet it was he, not Erasmus, who approached the scholastic view in holding that Christ could not have feared for himself.

From reflexive reactions to natural instincts

With the referral to "nature's way," in (4e) above, Erasmus shifts the focus from involuntary reactions and propassions directly to natural instincts and emotions. He was able to make a smooth transition to emotion because it too, he has shown, contradicting orthodox Stoicism, is involuntary. In either case the individual human is not responsible for what arrives on his doorstep. All humans are susceptible to involuntary reactions from *phantasiai* and all are born with natural instincts, including emotion. And yet, Erasmus is at pains to show, there are all-important differences. The one is externally imposed while the other is internally imposed. An individual can overcome involuntary reactions to external *phantasiai*, employing reason, but he cannot overcome the involuntary emotions he is born with. While involuntary reactions are momentary responses to harsh and unexpected events, natural instincts are central to a person's very being. The problem, Erasmus shows, is that Stoics have confused natural instincts with the *phantasiai* that lead to pre-emotions and the wiseman's refusal of "assent." This is evident, he demonstrates at length, in Gellius' illustration, reflecting Epictetus' thought, of the Stoic in the typhoon (above, Part IV.2). The illustration does not support the thesis Gellius thinks it supports. The problem is that Gellius/Epictetus wants to see the paleness and trembling of the Stoic in terms of a pre-emotion. Unlike those not wise, the Stoic held firm mentally, according to Gellius, notwithstanding the dire life-and-death situation that confronted him. Gellius sees the storm as equivalent to an external *phantasia* and believes the Stoic suffers not fear but involuntary reactions to this situation and that he would have suffered the emotion of fear only if he had "assented" to his involuntary reactions. But Erasmus shows that the actual situation is very different. The physiological and mental disturbances were not produced by the crashing of the waves and the bailing of water but from fear of the future, a fear of dying. This fear came from within himself, from the lower part of his mind, the location of natural instinct. Emotion is inherent to natural instinct. An instinct given at birth is not something that reason – even in theory – can deny or overcome. The Stoic had no control over the emotion itself – no matter how much he might counter mentally its effects. Nor was this fear something momentary, as with an external *phantasia*. It lasted as long as that which had instigated it.

As with Erasmus, the core issue for orthodox Stoics was not involuntary pre-emotions but emotion as such. The wiseman considered emotion errant reason and, being a paragon of reason, disposed of emotion effortlessly. The purpose of Stoic analyses of *phantasiai* and pre-emotions had been to confirm that the wiseman never gives in to emotion. Over time, however, the reality of emotion in worldly affairs and in the lives of individuals had been much attended to by Stoics – more so than in any other ancient philosophy. What especially interested them were the steps non-philosophers can take in advancing towards the rational model. Cicero has much to say about this in works such as *Tusculan Disputations* and *De officiis* – as do, at great length, Seneca in his *Moral Epistles* and treatises such as *Consolation to Helvia* and Epictetus in his *Discourses* and *Handbook*. There was also increasing emphasis on not only the nature of the human at birth – his self-preservation instincts and character traits – but also the stages of human development from this base and the relationship to the outlook of the wiseman. The revisionist Antiochus in Cicero's *De finibus*, Books 4 and 5, reflects and builds on this interest, as does Erasmus in his radical relocating of emotion.

While the theologians had analysed and reworked over and over the meaning in the biblical account of the word "began," Erasmus approached the subject from an entirely different perspective. "Began," as shown above, does not have an abstract logical meaning but a linguistic meaning. It refers to something that simply started. There is no necessary reason why the word should relate to either Jerome's "pre-emotion" theory or scholastic "small passion" theory. Although Christ was the Son of God, Erasmus shows that the same rules applied to him as to the Stoic wiseman. Orthodox Stoics had wrongly interpreted the place of emotion in the wiseman and theologians using similar reasoning – derived unknowingly from Stoic pre-emotion – had wrongly interpreted Christ's feelings in Gethsemane. Demonstratively, Christ had suffered true passion throughout. There is not just one type of "terror" but two, and the most devastating type by far is not that which originates from external *phantasiai* but that which originates in the mind itself, as the mind rationalizes about that which is before it (see Part IV.2–3). Christ experienced the latter type. His "terror" arose in his mind as a result of his foreknowledge of what awaited him in the near future. The beginning was not an external shock to the senses but internal, something deep within his being. There was a very fundamental reason why Christ suffered true passion, why his response to suffering was not tiny, not short, not halted prior to passion – contrary to what the theologians had wanted to believe. Like every human he was impelled by natural instinct, and fear of death was, emphatically, a natural instinct.

Erasmus shows that in the garden of Gethsemane Christ was not suddenly beset with *phantasiai* from outside his own mind. No soldiers at this time had pricked his skin, nor had he been mocked. Were one to apply the concept of propassion to Christ it would much more easily, we can see, relate to his crucifixion the next day than to the beginning of his passion in the garden. Richard Layton has pointed out that Origin's application of propassion to Christ's feeling in the garden is problematic for these very reasons. Origen failed to draw out how Stoic propassion actually relates to the garden scene and did not realize that the concept is much more applicable to the crucifixion.[104] Erasmus, in contrast, went out of his way to show that propassion is not applicable to Christ's experience in the garden – nor even the crucifixion. What is entirely applicable is the type of terror that originates internally. Christ experienced full-blown passion, extreme terror, in the garden.

The theologians, of course, accepted that Christ had a human nature (even if some, such as Hilary, had tried to mitigate even this), but what they did not see, Erasmus shows, was the composition and irrevocableness of this nature. Understanding Stoic natural instinct, as applied to emotions and located among things "indifferent," allows us to understand Christ. Although in Erasmus' view Christ suffered emotionally to a degree not comparable with any other human, his natural instincts and emotions did not differ in nature from other humans. The theologians, including Colet, had got it all wrong. Yes, Jesus was concerned about the fate of the Jews, but this did not trigger his fear of death. In the garden it was his foreknowledge of what was going to happen to him personally that triggered his fear and despair. And this was a fear that originated in the lower part of his soul, the location of inescapable natural instincts.

---

104 See above, pp. 193–4.

Equating the Christian state of innocence and Stoic natural instinct

A new philosophical understanding of emotion and reason led not only to a new understanding of the Passion but to new assessments of the afflictions Christ had taken on as a human and even the attributes he possessed in the state of innocence. Erasmus' understanding of the latter is radical.

Regarding the particular human afflictions Christ took on, Lombard had distinguished between "defects of guilt" (*defectus culpae*) and "defects of punishment" (*defectus poenae*)[105] and Bonaventure, Aquinas, and other scholastics held to this distinction and the belief that Christ took on only defects of punishment. Likewise, Erasmus holds that Christ took from fallen nature only handicaps imposed on us as punishment (*defectus poenae*) (1270B). That is, he took on no affliction that is a sin but only those that result from sin (1270C). Among the punishments he accepted only those, "as Bonaventure states," that are universal, "helplessness of childhood, frailty of old age, thirst, hunger, weariness, sorrow, pain, drowsiness and the thousand trials of our earthly life" (infantia, imbecillitas aetatis, sitis, fames, lassitudo, tristitia, dolor, dormituritio, and mille nostrae vitae hujus labores) (1270D). The "universal" punishments Bonaventure actually names comprise a much smaller list: hunger, thirst, death, and pain (fames, sitis, mors, dolor et consimilia).[106] Regarding bodily afflictions, medieval writers unanimously agree that hunger, thirst, and death originated in the Fall.[107] Regarding emotions that originated in the Fall and are universal punishments, the standard view was close to that of Aquinas: sadness and fear originated in the Fall but not love and joy. Love and joy, which

105 Lombard, *Sent.* III, d. 15, ch. 1 (ed. Coll. Bonav., p. 93).

106 Bonaventure, *Sent.* III, d. 15, a. 1, q. 2 (ed. Quaracchi, p. 332). Comparing Lombard's *Sentences* and Bonaventure's *Commentary*, Erasmus adds that Christ dispensed with afflictions that befall us as individuals, which as such were an affront to his dignity and immaterial to our salvation (1270D). Here too he names a greater number of afflictions than had Bonaventure (or Lombard): diseases, physical disabilities, mental defects arising from physical defects, deformity, monstrosity, and similar things. Cf. Lombard, *Sent.* III, d. 15, ch. 1 (ed. Coll. Bonav., p. 93) and Bonaventure, *Sent.* III, d. 15, a. 1, q. 2 (ed. Quaracchi, p. 333). Aquinas names leprosy and epilepsy and bad habits, such as inordinate eating. See ST III, q. 14, a. 4.

107 See Gondreau, *The Passions of Christ's Soul*, 159. Cf. Aquinas, ST III, q. 14, a. 1.

are "wholly subject to reason," existed before the Fall in the state of innocence.[108] As shown in chapter 1, Bonaventure and Aquinas discuss at great length the extent to which Christ assumed the emotion of sadness (and to a lesser degree anger and fear) – which originated in the Fall – concluding that he assumed it only as a propassion.

Erasmus states that the punishments that arise from sin but are not in themselves sinful, which he names and Christ took on (*defectus poenae*), "can be found alongside blameless virtue" (possunt cum summa etiam virtute cohaerere) (1270D). Why would he make a point of saying that the punishments named are on the same level as "blameless virtue"? Is this simply another way of distinguishing between *defectus culpae* and *defectus poenae*? He seems to have been building on the distinction represented by Bonaventure in his *Commentary on the Sentences*, responding to John of Damascus, between punishments that result from (intentional) ignorance and rebellion of the flesh and spirit (*defectus culpae*) and those that result from man's bodily nature – such as hunger, thirst, death, and pain (i.e., *defectus poenae*).[109] The latter differs from the former in that they are not in themselves, as Erasmus would have seen, intentional. But, still, why would Erasmus make the point that they stand "alongside blameless virtue"? And what is the place of emotion in the traditional view? Bonaventure's *Breviloquium*, which Erasmus had likely read, gives a more complete account of the traditional view:

> Again: since the damaging penalties, which are ignorance, weakness, malice, and concupiscence – four of the punishments incurred by original sin – are incompatible with perfect innocence, Christ could not be subject to them, nor did he in fact assume them. Other penalties, however, which give occasion for the practice of perfect virtue (quae sunt exercitativae virtutis perfectae) and testify to a humanity that is true not feigned – penalties such as hunger and thirst in the absence of nourishment, sorrow and fear (tristitia et timor) in the face of opposition – are characteristic of men in common; hence it was fitting for Christ to be subject to them, and He did in fact assume them.[110]

108 Aquinas, ST I, q. 95, a. 2; cf. *De veritate* q. 26, a. 8 and Augustine, *City of God*, 4.26.

109 Bonaventure, *Sent.* III, d. 15, a. 1, q. 2 (ed. Quaracchi, p. 333).

110 Bonaventure, *Breviloquium*, pt. 4, ch. 8.4 (in *Opera*, ed. Quaracchi, 5, p. 249); trans. José de Vinck, *The Works of Bonaventure*, 2:168.

In this instance Bonaventure names sorrow and fear, along with hunger and thirst, as punishments shared by all humans; affirms that Christ assumed the emotions of sorrow and fear as well as the physical afflictions of hunger and thirst; and points out that such physical and emotional punishments nevertheless allow humans "the practice of perfect virtue." All of this shows that Erasmus was not saying in itself anything new in holding that humans have the option of practising blameless virtue even in the face of the punishments and that Christ took on the punishments blamelessly.

What is new, analysis reveals, is the mentality of Christ when he took on the punishments and the meaning for Christians. The emotions Christ had in the state of innocence were not those of tradition and these emotions related directly to the way he took on human punishments and, in another context, his Passion.

Radically, Erasmus equates the state of innocence that existed before the Fall with Stoic nature and Stoic natural instinct.[111] Stoic-type "natural passions" were in that primitive state and Christ retained these primitive feelings:

> Jesus our redeemer took on all the feelings that would have existed in Adam had he continued in his original state: a sensible body and a sensible soul subject to the natural passions (naturalibus passionibus). (1270B)
>
> In fact, if you will allow me to address you [Colet] a little more philosophically, I shall venture to say – possibly with the approval of some theologians, and leaving to one side the question of sin – that it is only human nature to fear death, and that, such is the human condition, there would have been a place for it even in the state of innocence (etiam in statu innocentiae). (1270F)

But this was a striking departure from the accepted view. What theologian had ever allowed or even imagined fear, much less fear of death, in the state of innocence? Aquinas explicitly states that there were no emotions such as fear or sorrow in the primitive state, a state that lacked all evil but lacked no good.[112] Augustine saw the matter

111 Aquinas and the neo-scholastic thinkers who followed did not apply Aristotle's state of nature to Adam and Eve's condition but to "the human condition after the Fall but before the formal establishment of political society." See Monahan, *From Personal Duties towards Personal Rights*, 134.

112 Aquinas, ST I, q. 95, a. 2, *corpus*.

similarly.[113] Bonaventure, as evidenced even in my quote above of his *Breviloquium*, is only following common opinion in tying emotions such as sadness and fear in with the punishments of humans *after* the Fall. Contrast Erasmus. For him emotions such as sadness and fear did not come about only after the Fall but – considering the matter "philosophically," i.e., Stoically – existed even in the state of innocence. Since Christ lived in a state of innocence he retained the feelings that ordinary humans had had before the Fall – and this included fear of death.

Leaving nothing to doubt, Erasmus immediately ties the state of innocence, and the attendant emotions of fear and sadness, in with Stoic thought on the state of humans at birth (what moderns have sometimes referred to as the Stoic "cradle" theory).[114]

> Therefore the Stoics, who generally expect rather more of their wiseman than human frailty can bear, not only will allow him this fear of death, but even give it the leading place among the "first principles of nature" [The Latin reads: *τὰ κατὰ φύσιν πρῶτα,* id est, *inter naturae prima*]. For the earliest lesson that nature teaches us is to avoid; at first instinctively but later by reasoning too, anything that threatens her gentle rule, and still more anything that may destroy it entirely, and in every way to protect and cherish our existence. (1271A–B)

In short, Erasmus envisions Adam's original state in terms of Stoic natural instincts and Stoic "first principles of nature" and sees Christ, including his fear of death, in terms of these instincts and principles.[115] On Erasmus' extensive employment and development of Stoic thinking on "first principles of nature" and the self-preservation instinct see above, pp. 61–3, 105–8.

Somewhat further on, responding yet again to "Colet," Erasmus makes clear that he is assigning to the state of innocence not only Christ's fear of death but other emotions as well. "I am depicting the whole nature of the man [Christ], complete with all his emotions, fear, sorrow,

113 Augustine, *City of God*, 14.10.

114 Cf. Brunschwig, "The Cradle Argument in Epicureanism and Stoicism."

115 Bonaventure attempts in his *Breviloquium* to take away from Christ even the impulse to flee death. Humans, states Bonaventure, have a natural impulse to flee death and therefore Christ assumed the universal penalties only in a qualified manner. Complex distinctions regarding Christ's divine will, rational will, and natural will explain the matter. See *Breviloquium*, pt. 4, ch. 8 (ed. Quaracchi, p. 249).

hope, joy, desire, anger, hatred, and any others that may exist without vice" (Hominis perfectam naturam constituo, omnibus suis affectibus absolutam, metu, dolore, spe, gaudio, cupiditate, ira, odio, reliquisque, qui sind ejusmodi, ut citra vitium queant consistere) (1276F). In the state of innocence are found, that is, not only emotions that might seem positive, such as joy and hope, but also fear, sorrow, anger, and hatred. A follow-up statement shows that he recognizes again, and quite rightly, that he is saying something different and something others may consider problematic or even evil:

> I do not consider it wicked at all to give Christ these emotions, which certainly do lead to sin – but in us, not in him. (Atqui ego, Colet, neutiquam impium esse video, ea ponere in Christo, quae ad vitia quidem trahunt, sed utique in nobis trahunt, non in ello.) (1277A)

In stating that "in us" such emotions "lead to sin" he is affirming again that at birth they are not sinful but only potentially such. Even though humans had been forever laid open to sin as a consequence of Adam's Fall, they had emotions before the Fall – the emotions Christ has, including his "fear, sorrow, hope, joy, desire, anger, hatred" – and such emotions even after the Fall can exist – though perhaps seldom – "alongside blameless virtue." Most important, Christ did not become acquainted with emotions such as fear, sorrow, desire, anger, and hatred only in accepting human punishments for the Fall. Living in a state of innocence he himself possessed these emotions.

Erasmus' exposition of the state of innocence and its effects can be systematized. (1) Emotions such as "fear, sorrow, hope, joy, desire, anger, hatred" existed (unseen by the theologians) in the state of innocence. (2) In representing the state of innocence Christ had (unseen by the theologians) such emotions. (3) At birth humans also have these emotions, emotions they had (unseen by theologians) before the Fall. (4) But for humans there is at birth the potentiality, because of the Fall, of sinning through these emotions. (5) In taking on human punishments Christ had no potentiality of sinning through these emotions.

Is there a problem with Erasmus' logic? Were not Aquinas, Bonaventure, and other scholastics logically correct in distinguishing (assuming the Fall) the emotions that preceded the Fall from those brought on by the Fall? If sadness and fear were found in the state of innocence and did not originate as a consequence of the Fall, in what ways was the Fall a demotion? On the other hand, if the state of innocence was a beautiful time, how could there be emotions such as sadness and fear? And if in the state of innocence humans had possessed emotions such as sadness and fear, and these were emphatically not then punishments, what was the relationship of this sadness and fear to the sadness and fear that were, after Adam's Fall, punishments? How can it be that negative emotions – indeed the same negative emotions – can exist before the Fall as after? Was Erasmus imagining a difference in degree or a difference between a good and an evil fear? What kind of fear would have been "good" in the state of innocence?[116] The situation with Christ, as depicted by Erasmus, brings the issue to a head. Christ took on punishments such as sadness and fear but he already had sadness and fear in the state of innocence. So what was the difference? Christ exhibited the greatest possible fear in the garden and this, Erasmus is at pains to show, resulted from a natural instinct. But how could this instinct both reflect the state of innocence and the punishments he took on for our sake?

Consider carefully the following statement and most particularly the referral (again) to "natural passions":

> Since Christ took nothing from fallen nature except the handicaps imposed on us as punishment, and there was in him no capacity for sin, I shall boldly (audacter) ascribe to him the natural passions (passiones naturales) appropriate to mind and body respectively: grief, joy, hatred, fear, and anger in the mind; in the body hunger, thirst, drowsiness, weariness, suffering, death. (1277C)

Since Christ (a) accepted only *defectus poenae* from fallen nature and not *defectus culpae* and (b) had no capacity to sin, Erasmus (c) "boldly" ascribes to him mental and physical "natural passions." But what are "natural passions"? And why does Erasmus imagine that (a) and (b) entail them? Without defining these "natural passions," he had earlier shown that they exist in the state of innocence and as such were reflected by Christ: "Jesus our redeemer took on all the feelings (cum omnibus affectibus) that would have existed in Adam had he continued

116 Although in *The City of God* Augustine holds that there was no fear, sadness, or pain before Adam's fall (14.10) and that the first man "lived according to God in a Paradise both corporeal and spiritual" (14.11), he comments elsewhere that anger and lust, albeit now vicious parts of the soul, existed in Paradise but were "not then moved to do anything contrary to a righteous will" (14.19).

in his original state: a sensible body and a sensible soul subject to the natural passions (naturalibus passionibus obnoxiam)" (1270B). Now, however, we are given more detail. The natural passions consist of emotions deriving from the mind (grief, joy, hatred, fear, and anger) and bodily afflictions (hunger, thirst, drowsiness, weariness, suffering, death). Emotions, he has already shown, are in Christ those that existed in the state of innocence – which he has equated with Stoic natural instinct. But how can the physical afflictions be "passions"? By very definition this might seem untenable. More than this, it had been unanimously agreed among theologians, as noted above, that hunger, thirst, and death came about only *after* the Fall – as did the emotions of sadness and fear. But Erasmus has now transferred these physical needs, along with the negative emotions, to the state of innocence. What is his justification? And, again, what is the relationship of Christ's "natural passions" to the human punishments he took on?

Analysis shows that Erasmus is bringing in bodily and mental "natural passions" where he should be discussing, were he thinking in terms of tradition, bodily and mental punishments (*defectus poenae*). Although Bonaventure makes no mention of "natural passions" in either his *Commentary* or his *Breviloquium*, consider what he has to say about bodily and mental *punishments* in the latter work:

> He [Christ] assumed the corporal punishments, such as hunger, thirst, and weariness, and he assumed the spiritual punishments of sadness, anguish, and fear (Assumpsit enim poenalitates corporales, ut famen, sitim et lassitudinem; assumsit etiam spirituales, ut tristitiam, gemitum et timorem).[117]

Bonaventure, that is, lists "punishments" that are both bodily and spiritual and Erasmus lists "natural passions" that are both bodily and mental. The punishments Bonaventure lists are for Erasmus natural passions found in the state of innocence – as well as after the Fall. We can only conclude that Erasmus "boldly" turned punishments into "natural passions." Bonaventure wants to talk about the punishments Christ assumed; Erasmus wants to talk about Christ's "natural passions." Note four things: (1) Christ's "passions" are now considered bodily as well as mental. (2) These bodily and mental passions are not now seen in terms of punishments but as "natural." (3) "Natural

117 Bonaventure, *Breviloquium*, Pt. 4, Ch. 8 (ed. Quaracchi, p. 248), my translation.

passions" are passions that exist in the state of innocence. (4) "Natural passions," most importantly, is another way of talking about natural instincts. In short, the punishments Christ takes on are now seen as "natural" and "passions" that include not only instinctive emotions but instinctive physical responses. Just as Erasmus includes "grief, joy, hatred, fear, and anger" among the instinctive emotions found in the state of innocence, so too does he see "hunger, thirst, drowsiness, weariness, suffering, and death" as instinctive physical needs existing in the state of innocence.[118]

Why was Erasmus, contrary to all the authorities, so intent on "boldly" turning Christ's assumption of punishments into a referral to Christ's "natural passions"? Why did he want to see Christ's acceptance of bodily and mental punishments in terms of bodily and mental instincts – existing in the state of nature? The answer is that he wanted to see Christ's natural instincts at work even in his acceptance of our punishments. Looking at the world from his Stoic perspective, he wanted to see natural instincts as inherent in Christ's very nature. He wanted to show not only that Christ took on our punishments but exactly how he took them on, that he accessed them from the vantage point of the natural instincts found in the state of innocence. While Bonaventure and Aquinas, like other theologians, emphasized the innocence represented by Christ, Erasmus was deeply concerned with the content of this innocence.[119] He contended that it was filled with natural instincts. Included among these instincts were emotions such as sadness and fear (as well as hunger and thirst) – and not only emotions such as love and joy. Christ experienced sadness and fear and indeed *all* other human emotions before his acceptance of our punishments. Emotions such as sadness and fear were inherent in his very being.

118 Regarding hunger, thirst, and death, Aquinas mentions John of Damascus' referral to "natural and intractable passions." But John, he shows, is discussing universal punishments (not the state of innocence). See ST III, q. 14, a. 4.

119 In his discussion of the physical disabilities Christ assumed (ST III, q. 14), Aquinas states that Christ "took on human nature without sin, with all the purity it had in the state of innocence," but does not tell us what this primitive purity consisted of (ST III, q. 14, a. 3). Regarding the bodily disabilities of hunger, thirst, and death (resulting from the Fall) he comments that "human nature is unknown to us except as burdened by these bodily disabilities ..." (ST III, q. 14, a. 1).

Although Christ voluntarily took on human punishments (1283F), as Bonaventure, Aquinas, and all other theologians insist,[120] this misses the substantive issue: *He had voluntarily taken on that which is not voluntary.* The natural instincts he had in existing in a state of nature and of innocence were the natural instincts all humans have and the *defectus poenae* which humans have following the Fall are defects only in the sense that they can potentially lead to sin, whereas Christ had the same instincts but without the potentiality. Thus, when he took on human punishments for the Fall he took them on as an equal, the difference being that his reactions to natural instincts differed greatly from those who had the potentiality to sin (see further below). He had our emotions at the very core of his being and accessed the failings of humans from this standpoint. He retained his natural instincts and most certainly the emotions of sadness and fear even as he took on human punishments. Erasmus "boldly" concludes, in short, that Christ accessed the punishments suffered by humans as a consequence of the Fall as "natural passions." He accessed them, that is, in terms of a Stoic (as Erasmus sees Stoicism) state of nature, physical and mental instincts he had always had.

Again, however, what is the difference between the sadness and fear that Christ experienced in the state of innocence and the sadness and fear, as a consequence of the Fall, that he took over from humans? Although not sharing in original sin, Jesus was "a complete man subject to the ills of the human condition" (1282B). One could ask how he could be a complete man and how, even more, he could take on and experience human punishments, if it is the case, as alleged, that he took on our sadness and fear and the like from the standpoint of his natural passions. If this was the case, could it not be doubted that he really suffered in taking on human punishments? What was different about the sadness and fear he took on and the sadness and fear (not to mention hunger and

120 Bonaventure emphasizes that we have our defects from necessity while Christ took them on voluntarily, *Sent.* III, d. 15, a. 1, q. 3 (ed. Quaracchi, p. 334). Cf. Aquinas, ST III, q. 14, a. 2 and a. 3. Responding to Hilary's contention that "It was not because he was thirsty, hungry or weeping that the Lord is presented as having been thirsty, hungry or sad," Aquinas imagines that "Hilary does not want to exclude the reality of pain from Christ but the necessity" (ST III, q. 15, a. 5). Referring to Matthew 26: 38, "as his passion drew nigh his soul was grieved," Augustine states: "Truly, he accepted these emotions into his human mind for the sake of his own assured purpose, and when he so willed, just as he was made man when he so willed" (*City of God*, 14.9).

thirst) he already possessed? Are we to believe that he encompassed at one and the same time and in the same way emotions found in the state of innocence and the emotions that are punishments (*poenae*)?

Erasmus, however, would find that such questions overlook the core point. Christ easily felt our sadness and fear, not to mention our physical needs, precisely because he had these natural instincts even in the state of innocence. He was "a complete man subject to the ills of the human condition" not because he took on our punishments but because he already had, by natural instinct, all the human emotions. He accessed human physical and mental punishments in terms of his own "natural passions." There was a seamless web between his natural instincts and the way in which he interacted with human punishments.

In short, Christ was a person living in a state of innocence that closely resembled Erasmus' conception of the Stoic state of nature. It was a state of innocence less innocent than ever imagined, a state built from intractable mental and physical instincts – be they hunger and thirst, be they sadness and fear. And yet, though Christ had the same "natural passions" as others and as a result could deeply commune with the feelings and situations of others – and they with him – his Passion shows just how different his response to his emotions could be. As the following will show, his emotion had no effect on his reason and his reason had no effect on his emotion.

Reason had no effect on emotion

Reason – contra scholastics – had not the slightest thing to do with the origin, nature, and development of Christ's emotion. Reason did not precede his fear of death nor did it impregnate, accompany, express, guide, regulate, develop, or govern it. Nor, as has been shown in so many ways, was Christ's emotion a false judgment, as in orthodox Stoicism. In showing what is wrong with Gellius' interpretation of the Stoic in the typhoon, Erasmus shows what is wrong with orthodox Stoicism. The illustration actually shows that the Stoic's reason had absolutely no effect on his emotions – as long as what caused the emotion existed. Erasmus' ultimate purpose here was of course to show that Christ suffered emotional meltdown in the Passion and that his reason was powerless. More than this – going beyond the Stoic – reason was not even a player. While the reason of the Stoic was troubled but unable to act as long as what caused the emotion was present, Christ's reason was in no way touched by his extreme fear of death (Part IV.2–3).

Emotion is for Erasmus an involuntary and ineradicable natural instinct and as such is not "reasonable" and not responsive to reason. Ordinary humans can overcome evil expressions of their natural instincts with reason but they cannot overcome the instincts themselves. Christ's emotional suffering was incomparable because he, the Son of God (not susceptible to evil, with a unique nobility of body and mind [1271D]), had taken on human punishments for the Fall and yet was entirely unable as a human to escape natural instincts. In showing at length that the greater the handicap the greater the possibilities for virtue, Erasmus' ultimate purpose was to show that there was a direct relationship between Christ's unparalleled handicaps and his unparalleled achievements (above, pp. 120–6, 179–80).

Had Lombard, Alexander of Hales, Bonaventure, Aquinas, or other scholastics been presented with the contention that reason was irrelevant, that Christ's emotions were full-blown and entirely explained by involuntary natural instincts, they would have found this contention preposterous and blasphemous. As shown in chapter 1 above, scholastics believed that Christ's emotions had to have been saturated with reason or they would have partaken of evil, which was of course impossible. Here as elsewhere, many distinctions were made. Thinking inclusively, they attempted to find a place for large numbers of seemingly contradictory primary and secondary sources. Interpretation would set everything aright. What was needed was only to distinguish the many ways reason can be related to Christ's emotion – resulting in their conception of propassion – and the many ways reason appears to be at odds with emotion. "In Christ all the impulses of the sense appetite arose under the control of reason."[121] Even in the state of innocence, Aquinas concluded, reason preceded emotion:

> But in the state of innocence the inferior appetite was wholly subject to reason: so that in that state the passions of the soul existed only as consequent upon the judgment of reason. (In statu vero innocentiae inferior appetitus erat rationi totaliter subiectus, unde non erant in eo passiones animae, nisi ex rationis iudicio consequentes.) (ST I, q. 95, a. 2)

Christ made the choice to be human, as everyone agreed, but what he chose was not, Erasmus shows, voluntary. Being human meant being

121 Aquinas, ST III, q. 15, a. 4.

subjected to involuntary forces. And these forces had nothing to do with reason as such. Devoid of reason, his emotions reflected raw nature and there was no way he could have mitigated or controlled them. His fear, sadness, and other emotions were internal, an essential part of who he was. Human nature was no longer simply something to be worked out logically. It had deep biological content – and punch. Nor had earlier humanists (however much they may have looked at human nature through a rhetorical and worldly lens) imagined Christ in this way (as can be gleaned from Part I above). General opinion in the fifteenth century likewise saw nothing of involuntary biological instincts in Christ's human nature. According to John Bossy, "To show, in the fifteenth century, that Christ was a real man, it was not necessary to resort to biology, and not sufficient to see that he was a child of known parents: it was necessary to know that he was someone with a human kin."[122]

Emotion had no effect on reason

What sense, however, can be made of Erasmus' contention, the third of the four key statements quoted earlier (pp. 185–6, 221), that he does not object to the idea that Christ's reason was not dethroned?

> Si passionem appellant eam, quae rationem a statu suo dimoveat, si perturbari vocant a statu mentis dimoveri, non reclamo. (1285E–F)
>
> (3) If they [theologians] define "passion" (passio) as something that dethrones reason and "overwhelm" (perturbatio) as being driven out of one's mind, I do not object [to the distinguishing of *propassio* and *turbatio* from *passio* and *perturbatio*].

Like others, that is, Erasmus does not allow that Christ's reason could have been brought down or his mind overturned, but this is in actuality, he holds, not a problem. *Passio* and *perturbatio* did not conflict with his reason. He agrees with those who talk about *propassio* and *turbatio* should it be the case that *passio* necessarily dethrones reason and *perturbatio* necessarily drives one out of one's mind, but this is emphatically not the case. Christ's emotions had no effect on his reason. As stated with (4), emotion "not only disturbed Jesus' mind (or at least

122 Bossy, *Christianity in the West, 1400–1700*), 8.

the lower part of it), but most violently overwhelmed it" (non turbarit solum, sed vehementissime perturbarit) and yet his reason was absolutely uneffected.

Here again Erasmus travels from the Stoic in the typhoon to Christ. Against orthodox Stoicism he has shown that the Stoic's fear was not a false judgment and did not in fact unbalance his mind. Although the wiseman's fear in the typhoon was manifestly not momentary but lasted as long as what instigated it and he experienced full-fledged emotion, his reason was not dethroned. His reason remained active and his mind held firm throughout. All of which shows (see Part IV.2) that emotion does not necessarily unbalance the mind – "neque tamen eum loco dimoveat" (1277F, also 1278A). As alluded to in (3) above, the theologians assume and argue to the contrary, that passion necessarily "dethrones reason" (quae rationem a statu suo dimoveat) and perturbatio necessarily drives one out of one's mind (perturbari vocant a statu mentis dimoveri) but this was not in actuality the case with Christ. It can be the case for ordinary humans. Although reason is not able to take away our natural instincts or reverse the individual traits and feelings we are born with, when emotions go astray and become involved in evil our reason can be affected.[123] But Christ was without sin so his emotions could never have negatively affected his reason.

Again going beyond the Stoic, Christ's reason was entirely separate from what was occurring with his emotions. While the Stoic's reason struggled during the typhoon and his mind was not unbalanced, Christ's reason in Gethsemane did not struggle. His mind was not even touched (Part IV.3).

> He was afraid, not because his passions seized and overwhelmed his reason as ours do [lacking the type of wisdom practiced by the Stoic wiseman], but [unlike even the Stoic] in untroubled serenity of mind. (1283F)

Nor could Christ's mind have been touched:

> Christ was not alarmed, as the (Stoic) philosopher was, by an inescapable consequence of his human nature, and he did not possess a mind, unlike the Stoic, that could (potentially) be unhinged. (Neque enim illi

123 The *Enchiridion* is all about the ways in which humans can handle their natural dispositions. See below, Part VII.

pavor accidit necessitate conditionis, quaemadmodum Philosopho isti, neque mentem afficiebat, quae possit a statu dimoveri quemadmodum in Stoico.) (1278A)

Christ was not troubled not only because there was no possibility that fear, dread, and alarm could affect his reason but because the divine side of his soul had a nature that differed entirely from the natural instinct side (1284A).

They [emotions] did not dictate to his reason or in any way disturb his composure (aut ullo pacto a tranquillitate dimoverent). They did not dim the joy his soul (gaudium animae) found in endless contemplation of the divine, nor diminish the pleasure (laetitiam) his soul felt at the prospect of humanity's salvation. (1284A)

In the upper side of his soul was found not the eagerness of the martyr, his *alacritas*, but the contemplative, the person experiencing great joy in his soul (*gaudium*). Note relationships with *honestum* and the wiseman's spirituality and happiness.

A Stoic rewriting of "no redundancy"

Through multilayered distinctions, scholastics such as Thomas Aquinas had argued that Christ suffered in his Passion "no redundancy," meaning that there was no redundancy from superior (Christ's divinity) to inferior (Christ's humanness), that his suffering received no help from his higher nature. As John of Damascus had contended, "He permitted each of his powers to act according to its own laws."[124] But how can this be? Following Aristotle and Augustine, they distinguish a sensitive soul and an intellective soul but show throughout that the intellective soul is responsible for every aspect of the sensitive soul. Christ's propassions were created and governed by reason. As Aquinas even states, in referring to John of Damascus, Christ's humanity was "a kind of instrument of his divinity."[125]

Erasmus brings up the issue of "no redundancy" and states that he agrees (1289A, cf. 1284E), but here as with other issues gives an

124 Aquinas, ST III, q. 46, a. 6, resp. 3.
125 Aquinas, ST I-II, q. 112, a. 1, ad. 1; III, q. 18, a. 1, ad. 2.

interpretation that is anything but traditional – and far more supportable. The "no redundancy" he sees is built, as demonstrated throughout *De taedio Iesu*, from a Stoicism that comprises two distinct types of value and a unitary both/and frame of mind. Although he had greatly enlarged the second side, making self-preservation instincts at birth life-long and expanding their scope to include, most importantly, emotion, the unbending side was at all times in place. He now shows how this works, uniquely, with regard to Christ's Passion. "Redundance withdrawn," Christ "could be both willing and unwilling, could both dread and desire the same thing, in equal measure and at one and the same time ... both sublime joy and abject misery" (1289A). Not only did reason not affect his emotions and emotions not affect his reason, both were fully active at one and the same time.

> Bear all this in mind and you need not be afraid to combine in him complete dread and perfect eagerness, sublime joy and intense pain, supreme bliss and extreme suffering (summam reformidationem, cum summa mentis alacritate, summum gaudium, cum extremo dolore, summam felicitatem cum summis cruciatibus, copulare). (1284A)
>
> Given the qualities that we ascribed to Christ just now, there is no reason why the same person at the same time should not have dreaded and desired, welcomed and rejected, the same thing, and experienced the extremes of both joy (gaudio) and suffering during his ordeal. (1286B)
>
> To the extent that Jesus' soul was in touch with bodily sensation, he was afflicted by horrible suffering; to the extent that it was in touch with his divine nature, he was filled with triumph and boundless joy by precisely the same thing, his death. That intense feeling of dismay did not restrain his eagerness for death, but neither did his eagerness diminish his feeling of dread, because, in this exceptional case, the feeling in his rational part did not overflow into the sensible part of his soul. (1289B)

While the theologians had looked at Christ's Passion in terms of reason, revealing his human side by multifarious abstruse logical distinctions, Erasmus looked at the Passion in terms of natural instinct while holding unbendingly to spirit (and the reason therein). The Passion was unitarily both/and.

PART VI Beyond Devotionalist Assumptions

An important question has yet to be addressed. How do Erasmus' theses regarding Christ's emotional state and fear of death line up with the larger social, cultural, and religious environment in which he lived? Is it possible that his surroundings affected his outlook – notwithstanding what I have shown about his deeply personal motivations (in Part II.4) – far more than, up to this point, has been indicated? Was he simply reflecting, whatever his Stoicism, a view of the Passion of Christ embedded in late medieval culture, not least relevant being his youthful contacts with the Devotio Moderna? Even here, I will demonstrate, Erasmus' thinking had taken a radical turn.

The social, cultural, and religious milieu

In *Texts of the Passion: Latin Devotional Literature and Medieval Society*, Thomas H. Bestul sees the fifteenth century as "in many respects the great age of Western European devotional writing, and the Passion of Christ was at the center of it."[1] While in the early Middle Ages thought regarding Christ's Passion did not dwell on his suffering and there was little interest in his humanity, a major shift, represented by an immense and widely circulated body of literature, occurred in the period 1100–1500.[2] Over time these "devotionalist" accounts of Christ's

1 Bestul, *Texts of the Passion*, 60. See also Kieckhefer, "Major Currents in Late Medieval Devotion."

2 Covering the entire Middle Ages are two works of extraordinary importance: Viladesau's *The Beauty of the Cross* and Belting's *Likeness and Presence*. See also Constable, "The Ideal of the Imitation of Christ."

death, emphasizing his physical suffering and pain, became ever more elaborate. The theme also pervaded tools for meditation, such as prayer books, paintings and other forms of art, poetry, plays in various settings, liturgy, and music. While Giotto's paintings, around 1300, brought to bear on the Passion a greater naturalism and realism than found previously, painters of the later fourteenth and fifteenth centuries tended to develop this realism by depicting in grotesque detail the intensity of the pain.[3] The painter Hieronymus Bosch (c. 1450–1516), who inhabited the same world Erasmus grew up in, spending his life at s'Hertogenbosch in the Netherlands, stretched late medieval perspectives of the Passion "to the aesthetic screaming point."[4] Images of the crucifixion and relics of saints or Christ (seemingly everywhere present) were valued in ways now hard to comprehend. Before the Reformation (i.e., 1517), Hans Belting has shown, images were objects of veneration that possessed a tangible presence of the holy.[5] Like the paintings, sculpture, and other types of art, late medieval plays elaborately drew out the horror of Christ's flagellation and crucifixion. The plays also brought into being assorted villains and details about the grief of Mary not found in the biblical accounts. Passion plays were immensely popular. English town guilds, for example, staged elaborate Passion plays on outdoor wagons beginning in the late fourteenth century and lasting to the latter half of the sixteenth century.[6]

Treatises on the Passion continually attempted to heighten the emotional effect on the reader or listener. Indispensable sources were the *Historia scholastica* of Peter Comestor (d. 1179) and the *Legenda aurea* (*The Golden Legend*) of Jacobus de Voragine (d. 1298). Although a large part of the devotional literature of the late Middle Ages circulated under

3 See Viladesau, *The Beauty of the Cross*, 137–44 and 155–63, and Marrow, *Passion Iconography in Northern European Art*.

4 Marsden, "Bosch's 'Christ Carrying the Cross,'" 17. Walter Bosing has concluded, similarly, that "His [Bosch's] visual images were highly original; but they served to give a more vivid form to religious ideals and values which had sustained Christianity for centuries." See his *Hieronymus Bosch*, 96. How "Christ Carrying the Cross" (Ghent) relates to previous paintings of the same is made evident by the plates and figures, and pp. 40 and 163, in Marrow's *Passion Iconography in Northern European Art*. See also Gibson, "Imitatio Christi."

5 Belting, *Likeness and Presence*. On the demotion and reorientation of images brought about by Luther, and those who followed, see 458–70.

6 See Edwards, *Ritual and Drama*, and Sticca, *The Latin Passion Play*; also Happé, *English Drama before Shakespeare*.

the names of Anselm, Bernard, Bonaventure, and Augustine, much was inauthentic.[7] The way these authors were understood, therefore, could have as much to do with the inauthentic as the authentic. Translations, beginning in the thirteenth century, and then the printing press, beginning mid-fifteenth century, contributed to the circulation of these works, whatever their origins. Latin texts of the Passion treatises were among the first and most frequently printed.[8] Books that cover the entire life of Christ also focused on the Passion, particularly important being *Meditationes vitae Christi*, a late thirteenth-century Franciscan work emanating from northern Italy, and *Vita Christi* of Ludolphus of Saxony (d. 1377), written between 1348 and 1377. Eleven of one hundred chapters of the *Meditationes* are taken up with the Passion.[9] *Vita Christi*, by far the most learned treatment, brought together all the previous themes. One of the most popular works of the fifteenth century, it influenced even Loyola in the sixteenth. Bestul explains why: "The late medieval fascination with the physical particularities of the suffering of Christ is everywhere apparent, perhaps nowhere more prominently than in the section on the exact number of wounds received by Christ in his Passion, said to be 5,490, according to a revelation of a pious woman recluse."[10]

Popular culture, it is often held, was something very different from the rationalistic debate centred at Paris and Oxford. And yet there exists such a thing as "climate of opinion," and "paradigm shifts" do occur.[11] Climate of opinion cuts across high and low understandings of Christ's Passion.[12] That there was in fact no clear-cut distinction

7 See Constable, "The Popularity of Twelfth-Century Spiritual Writers in the Late Middle Ages," and "Twelfth-Century Spirituality and the Late Middle Ages."

8 Bestul, *Texts of the Passion*, 68. Regarding the complexity of relationships between Latin and the vernacular languages, see Bäuml, "Varieties and Consequences of Medieval Literacy and Illiteracy," and Chartier, "Texts, Printings, Readings."

9 Bestul, *Texts of the Passion*, 48.

10 Bestul, *Texts of the Passion*, 58. According to Bestul, in Middle English works is found "the idea that the body of Christ was so stretched out that all his bones could be numbered" (66).

11 "Climate of opinion" became a stock phrase following Becker's *Everyman His Own Historian* (1935), while "paradigm shift" became common parlance following Kuhn's, *The Structure of Scientific Revolutions* (1962). In *The Stripping of the Alters*, Eamon Duffy exemplifies ways in which climate of opinion (though he does not use the phrase) crosses high and low culture in religious practices.

12 Viladesau does much to show the crossover between high and low attitudes in *The Beauty of the Cross*.

between academic writers and devotional writers can be illustrated by the Franciscan Bonaventure (d. 1274). Although Erasmus, we have seen, takes note in *De taedio Iesu* of Bonaventure's massive *Commentary on the Sentences*, he would have known that there was another side to Bonaventure's writings. Bonaventure's devotional writings had a wide influence on later medieval authors, Franciscan or otherwise, who wrote on the Passion.[13] Particularly influential were his *Lignum vitae* (*Tree of Life*) and *Vitis mystica* (*Mystical Vine*). At centre stage, "verging upon obsession," is Christ's physical sufferings.[14] Although the incomparability of Christ's bodily sufferings with other humans was a commonplace, it appears that Bonaventure definitively articulated the theme.[15] Subjected to excruciating physical pain, Christ is deformed by injury and bleeding. Among other tortures he is crowned with thorns; his hands and feet are pierced; he is pulled, stretched, and hurled to the ground.[16] In *De perfectione vitae sorores* (*On the Perfection of Life Addressed to Sisters*) Christ's sorrow resulting from his physical pains is directly related to the blood flowing from all parts of his body. "Indeed, no sorrow was comparable to yours ... blood sprang from five parts of your body: the hands and feet in the crucifixion, the head in the crowning of thorns, the whole body in the flagellation, and the heart in the opening of your side."[17]

Individuals longed for union with the suffering Christ. St Francis' stigmata, 1224, was held to be a visual sign of an instance where this union had been accomplished. The goal, according to *Vitis mystica*, is to participate in Christ's suffering by impressing on our minds mental pictures of the event, seeing "with the eyes of the mind" – words also

13 See Bestul, *Texts of the Passion*, 43. He cites Fleming, *An Introduction to the Franciscan Literature of the Middle Ages*, 250–6. See now Roest, *Franciscan Literature of Religious Instruction*, 472–514, and the bibliographies given there. According to Heiko Oberman, during the two centuries before Erasmus and Luther, Franciscans dominated "spirituality, piety and theology outside the university halls." See *The Dawn of the Reformation*, 22, and his discussions of "the Franciscan hegemony," 5ff. Cf. Posset, "Preaching the Passion of Christ on the Eve of the Reformation." On the Franciscan influence on painting, see Derbes, *Picturing the Passion in Late Medieval Italy*.

14 Bestul, *Texts of the Passion*, 44.

15 See Gilson, "Saint Bonaventure et l'iconographie de la Passion," 424.

16 For a systematic illustration of these tortures in late medieval and early Renaissance paintings see Marrow, *Passion Iconography in Northern European Art*.

17 *De perfectione vitae sorores* 6.6. *Opera omnia* 8, p. 122, trans. Jose de Vinck, *Works of Bonaventure* 1:243.

used in his *Commentary on the Sentences*.[18] Carrying the theme a step further, we need to be, like Jesus, deformed outwardly in our bodies in order to be reformed inwardly.[19] Even the humanist Giovanni Pico della Mirandolla (1463–94) whipped himself in remembrance of Christ's passion.[20] Caroline Bynum has shown that in the late Middle Ages "imitation" of Christ came to have a literal meaning.[21] Imitation was a fact, not simply something done in remembrance. Catherine of Siena (d. 1380) "craved blood because she craved identification with the humanity of Christ, and she saw this humanity as physicality."[22] Catherine of Genoa (d. 1510) "consciously and explicitly chose food as her central image for mystical union."[23] Behind eucharistic devotion was the belief (the doctrine of transubstantiation) that "One *became* Christ's crucified body in *eating* Christ's crucified body." "Both priest and recipient were literally pregnant with Christ."[24]

Erasmus' education, leaving aside his precociousness, was encompassed by the Devotio Moderna. He attended a Brethren of the Common Life school at Deventer, in the Netherlands, from 1475 to 1484 and another at s'Hertogenbosch from 1485 to 1486. His schooling with the Augustinian canons at Steyn, from 1486 to 1493, was also structured by a version of the Devotio Moderna (see above, Part II.4). Although the exact teachings and practices of the Devotio Moderna, as well as their effects on Erasmus, have been much debated, the Devotio Moderna can be seen as a late version of the impulses described above. It was, first, in

18 *Vitis mystica* 4.1. *Opera omnia* 8, p. 166, trans. Jose de Vinck, *Works of Bonaventure* 1:158. Cf. *Commentary on the Sentences*, above, p. 219. On meditation as envisioning particular biblical scenes in Bonaventure's writings, see Despres, *Ghostly Sights*, 25–30.

19 *Vitis mystica* 5.7. *Opera omnia* 8, p. 171, *Works* 1:168.

20 See CWM 1, 209–28 and Lehmberg, "Sir Thomas More's Life of Pico della Mirandola."

21 See Bynum, *Holy Feast and Holy Fast*, 255–9.

22 Bynum, *Holy Feast and Holy Fast*, 178, cf. 245. Richard Kieckhefer describes Catherine's desire to shed blood for Christ as (simply) a desire for reciprocity. See *Unquiet Souls*, 69. On devotion to Christ's wounds and blood from the eleventh century on, see the bibliography in Constable, *Three Studies in Medieval Religious and Social Thought*, 209 n. 376.

23 Bynum, *Holy Feast and Holy Fast*, 185.

24 Bynum, *Holy Feast and Holy Fast*, 257. As an example of the parallelism between the eucharist and relics Bynum cites "the behavior of Hugh, Bishop of Lincoln, who chewed off a piece of Mary Magdalen's arm while visting Fécamp and defended himself to the horrified onlookers by replying that if he could touch the body of Christ in the mass, he could certainly apply his teeth to the Magdalen's bones" (255).

the Bernardine and Franciscan traditions.[25] According to G.H. Gerrits, the Christology of the founder, Gerard Grote (1340–84), was restricted almost entirely to Christ's humanity.[26] Stress was placed on individual identification with Christ's Passion[27] and, by some accounts, adherents seem to have had a preoccupation with death.[28] A lay movement, the emphasis was on renewal of ancient spiritual traditions, interpreted as humility, inwardness, simplicity, communalism, purity of heart, meditation, obedience, poverty, charity, spiritual training, progress in the virtues, and conventional pieties.[29] Prominent figures in the movement, besides Grote, included Florens Radewijns (1350–1400), Gerard Zerbolt of Zutphen (1367–98), and Johannes Mombaer (c. 1460–1501). Thomas à Kempis (1380–1471), author of *The Imitation of Christ*, was also a disciple.[30] Zerbolt's two handbooks for the religious life, *De Reformatione* and *De Ascensionibus*, though lacking great originality, were widely read in the fifteenth and sixteenth centuries.[31] Major influences on these works were Bernard's *Sermons on the Song of Songs* and Bonaventure's *De Triplic Via*.[32]

Linked to late medieval mentalities, including the Devotio Moderna, was the philosophical and theological thinking called Nominalism.[33]

25 Gerrits, *Inter Timorem et Spem*, 102. See also Post, *The Modern Devotion*, and Van Emgen, *Devotio Moderna*.

26 Gerrits, *Inter Timorem et Spem*, 104.

27 Cf. Gerrits, *Inter Timorem et Spem*, 121–3. The painter Bosch (c. 1450–1516), who spent his life at the heart of the Devotio Moderna world, at s'-Hertogenbosch, has St Anthony assume, like Christ, a position fully beneath the weight of the cross. St Jerome becomes one with Christ "through dwelling in his wounds." See Ruppel, "Salvation through Imitation," 6 and 10.

28 See Tracy, *Erasmus of the Low Countries*, 21.

29 See Van Engen, *Devotio Moderna*, 25–35.

30 Regarding the authorship and content of *The Imitation of Christ*, see Constable, *Three Studies in Medieval Religious and Social Thought*, 239–44.

31 Gerrits, *Inter Timorem et Spem*, 27.

32 Gerrits, *Inter Timorem et Spem*, 235. Zerbolt acknowledges Bernard more often than any other non-scriptural source (19). On the influence of Bonaventure, see 22 and 25 n. 90.

33 See in particular Knowles, *The Evolution of Medieval Thought*, and Leff, *The Dissolution of the Medieval Outlook*. Other works include Courtenay, *Schools and Scholars in Fourteenth Century England*; Hirvonen, "A Nominalist Ontology of the Passions"; Knuuttila, *Emotions in Ancient and Medieval Philosophy*, 260–82; and Nauta, "William of Ockham and Lorenzo Valla"; Oberman, *The Harvest of Medieval Theology*; and Trinkaus and Oberman, *The Pursuit of Holiness in Late Medieval and Renaissance Thought*. On the development of *Sentences* commentaries in the fourteenth and fifteenth centuries, see Rosemann, *The Story of a Great Medieval Book*, 93–193.

Represented most learnedly by Duns Scotus (c. 1270–1308) and William of Ockham (1270–1347), Nominalism arose almost immediately after the time of Bonaventure and Aquinas. "Names" were now held to be realities that exist only in individual things. While Aquinas held a "moderate realist" position (compared with Plato's "realist" contention that names have substantive existence) and had thought that reason and the intellect attest to larger realities, including the existence of God, Nominalists held that certitude could not be found through the intellect. God's existence is a matter of faith rather than reason. Knowledge comes from sense experience alone and it follows that salvation depends on God's will alone, not merit. In this context Christ's Passion was sometimes seen not as a sign of love but the warning of an unknowable and arbitrary god.[34] Rapidly evolving and dire social situations, brought about most especially by the Black Death, which carried off a third of the population of Europe, added to the appeal of this type of thinking.[35]

A relationship to *De taedio Iesu*?

It is clear that the devotionalist literature hammered home a belief that Christ's Passion involved unsurpassed violence and incomparable suffering. Was Erasmus somehow building on devotionalist writings and the social and cultural outlooks that surrounded them? The problem with this scenario is that *De taedio Iesu* is little concerned with Jesus' physical suffering. Erasmus does not doubt the extremity of the physical suffering but his interest is elsewhere. The most important use he makes of the pervading outlook is the claim, early in the treatise, long before his criticism of propassion and *turbatio*, that Christ's suffering was magnified by a unique nobility of body and mind. A comparison even here with the devotionalist literature reveals fundamental differences in meaning as well as context.

The idea that Christ's body was exceedingly tender is often found in the Passion narratives. It is one of five causes of Christ's pain set forth

34 Cf. Viladesau, *The Beauty of the Cross*, 154 and 162.

35 Cf. Kelly, *The Great Mortality*; Herlihy, *The Black Death and the Transformation of the West*; Tuchman, *A Distant Mirror*; and Meiss, *Painting in Florence and Siena after the Black Death*.

in *The Golden Legend*.[36] In his *De perfectione vitae ad sorores* Bonaventure words the matter as follows:

> You will see even more clearly how cruel was the death of Christ if you consider that whatever is more sensitive suffers more. In general, the body of a woman is more sensitive than that of a man; but never was there a body that felt pain as keenly as that of the Savior, since his flesh was entirely virginal, conceived of the Holy Spirit and born of the Virgin. Hence the Passion of Christ was as much more painful as he himself was more tender even than any virgin.[37]

Contrast Erasmus' statement, discussing Christ's fear of death:

> Moreover, the impact of this affront to nature [death] is all the keener and sharper on those who are by nature worthier and nobler than the rest. No human body was ever nobler than Christ's, no soul more worthy. Thus the impact on him was more painful by far than on anyone else, whether of the wounds that hurt his body and through it his soul, or those that directly struck at his soul's essence. (1271D)

Leaving aside the fact that Erasmus' statement is in *De taedio Iesu* peripheral while Bonaventure's statement reflects a central thesis, Erasmus' statement relates to Christ's fear of death while in *De perfectione vitae ad sorores* Bonaventure never mentions fear of death. Erasmus is giving reasons why Christ had more reason to fear death than ordinary mortals. Reflecting this context Erasmus' statement brings in, unlike Bonaventure, not only Christ's body but also his soul. Also not found in Bonaventure's statement is the referral to human nature. Erasmus specifies that it is Christ's uniqueness *within* nature that accounts for his incomparable bodily and mental pain. Most remarkable, however, is his distinguishing between wounds (a) "that hurt his body and through it his soul" and (b) "those that directly struck at his soul's essence." Regarding (a) Erasmus has little to say in *De taedio Iesu* not only about

36 Voragine, *Legenda aurea*, ch. 51. Edited Magioni, 1:337; trans. Granger Ryan, *The Golden Legend: Readings on the Saints* 1:204. In his *Summa Theologiae*, Aquinas affirms often that Christ suffered physically for us, as at ST III, q. 14, a.1 (where it is stated that he was "wounded for us") and sees Christ's extreme sensitivity of body and soul as one of four causes of his pain, ST III, q. 46, a. 6, reply 3, and hence 4.

37 *De perfectione vitae ad sorores*, 6.5. *Opera omnia* 8, p. 121, *Works* 1:242.

bodily suffering as such but even the "sorrow" or "torments" that arose, according to devotionalist accounts, from these extreme pains. Regarding (b), what concerns him is pain that strikes directly at the mind, lacking any instigation from bodily harm or bodily pain. This type of suffering finds no likeness in devotional writings.

Emotional suffering, that is, can be something entirely different than even the mental stress that results from excruciating physical pain. The most important suffering does not originate externally, from physical pain, but internally, in the mind itself – and it is this suffering which so "violently disturbed" Christ. While the devotionalist literature sometimes shows that Christ was sad for reasons other than his physical pain or the resulting stress, this is not a sadness that originates in the mind itself from natural instinct. In Bonaventure's *Lignum vitae* Christ sorrows and weeps tears because of human weakness, blinded hearts, and obdurate malice (and humans are advised to return the favour with tears of remorse),[38] a sadness out of concern for humankind, not at all a statement about emotion as such, much less any particular types of emotion suffered by Christ.

Colet, like the devotionalists and like the scholastics, could not comprehend the reality:

> It is logical to suppose that if his [Christ's] death was more painful physically than any other, then his fear of it must have been more excruciating mentally than any other. And as his boundless charity made the pain of his death no whit more bearable, so nothing lessened the intensity of his fear. Why will you [Colet] admit the one but reject the other? (1281D)

Mental pain is just as much a part of human nature, Erasmus insists, as physical pain. If Christ's physical pain was incomparable, it makes no sense to believe that his fear of death was not, likewise, incomparable.

It is surely not without cause that in his discussions of medieval devotional literature on the Passion, Bestul does not mention any source that holds that Christ feared death. What he does give us is an example of the contrary. He finds it very probable that the *Glossa ordinaria* (compiled in the twelfth century), which summarizes and codifies the biblical commentaries, is the source of the prevalent supposition that "Christ's

38 *Lignum vitae* 4.14. *Opera omnia* 8, p. 74, trans. Jose de Vinck, *Works of Bonaventure* 1:113.

sorrow in the garden was not from fear of his approaching Passion, but because of the loss of the wicked."[39] This is of course Colet's belief, the very view Erasmus is so determined to reject.

In short, the devotional literature provides only background and context. It tells us nothing about what Erasmus was up to in *De taedio Iesu*. The devotional literature centres on Christ's physical pain and the need to identify with and imitate this pain. Now and then note is taken of the mental suffering that must have accompanied this pain. But nowhere do we find belief that Christ could not as a human control his emotions, much less that he actually feared his own death.

A puzzle regarding Erasmus' criticism of St Bernard

What may seem puzzling is Erasmus' attribution of the *turbatio/perturbatio* distinction, which he rejects, to Bernard of Clairvaux (1091–1153) (above, p. 221). Why not Bonaventure, the author he was directly studying? Bernard appears to have made no comparable differentiation between *turbatio* and *perturbatio*.[40] And Bonaventure does not cite him in this regard. Nor is it likely that the distinction will be found in the great numbers of works wrongly ascribed in the late Middle Ages to Bernard.[41] Bonaventure distinguishes the words *turbatio* and *perturbatio* (above, pp. 213–17) in a very logical and thoroughly scholastic manner while Bernard, like those authors that would have been lumped with him, most certainly was not a scholastic. Contrast Bernard with his contemporary, Peter Abelard (1079–1142). Abelard's logic-driven methodology is linked with the foundation and very raison d'être of the University of Paris while Bernard is famous for his objections to that methodology.[42] And the gulf separating Bernard and scholasticism was

---

39 Bestul, *Texts of the Passion*, 30. He cites PL 114, col. 169.

40 Deeper study of Bernard's writings would confirm or disconfirm my assessment. See Bernard of Clairvaux, *Opera Sancti Bernardi*, and *Thesaurus Sancti Bernardi Clarevallensis* under *perturbare* and family and *turbare* and family, pp. 246 and 342. Simo Knuuttila summarizes Bernard's conception of emotions in *Emotions in Ancient and Medieval Philosophy*, 195–200.

41 See Constable, "The Popularity of Twelfth-Century Spiritual Writers in the Late Middle Ages," 14: "No less than seven out of the nine treatises in the 1491 edition of Bernard's works were spurious."

42 Among many works, see Sommerfeldt, *Bernard of Clairvaux on the Life of the Mind*; Doyle, *Bernard of Clairvaux and the Schools*; Evans, *The Mind of Bernard of Clairvaux*.

well recognized in later times. In the sixteenth and seventeenth centuries he was given the epithet "the last of the fathers."[43]

Nonetheless, the fact that Erasmus ties Bonaventure's *turbatio/perturbatio* contrast to Bernard is intriguing. What was there in Bernard's outlook that would make Erasmus go out of his way to rebuke him? Why would he have found cause to attribute to him the contention that Christ suffered *turbatio* but not *perturbatio*?

According to Giles Constable, in the late Middle Ages there was far more interest in Bernard than in any other twelfth-century writer, and in the fifteenth century this interest seems even to have been on the rise.[44] He was popular because his monastic, spiritualist, and experientialist outlook, emphasizing the humanity and sufferings of Christ and his mystical marriage with the Word, well fit the devotionalist atmosphere. The need was to seek intimate and tangible contact with Christ, working one's way upwards, following Christ's example, from flesh to spirit and mystical union with God.[45] While Bernard sought to stir up intense emotion, such as tears of loss and compassion, the late medieval treatises erroneously attributed to him focus even more on the bodily aspects of the Passion, a Christ that can be touched, felt, and gone into.[46] Among those who thought highly of Bernard were the Brethren of the Common Life.[47] Erasmus, not by chance, had contact with his writings in his schooling at Steyn.[48]

---

43 See Pranger, *Bernard of Clairvaux and the Shape of Monastic Life*, 163–4f. Bernard may have had more of an impact on Luther and even Calvin than on Erasmus: see Bell, *Divus Bernhardus*, and Lane, *Calvin and Bernard of Clairvaux*.

44 Constable, "The Popularity of Twelfth-Century Spiritual Writers in the Late Middle Ages," 7, 13, 18–19.

45 Cf. McGuire, *The Difficult Saint*, chapters 7 and 8, and Constable, *Three Studies in Medieval Religious and Social Thought*, 204–5.

46 McGuire, *The Difficult Saint*, 238–49.

47 Constable, "The Popularity of Twelfth-Century Spiritual Writers in the Late Middle Ages," 11, 13, 18–20.

48 Gerhard B. Winkler points to a 1488 letter to Servatius Roger (*Ep*. 15. Allen 1, 89/34–5, CWE 1, 20/36–8) in "Die Bernhardrezeption bei Erasmus von Rotterdam," 264. Erika Rummel notes similarites with statements of Bernard of a moralistic nature in Erasmus' *De contemptu mundi*, CWE 66, 141 n. 12, 142 n. 28, 149 n. 26, 150 n. 32, 163 nn. 27 and 28, 164 n. 35, 167 nn. 19–21. In his *Ratio Verae Theologiae* Erasmus censures Bernard for sloppy borrowings of the phraseology of scripture (H 287). Erasmus, *Moriae encomium* (1509, pub. 1511), recounts Bernard's story about a conversation with the devil and implies that Bernard is one of those, educated or not, who see entry into heaven as a matter of ceremonies. See *The Praise of Folly*, Miller translation, 65, ASD IV-3, 124.

Why Erasmus refers to Bernard had everything to do, we can deduce, with Colet. Colet had always made a big issue of his contempt for scholastic methodology and learning, mentioning Scotists and especially Aquinas. Erasmus points out Colet's antipathy to scholasticism in his introduction to *De taedio Iesu*[49] and in his conclusion (1290D–E). In contrast, Bernard's writings are clothed in language that Colet would have instinctively appreciated and tied into his own Christology.[50] As a rhetorician, Erasmus undoubtedly recognized that a criticism of the *turbatio/perturbatio* distinction found in Bonaventure's massive *Commentary on the Sentences* would not compare in effect with a criticism of Bernard. A number of other factors likely contributed to the referral to Bernard. (1) Although Bernard never contrasts or technically develops differences between *turbatio* and *perturbatio* he would surely have agreed, had Bonaventure's distinction been described to him, that Christ did not suffer *perturbatio*. (2) By bringing in Bernard, Erasmus made clear that his criticism was not aimed merely at Bonaventure's *Commentary*, which he had earlier mentioned, but at a vast sea of thought, going back to Bernard and beyond and coming up to Colet and the present day. (3) Erasmus did not want it to appear, considering the detailed nature of his own arguments, that he was arguing like Bonaventure, as a scholastic logician. (4) Bonaventure had radicalized propassion, making it something that was brought about by Christ's reason – rather than something, in all spirituality, Christ's reason had rejected – contrary not only to Jerome's view but Colet's. Bernard would not have agreed with Bonaventure's rewriting of propassion.

49 *Ep*. 108. Allen 1, 246/20–1, 247/26–31, CWE 1, 203/24–5, 31–4. See above, pp. 80 and 98. Erasmus gives more detail in a 1521 letter to Justus Jonas: *Ep*. 1211. Allen 4, 520/425–44, CWE 8, 238/462–83.

50 Eugene Rice long ago tied Colet to Bernard and the late medieval piety represented in *The Imitation of Christ*. See "John Colet and the Annihilation of the Natural," 153–4. John Gleason sees Colet as in the Franciscan tradition and often relates the devotionalist side of Bonaventure, contrasting (without recognizing Bonaventure's scholastic side) the "Thomistic-Aristotelian" school. See *John Colet*, 196–203. In his famous Convocation Sermon at St Paul's Cathedral, now dated 1510, Colet quotes Bernard in support of his contention that the false doctrines of heretics are less harmful and less heretical than the depraved lives of clergy. See Olin, *The Catholic Reformation*, 31–9 at 35. G.R. Owst shows the considerable influence of Bernard on fourteenth- and fifteenth-century sermons, including complaints about the wicked lives of priests. See *Literature and Pulpit in Medieval England*, 3, 268, 270–2, 277, 304 passim.

Bernard's Christology resembles Colet's: *Propassio* and *turbatio* tie with *alacritas*

Alacritas is another word Erasmus could easily have related to Bernard. The word *alacritas* was put into the mouth of "Colet" by Erasmus, I have shown (Part III.3), as a way of neatly summarizing and criticizing – by way of what is in Stoicism a negative emotion – a central facet of Colet's argument. Had Erasmus as author wanted to find a theological source for the "eager joy" represented by *alacritas* he could have done no better than name Bernard. *Alacritas* was a way of conceptualizing the Passion in terms that accord with "Colet's" *propassio/turbatio* thesis – directly tied to Jerome – and comes close to the actual views of Colet. Indeed, there is an inherent relationship between *propassio/turbatio* and *alacritas*. Immediately overcoming suffering and approaching death with eager joy are for "Colet" two aspects of the same thing. Belief that Christ suffered only *propassio/turbatio*, which he immediately overcame, was one with believing his Passion was about *alacritas*, about joyfully overcoming incipient emotions. In line with common opinion, Colet's Christ was a martyr of martyrs.

But Erasmus reveals a Christ that was not a martyr, not the person people have imagined. Christ, he shows, did not see himself as a martyr and he did not want to be considered a martyr. There was nothing of glory, nothing of *alacritas*, in his distress. His fear of death was entirely real, not a mere propassion, not merely a concern with the fate of the Jews. In fact, Erasmus contends, his fear of death, like his other emotions, was incomparably greater than ever felt by a human. Unlike martyrs and other humans he had no way of mitigating his fear. Martyrs overcome their fears and physical pain by holding to something higher: a vision of Christ, divine truth, angels, and the like. "In humans [Christ being the exception] any strong emotion is in competition with others, and as each one is more or less powerful, it either overwhelms or succumbs to the others" (1279C, cf. 1284E–F). What Christ experienced in contrast was only raw emotion. There was for him no way to hold emotion in check. He experienced total *passio* and total *perturbatio*. His reason had no role to play.

What Christ wanted in all this was not our admiration. Admiration is what we feel for martyrs, those who overcome their physical pains and fears (1289E, above, p. 180). Martyrs carry out what are considered glorious deeds. What Christ wanted was not glory but only our love – at the gut level. He wanted to move us by being, through natural instinct, one with us. His emotions were our emotions, magnified. He overcame nothing.

The Passion had nothing to do with *alacritas*, *propassio*, or *turbatio* for the simple reason that these concepts do not recognize natural instinct. Christ chose to become human but he made no choices with regard to natural instincts. To have done so would have been a contradiction in terms as there is no way to be human and not have (involuntary) natural instincts. He carried within his bosom all the natural instincts, including fear of death, found, according to Erasmus, in the state of innocence. The fear that came over him in the garden of Gethsemane was not voluntary but involuntary. Human emotions cannot be willed away. In this regard Christ was not representing reason or abstract truth. His feelings came from the depth of his being. And these feelings, most especially his fear of death, were on full display in the garden. What he experienced there, and what he wanted us to absorb from the event, was anything but mystical. Our instincts are his instincts and his fear of death was our fear incomparably magnified. We feel love rather than admiration because he was on the same emotional level as ourselves. At Gethsemane he did not feel what martyrs feel. He did not transcend nature.

Perhaps a single passage from Bernard's writings will allow us to glimpse what it was that Erasmus could not have accepted – and the relationship to his disagreements with Bonaventure and, most especially, Colet. The passage, from a sermon on St Andrew, accords not only with *turbatio* but with *propassio* and *alacritas*. Note carefully even the words used:

> Quid magnum fuerat, Domine Iesu, si, accedente hora propter quam veneras, intrepidus stares, tamquam qui potestatem habebas ponendi animam tuam, et nemo tollebat eam a te? Aut non longe gloriosius fuit, quando quidem totum propter nos agebatur, ut non modo passio corporis, sed etiam cordis affectio pro nobis faciat, et quos vivificabat mors tua, tua nihilominus et trepidatio robustos, et maestitia laetos, et taedium alacres, et turbatio quietos faciar, et desolatio consolatos? Lego quidem in Lazari resurrectione, quia infremuit spiritu et turbavit seipsum. Sed esto interim quia se ipse turbavit, non conditionis necessitate, sed suae beneplacito voluntatis. Nunc autem aliquid iam amplius audio. Usque adeo siquidem praevaluit ea quae fortis est ut mors dilectio, ut Christum Dei angelus confortaverit. Quis, quem? Evangelistam audi: Apparuit, inquit, angelus confortans eum.

> How great it was, Lord Jesus, as the hour for which you had come approached, that you stood intrepid as one holding the power to lay down your own life and not have someone take it from you. Yet only a little more glorious was it that you did all of this for our sake. You committed to us not only your body's suffering but also your heart's affection. Your death gave us life, your trepidation made us brave, your sadness made us joyful, your loathing made us eager, your trouble made us tranquil, and your desolation consoled us. I read that at the resurrection of Lazarus your spirit groaned and writhed in distress. Yet this happened not because it was forced on you, but because you consented to it out of kindness. Now I hear something else more clearly: For all this love, which is as strong as death, has prevailed, so that the angel of God could comfort Christ. Who comforted whom? Listen to the Evangelist: The angel appeared and comforted him.[51]

Two things stand out, both counter to the message of *De taedio Iesu*: (a) the effectual denial of Christ's *perturbatio* and (b) the effectual attribution of *alacritas* to Christ. Let us break this down.

(1) Contrary to Erasmus, Christ *was* a martyr. He "stood intrepid" as the hour of his crucifixion approached. His love was "stronger than death." Compare Colet: "As love grows fears decrease" (1271F). Not by chance the sermon in which Bernard's words are imbedded is dedicated to a person who followed Christ in martyrdom, St Andrew.[52] Regarding Matt 26:38, "my soul is sorrowful unto death," Bernard refers, in another sermon, to the comeliness of Christ's body and "the strength and imperturbability of his mental state" (fortitudinem vero in impertubabili statu mentis).[53] Christ was not simply a martyr but the ultimate model for martyrdom.

(2) Contrary to Erasmus, Christ's Passion was "glorious." This glory was for us. We need to follow in his footsteps. His suffering and glorious martyrdom gave us the tools to be martyrs. His *trepidatio, maestitia, taedium, turbatio*, and *desolatio* made us *robustos, laetos, alacres, quietos*, and *consolatos*. Martyrs, following Christ's example, go through the most horrendous ordeals bravely, joyfully, eagerly,

51 Sermon on St Andrew, 1.6. PL 183, 507A–B; *Bernard of Clairvaux: Selected Works*, trans. Evans, 44.

52 Erasmus refers to Andrew's martyrdom at 1280D–E.

53 Sermon 34.4. PL 183, 633A.

tranquilly, and entirely consoled – everything "Colet" meant by *alacritas*, as applied to Christ. Commenting on Bernard's writings, Jean Leclercq states: "Like the whole of his human existence from the moment of the incarnation, the suffering of Christ on the Cross was directed toward his glorification, which is made manifest in the brilliance of the ascension."[54]

(3) Contrary to Erasmus, our love for Christ comes about through a strictly down and up relationship. We admire Christ's glorious martyrdom and we realize that Christ "committed to us" his "bodily sufferings" and his "heart's affection" and that his distress (far from natural instinct) was "consented to out of kindness." Christ's Passion was about divinity descending from heaven and the effect on us. Accordingly, Bernard's *Sermons on the Song of Songs* is said to be, through and through, "a poetic description of the experience of being affected by divine love."[55]

(4) Contrary to Erasmus, Christ's emotional suffering was at all times voluntary. His human nature, that is, did not restrict his will.[56] In his Passion as at the resurrection of Lazarus his spirit "groaned and writhed" (infremuit et turbavit [John 11:33]), but in both situations this was not a matter of necessity but of choice. Had he not chosen suffering he would not have been able to show, it is assumed, "kindness" and "affection" towards us.

(5) Contrary to Erasmus, we learn in another writing by Bernard that Christ (merely) "began" to experience the miseries of the flesh. Whether or not Bernard was consciously thinking of Jerome, statements such as the following can easily be related to *propassio* and *turbatio*, not *passio* and *perturbatio*: "You see, then, that Christ has two natures in one Person, one which always

---

54 See his introduction to *Bernard of Clairvaux: Selected Works*, trans. Evans, 44. Leclercq states in the same place that Bernard "left more sermons on the ascension than on almost any other mystery, including the Passion."

55 See Knuuttila, *Emotions in Ancient and Medieval Philosophy*, 198. According to Leclercq, "The ascension symbolizes [for Bernard] Christ passing from the life of the flesh to glory in the life of the Spirit. This transition from flesh to Spirit can be accomplished in us because it has first taken place in Christ." See *Bernard of Clairvaux: Selected Works*, 44.

56 According to Coleen McClusky, Bernard argues that the will does not move without the intellect and that we always retain, even after the Fall, freedom from necessity. See "Bernard of Clairvaux on the Nature of Human Agency," 303 and 306.

was and another which began (coepit) to be ... began to know the miseries of the flesh."[57]

(6) Contrary to Erasmus, Christ's pain and suffering could be mitigated and was mitigated. The angel "comforted" him.

(7) Contrary to Erasmus, Christ did not demonstrate his love by experiencing natural instincts, most particularly fear of death, but "consoled us" from on high.

If Erasmus' depiction of Christ has no model within devotionalist thinking the frame of mind that surrounds it is even more remote. The Christian journey is not fundamentally about a flesh/spirit either/or but about a both/and consisting inseparably of natural instinct (including emotion), character traits, and situations on the one side ("things indifferent") and spirit/reason (unbending absolutes) on the other. His *Enchiridion* is all about this Stoic-based frame of mind.

---

57 "On the Steps of Humility and Pride" (De gradibus humilitatis et superbiae), Ch. 3, 12. PL 182, 948A, trans. Evans, *Bernard of Clairvaux: Selected Works*, 110.

PART VII Spiritual Warfare: Christianizing *Katorthoma/Kathekon*: The *Enchiridion militis christiani*

Erasmus' *Enchiridion militis christiani* (*Handbook of the Christian Soldier*) was inspired, through and through, by Stoic ways of thinking. It leans heavily on *De finibus*, particularly Book 3, and *De officiis* Book 3.[1] The explanation Erasmus gives for the title virtually copies what he had stated about *De officiis* in the preface to his 1501 edition.[2] The book is "an 'enchiridion,' that is, a sort of dagger, which you should never put aside, not even at table or in bed, so that if you are ever compelled to sojourn as a stranger among the affairs of the world ... you are not totally unarmed" (CWE 66, p. 38). Christians (like Stoics) need to be mentally armed against fortune,[3] and to this end the *Enchiridion* should always

1 My referrals to the *Enchiridion militis christiani* employ the Latin edition found in *Desiderius Erasmus Roterodamus, Ausgewählte Werke*, 22–136, and the translation found in CWE 66, 24–127. Among many works on the *Enchiridion*, see Augustijn, *Erasmus: His Life, Works, and Influence*, 43–55; Christ-Von Wedel, *Erasmus of Rotterdam*, ch. 4; *Enchiridion Militis Christiani*, intro. and trans. Festugière; Godin, *Érasme lecteur d'Origène*; Kaufman, "John Colet and Erasmus' *Enchiridion*"; Kohls, *Die Theologie Des. Erasmus*; Marcel, "*L'Enchiridion Militis Christiani*; McConica, *English Humanists and Reformation Politics under Henry VIII and Edward VI*, 16–35; O'Donnell, "Rhetoric and Style in Erasmus' *Enchiridion militis Christiani*"; Schoeck, *Erasmus of Europe: The Prince of the Humanists*, 28–40; Stupperich, "Das *Enchiridion militis christiani* des Erasmus von Rotterdam nach seiner Enstehung, seinem Sinn und Charakter"; and Tracy, *Erasmus of the Low Countries*, 32–40.

2 Cf. above, pp. 68–9.

3 Cf. *Tusc.* 5.19: Philosophy "will ensure that the man who has been obedient to her laws is always armed against the assaults of fortune (contra fortunam semper armatus), that he has within him all the support required for leading a good and happy life, that in fine he is always happy."

be kept at hand because it offers examples that deal (as does *De officiis*) with particular problems in life.[4] Just as *De officiis* was written for those not up to the standards of the Stoic wiseman, so too was the *Enchiridion* not directed at intellectual elites or the religious establishment, as such, but all members of the Christian order, particularly those lay persons and clerics involved in the hurly burly of life and concerned about their salvation. Book 3 of *De officiis* argues, and demonstrates at length, the oneness of the *utile* and the *honestum* and the *Enchiridion* follows suit, Christianizing this mindset. As shown in Part I, above, humanists before Erasmus had seen Stoicism in one-dimensional, rather than two-dimensional, terms.

Erasmus brings in many sources but he is not, as has been thought, a rhetorician swinging carelessly or fitfully from one source to another without a clear plan. Nor does he contradict himself. He uses the sources he brings in to develop, step by step, a thesis. His mind is set. He knows where he is going. Whether mentioning Plato or Origen or St Paul or a passage in the Bible or, now and then, some literary figure, he does not simply state a view and go on to the next. He very consciously revamps these sources, either directly or contextually, to make them fit a set way of thinking and outlook – one moulded by Stoicism.

As with *De taedio Iesu*, the origin and meaning of the *Enchiridion* cannot be explained outside Erasmus' own physical, mental, and emotional experiences. Extremely disturbed by the incompatibilities between himself and society, particularly church society, he had looked as a youth and young adult for underlying explanations (see above, II.4). What self-analysis uncovered, first of all, was that his mind loved freedom and disliked ritual and that his body was unable to withstand hardship. But his probing and excavating did not stop here. What he wanted to know above all was the origin of his feelings and behaviour and how these impulses should be handled. He latched on to Stoicism because he came to see that Stoicism, unlike other philosophies, answered his burning questions. What came into sharp focus was not only Stoic discussions of unbending truth – reason, virtue, the *honestum* – but the reality, at one and the same time, of natural instincts and character traits for which at birth a person is not responsible. All the issues of life relate, he came to believe, to these inborn instincts and traits. The Stoics rightly saw that

4 Of course the printing press made carrying around the *Enchiridion* much more doable than was possible when *De officiis* was written.

some things are in accord with nature and other things are contrary to nature – and that the distinctions are all important.

A particularly important tension point in Erasmus' youth was his perceived inability to fast. He ultimately concluded, I have shown, that "ceremonies" such as fasting are things "indifferent" and bear no necessary connection with spirituality. But what is spirituality? Readers have recognized that Erasmus saw no necessary spirituality in religious ceremonies but have not correctly assessed the spirituality he advises. What has not been discerned is the Stoic frame of thought within which spirituality is embedded. Things "indifferent" must always be seen – simultaneously – from two radically different standpoints. From the standpoint of unbending values "ceremonies" are "indifferent" in the common meaning of the word. But from the standpoint of bending values "indifferents" are all important. Here the differences between indifferents must always be carefully analysed and dealt with. On the unbending side Erasmus points to the force of Christ's precepts – their inescapable and unconditional demands – and their precise nature. In his view these precepts had been flaked away by the common assumptions of the masses and the scholastic distinctions of the educated, one result being the satisfaction found in religious ceremonies as such. On the bending side he focused on ways to differentiate and deal with the differences between all the happenings (*indifferentia*, "ceremonies") that make up human life. What he saw was that natural instincts and one's own particular bodily and mental traits are indispensable starting points.

Unbending values: The precept side of the both/and

First in rank among the precepts are belief that God exists and belief in the divine promises (CWE 66, pp. 55 and 56). Christianity demands unshaken trust in rewards and punishments for our sins, eternal life, and the immortality of the soul (27, 62). Such beliefs comprise Erasmus' "first rule." If an individual does not believe in these hard and unbendable truths he is not a Christian but a worldling (57). Faith reflects "the treaty struck with God at baptism" (25). It is the foundation of everything, the only avenue, and Christ is the exemplar, the sole archetype (61, 63, 84, 86, 88, 93, 104). Regarding things such as, honours, pleasures, health, and the life of the body, "We should strive after Christ, our only goal (scopum), with such great ardor that we have no time to attend to any of these things, either when they are given to us or when they are taken away" (63, H 65/18). We must hold to the mystery of the cross

(110) and the "rule of Christ" (ad regulam Christi) (86, H 91/5–6), and "measure the value of all things by their conformity with the standards of Christ" (88). Brahmans, Cynics, and Stoics hold with grim tenacity to their beliefs, no matter the protests of the world, and so too must Christians hold to the dogmas (decreta) taught by Christ (93, H 99/11).[5] These dogmas include (referred to often) the rejection of things such as anger, desire for revenge, lust, avarice, ambition, pride, arrogance, improper self-interest, ill-will towards others, and hunger for power. Another dogma referred to repeatedly – and, unlike the previous ones, not found as such in Stoicism – is adherence to charity.

Even lacking knowledge of Christian heaven and hell, some of the ancients, "preferred to sacrifice fame, wealth, and even life itself rather than depart from moral rectitude (ab honesto)" (105, H 111/26–7). Similarly, Christians, having no doubts, must hold to their precepts, "with resolute purpose, wholeheartedly, and with a trusting and, so to speak, gladiatorial heart, ready to suffer the loss of their fortunes or their life for Christ's sake" (56). It is one thing to talk about Christian truth, quite another thing to be so committed as to suffer personal losses. In counteracting the vices that sprout up in human life, "certain fixed resolutions (certa quaedam decreta) should be inscribed in the album of the mind, and they should be frequently renewed, so that they will not fall into disuse" (126, H 134/22–5). These "fixed resolutions" need to be fortified "by prayer, the sayings of wise men, the doctrines of Scripture, the example of pious men and especially of Christ" (126). Prayer and knowledge intertwine (30–1). Following St Paul, the weapons to be used are not of the flesh (2 Cor. 10:14). There are only two paths, one towards Christ, "mortification of the flesh," and one towards the devil, "gratification of the passions" (57). "The love of Christ, the love of the good (honestorum) and of the eternal will automatically bring with it a repugnance for passing things and a hatred of things vile (turpium)" (104, H 111/7–8).

Bending values: The *indifferens* side of the both/and

Emphasis on the stark reality of precepts and the need to hold unbendingly to them has led many readers to imagine that the work is in the contemplative tradition. This conclusion has been arrived at from

5 Cicero refers to Brahmans who throw themselves into the flames without uttering a word (*Tusc.* 5.77, cf. 2.52).

either/or debates as to whether the work is more concerned with *otium* or *negotium*. John O'Malley is in touch with many of these discussions when he decides that "For all its originality, the *Enchiridion* is related to the tradition of *contemptus mundi*," thinking epitomized by Thomas à Kempis' widely read *The Imitation of Christ* (15th cent.), and Erasmus "does not, therefore, propose engagement with the world."[6]

The problem here, it can now be seen, is not so much O'Malley's conclusion as the question itself. Erasmus was not concerned in the *Enchiridion* with deciding between worldly involvement and non-worldly contemplation. The *Enchiridion* is about Stoic "indifferents" and the fact that these indifferents inhere in a mindset that is unitarily both/and. The author's outlook was not one-dimensional, focused on an either/or contrast between spirit and flesh, but two-dimensional, comprising a spirit/indifferents both/and. While *De taedio Iesu* focuses on Christ's natural instincts and experience of the world, the *Enchiridion* concentrates on the natural instincts, particular bodily and mental traits, and worldly involvements of ordinary humans. The challenges of life are infinitely variable and trying, but a spirit/indifferents frame of mind needs to govern in every situation. Debates as to whether the *Enchiridion* is more concerned with *otium* or *negotium* have no meaning once one grasps the Stoic cast of the author's mind.

1 Correcting Origen on *Indifferentia*

While it is commonly held that Erasmus' reading of Origen, in the summer of 1501, was a prime inspiration behind the *Enchiridion*, what has not been seen is that he radically changes Origen – who was mainly a Platonist and biblical theorist – to make him fit what had some years before become a deeply embedded Stoic frame of thought. Although Origen had some knowledge of Stoicism, as evident in his discussion of pre-emotion, he little grasped or appreciated Stoic thinking on things indifferent and the unitary *honestum/indifferens* nature of Stoic ethical thought.

---

6 O'Malley, CWE 66, xxx, 265 n. 112, and xliv. Schoeck holds that "nearly every theme of the *Enchiridion* may be found in the *Imitation of Christ* as well" (*Erasmus of Europe: The Prince of Humanists*, 30). Simon Goldhill represents a widely accepted modern view where he states that the *Enchiridion* is "a laborious and conventional instruction kit for piety." See *Who Needs Greek*, 51.

I have shown that near the end of *De taedio Iesu* Erasmus rewrote the interpretation of spirit, flesh, and soul set forth by Origen (d. 254/5) in terms of Stoicism (above, Part III.2). He begins, it was shown, by setting forth a Stoic/Christian either/or, employing interchangeably the Stoic word *honesta* and the Christian word *spiritus* (spirit) and the Stoic word *turpia* and the Christian word *caro* (flesh). The soul and its will are like an iron bar pulled between two opposed magnets (1286F). One magnet pulls it towards good (*ad honesta*), the other towards evil (*ad turpia*). The metaphor well reflects, I demonstrated, Origen's view. In his commentary on St Paul's *Epistle to the Romans*, for example, Origen attempts to understand why Jesus' soul is *not* distinguished from flesh or spirit:

> It is my belief that the Apostle [Paul] is using the customary habit in this passage [Ps 16:10, Acts 2:27], knowing that the soul is always midway between the spirit and the flesh and that it joins itself either to the flesh, thus becoming one with the flesh, or it associates itself with the spirit and becomes one with the spirit. Consequently if it is joined with the flesh men become fleshly; but if it unites with the spirit they become spiritual. For that reason he does not explicitly designate the soul but only the flesh and the spirit. For he knows that the soul inevitably attaches itself to one of these two aspects, as in those to whom he writes, "But you are not in the flesh but in the spirit" [Rom 8:9], and, "Whoever unites himself with a prostitute is one body" [1 Cor 6:16], here calling "prostitute" the flesh or body. "But whoever unites himself with the Lord is one Spirit" [1 Cor 6:17]. (1.5.3)[7]

Paul did not explicitly designate the soul, Origen adds, because he did not want to "break apart the unity of Jesus" by distinguishing soul from flesh and spirit. With Jesus, that is, soul was one with spirit.[8]

But Erasmus goes far beyond this either/or, spirit/flesh, outlook. He shows in *De taedio Iesu* that the soul is substantive, inclusive, and

7 See above, p. 128 n. 42.

8 André Godin, whose book has been immensely influential, believes Erasmus follows Origen in seeing the soul as simply an either/or decider between flesh and spirit. See *Érasme lecteur d'Origène*, 37–43. This either/or way of looking at Erasmus' thinking has pervaded research for decades. Even before Godin's work David Marsh, for example, had offered excerpts from a number of Erasmus' writings, beginning with the *Enchiridion*, as proof that his thinking was either/or, spirit/flesh. See "Erasmus on the Antithesis of Body and Soul."

variable, something separate from spirit or flesh – and that Jesus' soul was one with this content. The soul is not something that simply decides and latches onto either spirit or flesh. It deals with and represents everything that is not spirit and not flesh, everything not good and not bad, beginning with the primary objects of nature discussed at length by Stoics. The soul is attracted "towards anything that is favorable to nature; and it recoils from anything that threatens our survival, or even our peace of mind" (1287C). Soul comprises not only natural instincts such as the need for food but even (building on Antiochus in Book 5 of *De finibus*) a fear of death which lasts throughout life. In its many forms, natural instinct is "so deeply implanted in human nature that it can be conquered but never eradicated" (1288A). Although Erasmus insists that he has not invented this tripartite division of humanity into spirit, flesh, and soul (*spiritum, carnem,* and *animam*), that he has followed the lead of Jerome, who followed Origen, who followed St Paul, in actuality he radically transforms the meaning and content of "soul." Far from being something that simply makes choices between spirit and flesh, the soul is deeply substantive and is found on the second side of a unitary (spirit/*indifferens*) both/and.

In his *Enchiridion* Erasmus again brings to the fore Origen's division of man into spirit, soul, and flesh (51). If humans did not have a body they would (in Origen's view) be all soul (here seen as "spirit") and perfect. If humans did not have a soul they would be all body and lack every vestige of perfection. As it is (Origen holds) humans relate by their very nature to both arenas, through "the middle soul" (41). The middle soul is situated at the crossroads (52). From the vantage point of the middle soul the task for humans is to decide which way (either/or) they will go, towards the spiritual or towards the carnal. "As in a republic rent by factions, the soul cannot but attach itself to one of the two sides; solicited on this side and on that, it is free to incline to whichever direction it wishes" (51).

Promptly a quite different picture emerges. Erasmus does not deny the opposition between spirit and flesh any more than he denies Stoic opposition between virtue and vice (*honesta* and *turpia*) but Origen, he saw, had in effect blotted out a thesis at the very heart of Stoicism, a thesis fundamental to being a human and fundamental to the Christian enterprise. Christianity is both/and as well as either/or.[9]

9 On later criticisms of Origen's view of the soul, by Erasmus, see above, p. 130 n. 46.

The "middle soul" is for Erasmus not simply a decider between flesh and spirit (Stoic *turpia* and *honesta*, vice and virtue, bad and good); it has an independent and material reality. Humans occupy "a third world," a state between the visible world and the invisible world (65), a state that is "neutral or intermediate" (62), consisting of things that are indifferent, "*indifferentia*." As in Stoicism, indifferents comprise everything in the world that is not virtue or vice.[10]

> Ergo spiritus deos nos reddit, caro pecora. Anima constituit homines, spiritus pios, caro impios, anima neutros. Spiritus quaerit caelestia, caro dulcia, anima necessaria. Spiritus evehit in caelum, caro deprimit ad inferos, animae nihil imputatur. Quicquid carnale, turpe est, quicquid spiritale, perfectum, quicquid animale, medium et indifferens. (H 53/33–7)
>
> The spirit makes us gods, the flesh makes us brute animals. The soul constitutes us as human beings; the spirit makes us religious, the flesh irreligious, the soul neither the one nor the other. The spirit seeks heavenly things, the flesh seeks pleasure, the soul what is necessary. The spirit elevates us to heaven, the flesh drags us down to hell, the soul has no charge imputed to it. Whatever is carnal is base, whatever is spiritual is perfect, whatever belongs to the soul as life-giving element is in between and indifferent. (52)

The soul is not a faculty that by its very nature ties itself to either flesh or spirit. Nor does it simply make choices from an in-between position. By its nature it is neither flesh nor spirit and has no connection with flesh or spirit. Comprised of things that are "indifferent" the soul "constitutes us as human beings," "seeks what is necessary," and is "the life-giving element." Substantive, inclusive, and variable, the soul is at the very core of what it means to be a human. Aspects of the soul that relate to particular individuals have to be studied – as indifferents – with all

10 "All things are indifferent and indistinguishable except moral worth (*honesta*) and baseness (*turpia*)" (*Fin*. 3.25, cf. Gellius 12.5.7). Discussing in 1517 Romans 13:1–7 and whether laymen should obey the authority of rulers, Erasmus' argument is here again Stoic based. He distinguishes between "good" and "heavenly" on one side, that which is "bad" and "sin" on the other side, and in-between situations that are indifferent (*neque bonum, neque malum*) but "nevertheless necessary for protecting the order and concord of the whole state." The choices made must never "conflict with the righteousness of Christ." *Paraphrasis in Ep. Ad Romanos* LB 7, 820C, CWE v. 42, 74.

care. The indifferents that first need dealing with, Erasmus will demonstrate, are the particulars of one's own body and mind. No assessment of spirituality can be made separate from analyses and employments of these indifferents. Spirituality is not one-dimensional but two-dimensional, comprising simultaneous adherence to *indifferentia* and spirit.

The soul depicted by Origen, in contrast, has no substance. It is a faculty that decides between flesh and spirit and its decisions, as evidenced by his *Commentary on Romans*, have nothing to do with material that is neither flesh nor spirit. As discussed in *First Principles*, the soul is "indifferent" in the sense that it has to make a choice between flesh and spirit, and, in practice, continually teeters back and forth between flesh and spirit (3.4.2).[11] It is better for the soul "to follow even the wickedness of the flesh than by remaining fixed in the sphere of its own will to occupy the position of an irrational animal" (3.4.3). At one point Origen recognizes that indifferents comprise all events that happen in the world but he gives this an abstract interpretation. Things that are indifferent happen neither by God's doing nor without. God restricts them to definite times and places (3.2.7). Further on he gives a more extended discussion of indifferents, naming physical beauty and strength as indifferents, but even here he does not escape his either/or frame of thought (4.9.3–10).[12] Things "are called indifferent and neutral according to their own nature because when attached to evil works they can be called evil and when joined to good works they can be designated good" (4.9.6). In short, Origen sees nothing of a soul that is independent, substantive, inclusive, and variable, a soul that takes in everything that surrounds us, everything between spirit and evil, heaven and hell. Not seeing that the soul has its own content and is not simply a faculty that chooses between spirit and flesh, he would have emphatically denied that soul "constitutes us as human beings," "seeks what is necessary," and is "the life-giving element."

Going even more deeply into the matter, Erasmus states that God "established a third and middle soul between the other two, which is capable of sensations and natural movements" (quae sensuum ac motuum naturnalium sit capax) (51, H 52/32–3). Note first the "capable of sensations and natural movements." It seems virtually certain that Erasmus was looking directly at Origen's definition of soul in *First*

11 Cf. also *Princ.* 1.8.3, 2.6.5, 2.8.4.
12 Cf. *Contra Celsum* 4.45.

Principles, in Rufinus' translation (only pieces of the original Greek survive) and assessing what was wrong with it. All living creatures have souls and soul, states Origen, has been well defined by those who lay down precise definitions:

> Definitur namque anima hoc modo, quia sit substantia φανταστικη et ορμητικη [phantastikè et hormètikè], quod latine, licet non tam proprie explanetur, dici tamen potest "sensibilis et mobilis." (2.8.1)
>
> For soul is defined thus, as an existence possessing imagination and desire, which qualities can be expressed in Latin, though the rendering is not so apt as the original, by the phrase, "capable of sensation and movement."

This statement is unquestionably Stoic based,[13] but notice the context. Origen goes on to apply the definition to angels (2.8.2). He further develops the definition in his discussion of freedom of the will in Book 3, arguing – modelling here too Stoicism – that animate beings are moved from within themselves, "when there arises within them an image (*phantasia*) which calls forth an impulse (*hormê*)." When such a *phantasia* arises, the "imaginative nature" (*phûsis phantastikê*) sets the impulse "in ordered motion" (3.1.2).[14] In the surrounding discussion (3.1.1–5), likewise built from Stoicism, he notes that animals such as spiders and bees seem to carry out their work by natural instinct.[15] Spiders "are stirred up in a most orderly manner by a *phantasia*, i.e., a sort of wish and desire for weaving, to undertake the production of a web, some natural movement undoubtedly calling forth the effort to work of this kind. Nor is this very insect found to possess any other feeling than the natural desire of weaving" (3.1.2). But – the central point – with a rational animal the situation is very different. Humans, unlike the

13 See Inwood's analysis of a more detailed discussion of soul in *De principiis* 3.1.2–3, in *Ethics and Human Action in Early Stoicism*, 21–6. Görgemanns and Karpp state that the definition at 2.81 is Stoic and cite Philo of Alexandria (20 BCE–50CE), *Allegories of the Law* II 7, 23 ("soul is a nature that possesses imagination and desire"). See *Origenes Vier Bücher Von Den Prinzipien*, 383 n. 4. For Aristotle's thinking, somewhat related, see *De anima*, 433b 25–30. The phrase "capable of sensation and movement" is not found, it appears, in Cicero's writings.

14 Translated and discussed by Patricia Cox, "Origen and the Bestial Soul," 126–7. See also Inwood, *Ethics and Human Action in Early Stoicism*, 21–6.

15 Cf. Seneca, above, p. 7.

spider, are rational beings, and reason governs all natural movements, all urges or desires.[16] Focusing on things which arrive at our senses from external sources he holds that we must either assent or not assent[17] and in so doing distinguish between good and evil. With regard to the human body, as differentiated from externals, he ridicules the idea that bodies can be blamed. "And if any one were to refer the causes of our faults to the natural disorder of the body, such a theory is proved to be contrary to the reason of all teaching" (3.1.5). Our faults are found in unchaste and intemperate living.

In looking at Origen's "capable of sensation and movement" definition of the soul, Erasmus did not see a definition that needed imitating but a definition that demanded correction.[18] He refers not just to a soul that has "sensation and movement" but to a "third and middle soul" consisting of sensations and "natural movements," "natural movements" having nothing to do with angels and everything to do with natural instincts. And while Origen sees the spider as governed by natural instincts and contrasts this governance with the reason of humans, reason that can deny assent to bodily urges or desires (*phantasiai*), Erasmus contends – expanding Stoic *oikeiosis* – that natural instincts are inextinguishable. And for Erasmus here again the real issue is not that of choosing between good or evil (though he by no means denies that good and evil are always at play). It is the "natural movements" – and their both/and relationship to spirit – that are of central importance. The "natural movements" are inborn and ineradicable "instincts of nature" (52, 53) and "natural propensities or traits of character" (53) – a thesis that relates directly to his criticism of Origen (and others) on first movements and pre-emotions (see above, Part V).

Erasmus' description of the soul as life-giving should also be seen as a direct rewriting of Origen. As quoted above, "Whatever is carnal

16 In orthodox Stoicism reason takes charge around ages 7–14. See Dyck, *A Commentary on Cicero, De officiis*, 291. Cf. D.L. 7.86. Erasmus takes account of this distinction in *De taedio Iesu*, 1271A–B.

17 See Inwood, *Ethics and Human Action in Early Stoicism*, 78–91.

18 Regarding Origen's definition at 2.8.1 (above), Erasmus remarks in his edition of Origen's works, published posthumously in 1536 (mainly Merlin's 1512 edition), "that *φανταστικη* may be rendered *imaginitiva*, which is the understanding: *ορμητικη*, *impulsiva*, refers to the affections." See Roberts and Donaldson, *Ante-Nicene Fathers*, 4:286. Erasmus was the first to recognize that the translator was not Jerome but Rufinus. André Godin makes no mention of Origen's definition or the apparent relationship with Erasmus' statement. See *Érasme lecteur d'Origène*.

is base, whatever is spiritual is perfect, whatever belongs to the soul as life-giving element is in between and indifferent" (Quicquid carnale, turpe est, quicquid spiritale, perfectum, quicquid animale, medium et indifferens). Commenting on various interpretations of the soul, Origen states: "Bodies are in their own proper nature dead and utterly lifeless, since it is from us, that is, from our souls, that the material body derives its life" (3.4.1). For Erasmus, unlike Origen, the soul is not something that gives life to a body that is either dead or evil, mere "flesh." Soul *comprises* one's bodily and mental makeup, not to mention other things that are indifferent. Erasmus may have appreciated Origen's admissions, at one point, that the necessities of our bodies are not evil, that natural instincts such as hunger or thirst and the desire for sexual intercourse would exist even were the devil not always at work (3.2.2), but here too the trajectory of Erasmus' thought is very different. The fact that the soul is dragged in two opposite directions, the spirit and the flesh, means, Origen goes on to say, that the needs of the body divert us from things of the spirit (3.4.4) – which again bypasses what is for Erasmus a "third world" and the inseparability of spirituality from inborn bodily and mental needs.

In short, either/or thinking and both/and thinking are not in Erasmus' thought contradictory, anymore than they are in Stoicism. He saw nothing wrong with Origen seeing spirit and flesh as antitheses, a contrast comparable to the Stoic contrast of *honesta* and *turpia*, but while Origen applied this either/or outlook indiscriminately, Erasmus' focus is on something else, the both/and relationship of *indifferentia* and *honesta* as in Stoicism. Spirituality is not simply a matter of choosing (either/or) spirit over flesh; most of all it is about working out the indifferents, which comprise everything between spirit and flesh, as one holds unbendingly (both/and) to spirit.

In my introduction I explained why the wiseman can rigorously develop the indifferent side without contradiction (pp. 7–8). Consider now what the Greek anthologist Stobaeus (5th cent. CE) reports on this matter:

> They [the Stoics] hold that the theory on these [indifferent things] starts from the primary things in accordance with nature and contrary to nature. For difference and indifference belong to things which are said relatively. Because, they say, even if we call bodily and external things indifferent,

> we are saying they are indifferent relative to a well-shaped life (in which living happily consists) but not of course relative to being in accordance with nature or to impulse and repulsion. (2.80.13, LS 58C)

As Epictetus states in his *Discourses*, "The materials of action are indifferent but the use we make of them is not indifferent" (2.5.1). From one standpoint *indifferentia* have no significance while from another standpoint – simultaneous – they are all important.

The Stoic Cato explains in *De finibus* how this indifference/difference way of thinking had come about:

> If we maintained that all things were absolutely indifferent the whole of life would be thrown into confusion, as it is by Aristo [3rd cent. BCE], and no function or task could be found for wisdom, since there would be absolutely no distinction between the things that pertain to the conduct of life, and no choice need be exercised among them. Accordingly, after conclusively proving that morality alone is good and baseness alone evil, the Stoics went on to affirm that among those things which were of no importance for happiness or misery, there was nevertheless an element of difference, making some of them of positive and others of negative value, and others neutral. (3.50)

Unlike Origen, Erasmus grasped and was deeply affected by this way of thinking. From the standpoint of the unbending type of value, *honestum*, everything is indifferent in the common meaning of the word while from the standpoint of the bending type of value the difference among things indifferent is of crucial importance. In evaluating particular differences one must decide whether they are "in accordance with nature (or not in accordance) or to impulse and repulsion," "making some of them of positive and others of negative value, and others neutral."

The problem for Christians, Erasmus argues, is that they no more grasp how it is that all things in life are indifferent than they grasp, from another angle, why the differences between these indifferents are all-important (the "third world," the arena of "soul"). In short, they miss what it means to be a Christian. On the one hand, they confuse "ceremonies," mere ritual, with the precepts of the faith and, on the other, fail utterly to see that spirituality must begin with the particulars that make up their own natures. Christianity requires – in confronting all the circumstances of life – both perspectives at every moment.

"Ignorant of their own natures" spirituality is impossible

Not recognizing that everything not spirit or flesh is indifferent, a "third world," humans take no heed of the larger problem, discovering and analysing the components of what is indifferent. They are, first of all, "ignorant of their own natures" (44). They do not see the unique ways in which their bodies and minds are put together, their particular constellation of instincts and physical/mental characteristics, much less the significance. Not something that comes to the surface easily, knowledge of oneself requires deep study. "I doubt whether anyone has an accurate knowledge of his body, and are we to think that anyone at all will be conscious of his own state of mind (mentis habitum)?" (40, H 40/33–4). At all times and in every aspect of life humans must accustom themselves to "shrewd self-examination" (53).

Without analysing the particulars of one's nature or at least taking a first step towards this end, spirituality is impossible (32). What is spiritual and what is not is relative to a particular person. What one can become, what road one should follow, can only be judged in terms of the attributes or disabilities one starts with and one's situation at any particular time in life. The pilgrim must not begin with abstract assessments of what should be his course in life or abstract assessments of what would be Christian but with hard analyses of the components of his own body and mind. The components are not in themselves goods or spiritual but they are the indispensable starting points of spirituality. From thence we must "set our minds on those things to which our nature is more inclined," one example, very relevant to Erasmus and his time, being whether to choose marriage or celibacy.

> The myth of the giants admonishes us that we must not do battle with the forces of heaven, that we should refrain from those desires from which nature recoils and should set out minds on those things to which our nature is more inclined (ad quae natura propensior es), provided they are morally acceptable (modo honesta sint). Thus, do not entangle yourself in marriage if celibacy is more suitable to your character, and conversely, do not vow yourself to celibacy if you seem more adapted to the married state (si coniugio videris utilior), for whatever you attempt against your natural inclination usually turns out to be unsuccessful. (68, H 70/30–6)

In deciding on marriage or any other endeavour two things are required, a deep knowledge of things indifferent, beginning with one's own nature, and a firm hold on the precepts of the faith, *honestum*.

Here again Erasmus' thinking is underpinned by Stoic or Stoic-based sources. His insistence that we need to study carefully our genetic makeup relates to the thesis, strongly influenced by the Stoic Panaetius, found in *De officiis* 1.107–14. As shown earlier (pp. 122–4), in analysing theses in *De taedio Iesu*, Cicero describes at some length in *De officiis* the wide variety of traits found among humans and argues that a person's path in life must be built on the traits one is born with, whatever their nature.[19] It is pointless to fight against nature – a contention Erasmus notes in the margin of the edition he edited (and mimics, seemingly, in his criticism above of the myth of the giants).[20] The task for each human, if he is to lead a meaningful life, is to "make a proper estimate of his own natural ability and show himself a critical judge of his own merits and defects" (1.114). What is a proper path for one person may be improper for another.

Erasmus was also holding in mind, as with *De taedio Iesu* (above, pp. 110–11, 123–4), Antiochus' contention in Books 4 and 5 of *De finibus* that it was not logical for Zeno to have held that the *honestum* is the sole good and yet hold that we desire, by nature, the things that are conducive to life (4.78). The self-preservation instinct is life long, not something taken over by reason (5.24). "The senses were not discarded when reason was created" (4.38). Bodily factors are not only *relevant* to *honestum* – "the only good," "virtue alone," "the happy life" – the highest good and happiness are built directly from natural instinct, "the first principles of nature" (4.43, 45).[21] Correlating even more directly with Erasmus' thesis is the need to study our bodily and mental traits and the contention that such study is not something common or obvious. "Our nature at all events at the outset is curiously hidden from us" (5.41). As we grow older, however, our knowledge of ourselves gradually increases. We look around and see we are different "and then commence to pursue the objects for which we are intended by nature" (5.42). We need to study what we are "in order to keep ourselves true to our proper character" (4.25), to preserve and perfect our nature (4.32–9). "The sole road to self-knowledge is to know our powers of body and of mind and to follow the path of life that gives us their full employment" (5.44).

19 See also Erasmus' comment and marginal notes on 1.107–14 in his edition of *De officiis* (1501), pp. 54–8 of the 1574 printing (Ioannem Kyngstonem).

20 *De officiis*, ed. Erasmus (Ioannem Kyngstonem, 1574), p. 57 (1.110).

21 On the differences between the "self realizationist" theses of Books 4 and 5 *De finibus* and Cato's discussion in Book 3, see above, p. 110 n. 13.

In stating a number of times that among the ancients (cf. *Fin*. 3.73) the first stricture was "know thyself" (40, 41, 46), Erasmus is likely holding in mind Socrates, but the frame of thought is demonstrably Stoic. In *Phaedrus* Socrates states that he has no time for thoughts about monsters and the like because "I am still unable, as the Delphic inscription orders, to know myself: and it really seems to me ridiculous to look into other things before I have understood that" (229E). What he wants to know in studying himself is whether he has "a share in a divine and genteel nature." In *Alcibiades* he makes a point of affirming that knowing thyself does not refer to the body but to the soul: "And let others take care of our bodies and our property" (132C). In *Charmides* he contends that to be "temperate" is the same as to "know thyself" (164E).[22] Socrates did not, that is, see knowing oneself as about ineradicable natural instincts and ineradicable character traits. Nor, for greater reason, did he imagine that spirituality is inseparable from one's particular instincts and traits.[23]

In looking inward Erasmus is not replacing ritual or ceremony, unlike what is so often imagined, with a contemplative type of piety. Nor is he abstractly moralizing about the precepts of the faith and "rules" that should be followed. Piety and true morality cannot take place without an evaluation of one's genetic makeup and present situation. Human bodies and minds are very different and the Christian life begins with these differences. There is no way to become spiritual without deep study of one's own particular nature. Throughout life even, true spirituality depends on continual evaluation of one's constitutional makeup and decisions based on these evaluations. Relating to his Stoic sources,

---

22 Cf. *Philebus* 48C ff, *Protagoras* 343B, *Alcibiades* 129A, 130E. See also Erasmus' *Adagia* 1 vi 95 (*Nosce teipsum*) (CWE 32, 62–3), number 108 in the *Adagiorum Collectanea* of his Paris days, published in 1500.

23 Erasmus Bartholin and Lynda Gregorian Christian assume that "know thyself" meant for Erasmus what it meant for Socrates. See "The Figure of Socrates in Erasmus' Works," 2. With regard to "know thyself," Cornelis Augustijn states – rewording the error – that Erasmus is saying "the most important part of self-knowledge is the realization that man in his soul belongs to the divine, but in his body to the animal world." See *Erasmus*, 43. According to Godin, Erasmus had been "convinced by Origen and all the ancient ethic that 'the highest part of wisdom' [one-dimensional] is 'self-knowledge.'" See "The *Enchiridion Militis Christiani*," 73. Christ-Von Wedel sees Erasmus' referrals to self-knowledge as one with the Platonism of Ficino, Pico della Mirandola, and Colet, a battle of the soul versus the body and the passions. See *Erasmus of Rotterdam*, ch. 4.

what is spiritual for one person may not be spiritual for another. How a person approaches the precepts of the faith varies in terms of his particular inborn makeup. Otherwise stated, the person with "a gladiatorial heart" (56) holds firmly to the precepts of the faith but his middle soul has, inseparably, a unique agenda, provided by his particular physical and mental constitution.

A powerful statement of this unitary both/and thesis, evidencing also the personal experiences from which it had sprung, is found in the conclusion to the work. "Being a monk is not a state of holiness but a way of life, which may be beneficial or not according to each person's physical and mental constitution" (127) (Monachatus non est pietas, sed vitae genus, pro suo cuique corporis ingeniique habitu vel utile ver inutile) (H 135.8–9). This statement, which was to become famous (Luther rewrote it as "Monachatus est impietas"), is very often quoted by modern authors, especially the "Monachatus non est pietas," but the larger meaning has been missed. Arrested by the contention that "being a monk is not a state of holiness but a way of life" readers have consistently passed over, as if little relevant, the second part of the sentence, the allegation that choosing a way of life depends on "each person's physical and mental constitution."[24] What is imagined, in one way or another, is that Erasmus is simply saying that the ritualized monastic life is not necessarily holy because inner piety is what matters and – levelling the playing field – those outside monasticism have as much opportunity as those within.[25] In fact, as the statement explicitly states, a person's "way of life" depends on his particular "physical and mental constitution." The thesis goes to the very core of everything Erasmus had experienced as a youth – and overcome with the help of Stoicism. Forced to concentrate on the uniqueness of his own bodily and mental characteristics and thus to think out the nature of Christianity, he had

24 Examples of the failure to address the referral to "each person's physical and mental constitution" abound. I will note here Augustijn, *Erasmus*, 54, and Tracy, *Erasmus of the Low Countries*, 39.

25 Erika Rummel states, and this seems to be the accepted interpretation, that Erasmus was saying (merely) that "piety could be obtained by anyone." See "The Theology of Erasmus," 36, and her "*Monachatus non est pietas*." Regarding the nature of this piety, a persisting view, repeated recently by Scott H. Hendrix, is that the "Monachatus non est pietas" passage replaces ceremonialism as the essence of piety with (merely) "the desire to love Christ and to follow him by loving the neighbor," in line with Thomas Kempis' *The Imitation of Christ*. See *Recultivating the Vineyard*, 32.

ultimately concluded that his situation was actually that of all would-be Christians. No matter whether monk or layman, a person's spiritual journey must begin with one's particular physical and mental constitution. More than this, spirituality is inseparable from one's unique constitution. Whether one chooses to be celibate or not celibate is like everything else between spirit and flesh, virtue and vice, a thing indifferent.[26] What makes the choice spiritual is only the way one works out one's particular mental and physical makeup – as one holds unbendingly to the precepts of the faith.

We must not attribute to virtue that which is indifferent

So-called Christians, Erasmus contends, are asleep. Not even seeing the problem, they do not analyse their natures and do not build from what they learn. What Erasmus tries to do in the *Enchiridion* is to shake them out of their slumber and make them see the difference between who they are, whatever this may be, and what being a Christian requires. What they are is not something obvious. They imagine that life is a Greek symposium (25) whereas in fact, "the life of mortals is nothing but an unremitting warfare" (24). The war is not with others but with oneself. Those who do not recognize the war and do not study themselves are, by that fact, engaging in non-spiritual behaviour. Unconcerned about the unique composition of their own bodies and minds they are oblivious to the fact that "know thyself" – interpreting the phrase in a way foreign to Socrates – entails a detailed knowledge of one's starting point and then "war with oneself" (40).

Incurious regarding their habitual behaviour and the sources of this behaviour, people just accept their impulses as a given and do whatever comes naturally (53). In the process they falsify words and thus reality. Making no distinction between natural impulses and reason, they follow their impulses "as if they were the dictates of reason, to such an extent that what has been prompted by jealousy or envy they call zeal for God" (44). Deceit becomes second nature. They bend reality to make it fit what they want to believe and what they want others to

26 Although Hilmar M. Pabel admirably works out Erasmus' statements on virginity and marriage, like others he fails to recognize that "Monachatus non est pietas" is not simply a particular contention but exemplifies things indifferent – a fundamental frame of thought – other examples being things such as money or political office. See his "Exegesis and Marriage in Erasmus' Paraphrases on the New Testament," 192.

believe about themselves and about the world. Passions which appear honourable, but which in fact are neutral and indifferent, are "disguised with the mask of virtue" (53). Taking pride in their habitual ways of expressing natural instincts and character traits they "attribute to their own virtue something that is in itself indifferent" (53). The person who gratifies his own inclinations acts out what is indifferent as if it were not indifferent but a positive attribute. An "instinct of nature" is one thing; piety is something else (53). Whether one does or does not have strong sexual urges is indifferent – irrelevant from the standpoint of spirituality. The same goes for fasting or not fasting, praying or not praying.

> Many people are attracted or repelled by certain things through natural propensities or traits of character (Plerique propensione naturae atque ingenii proprietate rebus nonnullis vel gaudent vel abhorrent). There are some who are never titillated by sexual pleasures. They should not attribute to their own virtue something that is in itself indifferent (*indifferens*). Virtue lies not in being free of lust but in conquering it. Another finds pleasure in fasting, attending religious ceremonies, going to church regularly, reciting as many psalms as possible. Submit his actions to the following criteria. If he is seeking a good reputation or gain, his action smacks of the flesh, not the spirit. If he is merely gratifying his own inclinations and doing what he feels like doing (Si tantum ingenio indulget suo, facit enim quod animo lubet), he has no reason to be inordinately pleased with himself – on the contrary, he has reason to fear. This is the danger you incur. You pray, and you judge one who does not pray. You fast, and you condemn your brother for eating. If someone does not do what you do, do you think you are better than he on that account? (53, H 54/31–55/6)

The person who is "attracted or repelled by certain things through natural propensities or traits of character," without analysing these traits and then building on them positively, holding to the precepts of the faith, is not a spiritual person. He is "merely gratifying his own [natural] inclinations" or, alternately, "gratifies his own character" (animo indulget suo) (53, H. 54/22). Building up our self image in terms of these inclinations, blindly following them without analysis, has no spiritual value and can lead to all sorts of evils. Natural inclinations, whatever they may be, are nothing a person has earned. The traits and instincts given at birth need to be studied not with the idea that they can be changed, they can't, but so that they can be seen and understood and then used to discover the path, holding to the unbending precepts of the faith, that would be most appropriate.

2 Correcting Origen and Socrates on the Origins of Human Diversity

It may be easy to say that all things not spirit or flesh, virtue or vice, are indifferent (even while zeroing in on the extreme differences among things indifferent) but what this entails is for most individuals, Erasmus recognizes, counter intuitive and a hard sell. Positive character traits are as indifferent as negative traits. Traits deplored are no more or less indifferent than traits admired. No matter their variety, that is, temperaments are morally indistinguishable. In demonstrating this contention and its importance Erasmus rewrites both Origen and Plato.

Erasmus *denies,* silently correcting Origen, "a fundamental diversity of minds"

> As one state is more strife-ridden than another, so one person is more inclined to virtue than another. Such differences do not proceed from any fundamental diversity of minds (quae differentia non ex animorum discrimine), but from the influence of heavenly bodies, or one's ancestors, or education, or physical make-up. (44, H 45/12–16)

Why does Erasmus find it necessary to deny that there exists a "fundamental diversity of minds"? Hasn't he been emphasizing the diversity of humans at birth and the seminal importance of this fact? It might be thought that he would here have strongly affirmed human diversity at birth. Even in the quote he allows that "one person is [at birth] more inclined to virtue than another." Why, finally, is the belief that there exists a "fundamental diversity of minds" at odds with a naturalistic explanation of human differences?

Without question he is once again correcting Origen's discussion. Origen makes a major issue in *First Principles* 2.9 of whether or not there exists "diversity in the nature of souls" (naturae diversitas animarum) (2.9.5), whether or not, that is, humans were created diverse.

Gnostics had argued, he shows, that souls are "diverse by nature" in that only divine determinism, or the chance or accidents allowed by a creator, can account for the diversities that everywhere surround us (2.9.5). Political (cf. Erasmus' "As one state is more strife-ridden than another") and racial alignments (whether barbarian or Greek, for example), social rankings, freedoms or the lack thereof, degrees of health, intelligence, and the like, did not come about by free will but were ordained, or at least allowed, by God (2.9.5). The fact that some persons would be born better than others, some rich and others poor, some in power and others not had nothing to do with an individual's choice (2.9.3).

Contradicting the views of Gnostics, Origen argues that the diversity that we see among humans is not the way they were created but is due to causes that predate their birth (2.9.7) and can be coupled with God's absolute impartiality and righteousness (2.9.4). Diversity does not reflect the capricious actions of an unjust God but the thoroughly just responses of God to the free-will decisions made by rational beings. A righteous God would have allowed free will, and this being the case there was no fundamental diversity, i.e., no diversity that was at birth dictated by God. All humans, he imagines, were in a pre-existent state created rational and good and the diversity comes about because God allowed humans, while in this pre-existent state, free will. Using their free will humans obtained various types of merits and demerits based on the degree to which they progressed or fell away from the imitation of God (2.9.6). The diversity is the result of these earlier merits and demerits. Every being, whether of earth or heaven, possesses "within himself the causes of diversity antecedent to his birth in the body" (2.9.7; cf. 3.3.5). The condition of humans at birth is not due to chance, nor does it result from "different creators or souls that are diverse by nature." The diversity exists because, in a pre-existent state, "divine providence arranges all creatures individually in positions corresponding to the variation in their movements and the fixed purpose of their minds (pro varietate motuum suorum vel animorum propositique)" (2.9.6).[27] What we see are the results not of a deterministic God but of "impartial retribution," God's very just responses to these earlier free-will decisions. The Creator places

27 Earlier in *First Principles* Origen theorizes that when the mind goes lower down on the scale it turns into soul but the fact that some humans are more intelligent than others shows that portions of mind are retained in the soul (2.8.4). When the soul sinks down too far sensation withdraws and the soul is changed into the insensate life of a plant (1.8.4).

people in positions exactly proportionate to their previous merit. "The inequality of circumstances preserves an equality of reward for merit" (2.9.8). In short, the diversity among humans is not "fundamental" because an unjust God does not cause it. It is brought about by the free-will decisions of humans in a pre-existent state – to which God with all justice responds.

Erasmus emphatically rejects this view of the origin of human differences, a view that would take away everything he has argued regarding the force of nature. He does not allow that the diversity among humans, their character traits or their situations, has anything to do with earlier free-will decisions. Although he in effect agrees with Gnostics in seeing that humans are "diverse by nature," lacking at birth any free will, he does not agree that this diversity results from divine determinism or chance. The differences come about from the workings of nature, Nature writ large. The nature that creates human diversity does not, following the Stoics, need any higher explanation. However varied their temperament and situation at birth, humans are not responsible for their differences. Although elsewhere in the *Enchiridion* he puts all the weight on genetic factors as determinants of bodily and mental differences, in the above quote, where he is responding to Origen, he spreads the causation, referring to "the influence of heavenly bodies," an explanation explicitly rejected by Origen (*Princ.*, pref. 1.5), "or one's ancestors, or education, or physical makeup." But the causation is still entirely naturalistic. The naturalistic origins of human character are not an odd point but a fundamental of the entire work. The "virtue" humans are born with has nothing to do with what one has merited. Such "virtue" or lack thereof is simply a product of nature. Morality has nothing to do with the existence of particular character traits or social situations. And what is admirable or not admirable about a person's qualities at birth does not make that person moral or not moral, spiritual or not spiritual.

What is not diverse at birth is the moral stature of an individual. Morality is all about what one does with what nature gives. And here too, we may be certain, Erasmus was holding in mind his "greater handicap" thesis (see above, pp. 120–6). The greater the opportunities for improving one's natural condition, i.e., the fewer attributes one has at birth, the greater the possibilities for virtue. Although it is Origen who sees the initial diversity of humans as due to free will, it is Erasmus who sees everything originating from nature. He focuses on and details the temperamental and bodily differences of humans. Nor does Origen talk about the need to learn what our natures are through careful study, much less that spirituality depends on this. Erasmus' thinking on the issue, unlike Origen's, was not prompted by any important contemporary intellectual debate but by a profound belief – contrary to the accepted opinion of his time – that his own physical and mental characteristics were ineradicable.

Origen illustrates his thesis by bringing in the story of the twins Esau and Jacob (2.9.7) and Erasmus, in direct rebuttal (though here again not pointing out that he is responding to Origen's view), gives a radically different, naturalistic, interpretation. Origen quotes the following from Romans 9:11–14:

> When they were not yet born and had done nothing either good or evil, that God's selective purpose might stand, based not upon men's deeds but upon the call of God, it was said that the elder should serve the younger, as it is written, "Jacob I loved, but Esau I hated." What shall we say to that? Is there unrighteousness with God? By no means.[28]

It was because of merits in a previous life, argues Origen, that God selected, prior to birth, the younger rather than the older and loved the former but hated the latter. God's preference for Jacob can only be explained, "if each being, whether of heaven or earth or below the earth, may be said to possess within himself the causes of diversity antecedent to his birth in the body" (2.9.7). Esau and Jacob had not yet had the chance, that is, to do good or evil in the world, but they had already merited or not merited in a pre-existent state.

For Erasmus, in contrast, the story exemplifies the nature of Christian spirituality after birth. The context for his discussion is Paul's referral to a first and second Adam, in 1 Corinthians 15:45–50. The living soul, the first Adam, precedes the life-giving soul, Christ, the second Adam (47).[29] The purpose of the story, at odds with what Origen wants to prove, is "to show that the carnal comes first, but the spiritual is preferred" (48). Making no mention of the discussion in Romans, where God pre-selects, Erasmus focuses instead on the lengthy historical account of Esau and

28 See also Origen's *Commentary on Romans*, 7.15.1–7.17, PG 14, 1142–7.

29 On Origen's view of Adam, see Bammel, "Adam in Origen."

Jacob in Genesis (25:22ff).[30] His concern is not with causes of the differing personalities of Esau and Jacob but with the goals that humans need to have after they are born. Due to entirely different physical and mental genetic natures the twins were in conflict in the womb and the differences continued after they were born. But spirituality is something else. Only later did the mother consult the Lord about the great difference between the two brothers – and was told that the older would serve the younger. Contrary to the Romans account, that is, the Lord did not decree while they were still in the womb that the older would serve the younger. What matters is only what happens after birth. Again, "Whatever is carnal is base, whatever is spiritual is perfect, whatever belongs to the soul as life-giving element is in between and indifferent" (52). Humans have the chance to work out temperaments and situations that are indifferent, holding at the same time to that which is spirit. The fact that Esau and Jacob were temperamental and physical opposites in the womb, as well as later, says nothing about spirituality. Esau was the firstborn and had a harsh temperament but such factors are as such immaterial. What matters for spirituality is only what one does with that which is given at birth. Esau had the same chance, considered in terms of his own particularities (actually more opportunity, according to Erasmus' "greater handicap thesis"), to become spiritual as Jacob. But it was Jacob who, as it turned out, became the more spiritual – and this is why he was later preferred by God.[31]

---

30 Later, in his *Annotations on Romans* (1516) (CWE 56, 255–60) and *Paraphrases on Romans* (1517) (CWE 42, 54–6) Erasmus does discuss the passages in Romans that Origen focuses on (9:11–14). Regarding Erasmus' attempt to explain Romans 9:16, "So it depends not upon man's will or exercise, but upon God's mercy," see Rabil, "Erasmus's Paraphrases of the New Testament," 151 and Scheck, "Erasmus's Reception of Origen's Exegesis of Romans," 151–6. Denying in his *Annotations* that Romans 5:12 supports the doctrine of original sin, Origen is said to be "often slippery in argument" (CWE 56, 142).

31 Although Erasmus rejected Origen's thinking on the original causes of diversity, he was undoubtedly impressed by Origen's focus on human potentiality, freedom, responsibility, and God's mystery. According to Elizabeth A. Clark, Jerome and others opposed Origen's views because they wanted to uphold hierarchy among Christians. The condemnation of both Origenism and Pelagianism, "made effective in the west the flourishing of a Christian theology whose central concerns were human sinfulness, not human potentiality; divine determination, not human freedom and responsibility; God's mystery, not God's justice." See *The Origenist Controversy*, 8 and 250. Cf. Trigg, *Origen*, 115.

Putting the argument in personal terms, Erasmus was saying that his own temperament, at odds with religious and societal norms, was no worse and no better than any other temperament. What matters is only what he or others do with their particular temperaments.

Rewriting Socrates' fable of the good and bad horses (Temperaments are equal, morally) (Empathy belongs with the bad horse, not the good horse) (The "greater handicap" thesis, again)

Erasmus' referral to Socrates' fable about the charioteer and the good and bad horses, in Plato's *Phaedrus* (246A–B, 253C–254E) (44–5), highlights his use of sources, way of thinking, and core theses. Not least, it brings to light major errors in modern interpretations, exemplified by James D. Tracy's analysis in *Erasmus of the Low Countries* (1996). The difference between Tracy's work and the mass of research on the *Enchiridion* is that he does not simply gloss accepted interpretations but gives us concise reasons. But are these reasons correct?

With regard to Socrates' fable Tracy refers to Erasmus' own words (T 35):

> (Socrates' fable about the charioteers and the good and bad horses is no old wives tale.) Some are born with such a moderate disposition and are so tractable and compliant that they can be instructed in the path of virtue without difficulty (and make progress on their own accord without any prodding). (Non anilis est illa Socratis fabula de aurigis et equis bonis ac malis. Videas enim nonnullos ita moderato ingenio natos, ita tractabiles ac faciles, ut sine ullo negotio ad virtutem instituantur ac sine calcaribus ultro praecurrant). (44, H 45/16–20)

According to Tracy, Socrates shows that the good horse is easily controlled by the charioteer because of its sense of shame, shame that is connected with anger (*thumos* or spiritedness),[32] while Erasmus, in contrast, makes the shame of the good horse – which Tracy connects with an earlier referral to "fear of disgrace" – represent "gentle and humane

32 Tracy does not cite Plato directly. The connection of sense of shame with anger is not made in Socrates' fable. The connection of anger with spiritedness is found in the *Republic* 4.439E.

qualities" unconnected with anger (T 35).[33] A major thesis of Tracy's book is that Erasmus idealized this moderate, tractable, and humane disposition (a thesis readers everywhere seem to assume) and that this is the point Erasmus wanted to make in bringing up Socrates' fable.

Demonstrably, Erasmus is not, in the fable, talking about or admiring "gentle and humane qualities" in the horse that is born with a moderate and tractable disposition. He does not say here, or elsewhere, that the person with a moderate disposition is better than the person with a harsh disposition. He is making the point, poles apart and fundamental for his entire thesis, that the person with a mild disposition is no better than the person born with a very rebellious body. Quite a difference! And his sympathy is more with the latter than the former. There is nothing even remotely like this in Plato's fable, much less Origen's thought.

Both before and after the referral to Socrates' fable Erasmus insists that whether a disposition is moderate or immoderate the moral standing is the same. Spirituality only begins when one goes beyond what one is born with.

> If instead (of a bad temperament) you have been endowed with a good temperament, this is not to say that you are better than another, but merely more fortunate, and since more fortunate, also more beholden. (Quod si bonam mentem nactus es, non hoc protinus alio melior es, sed felicior, at rursum ita felicior, ut obligatior). (45, H 45/26–7)

An accident of birth makes the life of the person with a good temperament easier than that of a person born with a bad temperament but since the person with a good temperament has had nothing to do with his good fortune at birth he is more indebted to nature than the person with a bad temperament – and more obligated to make something positive of his good fortune. Erasmus is here describing an aspect of spirituality, not illustrating the inherent goodness of "gentle and humane qualities." Such qualities may be admired and sought but they have in themselves nothing to do with spirituality.

---

33 The "fear of disgrace" (Socrates' "sense of shame") which Tracy sees Erasmus tying in with gentle and humane qualities is not a motif of the *Enchiridion* and not textually connected with the fable but merely a single usage that is, in fact, expunged by Tracy from a number of other traits, such as respect for one's parents, compassion for the afflicted, and the desire for good reputation (42). The Stoics, and Cicero in their train, emphatically rejected Plato's discussion, in Book 4 of the *Republic*, of *thumos* or "spiritedness." See *Tusc.* 4.51 and Graver, *Cicero on the Emotions*, 167.

In fact, he is making an opposite point. People are not born with any inherent goodness. Nor are they born with any inherent badness. Temperaments are indifferent. The person born with a tractable disposition is, by that fact, no better than the person born with a harsh disposition. At birth neither individual has made a single step towards spirituality. That different bodily and mental conditions do not make one person superior to another is a fundamental of the entire work. "Temperament," one's mental and bodily constitution, is not something an individual can legitimately take pride in for he has had nothing to do with its creation. Temperament results (as stated in the immediately preceding correction of Origen) from either "the influence of heavenly bodies, or one's ancestors, or education, or physical make-up" (44).

The good horse is not even Erasmus' prime focus, contrary to Tracy's presentation. What most interests him is the bad horse, a stand-in for the human who has a rebellious body. Erasmus' heart goes out to the person allotted such a body, a body "which the trainer for all his exertions can barely keep in check" (45). Such a person must not lose hope but, instead, strive all the harder. He should see this very severe handicap as affording an even greater opportunity for virtue than is the case with mild temperaments. The distance between a person born with a handicap – such as extreme sexual desire or a hot temper or a bodily inability to fast – and a desirable counter value is greater than it is for a person with a mild and tractable disposition, and this being the case, his achievement in reaching the desirable value is morally superior. Indeed, *De taedio Iesu* shows that Christ himself proved the point. His handicaps were greater than ever experienced by a human and it was precisely these handicaps that allowed his incomparable achievements.

This insistence that temperaments are all equal, as well as the "greater handicap" thesis, relates directly, of course, to Erasmus' own youthful experiences.

Clearly Erasmus is not thinking in Socratic terms. His referral to Socrates' famous fable is only a beginning ploy, a platform from which he can develop his real concerns – a methodology he often employs, as evident in his rewritings of Origen, Gellius, and Bonaventure.[34]

34 For other examples of Erasmus' use of Plato in developing in the *Enchiridion* his own Stoic based arguments, see below, pp. 297–305. While Erasmus places Plato within a Stoic frame, the Florentine Marsilio Ficino (d. 1499) had moved Plato in the opposite direction, making him a Neoplatonist. And Ficino had discussed the fable about the charioteer and the good and bad horses at length in his *Commentary* on *Phaedrus*. See Ficino, *Marsilio Ficino and the Phaedran Charioteer*.

3 Not Flesh/Spirit but *Indifferens*/Spirit

Like others, Tracy sees Erasmus' thinking as throughout representing a spirit/flesh either/or, one aspect of this being Socrates' fable of the charioteer driving the good and bad horses discussed above. In support of this outlook he brings in André Godin's arguments regarding the influence of Origen on Erasmus, in *Érasme lecteur d'Origène*.[35] Following Godin he contends that,

> [Origen is] central for Erasmus' doctrine of human nature. The crucial identification of St. Paul's distinction between "flesh" and "spirit" with the philosophical distinction between "reason" and "emotions" comes from Origen. (T 33)

In fact we now know that Erasmus had come to see problems with this "philosophical distinction" long before reading Origen. Stoicism had taught him to see that truth is not simply either/or (*turpia/honestum*, flesh/spirit) but fundamentally both/and (*indifferens/honestum*, indifferent/spirit) – and so too, he believed, is Christianity. And in expanding Stoic thinking on natural instinct (*oikeiosis*) he had transferred emotion (going far beyond even late Stoicism) from the realm of reason to the realm of natural instinct – and therewith things indifferent.

Without question the *Enchiridion* does make either/or distinctions between spirit and flesh and between reason and emotion – where emotion has been evilly employed – and relates these distinctions to Christianity. "The authority of the philosophers would be of little effect if all those same teachings [regarding the inner and outer man] were not contained in the sacred Scriptures, even if not in the same words. What the philosophers call reason Paul calls either spirit or the inner man or the law of the mind. What they call emotions he calls the flesh, the body, the outer man, or the law of the members." "If by the spirit you annihilate the deeds of the flesh, you will live" (47). Later on, directly mimicking Stoic words and thinking, he states that it is impossible to remain long in the grip of wickedness if one has become convinced and has assimilated into the very substance of his soul that virtue alone (solam virtutem), by the very nature of things (ipsa natura rerum), "is best, most pleasing, most beautiful (pulcherrimam), most honorable

35 On Godin's work see also p. 127 n. 41 and above, nn. 8, 18, and 23.

(honestissimam), and most useful (utilissimam), and that on the contrary immorality alone is evil (turpitudinem unicum esse malum), foul torment, shameful, and ruinous" (85–6, H. 90/19–25).[36] God "is virtue itself by his very essence and father and author of all virtues. The dregs of impurity accumulated from every species of vice is called 'stupidity' (stultitia) [because contrary to reason] by the Stoics, valiant defenders of virtue, but in our holy writings it is called 'malice' (malitia). Similarly, the purest virtue, perfect in every respect, is called wisdom (sapientia) in both traditions. Now is it not true that wisdom conquers malice?" (38, H. 38/13–18).[37] Spirit is "the eternal law of goodness, drawn from the archetype of his own [divine] mind, by which we are glued to God and made one with him" (51).[38] On the one side is spirit, reason, and virtue (*honestum* in Stoicism) and on the other flesh, unreason, and baseness (*turpia* in Stoicism).

Expanding on the spirit/flesh polarity that he finds in the work, Tracy brings in at one point (T 36) a statement found in the "Fifth Rule": "The flesh, slavery, disquiet, and contention are inseparable companions, as are (on the opposite ledger) the spirit, peace, love, and liberty. The Apostle [Paul] drives this home over and over again" (78–9).[39]

My question is this: Does the larger context of Tracy's quote support a singular thesis, that being spirit/flesh, or is it not the case that the either/or discussions found in the Fifth Rule (and elsewhere in the work) are framed by something far more fundamental?

---

36 Erasmus builds on these words and Stoic concepts in one of his last works, *Ecclesiastes* (1535) – a work on rhetoric. Cf. ASD V-4, 312/593–4, 314/631–4, 669–73, 356/776–7.

37 Cicero uses *malitia* (for the Greek *kakia*) at *Tusc.* 4.34 and *stultitia* (contrasted with *sapientia*) at *Tusc.* 5.54.

38 Cf. D.L. 7.88: Right reason (equated by Erasmus with spirit) "pervades all things, and is identical with this Zeus, lord and ruler of all that is." Virtue, states Cicero, is "the same in human and god" (*Leg.* 1.25). On the Stoic vision of a cosmic city, a community of Gods and men on a universal scale (cf. *Fin.* 3.64), see Schofield, *The Stoic Idea of the City*, and Vogt, *Law, Reason, and the Cosmic City*.

39 C. Augustijn likewise emphasizes that the *Enchiridion* argues throughout an either/or, spirit/flesh, thesis. See *Erasmus*, 47–55. In line with many, R. Marcel sees the invisible/visible thesis in Platonist terms. See "*L'Enchiridion Militis Christiani*," 625. See also John B. Payne's influential *Erasmus: His Theology of the Sacraments*, 35, 54–70, and Pineau, *Erasme, sa pensée religieuse*. Others, such as Peter Kaufman, find in the *Enchiridion* "the subordination of sacramental observances to ethical behavior." See "John Colet and Erasmus' *Enchiridion*," 310. Anne O'Donnell holds that the *Enchiridion* sets forth a "rationalistic" approach to the life of virtue. See "Rhetoric and Style in Erasmus' *Enchiridion militis Christiani*," 37, 49.

Missing the *indifferens/spiritus* both/and

What discussions of the spirit/flesh either/or leave out is what the *Enchiridion* is really about. It is *indifferens/spiritus* both/and thinking that the text focuses on. Origen developed the spirit (reason) side of the Stoic both/and but left the other side, comprised of things indifferent, undeveloped. Not Erasmus. The *Enchiridion* centres on things that are indifferent, everything *not* either/or, *not* virtue or vice, *not* spirit or flesh. At every step the Christian necessarily confronts things that are indifferent – bodily and mental things, family things, church things, social things, economic things, political things.[40] How one deals with indifferents shows what kind of Christian one really is.

The secondary literature emphasizes the spiritualist purposes of the *Enchiridion*, piety in life as against scholastic logical abstractions or the "ceremonies" of the monks and the masses, but fails to grasp the type of mindset Erasmus was actually proposing, what he means when he refers throughout to spiritual "warfare," "the method and rules of a new kind of warfare" (126). The "new kind of warfare" he describes is not at root an either/or, flesh/spirit, warfare. It does not take away the reality of flesh/spirit any more than Stoicism takes away the reality of vice/virtue, but what it swirls around is an *indifferens/spiritus* both/and – just as Stoicism swirls around an *indifferens/honestum* both/and. There is all the difference between an either/or and a both/and frame of mind.

Like others, Tracy sees the Fifth Rule, the longest section in the work (65–84), as about progress from flesh to spirit (worldly to non-worldly, visible to invisible) and central to the meaning of the *Enchiridion*. He considers the Fifth Rule not merely devotionalist but Neoplatonist, mentioning Ficino and Pico.

The Fifth Rule begins with the statement, "perfect piety is the attempt to progress always from visible things, which are usually imperfect or indifferent (quae fere vel imperfectae vel mediae sunt), to invisible, according to the division of man discussed earlier" (65, H 67:24). Note immediately one thing: The division of man "discussed earlier" (at 41–2) focuses on Plato's dichotomy between that which is bodily and that which is divine. Nothing is said in that discussion about a third category, that of *indifferentia*. All of which shows yet again that

40 Cf. *Fin.* 3.60–1: "All our deliberations are said to be directed at" intermediate things, that is, indifferents. "Directly under the judgment of the sage are the primary things in accordance with nature and contrary to nature."

Erasmus is not bringing in sources helter-skelter but gradually developing a thesis. He develops his opening statement by explicitly distinguishing not two worlds but three worlds: the visible, the intelligible, and the world of man: "Then there is man, who constitutes, as it were a third world, participating in the other two, in the visible world through the body, and in the invisible through the soul" (65). The "third world" constituted by man is not an either/or, spirit/flesh, virtue/vice, reason/unreason world. Unlike with Origen, the space between spirit and flesh is not occupied by a (Platonist) middle soul that simply makes decisions whether to go to spirit or to flesh. Employing different words, this "third world" has already been described with precision. It comprises the material of life,[41] everything that goes on in the world that surrounds us. It is "soul," "life-giving element," "that which is necessary"[42] (52). And everything in this "third world," as described here and elsewhere, is indifferent. Spirituality that does not deal with *indifferentia* is not spirituality. Spirituality is unitarily both/and.

The indifferents focused on in the Fifth Rule are ceremonies, an issue central to the entire book. Religious ceremonies are not flesh or spirit, vice or virtue. Celebrating the mass, fasting, venerating saints, saying a certain number of prayers, lighting candles, dressing in a certain fashion, and the like have no value in themselves. They are nothing but "silly little ceremonies" (74). "After the last supper, with what anxiety and emotion Christ orders his apostles not to observe prescriptions about food and drink but about mutual charity!" (John 13:34–5, 15:12) (79). The prescriptions are in themselves merely indifferent. The problem is that the majority of monks, priests, and theologians, not to mention the mass of lay persons, see such ceremonies as having in themselves great value, practices that take them ever closer to heaven. They see no relationship between the ceremonies they carry out and their thoughts and actions, their anger, greed, quarrelling, self-centredness, and the like. They imagine that "flesh" is restricted to lust and sensuality and cannot apply to ceremonies. In themselves, however, ceremonies do

41 Cf. *De taedio Iesu* 1275B (above, pp. 120, 121 n. 25) and 1275D–F (above, p. 158). In a long and important letter to William Croy, in 1519, criticizing Croy's one-dimensional view of Stoicism, Erasmus states that worldly goods and benefits "must be turned into opportunities and materials for virtue" (*in materiam organumque virtutis*). *Ep.* 959. Allen 3, 569/28–30, CWE 6, 345/36–8. Cf. Plutarch, *C.N.* 1071A, B, 1069E ("virtues matter"); Epictetus, *Disc.* 2.51; Cicero, *Fin.* 3.61 ("*materia sapientiae*").

42 Cf. *Ecclesiastes* (1535). ASD V-4, 314/642–53.

not amount to spirit, as so many assume, and can, like any other indifferent, be turned into flesh. In fact all sorts of evils are carried out in the name of fasting and even while fasting (80). Everywhere the precepts of the faith are either missed or glossed over. "Where is charity, where is that joy of the mind? Where is peace toward all men? Where is patience, long-suffering, goodness, kindness, gentleness, faithfulness, modesty, self-control, chastity? Where is the image of Christ in your morals?" (75). The image of Christ is here the image of spirit. The image does not exist if not one with Christian behaviour in the world. Ceremonies can have value only if they allow one to advance in spirituality, to develop their indifferent status holding at one and the same time to the precepts of charity, goodness, self-control. "With great veneration you revere the ashes of Paul, which I do not condemn (since they are things indifferent), if your religion is consistent with your devotion (i.e., both/and)" (72). Ceremonies are indifferents that can reflect, depending on their use, either vice or steps (both/and) on the spiritual path. Spirituality goes nowhere lacking recognition that ceremonies are indifferents and then gauging, both/and, one's motivations in carrying them out. Spirituality entails making a ceremony more than an indifferent, determining while carrying out a ceremony how one can help, for example, a particular neighbour (a "preferred indifferent" in Stoicism) at the same time as one holds to "spirit."

The secondary literature sometimes points out that Erasmus allows that ceremonies are not necessarily bad (explicitly stated, 73) but what is missed is the larger context. Ceremonies are just one example of things that are indifferent. The material of life is through and through indifferent. Money, for example, is a much-discussed indifferent (63, 118–21). Not grasping the Stoic both/and frame of thought, Tracy imagines that the discussion of money is contradictory and reflects "bourgeois sagacity" (T 37). What Erasmus actually shows is that from the hard side of the (Stoic) unitary both/and money is scorned whereas on the indifferent side it is condoned, provided one appropriately works out monetary advantage (a preferred indifferent) as one holds unflinchingly to the absolutes. Where this unitary both/and mindset is in play – where money is at one and the same time both disdained and approved – there is true spirituality.[43]

43 Chrysippus, states Dyck, "held both a concern and a lack of concern for wealth to be folly (cf. SVF 1, 33.27ff)." See *A Commentary on Cicero, De officiis*, 197. As Epictetus states: "It is, indeed, difficult to unite and combine these two things – the carefulness of the man who is devoted to material things and the steadfastness of the man who disregards them, but it is not impossible. Otherwise happiness were impossible" (*Disc*. 2.5.7–9).

Buttressing Christ's view that "It is easier for a camel to go through the eye of a needle than for a rich man to enter the kingdom of heaven" (Luke 12:20) (120), Erasmus refers to Epictetus' division between the virtue of the soul and everything else (i.e., things indifferent) and states that nothing is so outside the virtue of the soul as money and also of so little utility, considering all the evils that come about as a result of money (119).[44] Not without reason, the pagan philosophers all despised money (118, H 126/1–2)[45] and placed riches in last place among useful goods (119, H 127/1–2). And yet, considered in terms of another type of value, the second side of the both/and, money can be of help:

> At the same time I have no great admiration for those who abandon their whole fortune all at once so that they can shamelessly beg what belongs to another. There is nothing wrong with possessing money, but the worship of money [where the hard side of the both/and is not in play] is allied to vice. (119)[46]

---

44 Both Epictetus' *Discourses* and his *Enchiridion* begin with the distinction between "things which are in our power and things not in our power." The "division" between what pertains to man and what does not pertain (his version of the Stoic both/and thesis) is a constant refrain of the *Discourses*. Cf. Long, *Epictetus*, 33, 180–9, 227–8.

45 The CWE editor relates the disdain of money to Plato, *Alcibiades* 134B, and Aristotle, *Politics* 1323A–B. There is nothing comparable in the passages cited. Aristotle states only, at 1323A–B, that happiness is most evident in those who have a cultivated mind "and have only a moderate share of external goods." In his *Republic* Plato refers to a philosopher as that person who is "moderate and not at all a money lover" (6.485E, cf. 3.390D). For Stoics virtue is a good, the only good, while wealth, health, and the like are not goods (cf. *Fin.* 3.49–50). Commenting on *De officiis* 1.68, Dyck shows that the "despising" of money is not Aristotelian but Stoic. See *A Commentary on Cicero, De officiis*, 197. On the need for carefulness and thrift in the use of money (as an indifferent) see *Off.* 2.87.

46 Galen takes Chrysippus to say that "the opinion that possessions are a good is not yet an ailment, but becomes so when someone takes them to be the greatest good and supposes that life deprived of property is not worth living" (LS 65L). Augustine's famous distinction between use and enjoyment of the world has a quite different tone and setting in that he sees the invisible in terms of the visible rather than as in Stoicism one side of a unitary both/and comprised of two radically different types of value. "This world must be used, not enjoyed, so that the invisible things of God may be clearly seen, being understood by the things that are made – that is, that by means of what is material and temporary we may lay hold upon that which is spiritual and eternal" (*On Christian Doctrine*, 1.4.4, PL 34). Reflecting, it appears, Augustine's view Erasmus refers at one point to "use, not enjoy" but the context is thoroughly Stoic. "Even for the philosophers there exist certain imperfect and intermediate ends, at which we should not stop and which it befits us to use, not enjoy (*uti, non frui*). But of these neutral qualities, not all are equally useful ..." (62, H 64/5–8).

The both/and mindset is brought out yet again in a closing sentence.

> Whoever is an admirer of gold hates a natural tendency toward virtue, and hates honorable occupations. (Odit enim virtutis indolem, odit honestas artes, quisquis admirator est auri.) (120, H 128/9–10)

Note carefully the meaning. Whoever admires gold hates both unbending truth and bending truth; hates, that is, both virtue (*honestum*), the disdain for things such as wealth, and wealth (*utile*) that is employed for honourable worldly ends – holding, without avarice, to unbending truth.

Erasmus explicitly states that what is said about money, "you may apply also to honors, pleasures, health, and even the life of the body (sex and food)" (63). At one point he shows that such things can be ranked: "Knowledge holds the first place among neutral things; then come good health, intellectual gifts, eloquence, beauty, strength, rank, influence, authority, prosperity, reputation, race, friends, and family possessions" (62).[47] In short, Erasmus' rejection of the common belief that carrying out a religious ceremony is a spiritual act has a much larger context. Stoicism had shown him that everything between virtue and vice – religious ceremonies being only one example – is indifferent.

In his analysis of ceremonies and all other indifferents, virtually the whole of life, Erasmus transfers the Stoic both/and way of thinking (first worked out in his edition of *De officiis*) to the heart of Christianity. It bears repeating that at the very core of Stoicism is the contention that "appropriate action" (*kathekon, officium*) is common to both the virtuous and the non-virtuous (cf. "ceremonies") but "right action" (*katorthoma*) applies only to the virtuous (the wiseman, a person at one with Zeus). "Appropriate action" takes place in the realm of things indifferent (things like "ceremonies"). "Right action" requires the addition of a higher type of value. The difference between "perfect" and "imperfect" appropriate actions is the moral character of their agents.[48]

47 Cicero holds that Panaetius overlooked the need to weigh one expediency against another (*Off.* 2.88, cf. 1.10).

48 "Intermediate appropriate actions," Long and Sedley note, "are neither good nor bad, when considered in abstraction from their agents, but in reference to these they are either 'perfect' or 'imperfect,' right actions or wrong ones" (LS 367).

A Stoic Socrates

In pointing to the either/or thinking found in the *Enchiridion*, I noted above (pp. 290–1) Erasmus' use of Stoic words but did not note that the illustration given also depicts both/and thinking. It is impossible, we read, to remain long in the grip of wickedness if one has become convinced and has assimilated into the very substance of his soul that virtue alone (solam virtutem), by the very nature of things (ipsa natura rerum), "is best, most pleasing, most beautiful (pulcherrimam),[49] most honorable (honestissimam), and most useful (utilissimam), and that on the contrary immorality alone is evil (turpitudinem unicum esse malum), foul torment, shameful, and ruinous" (85–6, H 90/19–25) (cf. D.L. 7.98–102). *Honestum* and *turpe* contradict each other but *honestum* and *utile* are inseparable. Virtue *(honestum)* is most useful (*utilissimam*) while *turpe* is not useful. There is an inseparable tie between *honestum* and what works in the world. The most practicable, decorous, and useful thing is also the most principled.

It may be wondered, however, why it is that Plato's thinking provides the lead up to this Stoic-based statement. Plato holds in his *Republic*, Erasmus notes, that virtue cannot be preserved without firm ideas of good and evil (*de turpi atque honesto*). Correlating with the contention that Christ is the sole archetype and that we must hold without deviation to "convictions worthy of Christ," Plato insists that the guardians of the state he envisions must hold to unwavering principles as to what must be sought and what avoided, *"fugiendis atque expetendis"* (85, H 89/15–16).[50] Adding depth to the argument, a correction of Socrates' view by Aristotle is denied:

> Such (the necessity of firm ideas *de turpi atque honesto*) was the meaning of Socrates' saying – criticized by Aristotle, but not at all to be deemed absurd – that virtue is simply the knowledge of what is to be sought after and what avoided. (Huc enim pertinet illud a Socrate non absurde dictum,

49 Note Erasmus' use of the word *pulcrum*. *Honestum* is a translation of the Greek *τὸ καλόν* and *τὸ καλόν*, as Chrysippus states, is that which is inherently beautiful (D.L. 7.101). Cicero uses a cognate of *pulcrum* in describing the inherent nature of *honestum* (*Fin.* 2.47, 49). Virtue accords with the nature of man and is thus something to be desired, something beautiful. Cf. *Ecclesiastes* (1535). ASD V-4, 356/776–7.

50 Cf. *Republic*, 412D.

> quamquam ab Aristotele reprehensum, virtutem nihil aliud esse quam scientiam fugiendorum atque expetendorum). (85, H. 90/2–5)

Aristotle's objection is clearly stated in his *Nicomachean Ethics*.

> In thinking that all the excellencies were forms of practical wisdom he (Socrates) was wrong, but in saying they implied practical wisdom he was right. (1144B 19–20)

Against Aristotle, Erasmus holds that Socrates was right in holding that knowledge and practical wisdom are one. He follows up with a referral to Socrates' discussion in *Protagoras* which proves, he argues, the inseparability of (worldly) virtue from knowledge and that sin arises from false opinions (85). Turning to *Protagoras* we read: "For you agreed with us (states Socrates) that those who make mistakes with regard to the choice of pleasure and pain, in other words, with regard to good and bad, do so because of a lack of knowledge, and not merely a lack of knowledge but a lack of that knowledge you agreed was measurement" (357D). Measurement is "the art of the greater and the lesser" (357A), "of relative excess and deficiency and equality" (357B). Following the dictates of knowledge and intelligence allows a person to know what is good and bad and to act accordingly (352C).

What Erasmus is doing here is bringing in Socrates to support – though he deeply understood a fundamental difference (see below) – the Stoic unitary both/and. The inseparable tie between the Stoic wiseman's virtue and his management of worldly affairs ties in more closely with Socrates' thought than Aristotle's. In effect he is recognizing a reason why orthodox Stoics had from the beginning so admired Socrates.[51] The orthodox Stoic wiseman carries out appropriate actions and his moral stance makes these actions "perfect appropriate actions." Otherwise stated, his worldly choices are never at odds with the *honestum*. In Seneca's rendering, whatever happens the wiseman always has at hand a reservation clause (see above, p. 44). In demonstrating in Book 3 of *De officiis* that it can never be the case that the *utile* can conflict with the *honestum*, Cicero gives his version of the thesis – transposing the wiseman to the world of ordinary mortals. Just as the *utile* and the *honestum* are one in Stoicism so, too, Erasmus is here alleging, are

51 See above, p. 143 n. 63.

practical wisdom and knowledge one with Socrates and Plato. In both cases worldly affairs depend on absolute truth and this is the case with Christianity also.

And we may do well to look again at Erasmus' editing of *De officiis*. Preceding Cicero's statement in Book 2 that nothing more pernicious can be imposed on human life (nulla pernicies maior hominum vitae potuit afferri) than the doctrine that the expedient (the *utile*) may not be morally right (*honestum*) (2.9), Erasmus comments that *utilitas* is not just any type of profit but "quae cum honesto sit coniuncta, & ad vitae societatem pertineat."[52] The *utile* is (a) one with the *honestum* or it is not actually useful and (b) that which is truly useful pertains, unlike that which is only apparently or speciously useful, to the actual needs of society. Note also Erasmus' intertextual comments preceding Cicero's statement that the general rule or formula he is setting forth, by which the *honestum* is also the *utile* and the *utile* is also the *honestum* (3.20), is "in perfect harmony with the Stoics' system and doctrines."[53]

Often the *Enchiridion* points to a correlation between the precepts of the faith and truly workable and happy worldly practices. Even without a knowledge of heaven and hell many ancients saw the harm of things like fame and wealth lacking moral rectitude (105). Indeed, where *honestum* is in play one can see that some neutral things are not only not evil but more useful than other neutral things (62). In fleeing from the world to Christ, "you are not relinquishing the advantages of the world but exchanging trivial things for those of greater value" (60) – and this is true even without consideration of eternal life (58). A thousand disadvantages attend the sinner (105). Lust, for example, may be a momentary pleasure but its larger consequences are self-defeating (113–18).

But Socrates' outlook is only one-dimensional

What Erasmus does not point out in showing a correspondence between Socrates and Stoic thought is the radical difference between them, which he more than any of his contemporaries deeply grasped. In bringing in Socrates he is again simply setting forth a platform (employing in this regard his rhetorical skills) from which he can develop a larger way of

52 *De officiis*, ed. Erasmus 84. See above, p. 66.
53 *De officiis*, ed. Erasmus 133. See above, p. 65.

looking at issues. Unlike Socrates, for whom all virtue is one, a single knowledge, "a rationally based expertise at deliberation and decision,"[54] Erasmus is envisioning not just one type of value but two. Socrates saw the importance of "avoiding and desiring" (fugiendis atque expetendis) (85, H 90/5) in terms of absolute knowledge and Cicero states in Book I of *De officiis* that prudence is "knowledge of things to be sought and things to be avoided" (quae est rerum expetendarum fugiendarumque scientia) (1.153) but Socrates failed, from the standpoint of Stoicism, to see that "avoiding and desiring" is actually a second type of value, a value that begins at birth with the self-preservation instinct and then at the age of reason (from ages 7 to 14) is analysed in terms of preferred and dispreferred indifferents.[55] Actions that build on things indifferent must be in accord with the absolutes but they are not like absolutes. In the first place they are entirely pliable in terms of natural instincts and situations. In the second place a very different type of reason governs responses to things indifferent, things neither good not bad. As *De finibus* puts it, "An appropriate act is an act so performed that a reasonable account can be rendered of its performance" (3.58). Erasmus makes this point many times.[56] What makes an appropriate act morally correct is something else – which is not true for Socrates. Albeit worldly "seeking and avoiding" cannot be at odds with unbending truth, *honestum*, "seeking and avoiding" is not something that can ever be spun off, as with Socrates, from the absolutes of knowledge and intellect.

Earlier and in previous parts I have in fact already described at some length the ways Erasmus works out "seeking and avoiding." Against Origen he shows the materiality of things indifferent and that from birth humans are ineradicably involved in "seeking and avoiding" – from natural instinct. God "established a third and middle soul between the other two, which is capable of sensations and natural movements" (quae sensuum ac motuum naturnalium sit capax) (51, H 52/32–3). Indeed,

54 *Plato: Complete Works*, ed. Cooper, 746.

55 As the Stoic Cato states, "all appropriate actions proceed" from things that are intermediate, that is, indifferent, and "what falls under the judgment and selection of the wiseman are the primary things in accordance with nature or against nature" (*Fin*. 3.60, cf. D.L. 7.88). Some things are found to be preferred and other things are rejected (*Fin*. 3.69). Diogenes Laertius refers to Stoic indifferents as things that can excite inclination or aversion (7.104). Some indifferents, Gellius reports, are *προηγμένα* or "things desirable," and *ἀποπροηγμένα*, or "things undesirable" (12.5.7).

56 See, for example, Erasmus' discussion of the situation of a judge below, pp. 307–8.

spirituality depends on studying one's natural instincts and character traits. And just as he here corrects Origen so too does he recognize what is lacking in Socrates' thought. In his edition of *De officiis* he describes in his own words the self-preservation instinct and what this means for humans. From cover to cover *De taedio Iesu* is about the "seeking and avoiding" that is built – "my Stoics" versus "Colet's" one-dimensional outlook – into humans from birth. The greatest exemplar of this is held to be none other than Christ himself.

Socrates fails to appreciate the senses

Before bringing into the picture Stoic indifferents and his own thinking on the emotions, Erasmus relates Socrates to orthodox Stoicism not only with regard to "seeking and avoiding" but to their view of the senses. Here too it is abundantly clear that he brings in Socrates in support of only a small piece of his thought and to give context for his larger, Stoic-based, outlook. He is building – as always – a thesis.

> The Stoics believe that when you have used as guides those emotions that are awakened most directly by the senses and have arrived at the point of being able to judge and discriminate what is to be sought after and what avoided (expetendorum et fugiendorum) [age 7–14], then they should be abandoned altogether. From then on not only are they useless for the attaining of wisdom, but even detrimental. For this reason they wish that the perfect wiseman should be free of such promptings as if they were diseases of the mind. The more indulgent among them scarcely concede to the wiseman even those first impulses that precede reason, which they call *phantasias*. (44, H 44/25–45)
>
> Socrates in the *Phaedo* (64A) appears to agree with the Stoics when he says that philosophy is nothing other than meditation upon death, that is to say, that the mind should withdraw itself as much as possible from corporeal and sensible things and transport itself to those things that are perceived by reason, not by the senses. (44, H 44/6)

Here both orthodox Stoics and Socrates see reality in one-dimensional terms. The Stoics reject emotions aroused by the senses, and some even reject the reflexive pre-emotions that result from *phantasiai*.[57] Socrates

57 On diseases of the mind, see *Tusc.* 4.23–33, Seneca, *Ep.* 75.8–14, 85.10.

"appears to agree" in that he claims in *Phaedo* that philosophy is nothing but meditation on death in that it is about rejection of the senses and a concentration on reason.

But *De taedio Iesu*, we now know, had already worked out in great detail and with a level of analysis perhaps never exceeded in later writings everything the author had found wrong with orthodox Stoic rejection of emotion – building on and going far beyond late Stoicism. So if orthodox Stoicism is related to Socrates' views, we know there is something lacking in Socrates' views. Clearly, Erasmus is simply setting in place a context from which a more comprehensive outlook can emerge. And indeed what this larger picture is becomes ever more clear in succeeding discussions, discussions which silently rewrite Origen from the standpoint of Stoic indifferents, discussions which reveal that emotions are not evil but merely things indifferent, that in fact philosophy and spirituality require oneness with corporeal and sensible things. In short, bringing in orthodox Stoicism and Socrates and tying them together does not represent a helter-skelter use of sources. The author is using rhetorical, not logical, tools to build a unitary both/and philosophy.

And yet, in arguing the need to hold uncompromisingly to the unbending side of truth, bringing in *Phaedo* made for Erasmus good sense. He was making an important point even if, in his mind, lacking a proper context. Abstract truth is unbendable and nothing valid in life can be accomplished without this truth, a truth which has as its goal eternal life. Christianity is about holding to Christ as the *scopum* and thus hope for eternal life, and it is in this regard we read early in the *Enchiridion* that Socrates and the Platonists come closest to Christianity. "Of the philosophers I should recommend the Platonists because they are closest to the spirit of the prophets and of the gospel" (33). The *Phaedo* agrees with the (orthodox) Stoics in that both see reality as residing in reason and the moral character of their agents, rather than emotion and the senses.

Even Cicero ties Socrates' discussion in *Phaedo* with Stoicism, in *Tusculan Disputations*, Book 1. In death the Stoic Cato and Socrates had something in common:

> Cato departed from life with a feeling of joy in having found a reason for death; for the God who is master within us forbids our departure without his permission; but when God himself has given a valid reason as he did in the past to Socrates, and in our day to Cato, and often

> to many others, then of a surety your true wiseman will joyfully pass forthwith from the darkness here into the light beyond ... For the whole life of the philosopher, as the same wiseman says, is a preparation for death. (1.74)

In bringing in *Phaedo* Erasmus was likely holding in mind not only what he had read in the first book of *Tusculan Disputations* and Plato directly (probably in the translations of Ficino), but the Neoplatonist doctrines emanating from Florence.

From Erasmus' larger perspective, however, *Phaedo* presents only one side of truth. While Erasmus is intent on showing that the senses are an indispensable part of philosophy and religion and that truth is two-dimensional, Socrates argues not only that "the one aim of those who practice philosophy in the proper manner is to practice for dying and death" (64A) but that bodily things, including food, drink, and sex, should be of no concern to the philosopher and even despised.

> Do you think it is the part of a philosopher to be concerned with such so-called pleasures as those of food and drink? By no means. What about the pleasures of sex? Not at all. What of the other pleasures concerned with the service of the body? ... I think the true philosopher despises them. Do you not think, he said, that in general such a man's concern is not with the body but that, as far as he can, he turns away from the body towards the soul? I do. So in the first place, such things show clearly that the philosopher more than other men frees the soul from association with the body as much as possible? Apparently. (64D–65A)
>
> No thought of any kind ever comes to us from the body. (66D)
>
> While we live, we will be closest to knowledge if we refrain as much as possible from association with the body. (67A)
>
> It is only those who practice philosophy in the right way, we say, who always most want to free the soul; and this release and separation of the soul from the body is the preoccupation of the philosophers? So it appears. (67D)

Equally alien to the central message of the *Enchiridion* is the summary Erasmus gives, before going on to develop his own theses, of Plato's layering of the emotions in the *Republic* and *Timaeus*. Following closely the wording of *Timaeus*, 70D–E, he states that the appetitive instinct, attracted to food, drink, and sex, is confined "to the region of the liver and the belly, far from the royal seat, so that it might live there in a stall like a wild, untamed animal" (43).[58]

The food and bodily needs, which Socrates is contemptuous of and Plato would confine to "a stall like a wild, untamed animal," are at the very core of Erasmus' youthful sufferings and intellectual development and central to the spirituality he describes in the *Enchiridion* – not to mention *De taedio Iesu*. No progress in spirituality is possible lacking attention to ineradicable natural instincts and character traits. In fact the comparison with *Phaedo* comes immediately before Erasmus criticizes at some length those "ignorant of their own nature."

Socrates' reasoning in *Phaedo* also contradicts everything Erasmus had taken such pains to show in *De taedio Iesu* about Christ's nature. Listen to Socrates:

> And if this is so [that a true philosopher seeks pure knowledge], then, as I said just now, would it not be highly unreasonable for such a man to fear death? It certainly would, by Zeus, he said. Then you have sufficient indication, he said, that any man whom you see resenting death was not a lover of wisdom but a lover of the body, and also a lover of wealth or of honors, either or both. It is certainly as you say. (68B)

In Erasmus' mind Socrates is in effect criticizing Christ himself. Christ suffered incomparable fear of death. He suffered this fear because (a) he was human and as such had even in the state of innocence all the emotions and (b) he wanted to send a message to humans, the message that natural instincts and character traits are inseparable from Christianity.

Once again Erasmus is using his rhetorical skills to develop an overriding philosophical thesis. His bringing in of *Phaedo* (43–4) is only a build up to his rewriting of Origen to show that "soul" is about things indifferent, the material of life, and that Christianity is unitarily both/and. Against what has been believed the *Enchiridion* is here as elsewhere organized and purposeful. The author is dealing very carefully with philosophic ideas but he is setting them forth by means of rhetorical tools (a very loose rendering of Cicero's methodology). He saw an important truth, closely related to the rigid side of Stoicism, in Socrates' contention that philosophy is about meditation on death, but he knew

58 Augustijn assumes that the latter is Erasmus' actual view (*Erasmus*, 51), as does Schoeck (*Erasmus of Europe*: The Prince of the Humanists, 37).

something Socrates did not, that philosophy – and most important Christianity – is two-dimensional. Platonist and Origenist views add something to the discussion, as points of reference, but they are always to be placed, in Erasmus' mind, within a Stoic frame.

A consistent reconceptualizing of Socrates and Plato

What needs to be taken note of is that Erasmus consistently rewrites Socrates and Plato in terms of Stoicism, specifically *oikeiosis* and the two-dimensional unitary both/and.

We are shown in *De taedio Iesu* that Socrates was not necessarily brave in taking the hemlock in that every human has distinctive and ineradicable inborn traits and this being the case outward appearances or actions cannot tell us whether or not a person is brave (see above, pp. 116–19). In the same work he brings in Socrates' one-dimensional claim that bravery (abstract virtue) is *knowledge* of what is endurable and unendurable only to show that Socrates' meaning needs to be understood in two-dimensional Stoic terms (see above, pp. 141–3).

In the *Enchiridion* he gives Socrates' famous "know thyself" a radically different, Stoic-based, "inborn traits" meaning (pp. 278–80); rewrites Socrates' myth of the good and bad horses, concentrating on the latter (pp. 287–9); demonstrates that Socrates' conception of "unwavering principles" is faulty in that such principles do not take account of a second type of value (pp. 299–301); and shows that the senses are not in themselves negative, as *Phaedo* has it, but fundamentals of human nature and things indifferent (pp. 301–5).

Elsewhere I will demonstrate that in *The Praise of Folly* Erasmus rewrites Plato's myth of the cave in two-dimensional terms and shows that the rhetoric-based flattery denigrated by Plato is untentable in that flattery is first of all a philosophical concept and, as such, an indifferent that can be employed either positively or negatively.

In short, Plato may have been the vogue among contemporary humanists, cycling out from Florence, but the author of the *Enchiridion* shows us over and over why he is not – against the prevailing modern belief – a Platonist, much less a Neoplatonist. If it is true, as long alleged, that Erasmus refers to Plato (or his Socrates) more often in the *Enchiridion* than any other pagan figure, what has never been recognized is that in each instance he rewrites the meaning in Stoic terms. More precisely, in each instance Plato affords a base from which he can lead into and pinpoint his own radically different theses – a method also employed in his discussions of Gellius, Bonaventure, and Origen.

Piety is "not a matter of feeling"?

James D. Tracy, the most analytic of recent Erasmian scholars, has come closer than anyone to seeing a frame to Erasmus' thought in the *Enchiridion* but the frame is strictly either/or, not only spirit/flesh and virtue/vice but reason/emotion. Strikingly, Tracy deduces and emphasizes that for Erasmus "piety is not a matter of feeling." With Erasmus, reason or understanding "must always be clearly distinguished from emotion of any kind" (T 34). Reason is incompatible with emotion. Reason and spirit tie together and so too do flesh and emotion (unreason). Erasmus depicted a one-dimensional Christ, a Christ representing reason and spirit but lacking a touch of emotion, a Christ that saw the world in either/or, spirit/flesh, virtue/vice terms. Against the enslavement of reason to emotion, Christ brought, alleges Tracy, a sword (T 36). Erasmus' statement that humans should seek "convictions worthy of Christ" (85) refers, in Tracy's logic, to this one-dimensional and emotionless Christ (T 34, 47).

Where Erasmus argues that "merely gratifying one's own inclinations" is unacceptable (53) Tracy contends he is disallowing feeling. These inclinations are emotions and piety has nothing to do with emotions:

> [A person] has no reason to be pleased with himself "if he is merely gratifying his own inclinations." Thus piety is not a matter of feeling; the key is to have imbibed "convictions worthy of Christ." (T 34)

But this deduction is entirely unsupportable – and lays open a serious misunderstanding. Earlier I demonstrated that "merely gratifying one's own inclinations" refers to those who do not advance spiritually but merely accept the physical and mental makeup they were given at birth and act it out (pp. 280–2). Erasmus is not saying that there is anything wrong with feeling or emotion. Nor is he in any way commenting on feeling or emotion as such. What he is saying is only that deploying in life the traits and feelings one is born with wins no points. "Whatever comes from nature cannot be ascribed to merit" (52). Doing what comes naturally has nothing to do with spirituality. There is no thought here of denying emotions or other instincts or traits. He is talking about an entirely different issue. Humans tend to enact and take pride in the traits they were born with, without thought or examination. Erasmus sees this as only a "mask of virtue" (53).

In fact, Erasmus goes all out to demonstrate the very thing Tracy denies, that emotion is an ineradicable natural instinct and, as such, not a false judgment or vice (as in orthodox Stoicism) but located among things that are indifferent. Seeing Stoic *oikeiosis* as life-long and transforming late Stoic concerns with the worldly realities of emotion, *De taedio Iesu* shows at length – rejecting a thousand years of theology – that Christ, more than any individual who has ever lived, was overcome and could not help being overcome by emotion (specifically fear of death), a natural instinct. The *Enchiridion,* written shortly thereafter, shows throughout the existence of emotion as a natural instinct and thus neither spirit or flesh and that the problem is not emotion but only what one does with emotion. And yet, not once in *Erasmus of the Low Countries* does Tracy see anything of natural instincts or inborn character traits in humans, much less their inextricable tie to spirituality – and imagines (building on the spirit/flesh dichotomy that other scholars see) that Erasmus is actually depicting an emotionless Christ.

The following is just one of innumerable examples (the lettering is mine) that demonstrate both the pervasiveness of emotion in the *Enchiridion* and the frame of thought that surrounds it:

> If you are not careful, you can be deceived by certain emotions (*affectus*) that seem honourable in appearance and are disguised with the mask of virtue. (a) A judge inveighs sternly against a criminal and thinks of himself as incorruptible. Shall we discuss this case? If he gratifies his own character and yields to a certain native rigidity, without experiencing any feelings of remorse, in fact deriving a certain satisfaction, but never deviating from his role of judge or feeling too complacent with himself, then what he does is ordinary, neither virtue nor vice. (b) But if he abuses the law for his own private hatred or cupidity, his action is carnal, and he commits a murder. (c) If he feels immense sorrow in his heart that he must sentence to death one whom he would prefer to be free of blame and not in danger of death, if he inflicts the deserved penalty upon the accused with the same sentiments that a father has in ordering his dearest son to be cut open and cauterized, then only is his action spiritual. (53, H 54/20–31)

The prefacing sentence refers here again to emotions that are tied to instincts and character traits that are simply things given, accepted without analysis or even thought – "the mask of virtue." The sentence immediately preceding reads: "It is a great error of mankind to think that what is merely an instinct of nature is perfect piety." "Shrewd self-examination" is required. Lacking analysis of their own particular makeups, humans tend to imagine that the feelings and behaviour they represent are admirable. In fact such feelings and behaviour are not virtuous but simply things indifferent.[59] Analysis of the statements that follow the prefacing sentence clearly demonstrates not only the reality of emotion but the place of emotion within Erasmus' Stoic frame of mind.

(a) gives an example of behaviour that is not vice but indifferent, a judge that simply does what comes naturally, "gratifies his own character and yields to a certain native rigidity." His decision in this case is properly thought out and appropriate but lacks any higher-level emotional involvement. In short, his emotions and behaviour are indifferent, "neither virtue nor vice."

(b) is not indifferent behaviour but vice in that his decision is based on evil self interest rather than the law.

(c) represents the unitary both/and, building on things indifferent as one holds to spirit. Clearly, emotion as such is not considered a vice. It occupies an in-between position that can be turned into vice or virtue – or remain in a state of indifference. There are, that is, not two options but three. The judge subjects himself to both "shrewd self-examination," including analysis of his own natural instincts and character traits, and holds unbendingly to the precepts of the faith. Now his emotions are not indifferent but infused with spirit.[60] The judge simultaneously unites two different types of value, a value that evaluates and positively responds to things that are intermediate, deciding the case in the most appropriate way possible (the realm of "preferred indifferents") and a value that resolutely clings to a few absolutes of the faith. "Then only is his action spiritual." Spirit, virtue, reason (all of which are aspects, in Stoicism, of *honestum*) are here inseparable, although representing a different type of value, from the *indifferens* (and the *utile*).

---

59 The thinking is, of course, the same for things external as internal. "If it [honour] is given for something that is by nature indifferent, such as beauty, strength, wealth, or family, then it cannot rightly be called honour" (121).

60 Further illustrating the tie to spirit, an example shortly after, relating to treatment of one's wife, concludes: "you love her above all because you perceive in her the image of Christ" (53).

Regarding (c), compare the following statement – which is followed by a discussion of the three (Stoic) categories of *turpia, honesta,* and things in-between, *media*:

> But if your eye is not sound and you look elsewhere than towards Christ, even if you have acted with propriety, your actions will be unfruitful or even harmful. For it is a fault to perform a good action in an improper way. (Quod si nequam erit oculus tuus et alio quam ad Christum spectaris, etiam si qua recta feceris, infrugifera fuerint aut etiam perniciosa. Vitium enim est rem bonam non bene agree.) (61, H 63/24–7)

Reworded, the judge may have ordinary emotions, emotions that seem upright to himself and others, and may make a decision that is appropriate (as in "a" above), but spirituality is something else. Spirituality requires in addition a moral stance. Holding to the precepts at the same time as he assesses his own character traits and the law, the judge's actions are undertaken with the "sentiments" of a father and "immense sorrow." Spirituality, in short, is both/and. The charitable feelings of the practitioner, his "sentiments" and "immense sorrow," may diverge from Stoicism but the frame of thought is through and through Stoic.

Throughout the *Enchiridion* Erasmus is intent on showing, in accord with Stoicism, the difference between *medium officium* and *perfectum officium*. (a) above represents *medium officium* and (c) represents *perfectum officium*, all of which takes us directly back to Erasmus' unparalleled editing of *De officiis*. In that work, we may remember, he shows, pointing to specific passages in *De finibus* and *De officiis*, that *katorthoma*, or *perfectum officium* (absolute duty) is that which is right (*rectum*) and is attainable only by the wiseman while *kathekon*, or *medium officium* (ordinary duty), "is duty for the performance of which an adequate reason may be rendered" (quod cur factum sit, ratio probabilis reddi possit). *De finibus* 3.58–9, he points out, shows that the wiseman, unlike others, combines right actions *(katorthomata)* with appropriate actions *(kathekonta)*.[61] Appropriate actions are choices made between things that are indifferent, neither good nor evil, on the basis of what accords with

61 The Greek words are not used at *De finibus* 3.58–9 but at 3.20 (*kathekon*) and 3.24 and 3.45 (*katorthoma*).

nature and what is against nature. Both the wise and the unwise make such choices but when the wise selects, this is *perfectum officium*. While restoring a trust on principle exemplifies a right act (*recte factum*), and *perfectum officium*, merely restoring the trust is only an appropriate act (*medium officium*). In other words, *perfectum officium* (*katorthoma*) is unitarily both/and.

The *Enchiridion* is about spiritual "warfare" (24, 126 passim) and the tools required are right actions and appropriate actions. Emotion in Erasmus' analysis comprises one of the materials of life – and as such can be employed either positively or negatively. Spirituality always embodies deep emotion.

"Two [contradictory] ethical imperatives"?

Although Tracy contends that the *Enchiridion* revolves around a spirit/flesh either/or and, this being the case, disallows all emotion, he also finds that Erasmus values, incongruously, "humane emotions":

> One thus finds in the *Enchiridion* a tension between two ethical imperatives: the subjugation of all emotion to the rule of the spirit [and reason], preached by Origen and the Stoics, and the inherent goodness of humane emotions, a point of view more distinctive to Erasmus. (T 36)

The picture of Erasmus that emerges here is that of a rhetorician picking and choosing, unsystematically, in accord with either the needs of his own psyche or the philosophical/religious thinking that happened to cross his mental landscape. In short, according to Tracy Erasmus' thinking was muddled. As commonly believed, he was not a philosopher but a rhetorician, not a person given to logic or heavy thinking but a person who pulled in arguments at will. In building up to his analysis of the *Enchiridion* Tracy plays, like so many others, on Erasmus' interest in the "rhetorical theology of the Church fathers," the "*humanitas*" advocated by Cicero, and "humane studies" (T 25, 29, 30). Erasmus was a person with "sturdy good sense" (T 22). What Erasmus most admired were the "human qualities" in others and he "liked to think he possessed" such (T 29). Out of this diverse mixture emerged, we are now shown, two contradictory "ethical imperatives," the one rejected all emotion and the other recognized "the inherent goodness of humane emotions."

The first view was built from Origen and the Stoics. The second came, somehow, from Erasmus himself.[62]

In fact, there was a deeply rational and logical frame to his thought. He was a philosopher as well as a rhetorician and none of Tracy's allegations regarding "two ethical imperatives" can withstand analysis.

Considering what has already been shown we can immediately reject the first of these "ethical imperatives." Erasmus never in the *Enchiridion* sees emotion as vice. Emotion may be employed in evil ways but emotion itself is not evil. Nor does he see emotion as spirit, although it can represent highest spirituality (as with "c" in the judge example above). Emotions are natural instincts and things indifferent – like everything else, internal or external, that comprises the material of life. In short, there is no "subjugation of all emotion to the rule of the spirit [and reason], preached by Origen and the Stoics."[63]

More than this, the *Enchiridion* builds on *De taedio Iesu* and the central purpose of *De taedio Iesu* was to demonstrate the ineradicable and incomparable emotion (fear of death) experienced by Christ. In being uncontrollable as well as ineradicable, his emotion could be compared to Socrates' bad horse – just as, in a different way, Erasmus saw his own mental and emotional disposition as related to the bad horse in being uniquely negative with regard to the expectations of the world around him, and ineradicable.

But how valid is the other alleged "ethical imperative"? Did Erasmus both argue for and represent in his personality "the inherent goodness of humane emotions"? Let's bring in here another statement by Tracy:

> The hierarchy of possible temperamental endowments which favors dispositions like modesty and docility comes neither from St. Paul nor Plato

---

62 In an earlier work, discussing Erasmus' thinking on free-will, Tracy speaks of "the unresolved tensions" and "warring impulses" of his mind. Whatever else may be said, Erasmus was "not a consistent or systematic thinker." There were in fact "two Erasmuses," and Erasmus himself "was conscious of the ambiguity of his position." See Tracy "Two Erasmuses, Two Luthers," 57, 56, 57, 37 resp.

63 Although Cicero states at one point in *De officiis* (1.101) that reason commands and impulse follows, which correlates with Tracy's "subjugation of all emotion," orthodox Stoics, unlike Plato and Aristotle, did not divide the soul into conflicting parts. Impulse automatically follows judgment.

> but from wellsprings of Erasmus' personality which lie beyond the historian's ken. (T 36)

Having no way to explain what he sees as a belief in "gentle and humane qualities," "the inherent goodness of humane emotions," and a favouring of "dispositions like modesty and docility," and that Erasmus himself had "a modest and gentle disposition," Tracy turns to the deep waters of Erasmus' psyche. The "wellsprings of Erasmus' personality" "lie beyond the historian's ken." In favouring such dispositions Erasmus was expressing something that emerged from the depths of his being, an area perhaps open to the speculations of psychologists or psychiatrists but not open, in Tracy's estimation, to historical investigations.

Questions are in order:

(a) Is it true that Erasmus favours within a "hierarchy of possible temperamental endowments" "dispositions like modesty and docility" and "humane emotions"?
(b) Is it true that this favouring of modest and docile temperaments came not from St Paul or Plato – or Origen and the Stoics – but from "wellsprings of Erasmus' personality"?
(c) Is it true that these "wellsprings" are unknowable, things that "lie beyond the historian's ken"? This assertion, it may be noted, allows the historian to present as true statements about a person's deepest beliefs and personality and then hold, conveniently it may seem, that further investigation of these allegations is impossible in that the origins cannot be known.

My answers are as follow:

(a) He did not favour "dispositions" like modesty and docility.
(b) He did not have a modest and gentle disposition.
(c) The "wellsprings of Erasmus' personality" are knowable.

(a) To say that Erasmus *favoured* moderate and docile temperaments, as such, is not only incorrect, it entirely misses the point.[64] Above it was

64 Also unrelated is Tracy's belief that Erasmus was early on influenced by Cicero's support for *humanitas*, humane feeling for others (T 30).

shown that a passage quoted by Tracy in this regard is misinterpreted (pp. 287–9). Clearly, some temperaments are, for Erasmus, as for most humans, more desirable than others. Some people are born, he emphasizes, with more amenable and virtuous characteristics than others. But spirituality has a different footing – and this point is brought out over and over. One can have a disposition more moderate than anyone and yet lack spirituality. Humane emotions are not "inherently" good from the standpoint of spirituality. The person driven by harsh, unattractive, unsocial, or unusual impulses, possibly at odds with some church practices, has the option of being far more Christian than the person with a moderate disposition ("the greater handicap thesis"). Disposition, as such, has nothing to do, of cardinal importance, with spirituality. So even if one were to hold, which is not the case, that Erasmus had, or saw himself as having, a "modest and gentle disposition," he does not allow that this or any other dispostion says in itself anything about spirituality.

(b) Nor does evidence in the *Enchiridion* itself indicate that the author saw himself as having a "modest and gentle disposition." To the contrary, in distinguishing the traits of Socrates' good and bad horses, he does not see himself in terms of the good horse, the horse representing a good temperament, moderate and tractable (gentle and humane qualities in Tracy's interpretation), but the bad horse, the horse with a bad temperament, immoderate and stiff, the horse with the rebellious body. Directly at odds with Tracy's contention, that is, he ties in his own feelings and sympathy with the bad horse, not modesty, gentleness, or humaneness. That he sees himself in terms of the bad horse is not surprising once one understands what the "wellsprings" of his personality really were, as evidenced by his youthful sufferings – and that they very consciously affected his entire life, outlook, and writings. The *Enchiridion* was through and through an attempt to relate what he had learned from his youthful sufferings, with the help of Stoicism, to Christianity and the lives of other humans.

(c) We now know a great deal about what made Erasmus tick. Most particularly we understand the key psychological problems he suffered as a youth, his struggle to deal with his body and emotions and to come to grips with the world that surrounded him. More so than perhaps any intellect of the time, he had deeply thought about and analysed his character traits and their causation. The modesty, docility, and humane feelings described by Tracy do not tie in with anything unravelled in Part III.4 regarding his youthful feelings, problems, or outlook. What he had so intensely wondered about was not only the unusual nature of his bodily needs, emotions, and character traits but, most of all, their roots. He was distressed because he saw these needs, emotions, and traits as very much at odds with society. He never imagined in his youth or early adulthood that there was anything "modest" or "gentle" or "humane" about the way he felt about himself – or even the world surrounding him. What had for so long troubled him was his inability to control his bodily, mental, and emotional needs or desires, beginning with a body that had to have food, even against religious rules, and a mind rebelliously wanting freedom.

In short, we not only know a great deal about the "wellsprings" of Erasmus' personality, but what we know runs directly counter to the picture presented by Tracy – and so many other analysts.

Let's look at yet another discussion – related to Christ himself – cited by Tracy in support of the claim that Erasmus favoured "temperamental endowments" such as modesty and docility. As quoted and paraphrased by Tracy (T 35–6), Erasmus states the following:

> Just as "pernicious arrogance" always follows the diabolical wisdom of the world, "modesty and docility" are the attendants of the wisdom of Christ. (Cf. *Ench.* 40)

Without doubt Erasmus does make such statements in his discussion, surrounding them with many biblical referrals, but let us look at the context and framework. The statements are embedded in a section (38–41) titled "That the beginning of wisdom is to know oneself, and on true and false wisdom." Earlier I demonstrated that "know thyself" does not have Socratic meaning for Erasmus but relates directly to inborn instincts and character traits. After aligning Stoic and Christian words for vice, "stupidity" (*stultitia,* foolishness) and "malice" (*malitia*) respectively, and stating that perfect virtue is called "wisdom" (*sapientia*) in both traditions (38, H 38/14–17), Erasmus contrasts the peace described by philosophers (the Stoics, holding to *honestum*) with the peace (that is eternal) brought about by Christ and contrasts earthly wisdom with the wisdom of Christ, "the author of wisdom." Referring to St Paul and others he sees worldly wisdom as attended by vices such as "pernicious arrogance," blindness, tyranny of the emotions, and insensitivity to evil. Considered foolishness by the world (cf. Stoic virtue and reason), the wisdom of Christ is not attended to by arrogance but by modesty and docility (*modestiam et mansuetudinem*) (40, H 40/12). But why does the wisdom of Christ require modesty and docility? We are immediately told that "Docility makes us capable of receiving the divine spirit," but why is this the case? Clearly he is not imagining some type of mystical union for he refers to an interior joy, "which neither vanishes nor is taken away from us with the pleasures of the world" (40).

A few sentences later a serious rationale, reflecting the title of the section and a central theme of the *Enchiridion*, comes into focus: "The beginning of this wisdom is to know thyself." Ability to receive the divine spirit is possible only if one has deeply studied one's own particular physical and mental nature but this is not possible lacking modesty and docility. Modesty and docility are necessary not for abstract moralistic or mystical reasons or because Erasmus was making an intellectual choice among a "hierarchy of possible temperamental endowments"[65] but because serious study of one's constitution is impossible as long as one displays the arrogance that self satisfaction and lack of modesty regarding one's natural instincts and character reflect. Lacking openness to discovery of one's true self – comprised of things indifferent, not vice – there is no chance that one can begin a spiritual trek.[66] People want to imagine they are what they think they are and what they appear to others to be, and it is in this sense that they are "arrogant." There has to be a compelling motivation or self-study of one's actual physical and mental characteristics will not occur. It is not something that comes about naturally but requires a "war with oneself." Building positively and spiritually on what is learned also takes courage, as well as being extremely difficult and always lacking. "I doubt that anyone has an accurate knowledge of his body, and are we to think that anyone at all will be conscious of his own state of mind?" (40). Even St Paul saw that he was lacking in knowledge of himself. Spirituality relates directly to the degree of self-knowledge one has and how one deploys it (41).

Erasmus is not "favouring" here anymore than elsewhere particular temperaments, much less his own. Nor is he emphasizing the need for

65 In developing his thesis Erasmus brings in Plato's hierarchy of emotions (42–3), which "king reason" tries to control, derived from the *Republic* and, especially, *Timaeus* (70D–E). See above, pp. 303–4.

66 In one form or another Erasmus comes back to the theme repeatedly in later writings. In the introduction (Letter to Paul Volz) to the second edition of the *Enchiridion* (1518) he states, in the concluding paragraph, "No one is further from true religion than the man who thinks himself truly religious" (*Ep*. 858. Allen 3, 377/587–8, CWE 6, 90/621–2).

modesty and docility for unknowable psychological reasons. Modesty and docility are attendants of the wisdom of Christ because he was convinced that such sentiments are essential *preliminaries* to the analysis of one's particular human nature and because spirituality can occur, if it is going to occur, only where there is such an analysis.

4 A New Type of Warfare: Syncretizing Two Opposite Types of Value

Is it really possible to hold in all types of situations, no matter how variable, to two utterly different types of value, one rigid the other bending? It is one thing to recognize that one's inborn bodily and mental traits are *indifferentia* and to then courageously analyse them, but quite another thing to then grapple with the *indifferentia* found in everyday affairs. The two-dimensional way a transformed mind would respond to things like religious ceremonies or money or legal judgments was described above and yet there are situations that require even greater abilities, situations that are not so directly under one's control. Can this *spiritus/indifferens* mindset, "the philosophy of Christ," actually work if applied to larger social and political situations – as Erasmus wants us to believe?

In his reading of the New Testament Erasmus found that Christ's injunctions – such as charity and the denial of warfare – were meant and were not things that could be watered down by worldly practices or the logical subtleties of scholastic theologians. There can be no distance, his *Enchiridion* emphasizes, between precepts and worldly actions. Claiming faith without actions in accord with the faith may be worse than having no faith. *Spiritus* is two-dimensional, at once non-worldly and worldly.

> One thing is certain beyond the shadow of a doubt, and that is that faith without morals worthy of faith is of such little worth that it even contributes to one's damnation. (86)

This statement has been related to James 2:14,[67] but what Erasmus states is not the same. James shows that the faith still exists but has no effect. For Erasmus the person who alleges faith but does not implement such

---

67 CWE 66, 86 n. 14.

proves by that very fact that he has no faith. Worse, it shows that such a person is engaging in deceit. In effect, it would be better to deny faith than to lie about it. All of which contributes to a persons' damnation. Faith is unitarily both/and.

Compare Erasmus' binding together of faith and action, and even the way he read the New Testament, with Stoicism – however different the tone. In Stoic discussions, as I have shown so many times, the wiseman holds unbendingly to *honestum* and at the same time searches out worldly solutions that are in accord with nature and appropriate. A wiseman is not a wiseman if he does not at all times correctly practise both types of value. Book 3 of *De finibus* is all about the oneness of *kathekon* and *katorthoma* and Book 3 of *De officiis* is all about, and illustrates over and over, the inseparability of the *utile* and the *honestum*.

As in orthodox Stoicism, even performing an appropriate action is a fault if the precepts are not present (61, H 63/27). More than this, as Cicero in effect shows over and over in *De officiis*, "He who does not wish to be perfect will not be good either" (Quamquam ne bonus quidem est, qui perfectus esse nolit) (97, H 103/15–16). Christ is "virtue alone," the "sole good," and in effect everything represented by *honestum*, but much more in that he stands for charity and eternal life (61, H 63/17–18).[68]

A new, two-dimensional understanding of charity

Charity and its gentleness (*mansuetudo*) (cf. 75, H 78/3; 79, H 83/3) is not a Stoic theme,[69] though some relationships can be found,[70] and yet here too the frame of thought is built from Stoicism. Charity, in Erasmus'

68 In holding here to Christ as the goal (*scopum*) Erasmus brings in three Stoic theses (61, H 63/34–64/1): (a) "Nothing can harm a good man except for evil alone." (b) In between good and evil are things indifferent, "[preferred indifferents] such as good health, beauty, strength, eloquence, learning" (cf. D.L. 7.102). And (c) unlike either evil or things indifferent some things "are so intrinsically good that they cannot become evil, such as wishing well to all men, helping one's friends by honest means, hating vice, and enjoying pious conversations." The latter statement seems to derive from Diogenes Laertius' account of Stoic good emotions, where he states that "under wishing they bring well-wishing or benevolence, friendliness, respect, affection" (7.116).

69 The Stoics speak of "gentleness" (*lenitas*) (*Tusc.* 4.43), but this is the condition of the person who never gets angry at all (Graver, *Cicero and the Emotions*, 166), not a referral to the person who is gentle and tolerant of others.

70 In *De finibus*, for example, the Stoic Cato shows that "we are born for society and intercourse, and for a natural partnership with our fellow men" (3.65).

mind, is simultaneously unbending (Stoic "right action," *katorthoma*) and bending (Stoic "appropriate action," *kathekon*, *officium*). It is inseparably a core precept of the faith and a way of behaving – comparable to the Stoic cardinal virtues. As a precept, charity ties in not only with the precepts I listed earlier (pp. 265–6) but most remarkably to Erasmus' denials, based on his reading of the New Testament, that Christians can repel force with force (96–7). And yet, by its very nature, charity takes account of the particular personalities and situations of humans, and works out the most appropriate possible solutions.

But where, Erasmus wants to know, do humans recognize that charity is a precept, much less take account of – and practise – its both/and nature?

> ... where are the fruits of the Spirit? Where is charity, where is that joy of the mind? Where is peace toward all men? Where is patience, long-suffering, goodness, kindness, gentleness, faithfulness, modesty, self-control, chastity? Where is the image of Christ in your morals? ... But men who are skilful at indulging their own vices, and quick to criticize the vices of others do not think that this has anything to do with them. What Paul said about walking in the flesh [*Rom*. 8:1–8] they apply only to adulterers and whore-mongers. (75)

Failing to learn from scripture so-called Christians simply mouth – ever so conveniently – their unexamined and habitual ways of seeing themselves and others. Charity and related doctrines are nowhere to be found.

Is there not, however, a problem in attempting to apply the unbending precepts of the faith to one's interaction with other humans and all the variables of personality and situation? How can one in actual practice deal charitably – in all "gentleness" – with those who do not in fact hold to the precepts, the mass of humans? Won't the precepts be inevitably compromised? How can one deal with people on their own terms – even if one's communication skills have been perfected by the study of rhetoric – without corrupting oneself? Won't one inevitably end up by adapting Christ to men's lives rather than adapting men's lives to Christ (86)?[71] By definition, it might seem, how can worldliness

71 Over and over in his writings Erasmus contends, often with examples, that humans twist Christ's teachings to make them fit, ever so conveniently, evil self-interest. Cf. *Enchiridion* H 91/1–2, CWE 66, 86; *Bellum* ASD II-7, 32/601–2, CWE 35, 423; *Adagia* I v 93 (493), ASD II-1, 563–4, CWE 31, 465; and *Paraclesis* (1516): "We drag heavenly

not result in a breakdown of that which is non-worldly – and deceit of others as well as oneself? Erasmus has an answer:

> Hold the common crowd with its opinions and actions in complete contempt and take hold sincerely and entirely of Christian principles ... But wait! While I wish that you forcefully separate yourself from the common crowd, at the same time I do not want you to revive the practices of the Cynics by snarling indiscriminately at the beliefs and deeds of others ... You, too, must be all things to all men [1 *Cor*. 9:22], so that you may win everyone to the side of Christ, as far as it is possible, without giving offence to piety. Adapt yourself to everyone exteriorly, provided that interiorly your resolution remains unshaken (ut intus quidem immotum sedeat propositum). (104, H 110/14–30)

(a) On one side of one's two-dimensional mindset hold common opinions in contempt and (b) on the other side adapt to the physical/mental/emotional state and situations of everyone. And yet (c) this worldly adapting must never take away from one's absolute adherence, interiorly, to the precepts of the faith. The Stoic wiseman in all his actions and in all the perils of life, no matter the outcome, has a fixed inner intention[72] and so too does the Christian "inner man" (62, cf. 47). The purposes of this inner man are unbendable, wholehearted, and "gladiatorial" – regardless of what happens to the outer man (56). And yet in holding to right intention the Christian, like the Stoic, attempts to bring about the best possible worldly outcomes.[73] Charity is one aspect of this

---

doctrines down to the level of our own life as if it were a Lydian [or Lesbian] rule," LB 5, 141E, Olin 100.

72 Cf. *Tusc*. 3.34, 4.37, *Fin*. 3.22, 32, 5.20, *Par*. 22; Seneca, *Ben*. 4.34.4–5, 39.3, *Tr*. 13.2–3; D.L. 7.88.

73 Erasmus makes full use of rhetoric in his *Adages* (1500, 1508, 1515, and later) but Kathy Eden fails to distinguish in her discussions of these proverbs Erasmus' Stoic-based mindset. Commenting on the fact that the adage "Walk not in the public highway" (LB II, 20C, CWE 31, 41) is contradicted by the adage "Do not walk outside the public highway" (LB II, 21BC, CWE 31, 42) Erasmus states, quoted by Eden: "We need not be surprised at this contradiction since, as has been rightly laid down, one should speak like the many but think like the few, and yet at the same time there are matters in which it is the part of a skillful man to agree with the multitude, and others in which a good man must entirely differ from it." Eden believes Erasmus is merely reaffirming "a special rhetorical property of all proverbs." See *Friends Hold All Things in Common*, 136.

undeviating inner intention and as such is bending as well as unbending, imperfect as well as perfect.

Two-dimensional pacifism

The two-dimensional but unitary nature of Erasmus' outlook is evident even in his discussion in the *Enchiridion* of war, a subject Erasmus would develop in major works.

> "It is right to repel force with force," they say. I make no objections to what the laws of the empire permit; but I wonder how such statements could have found acceptance among Christians ... [he then quotes Matt. 5:39–41, 44–5, 46]. Listen to Paul ... Return no one evil for evil ... If it is possible, as far as in you lies, be at peace with all men [Rom. 12:14, 17–21] ... If you can avoid or repel evil without committing evil yourself, no one forbids you to do so. But if not, beware of saying: "It is better to do than to have done to you." If you can, correct him either by overwhelming him with good deeds or by winning him over by gentleness. If not, it is preferable that one perish rather than both. (97)

If Christ rejected the "right to repel force with force" and advocated winning over evildoers by "gentleness," does this not make Erasmus, as commonly believed, a pacifist – albeit a pacifist who engaged in wishy-washy rhetorical thinking and often contradicted himself? Note first of all that there are, as with charity, two types of value at play: one hard and unbending, the other bending. On the bending side the need is for expedient techniques in dealing with violence or potential violence, beginning with good deeds and a gentleness that recognizes differing attitudes and customs. Further on he states that contention, feelings of anger, and desire for vengeance simply make the problem worse (123).[74] On the hard side one must at all times hold to Christ's rejection of war. Whether bending to the situations and animosities of others is successful or not one must never compromise this fundamental of Christianity.

---

74 Although the relationship is tenuous, compare Erasmus' contention that one remedy against anger is to realize that God will pardon you if you pardon the offender (124) with *Fin.* 3.66: "But how inconsistent it would be for us to expect the immortal gods to love and cherish us, when we ourselves despise and neglect one another!"

One must at all times hold common opinion regarding the allowableness of war in complete contempt.

Taking into account the two types of value referred to, was Erasmus actually rejecting all involvement in warfare? Note the "as far as in you lies, be at peace with all men" and the need to "avoid or repel evil without committing evil." Would it be possible for a Christian to become involved in warfare, as a last resort, should he (a) reject common opinion and formal justifications of warfare (including Roman law), (b) unbendingly hold high Christ's denial, and (c) practise – as a concomitant of unbending truth – expedient worldly techniques?

Consider what I have demonstrated in some detail elsewhere – even before grasping the Stoic base – regarding Erasmus' extensive writings on war, particularly *Dulce bellum inexpertis* (1515), *Querela pacis* (1517), and *Utilissima consultatio de bello Turcis inferendo* (1530).[75] A central and entirely consistent theme in these writings – in conscious opposition to the way of thinking found in the massive tomes of scholastics – is that a Christian never allows himself to believe that Christ did not prohibit all warfare. "The entire Christian philosophy, that is the gospels and the apostolic letters, discourages war."[76] If Nature (the *doctrina naturae*) is a reason why war should be denied, Christ's precepts (the *doctrina Christi*) are the higher reason.[77] "Do not sully that heavenly philosophy of Christ (coelestem Christi philosophiam) by confusing it with the decrees of man."[78] Christ absolutely forbade Christians to resist evil and ordered them to return good for evil [Matt. 5:39, 44].[79] And yet Erasmus sees no contradiction – unlike modern scholars – in holding that Christ also shows Christians how to cope with the real-life reality

75 Dealy, "The Dynamics of Erasmus' Thought on War," 53–67.

76 *Apologia adversus rhapsodias Alberti Pii* (1531), LB 9 1193B, cf. CWE 84, 349. Cf. *Institutio principis christiani* (1516), ASD IV-1, 215/511–17, CWE 27, 284. Note that preachers at Rome from c. 1450 to 1520 urged war against the Turks, often saw the Turks as the cause of Christianity's problems, and sometimes portrayed Jesus as a person who gained victory through war. See O'Malley, *Praise and Blame in Renaissance Rome*, 61, 81, 115, 166–7, 196, 198, 206, 233, 234.

77 *Querela* ASD IV-2, 64–5/113–18, CWE 27, 296.

78 *Ep.* 858 (introduction to the 1518 *Enchiridion*). Allen 3, 367–8/227–31, CWE 6, 79/242–4.

79 *Querela* ASD IV-2, 74/307–8, CWE 27, 302. Cf. *Bellum* ASD II-7, 26/449, 35/688–9, CWE 35, 417, 427; *Sileni Alcibiadis* (1515) ASD II-5, 184/517–19, CWE 34, 277.

of war, how to make war less attractive, less practised, and less evil.[80] In this regard Erasmus emphasizes that warfare can be eliminated only gradually, little by little.[81] Christ "does not quench the smoking flax nor break the bruised reed, as the prophecy said, but cherishes and tolerates the imperfect until it could become better."[82] The task is to carry out prudent and expedient actions as one holds unbendingly to the absolutes – absolutes that at all times require appropriate deeds.[83] Against the Turks, for example, the Christian will begin with good examples – as contrasted with the bad examples they are every day presented with.[84] The problem is that without the absolutes one cannot even see what is truly expedient and prudent. Decorum and prudence are not, for Erasmus, independent variables. One cannot implement a part of Christianity by starting with decorum and prudence. The prudential is laudable but people use prudence in order to live any way they want – lacking absolutes.[85] Bereft of the unitary both/and mindset not only kings but popes and priests everywhere engage in war employing evil prudence and dissimulation – to the detriment of not

---

80 Like many, J. Mulryan sees Erasmus' attitude towards war as ambivalent and explains this by an "inability to reconcile humanistic ideals with experiential truth." See "Erasmus and War," 15. Christine Christ-Von Wedel admirably shows that Erasmus incorporates historical context into his many discussions of war but like others she fails to grasp his Stoic based unitarily two-dimensional mindset – a "pacifism" that does not contrast with "realism" but demands exactly what she points to, worldly (Christian) responses in accord with time and place circumstances. See *Erasmus of Rotterdam*, ch. 17. According to Erika Rummel Erasmus' books on war are "rhetorical compositions and offer clichés rather than Erasmus's personal opinions." See "Secular Advice in Erasmus's Sacred Writings," 16 (Abstract).

81 *Consultatio* ASD V-3, 82/142–50, CWE 64, 265.

82 *Bellum* ASD II-7, 40/838–41, CWE 35, 433.

83 Cf. *Querela* ASD IV-2, 72/249–52, CWE 27, 300; *Paraphrasis in Marcum*, LB 7, 154, CWE 49, 10; *Paraclesis* LB 5, 140F, Olin 98.

84 *Bellum* ASD II-7, 40/869–71, CWE 35, 434–5; *Querela* ASD IV-2, 84/558–637, 96/836–9, CWE 27, 310, 319. In far away New Spain, Vasco de Quiroga took to heart Erasmus' thinking on good example (and even more the thinking of More's Utopians) in building, beginning around 1531, communities for Indians. See my *The Politics of an Erasmian Lawyer, Vasco de Quiroga*, derived from a much larger work, "Vasco de Quiroga's Thought on War."

85 See, for example, the colloquy *Ἰχθυοφαγια* (A Fish Diet) (1526), ASD I-3, 530/1304–11, CWE 40, 715/1–9. Christian decorum, on the other hand, "is the guiding principle not only in art but also in all the actions of life." We must adapt ourselves "to the prevailing circumstance" and learn "to perform the play of life." *Morae encomium* ASD IV-3, 96/443, 106/613–14, 619, Miller, 34, 44.

only their souls but of perceived external enemies and, not least, he demonstrates in great detail, their own people.[86]

What can be seen here is a frame of mind that is very much at odds with modern, one-dimensional understandings of pacifism. Pacifism (if we want to use the word) is for Erasmus two-dimensional, hard and unbending, an unchanging inner intention, and yet at one and the same time prudential and appropriate. And there is here no contradiction or vacillating. The Stoic wiseman always protects himself, his core principles, from anything that may happen in the world – even as he does everything possible to correct worldly situations – and so too with regard to war, as with other issues, does the true Christian.

Erasmus does not in *Dulce bellum* contradict himself where he states "our one aim in life is to take flight from life"[87] and, not far away, "the end and aim of the faith of the Gospel is conduct."[88] Taking flight from life, holding to one type of value, allows one to engage in life, holding to another type of value, in the best possible ways. In representing this Stoic based *katorthoma/kathekon* mindset Erasmus ridicules over and over the voluminous scholastic distinctions on "just war," particularly their logicizing regarding "proper authority," "just cause," and "right intention."[89] Turning Christ's precepts into mere counsels scholastics approve indirectly, he demonstrates, what Christ forbade absolutely.[90] The multitudes of "conditions" and "distinctions" scholastics make are in both theory and practice covers for deceit – ways of evilly rationalizing away Christ's teachings and the realities of the human situation. Scholastics hold, for example (cf. ST II-II.40.2), that "priests and monks are not allowed to

---

86 The warring Pope Julius II (1503–13) epitomizes for Erasmus evil dissimulation and evil prudence. See *Dialogus Julius exclusus e coelis* (c. 1513, pub. 1517), *Erasmus Opuscula*, 65–124, esp. 108–14/866–943, CWE 27/189–90.

87 *Bellum* ASD II-7, 43/943–46, M.M. Phillips, *The* Adages *of Erasmus* (Cambridge, 1964) 351 [CWE 35, 438].

88 *Bellum* ASD II-7, 40/834–5, Phillips, The *Adages* 346 [CWE 35, 433]. Cf. *Institutio* ASD IV-1, 147/338–41, CWE 27, 216.

89 Still influential is J.A. Fernandez-Santamaria's belief that Erasmus held to all the just war assumptions of scholastics but unlike scholastics lacked philosophical acuity resulting in emotional diatribes, "utopian" pacifism, "narcissism," and "moralizing maxims." See "Erasmus on the Just War," and *The State, War and Peace*, 110, 132, 158, 194, passim.

90 *Bellum* ASD II-7, 34/647, CWE 35, 425. Building on Augustine, scholastics held that Christ's Sermon on the Mount justified war and that war as such is not a sin. See Russell, *The Just War in the Middle Ages*, 16–17.

brandish a sword, but they can be present and take command" – against everything, Erasmus contends, Christ stood for.[91] What they call "right intention" ("zeal, piety, and fortitude"), to give another example (cf. ST II-II. 66.8, response), is simply a name whereby one can cruelly "whip out his sword, stick it into the guts of this brother, and nevertheless dwell in that supreme charity."[92] "Right intention," that is, is for them a logical justification which covers up that which is at the very heart of Christianity: a unitary two-dimensional mindset.[93] One cannot rationalize away Christ's precepts. There is in actuality no difference between precept and counsel, "no difference between those things which are to be kept in spirit only and what is to be done externally."[94] If a war is now and then necessary this can be ascertained and carried out only by those who hold high the absolutes of Christ's teachings – with undeviating inner resolve and "horror of wars and capital punishment"[95] – at the same time as they respond prudently, appropriately, and expediently to "the immense burden of events,"[96] in accord with the bending side of Christ's teachings.

Responding to widespread condemnation of his "pacifism" Erasmus over and over, in early as well as late writings, denied that he was rejecting all warfare.[97] In truth, what would have contradicted the philosophy of Christ is the very thing his critics accused him of: one-dimensional pacifism. He not only restated his position but explicitly referred to previous statements and showed why they had been misinterpreted[98] – but

91 *Bellum* ASD II-7, 34, 640–1, CWE 35, 425.

92 *Moriae encomium* ASD IV-3, 174/821–5, Hudson 101.

93 Scholars have repeatedly claimed the contrary, that Erasmus promoted scholastic "right intention." See, for example, A.G. Weiler "The Turkish Argument and Christian Piety in Desiderius Erasmus' *Consultatio de Bello Turcis Inferendo* (1530)," 38.

94 *Apologia adversus rhapsodias Alberti Pii* (1531) LB 9, 1140 F, CWE 84, 173. Erasmus is here responding to criticism of *The Praise of Folly* (1511).

95 *Consultatio* ASD V-3, 60/143–8, CWE 64, 239.

96 *Institutio* ASD IV-1, 134/35–7, CWE 27, 203.

97 See, for example, *Dulce bellum inexpertis* (1515), ASD II-7, 40/867–9, CWE 35, 434.

98 See, for example, Erasmus' *Letter to Paul Volz*, which prefaced the 1518 *Enchiridion*: *Ep.* 858. Allen 3, 371/378–87, CWE 6, 84/401–11; also *Apologiae contra Stunicam* (1522), LB 9, 370B–D; *Supputatio calumniarum Natalis Bedae* (1527), ASD IX-5, 342/939–64, 424–6/854–916; *Divinationes ad notata Bedae* (1527), LB 9, 462E–463B, 493C; *Responsio ad notulas Bedaicas* (1529), LB 9, 708F–709B; *Apologia adversus rhapsodias Alberti Pii* (1531), LB 9, 1138A–C, 1141A–B, 1192F–1193E, CWE v. 84, 166, 174, 347–51; and *Declarationes ad censuras Lutetiae vulgatas* (1532), LB 9, 840D–843B, 906E–907B, CWE 82, 61–7 (worldly prudence with regard to warfare must not be separated from "the absolute archetype," 67), 217–19.

he was shouting into the wind. Humanists may have been variously interested in Erasmus' views on war but like scholastics – or, for that matter, modern readers – they little grasped the frame of his thought, much less the philosophy on which it was built.[99]

Everyday warfare

But in what sense did Erasmus see Christianity as – by its very nature – a type of warfare? Was there any particular or meaningful reason why he titled the book at hand *Enchiridion militis christiani* (*Handbook of the Christian Soldier*); why he refers often in this work to spirituality as a kind of warfare, as where he quotes Paul, "O Christian soldier" (cf. 2 Tim 2:3–5) (26) or speaks of "The armour of the Christian militia" (30) and insists that a person must never lay down his weapons and surrender (109)?[100] In a concluding paragraph he claims to have shown the reader "the method and rules of a new kind of warfare." Is this statement justified or simply rhetorical hyperbole?

Modern readers seem to have seen nothing significantly new about the warfare referred to. They have seen it as simply a type of traditional moralizing, pervaded by rhetorical interests. The fathers of the church often used warfare terminology[101] and so too, it is imagined, did Erasmus. Ernst-Wilhelm Kohls sees Erasmus' military topos as simply a fight (either/or) between God and "anti-God powers of the world."[102] Most often what Erasmus means by "warfare" is simply not addressed. In his introduction to the work John O'Malley states that Erasmus did not want to use technical language, unlike scholastics, and as a result his metaphor of the Christian soldier "helps obfuscate rather than clarify the issue."[103] Adding to this picture, readers have considered Erasmus' outlook and personality "weak," the very opposite of warlike. Long

---

99 The one humanist who did thoroughly grasp Erasmus' meaning, I will demonstrate elsewhere, was his friend Thomas More.

100 In his *Paraphrase on Acts* (1524) Erasmus sees Paul's missionary activity, according to Robert D. Sider, in terms of "the mythic images of cosmic warfare." See "Paul in Erasmus' Paraphrases on the Pauline Epistles," 103.

101 See Harnack, *The Expansion of Christianity in the First Three Centuries*, 2:19–22.

102 See "The Principal Theological Thoughts in the *Enchiridion Militis Christiani*," 62. Kathy Eden sees the meaning of the title, *Handbook of the Christian Soldier*, in the same way. See *Friends Hold All Things in Common*, 21.

103 CWE 66, xxiii, xliii.

ago Johan Huizinga stated, and this is close even now to the accepted view, that "Erasmus is a delicate soul in all his fibers."[104] The reasons given by Huizinga and others for this assessment are many. They note his youthful physical problems and sicknesses, his inability to fast, the possibility that he had homosexual tendencies, his desire for concord and lack of contention, his pacifistic writings, his interest in accommodation, his use of rhetoric rather than scholastic logical subtleties, his literary interests.

In fact Erasmus knew – as shown throughout Parts II–VII – that he was talking about a "new" kind of warfare because he knew that his way of thinking was unprecedented. Previous Christian thought had not taken into account the Stoic discussions of natural instinct and the unitary *honestum/indifferents* mindset that had transformed his own life and outlook. The title was meant to highlight the extreme strength of mind required by this two-dimensional but unitary Christian outlook. While the *Enchiridion* unravels the workings of this mindset opposite the everyday challenges of laymen,[105] his writings on war set forth the same outlook against those responsible for, or carrying out, physical warfare. Nor did Erasmus think he had a weak, tractable, or modest disposition – or even favour such dispositions.

In short, the combat Erasmus describes, far from being weak or confused or merely rhetorical, is built from the two-dimensional military stance of the Stoic wiseman. As in Stoicism the core fight is with ourselves, not others[106] – and is not one-dimensional but two-dimensional. In all situations, states Seneca, the wiseman sees himself "a citizen and soldier of the universe" (*Ep.* 120.12).[107] Claiming for virtue the entire earth (*Tr.* 4.4), the wiseman holds that there is no contemplation without action and no action without contemplation (*Ot.* 7.2). The wiseman does not whine or complain, he knows that there are problems everywhere, that in one way or another "all life is servitude" (*Tr.* 10.4). Epictetus avers that in this world "each man's life is a kind of campaign, and a

104 *Erasmus and the Age of Reformation*, 18–19.

105 Discussing "the philosophy of Christ" in the *Paraclesis* (*Exhortation*) which prefaces his *Novum instrumentum* (*New Testament*) (1516) Erasmus lays out "a disposition of the mind" which is clearly built from a Stoic frame however rhetorical the employment. See LB 5, 140E, Olin 98–9.

106 See Nancy Sherman on *Discourses* 3.215.1–5, in *Stoic Warriors*, 35.

107 On Seneca's use of military metaphors see Wood, "Some Aspects of the Thought of Seneca and Machiavelli."

long and complicated one at that. You have to maintain the character of a soldier and do each separate act at the bidding of the general [Zeus], if possible divining what he wishes" (*Disc.* 3.24.34).

"Fixed [unitary both/and] procedures"

Commenting on his utilization of ancient authors Erasmus states, near the beginning, "No matter where you find truth, attribute it to Christ" (36)[108] – which is exactly the way he had defended, a very short time before, "my Stoics" against "Colet."[109] In the body of the work he brings in St Paul, Origen, Augustine, and Plato, among others, but what has not been understood, I have shown, is that he very consciously rewrites or reinterprets the thought of each – in terms of Stoicism. As in *De taedio Iesu* (see Parts III–IV) he shows in detail what is wrong with seeing Christianity in either/or, *spiritus/caro* (cf. *honestum/turpe*) terms. In essence Christianity is both/and – *spiritus/indifferens*. Origen's understanding of Christianity was flawed at its very core in that he did not grasp Stoic thinking on *indifferentia*, the substantive reality of that which is in-between spirit and evil, and the oneness of *spiritus* and *indifferentia*.

Erasmus brings to life, I have now demonstrated, a way of thinking and mindset that had not existed for a thousand years. Previous humanists, such as Lovati, Mussato, Petrarch, Salutati, Bruni, Niccoli, Palmieri, Valla, Ficino, Poliziano, and Giovanni Pico (see Part I), not to mention Colet (see Parts III–V), had seen nothing of this two-dimensional but unitary Stoic frame of thought.

Many times Erasmus points out that his work has been motivated by a certain way of thinking, but his statements have been passed over or misinterpreted. In a 1504 letter to Colet regarding the *Enchiridion*, he explicitly refers to "fixed procedures":

> What I have tried to do, in fact, is to teach a method of morals, as it were, in the manner of those who have originated fixed procedures in the various branches of learning. (Conatus autem sum velut artificium quoddam pietatis tradere, more eorum qui de disciplinis certas rationes conscripsere.)[110]

---

108 See also *Antibarbarorum liber* (*Book against the Barbarians*) (circa 1489–95), discussed above, pp. 52–3.

109 *De taedio Iesu*, 1275D, discussed above, p. 157.

110 *Ep.* 181. Allen 2, 405/50–2, CWE 1, 87/57–60. Cf. Erasmus' paraphrase of *De officiis* 3.33, above, pp. 71–2.

As the first sentence of the *Enchiridion* puts it, the book is "a kind of summary guide to living," so that readers may attain "a state of mind worthy of Christ" (24).[111] This "state of mind," the work demonstrates, is two-dimensional but unitary and needs to be applied first to oneself and then to others and the surrounding world. There are no answers that are "correct" in an absolute sense. What matters is how one approaches issues. In accord with his own particular character traits, habits, and situations, each person needs to develop and carry out an appropriate unbending/bending plan of action – "so that whenever circumstances demand it he will be ready" (110). Throughout, Erasmus demonstrates the difficulty of the enterprise, why the outlook he proposes – and illustrates with remedies for various afflictions – is at all times an extreme type of warfare. The language used is sometimes striking: "When you do battle with the enemy, do not be satisfied with deflecting his blow or even repelling his attack, but bravely seizing the weapon, turn it back upon the attacker, cutting his throat with his own sword" (107).[112]

In working out, step by step, the various arguments found in the *Enchiridion* I have opened up a cohesive work – at odds with the rhetorical hodgepodge previous readers have seen. The author was not throwing together material but throughout developing a thesis, a set way of thinking, built from Stoicism as not scholastic logical methodologies, and employing in the process his rhetorical skills. Christ's yoke is light (59) in the sense that Judaizing rules are not required but spirituality is extremely demanding, a type of warfare, in that it requires a certain "method" and "state of mind" and goes from one challenge to another.

A concluding paragraph forcefully restates the central thesis. The author's concern has not been with uniform or doctrinaire responses to the issues that arise in life but rather, as mentioned above, "the method

---

111 "Efflagitasti non mediocri studio, frater in domino dilectissime, ut tibi compendiariam quandam vivendi rationem praescriberem, qua instructus posses ad mentem Christo dignam pervenire" (H 22/5–8). Robert Stupperich contends that Erasmus is not talking about a "theory of spirituality" but merely "suggestions" for piety ("Das *Enchiridion militis christiani*," 23).

112 In *Antibarbarorum liber* Erasmus had referred to the need to use the learning and oratory (the "arms and weapons") of the pagans to overcome pagan outlooks, "cut the enemy's throat with his own sword, as they say." See ASD I-1, 46, CWE 23, 25/16–19. Jerome uses very similar language. See Eden, *Friends Hold All Things in Common*, 19.

and rules of a new kind of warfare," a type of warfare that responds, in a unitary both/and way, to all the variables of situation and individual makeup.

> Tantum volui, quod tibi satis fore credebam, rationem et artem quandam novae militiae commonstrare, qua te posses adversus pristinae vitae repullulantia mala communire. Itaque quod nos in uno atque altero exempli causa fecimus, id teipsum oportebit facere cum in singulis tum potissimum in his, ad quae cognoveris te sive naturae sive consuetudinis vitio peculiariter instigari. Adversus haec certa quaedam decreta in albo mentis nostrae describenda sunt atque ea, ne desuetudine obsolescant, subinde renovanda. (H 134/17–25)

> I merely wished, thinking that it would be sufficient, to show you the method and rules of a new kind of warfare, by which you might arm yourself against evils of your former life, which continue to sprout up again. Therefore, what I have done by way of example for this or that vice you should do for each vice, especially those to which you know you are particularly inclined either by a natural defect of character or by habit. Against these vices certain fixed resolutions should be inscribed in the album of the mind, and they should be frequently renewed so that they will not fall into disuse. (126)

Note the difference here between an imperfection (*vitium*) and something evil or base (*malum, turpe*). Imperfections of nature or custom are things indifferent while *malum* and *spiritus* contradict each other. Erasmus saw himself as having major imperfections, in particular a weak body, an inability to fast, and a desire for untrammelled freedom of mind. Spirituality is about studying one's particularities, as such things indifferent, and then building on what one discovers (distinguishing as it were Stoic "preferred indifferents" from "dispreferred indifferents"), never allowing at any moment a conflict between these worldly choices and certain "fixed resolutions" (*decreta*) "inscribed in the album of the mind."[113] As in Stoicism one needs to always be ahead of future problems or circumstances, always "armed" (cf. also 106).

113 Cf. *Off.* 1.6: "No fixed, invariable, natural rules of duty can be posited except by those who say that moral goodness is worth seeking solely or chiefly for its own sake." Note Seneca's employment of the words *decreta/praecepta* in Letters 94 and 95, above, pp. 44–5.

Intention and the freedom of a Christian

Spiritual warfare is utopian in that it is totally at odds with everyday ways of thinking, feeling, and behaving. Where Erasmus refers to the freedom of a Christian (78) and the fact that Christ's yoke is light (59) he is describing what it means to be freed from the tyranny of unexamined inborn character traits and habits and from the authority of common practices and formal rules – not the least being religious ceremonies – as one holds to the unbending precepts of the faith. Otherwise stated, what frees one is a unitary two-dimensional mindset.

Compare again the mindset of the Stoic wiseman. The Stoics, states Diogenes Laertius, "declare that the wiseman alone is free and bad men are slaves, freedom being power of independent action" (7.121). In harmony with Nature and the will of Zeus, the wiseman is "free" in the sense that nothing external to himself impairs or hinders him. He is a true king because he alone is subject to no authority (*Fin.* 3.75–6). And we may do well to remember here Erasmus' all-consuming desire in his youth for mental freedom and the reasons for his initial attraction to Stoicism (II.4) – and the mental and physical freedom he sought throughout his life.

Of great significance, spiritual warfare centres on something that ultimately cannot be seen – intention.[114] Who can truly discern intention other than oneself – and God (81)?[115] Compare again the difference – unlocked by Erasmus in his editing of *De officiis* – between Stoic *kathekon* and *katorthoma*. The same action is represented by *kathekon* and *katorthoma*, the difference being that *kathekon* lacks the intention. Although the perfectly performing Stoic wiseman never deceives himself and never lacks correct intention (whatever happens), Erasmus never imagined that this was a possibility for the Christian practitioner. But a Christian would at all times hold to the ideal. "What good is it to do good exteriorly if interiorly one's thoughts are quite the opposite?" (82). What is your intention? "It is a fault to perform a good action in an improper way" (61).

> Judge everything you do by this rule. If you exercise a trade, well and good, if you do so without fraud. But what is your goal? ...

114 See above, pp. 319, 323.

115 If Erasmus in some way "laid the egg that Luther hatched," as often held, the context is very different.

> Or suppose that you are fasting, a pious action at least in appearance. But what is your design in fasting? To preserve your larder? To be regarded as more religious? Your vision is corrupted.
>
> But suppose you fast in order not to fall ill. Why are you afraid of illness? That it may deprive you of sensual pleasures? Your vision is very faulty. Then suppose that you say that you wish to be in good health in order to have strength for your studies. But what is the purpose of your studies? To procure some priestly position? What is your motivation in seeking the priesthood? To live for yourself, not for Christ. You have departed from the standard which every Christian should have before his eyes.
>
> On the other hand, suppose you take food [rather than fast] in order to be healthy of body [required by one's constitution]. If you wish to be healthy of body so that you may have sufficient strength for holy studies and holy vigils, then you have hit the mark. But if you take care of your health in order not to become less attractive and less capable of satisfying your lustful desires, then you have fallen away from Christ and fashioned another god for yourself. (H 65/24–66/3)[116]

Clearly, Erasmus was thinking here of himself as much as anyone else.

As in Stoicism, much leeway is allowed the bending type of value as long as – and here's the rub – the unbending type is firmly in place. In Stoicism only the wiseman is free and for him even cannibalism can be acceptable, "under stress of circumstances" (D.L. 7.121)[117] – since he acts from a unitary *honestum/indifferens* frame of mind. Erasmus thinks in related terms in the *Enchiridion*:

> No one will impute it to you as a crime if after the example of Solomon you maintain sixty queens and eighty concubines under your roof [Sol. 6:8], and countless young girls endowed with secular wisdom, provided that divine wisdom above all the others is your one and only, your fairest, your dove. (34)

Although Erasmus states this in discussing the allowableness of secular literature, quoting Titus 1:15: "all things are pure to the pure while to the impure nothing is pure," the thinking is directly applied to his

116 The translation is adapted from *The Enchiridion of Erasmus*, trans. Raymond Himelick, 98, and CWE 66, 63.

117 Cf. Erasmus, *Bellum*, ASD II-7, 18/165–9, CWE 35, 406.

discussions, further on in the work, of things that are indifferent, the material of life.[118] We must measure the *utilitatem* or *inutilitatem* of things in-between *honesta* and *turpia*, things that are for the Stoic philosophers imperfect, intermediate, and neutral – whether literature or money or something else – in terms of our "virtuous intent" and the degree to which they lead to virtue and Christ (61–2, H 63/28–65/1).

The problem, in Erasmus' eyes, is that most actions in the world are governed by deceit. Rationalizations block out the natural and spiritual bases of existence. Not analysing themselves and building from what they learn and not simultaneously seeing or holding to the absolutes, humans simply gratify their habitual ways of thinking and acting and in the process deceive themselves and others. They are blind, in short, to spiritual warfare – and the freedom of a Christian found therein.

The Stoic wiseman is utterly free and so too is that person who is truly Christian. And just as this wiseman looks at existence through a two-dimensional but unitary (*katorthoma/kathekon, honestum/indifferens, honestum/utile*) lens so too does the Christian. But the Christian knows things the Stoic does not and it is within this very different context that the "fixed procedures" must be worked out and practised – building, that is, "the philosophy of Christ" from "the philosophy of Stoicism."

118 In his *Paraphrasis* in *Ep. Ad Romanos* (1517) Erasmus criticizes "superstitious" customs regarding food and holidays and, alluding to his own earlier struggles as well as Jewish practices, emphasizes here again that "nothing is impure in itself." What matters is intention, conscience, mental fortitude, and constancy as one responds with "the spirit of Christ" to natural needs and worldly circumstances – which are in themselves neither good nor bad but indifferent. LB 7, 820B–826C, CWE 42, 73–83.

Conclusion

Erasmus may have been precocious but his core outlook did not come about through the reading of books or abstract intellectualizations. What was unique about the young Erasmus – and throughout his life – was not just the acuteness of his mind but unusual physical and emotional needs. Contrary to what has been believed, Erasmus' later descriptions of his youth as traumatic were essentially true. His unending desire for physical and mental freedom, including a dislike of ritual, and his unending problems with his body, including an inability to fast or eat fish, had repeatedly clashed with societal standards and societal views of Christianity. In his youth and early adulthood as later in life he was particularly bitter over the fact that others were managing his life – taking away his freedom – after the death of his parents at age fourteen and that he had been browbeaten at age sixteen into joining the Augustinian order, for which he found himself entirely unsuited. What is most significant however is Erasmus' determination – in the years immediately preceding a 1499 debate with Colet at Oxford – to study himself, to look inward as well as outward. What concerned him was why he had these particular temperamental characteristics and particular bodily needs and what could be done about them. He concluded that these idiosyncrasies were engrained and no amount of will power could overcome them. It was not merely that he had always sought freedom and had always had special physical needs; there was a deep underlying reason for these traits. They were embedded in something that was inherently unchangeable, a human nature that had been imprinted at birth and was not a matter of choice – however much those around him refused to recognize the fact.

Deeply impressed by the intractableness of his physical and mental needs, needs which he dealt with every day, Erasmus looked for help in thinking out the implications of this reality and he found it – some time before 1499 – in the Stoics. Unlike any of his fourteenth- and fifteenth-century humanist predecessors Erasmus had every reason to see and deeply appreciate Stoic thinking on natural instincts at birth, ineradicable character traits, and the relationship between worldly variables and unbending principles. He would work out this thinking in his edition of Cicero's *De officiis* (1501), *De taedio Iesu* (1499–1501), and the *Enchiridion* (1503).

The difference between Erasmus' writings before the impact of Stoicism and after is radical. In *De contemptu mundi* (c. 1485–8) and *Antibarbarorum liber* (c. 1489–95) Erasmus sees Christianity in one-dimensional terms. *De contemptu mundi* glorifies the monastic life, the fasts, the labour, the solitude, the silence, the contemplation of heaven. The world is evil. Physical pleasures are "utterly disgusting" and have nothing to do with spiritual pleasure. A major problem here is that scholars have believed that *De taedio Iesu* and the *Enchiridion* are simply continuations of this way of thinking. In this regard they see what Erasmus would come to refer to as "the philosophy of Christ" as simply a figurative way of speaking, however defined, having nothing to do with a philosophy or a systematic way of thinking but everything to do with rhetoric and a struggle between worldly and non-worldly, flesh and spirit, visible and invisible, letter and spirit, temporary and eternal, darkness and light.

In his edition of Cicero's *De officiis* (published 1501) Erasmus shows that he had come to see truth and reality not in either/or terms but in unitary both/and terms. Unlike anyone in a thousand years he saw that *De officiis* was built from Stoicism, not the one-dimensional abstract life and emotion denying Stoicism, seen by fourteenth- and fifteenth-century humanists, but two-dimensional Stoicism. Noticing that Cicero states at the beginning of *De officiis* that he is following the views of the Stoics and refers to the Greek words *katorthoma* and *kathekon*, Erasmus turned to Cicero's *De finibus* (a much more technical work) for the precise meaning of these words, words that go to the very core of Stoicism. There he learned that there are two types of duty and that for the Stoic wiseman they are inseparable. *Katorthoma*, or *perfectum officium* (absolute duty), is that which is right (*rectum*) and is attainable only by the wiseman. *Kathekon*, or *medium officium* (mean duty), "is duty for the performance of which an adequate reason may be rendered" (quod cur factum sit, ratio probabilis reddi possit). Unlike ordinary humans the wiseman combines right actions *(katorthomata)* with appropriate actions *(kathekonta)*. Appropriate actions are choices made between things that are indifferent, neither good nor evil, on the basis of what accords with nature and what is contrary to nature. Both the wise and the unwise make such choices but when the wise selects, this is *perfectum officium*. Erasmus also well understood the relationship of the *honestum* and the *utile* focused on in *De officiis* to the Stoic way of thinking. As he states in a marginal comment, an action carried out in terms of *honestum*, the sole good, that which merits praise even if not praised, is a right action (*recte factum, katorthoma*). Just as *katorthoma* and *kathekon* are at root inseparable so too are *honestum* and *utile*. Within this frame Erasmus was deeply affected by Stoic thinking on natural instinct, *oikeiosis*, the belief, as he correctly words it, that "all living creatures are motivated at birth by a desire for self-preservation." This desire "is a law of nature that humans have in common with animals and is called in Greek *κατὰ φύσιμ πρα τομ*, that is, *secundum naturam primum*." He had found the Greek wording in Gellius' discussion (c. 180 CE) of the Stoic Epictetus' *Discourses* in *Attic Nights* and the Latin wording in *De finibus*.

But how was it that Erasmus could so easily relate Cicero's discussions and exemplifications of Stoicism to the realities – 1500 years later – of his own world? Although the Stoicism described and illustrated by Cicero was a product of the social and intellectual world of Greece and Rome what Erasmus saw that others did not is that the purpose of Stoicism and of *De officiis* was not so much to show the solution or solutions to particular social, political, and intellectual problems as to show how to go about solving such problems. There is a "method" (*artem*) to the issues of life and those who do not believe this, Cicero contends in *De officiis*, are seriously misguided. Every situation requires application of the *honestum/utile* "formula" or "rule." The formula is not something abstractly imposed. It must be worked out in every circumstance. To become "good calculators of duty" the relevant questions must be asked over and over. Experience and constant practice are necessities. It was for these reasons that Erasmus holds in his introduction to *De officiis* that the work is "a pocket handbook" (*enchiridion*) or "tiny dagger" (*pugiunculus*) that needs to be carried about and constantly thought about. *De officiis* is a dagger and a handbook because it reveals the fixed procedures to be applied to all the variables of life, a theme reinforced in his 1519 preface to the second edition where he praises Cicero's "rules for living" and the "attitude of mind" he demands of those who govern. Thinking of these rules and this attitude Erasmus marvels in the preface to his edition of Cicero's *Tusculan Disputations* (1523) at the steady progression of philosophy from mere contemplation of the natural world to the worldly stage. While the progression began with Socrates, and Plato and Aristotle took philosophy into the courts of kings, the legislature, and law-courts, it was only with Cicero that philosophy "has learned to speak in such a fashion that even a miscellaneous audience can applaud." And Erasmus deeply felt the religiosity in this Stoic and Ciceronian way of speaking. As stated in his 1501 preface, *De officiis* is a work about "divine" (two-dimensional) *honestum.*

The problem for Erasmus was that he did not want to believe and did not want others to believe that his radically new understanding of natural instinct and of the relation between absolute values and worldly values was not thoroughly Christian. Since it was an article of faith that Christ was human as well as divine, what was needed, he saw, was a careful working out of the application of his new insights to Christ, particularly Christ's human nature. The debate with Colet at Oxford in 1499 was all about setting forth his views against Colet's tradition-based arguments. While Colet held that Christ suffered no fear of death in that he was a martyr of martyrs and martyrs overcome human nature and worldliness with extreme joy, Erasmus contended that fear is a natural instinct and that natural instincts are as such ineradicable.

Working out his thinking in *De taedio Iesu* (1499–1501), Erasmus argues that the Stoics consider fear of death a natural instinct and even give it a "leading place" among the first principles of nature. Although he well recognizes that orthodox Stoics had considered death unworthy of fear in that death is not an evil and that fear of death is like other emotions simply a false judgment of reason, Erasmus shows in carefully thought-out arguments that rightly understood fear of death and other emotions are not judgments of reason but are one with Stoic natural instincts (*oikeiosis*). Analysis shows that he was very much taken with Antiochus' revisionist contention set forth by Cicero in Books 4 and 5 of *De finibus* that even the wiseman feels, from natural impulse, fear of death and other emotions and that *honestum* is, in fact, built from natural instinct. And yet Erasmus does not allow Antiochus' linear view. He embeds emotion in a fundamental Stoic category, things indifferent (*indifferentia*), located on one side of a unitary both/and frame of thought (*katorthoma/kathekon, honestum/indifferens, honestum/utile*).

Erasmus also places a great deal of weight on the views of the late Stoic Panaetius (d. 110 BCE), and here he is very explicit regarding the source of his thinking. Panaetius considered insensibility (*ἀναλγησία*) and lack of feeling (*ἀπάθεια*) "incompatible with being human." He had found his information regarding Panaetius' thinking on this subject not in *De officiis*, so clearly dependent upon Panaetius, but in Gellius' discussions of the views of the Stoic Epictetus (d. 135 CE).

But if natural instincts are as such ineradicable what is the nature of bravery? Erasmus shows that the brave person begins by recognizing and accepting the reality of fears arising from natural instincts while the coward tries to ignore them. "Someone is not lacking in bravery if, when danger approaches, he shudders inwardly, his face turns pale, his heart beats faster, his blood ebbs away, and his suffering wrings from him a groan." We have differing biological makeups and thus respond to danger in all sorts of ways. "Socrates was not necessarily brave because his expression did not change as he took the hemlock; nor would he have been a coward if in the same circumstances he had happened to turn pale." Observable reactions to danger show nothing about bravery. Christ feared death but this fear reveals only natural instinct, something ineradicable.

A major thesis is that natural disabilities do not decrease opportunities for virtue but increase these opportunities. Those born with attributes that make it easy to respond to a dangerous situation have actually been given something unhelpful, since an appropriate temperament allows less opportunity for virtue than an inappropriate. Although Erasmus was much impressed by the argument of Panaetius/Cicero in *De officiis* that we must "follow the bent of our own particular nature," in one regard he saw the issue differently. Contrasting with Panaetius/Cicero he considered some inborn traits positive, in that they make it easy to respond to worldly situations, and others negative, in that they make it difficult to respond to worldly situations, and contended that the arena for bravery is much greater for the negative than the positive. All of which leads to Christ (and silently to Erasmus himself). It was because Christ's natural disabilities were greater than ever experienced by a human that he had opportunities for virtue that exceeded that of any human – and he used these opportunities to the full.

The influence of the Greek father Origen (d. 255) on Erasmus beginning around 1501 is often noted with regard to the *Enchiridion* but what has not been seen is Erasmus' all-out rejection in *De taedio Iesu* of Origen's outlook regarding the soul. While Origen saw the soul as something insubstantial and incorporeal that must by its very nature attach itself to either spirit or flesh, good or evil, Erasmus shows that the soul is independent and profoundly substantive, not something that simply attaches to either spirit or flesh. There are not just two factors in play, spirit and flesh, but three. The third is natural instinct and natural instinct equates with soul. Soul is something that comes about naturally, without any free-will. Spirit equates with Stoic *honestum* and sin equates with Stoic *turpe* while soul, the realm of natural instincts, is one of the things that comprise in Stoicism *indifferentia*. At one with Stoic *oikeiosis* (the self-preservation instinct at birth), natural instinct ("soul") is attracted – independent of spirit or flesh – "towards anything that is favourable to nature" and recoils "from anything that threatens our survival." Nor is Erasmus deterred by the fact that "some theologians call flesh (*carnem*) what I here call soul (*animam*)." In holding that natural instincts, fear of death being one, are not "flesh" a sizable part of what had been flesh (*caro*) now had a huge increase in status. Humans are responsible for evils of the flesh but they are not responsible for natural instincts. Natural instincts simply exist. "Soul," unlike "flesh," is about that which in human nature is unalterable. Spirituality now embodies both sides of the Stoic unitary *honestum/indifferens* frame of thought. What differs from orthodox Stoicism is not the frame but the content of the frame, the fact that Erasmus moves emotion from the cognitive realm to the realm of natural instinct, character traits, and things indifferent.

In developing the unbending side of his two-dimensional outlook Erasmus silently employs statements found in Gellius' rendering of Stoicism in *Attic Nights* and in Cicero's *Tusculan Disputations*, statements that show that the brave person steadfastly endures everything except lack of virtue and principles. Interestingly Erasmus' statements here incorporate the way Socrates died into the hard side – as not the bending side – of the two-dimensional Stoic frame. He goes on to show that there is all the difference between holding to unbending principles and martyrdom. Colet considered Christ, as evidenced by his Passion, a super martyr. Christian martyrs had accepted the most inhuman tortures with eager joy (*alacribus*), exalting and taking pleasure in pain and Christ, according to Colet and common opinion, was the unequalled example of martyrdom. In claiming that Christ feared death Erasmus was wallowing, according to Colet, in human nature and sin. In criticizing Colet's view Erasmus concentrates on the word *alacritas*, a word Cicero uses in *Tusculan Disputations* to describe one of the four types of false emotion. *Alacritas* (which Cicero associates with Epicurus' outlook) is a mental aberration, something alien to right reason and nature. Building on this thinking Erasmus argues that in Christ's entire life, not just his Passion, there was nothing of the martyrs' eagerness, his *alacritas*. *Alacritas* goes beyond human nature, beyond natural and ineradicable instincts. As a human Christ had no way of escaping these instincts. Had he faced death with exaltation, as did martyrs, he would not have been able to truly demonstrate (versus what Colet imagines) his love. Combined in Christ as in Stoicism were two types of value, one unbending the other bending. While one side of his mind was constant, enduring, contemplative, and filled with joy (not *alacritas* but *gaudium*) the other side was at one and the same time overwhelmed by uncontrollable natural instincts: fear, terror, and anxiety.

Colet the person, in fact, knew nothing about Stoicism but Erasmus in his write-up of the debate in *De taedio Iesu* has "Colet" represent orthodox Stoic views – against, remarkably, Erasmus' position. At centre court here is the pre-emotion thesis (Greek *propatheia*), as represented by Epictetus, which goes back to Zeno and Chrysippus. The wiseman may experience terror from an external shock, such as a bolt of lightening, but he never fears. Immediately he overcomes this pre-emotion by means of reason. Terror is something that relates to the senses and is involuntary while fear is a judgment of reason and is voluntary. The wiseman never "assents" (a key word) to such preliminary impressions. But Erasmus has the nerve to say, "Colet" exclaims, that Christ "assented," gave in to the fear of dying – which is wicked to even imagine! Christ feared death but overcame this "pre-emotion" immediately. The Stoic holds unbendingly to virtue and truth and in so doing is always happy and Christ, similarly, went to his death with extreme joy, *alacritas*.

While theologians for a thousand years had argued over and over the pre-emotion thesis with regard to Christ's Passion without recognizing the Stoic origins of this view Erasmus was determined to place this traditional outlook within the original Stoic context and yet was equally determined to show that on this point orthodox Stoicism goes awry. Different conclusions can be and must be drawn, he shows, from Stoic thought. Christ did not suffer mere pre-emotion ("propassion") but full-blown emotion ("passion"), extreme fear – a position that was for Colet the person, who did not allow even pre-emotion, beyond comprehension, a sign that Christ was weak and involved with evil.

Although Erasmus continues to consider himself a Stoic, notwithstanding "Colet's" rendering of orthodox Stoic views, he mounts an all-out and original rewrite, in no way dependent on ancient criticisms, of Stoic thinking on emotion. Pre-emotion resulting from *phantasiai* (things like a bolt of lightening) may exist but this does not come near the real problem. What about, for example, emotion that arises from fear of something that may happen but has not happened? Erasmus shows that Gellius' own illustration of Epictetus' thought with regard to this issue cannot withstand analysis. Recounting his experience on board a ship in the midst of a typhoon, Gellius states that he was surprised to see a Stoic white with fear. Later the Stoic advised him, in explanation, to consult what Epictetus has to say about *phantasiai*, where it is shown that the wiseman is subject to such things but he does not "assent" to them and overcomes his involuntary reactions almost immediately – and thus does not fear. In rebuttal Erasmus points out that what actually happened during the typhoon does not tie with either Gellius' account or Epictetus' theory. The Stoic demonstrably did not immediately overcome the assault on his emotions. The typhoon lasted a day and a half and the Stoic did not recover his composure before the crisis ended. All of which proves that the Stoic was in fact experiencing true emotion, full-blown emotion, emotion that was not overcome and could not have been overcome before the cause of the emotion ceased to exist. During the storm the Stoic's reason was unable to affect in any way his emotions, notwithstanding that his reason was not overcome. The fear was a reality. True emotions exist and come about internally, from an ineradicable natural instinct.

Epictetus, a late Stoic (d. 135 CE), had focused on "decrees of nature and necessity" that reason cannot overcome, such as sickness, but no Stoic prior to Erasmus had contended that emotion, as such, is a decree of nature and necessity that can never be overcome by reason. Fear and hunger are equally ineradicable natural instincts. The human psyche, he shows, is by its very nature unitarily two-dimensional and the emotion side is just as integral and important as the reason side.

Erasmus' depiction of Christ's fear in Gethsemane is a development of everything he unravels and corrects regarding the Stoic's experience and response in the typhoon. The typhoon lasted for one and a half days and so too, Erasmus appears to recognize, did Christ's Passion. At no time during the ordeal did Christ, any more than the Stoic, overcome his fear. The difference between these two events is that Christ's emotional distress was far greater than ever experienced by a human and yet his reason was aloof and serene, at one with the contemplation of heaven, entirely oblivious (also unlike the Stoic) to what was happening with his emotions. The fact that his emotional suffering was (for many reasons) incomparable relates directly to Erasmus' "greater handicap thesis." The greater the handicap the greater the possibilities for true bravery – which Christ incomparably demonstrated. And yet this bravery was not for Christ about martyrdom and he did not want other humans to attempt martyrdom. The greater the worldly vulnerability and despair the greater the love revealed. Had he set himself up as mere divinity, "with eager joy on his face and in his words, like a man practically devoid of feeling," he would have gained only our admiration, not our love. In advising gentleness and humbleness Christ was not, in Erasmus' view, thinking of mushy abstract ideals but something close to the opposite. Erasmus sees Christ's gentleness and charity as residing in his ineradicable natural instincts, "this natural weakness (*infirmitas*), so deeply implanted in human nature that it can be conquered but never eradicated." In conceptualizing the "weakness" Christ exhibited and advised we need to recognize that Erasmus was building on his own experience and feelings, the fact that in his youth he had tried, unsuccessfully, to override his natural instincts, character traits, and environment and in the process had not felt gentle, humble, or charitable towards himself or towards the makeup of other humans.

It was one thing to rework ancient Stoic thought and to relate the finished product to Christ's Passion but quite a different thing to contradict a thousand years of theological thought on Christ's Passion. Early on in *De taedio Iesu* Erasmus advises interested readers to look at Bonaventure's "skilful" discussion of Christ's Passion in the relevant section of his massive *Commentary on the Sentences of Peter Lombard.* Modern researchers have simply assumed that he is agreeing with Bonaventure (d. 1274), in essentials at least, but nothing could be further from actuality. Just as Erasmus radically rewrites Origen and Gellius without overtly criticizing them, so too is this the case with Bonaventure. In referring to the *Commentary* he is simply setting the stage for a radically different thesis, a thesis that denies not only the view of Bonaventure and other scholastics but even the view of Jerome and other fathers of the church. While Hilary of Poitiers (d. 367) had argued that Christ felt no fear in his Passion, a view that appeared to verge on heresy after the Council of Chalcedon (451) established that Christ was human as well as divine, the view that came to dominate discussion was that of Jerome (d. 420). Building on Origen and Didymus (though probably not grasping the Stoic base) Jerome argued that Christ in his Passion did not suffer full-blown emotion (*passio*) but only pre-emotion (*propassio*). Core features of Jerome's argument were that the Bible does not state that Christ "was" sad but only that he "began" to be sad and that this was a *propassio*, a sudden and involuntary movement, to which there was no assent. This understanding of *propassio* was greatly revised by scholastics, beginning in the twelfth century, who employed logic-based ways of analysing differing or contradictory statements or opinions. In his *Book of Sentences* (c. 1150) Peter Lombard does not see *propassio* as something that results from a shock of some sort but as something having to do with the lack of movement of the mind, fear and sadness that is "not moved from rectitude and contemplation of God." Bonaventure goes much further, arguing elaborately that with Christ *propassio* was preceded by and governed by reason. Entirely reversing Jerome's position (which he does not, for good reason, mention), Bonaventure argues that Christ's sadness (and fear of death) was not an involuntary reaction but something *brought about by* "the dictate and sway of reason."

Against Jerome's long-enduring thesis that Christ in his Passion only "began," according to scripture, to be sad and that this means that he suffered only propassion, Erasmus contends that "began" does not have the meaning attributed to it. Employing his language interests and skills he argues that there is, in fact, no real difference between *being* sad and *beginning* to be sad. "Began" does not entail a limitation of sadness but merely points to when the sadness started. The fact that an emotion begins does not entail that it is tiny and not at that point fully developed. Then too the words used to describe this beginning also need to be changed. Christ was not simply sad but filled with "distress and dismay." From the very beginning he was feeling not a pre-emotion but full-blown emotion, not propassion but passion. In fact his fear did not just disturb him, it "violently overwhelmed" him. And these feelings (which lasted, as with the Stoic in the typhoon, around twenty hours) "left him only with life itself."

Though Christ's fear was activated by what he saw was going to happen, he possessed this instinct and all human natural instincts from the beginning, in the state of innocence. While theologians had unanimously held (Augustine and Aquinas are very explicit) that sadness and fear came about only after Adam's Fall, Erasmus, in his own words, "boldly" places these emotions in the state of innocence that existed before the Fall and ties the state of innocence with Stoic nature and Stoic natural instinct. In that primitive state – which had always been considered a beautiful time – Christ had "natural passions." "Natural passions" include instinctive emotions such as "grief, joy, hatred, fear, and anger" as well as instinctive physical needs such as "hunger, thirst, drowsiness, weariness, suffering, and death." What Bonaventure had seen as punishments suffered by humans as a consequence of the Fall and assumed by Christ Erasmus sees as "natural passions" found in the state of innocence (now less innocent than ever imagined). Erasmus shows that Christ's physical and mental instincts were at work even in his acceptance of our punishments. He was "a complete man subject to the ills of the human condition" not because he took on our punishments (which he did) but because he already had, by natural instinct, all the human emotions – and could thus feel everything ordinary humans feel. Having far greater handicaps than anyone (from being, Erasmus shows, who he was) and thus having far greater possibilities for virtue, Christ's response to each side of his unitary both/and mindset was unique. On the emotion side the Passion brought about a total meltdown, the most extreme emotion ever known. On the reason side it brought about incomparable joy (*gaudium animae*) "in endless contemplation of the divine." Contrary to Bonaventure, Aquinas, and other scholastics, reason did not precede his fear of death nor did it impregnate, accompany, express, guide, regulate, develop, or govern it. Human nature was no longer something that could be worked out employing multifarious abstruse logical distinctions. It had deep biological content. Christ's Passion was not about the triumph of spirit over flesh but about the workings of natural instinct and spirit. Not only did reason not affect his emotions and emotions not affect his reason, both were fully active at one and the same time. Christ "could be both willing and unwilling, could both dread and desire the same thing, in equal measure and at one and the same time ... both sublime joy and abject misery."

Erasmus' depiction of the Passion revolutionized not only high-level educated opinion but the "devotionalist" outlooks so pervasive in European society and culture – and taught at the schools Erasmus attended in the Netherlands from 1475 to 1493. A subject of great concern for virtually everyone in the later Middle Ages, and especially in the fifteenth century, the Passion was represented in an immense and widely circulated body of literature as well as in prayer books, paintings, poetry, plays, liturgy, and music. Standing out in all this is the depiction of Christ's physical suffering. Subjected to excruciating physical pain he is deformed by injury, bleeding, crowned with thorns. His hands and feet are pierced. He is pulled, stretched, and thrown to the ground. Individuals longed, in ways that are now hard to imagine, for actual physical union with Christ and the sharing of his blood. But nowhere in all this was there anything of Erasmus' concern. His focus was not on Christ's physical suffering but his emotional suffering – and the relation of this to the meaning of his life and the nature of Christianity. Though no one was more highly regarded in the fifteenth century and the later Middle

Ages than Bernard, a saint who had focused on spirit versus flesh and mystical union with God, it is not of little significance that Erasmus makes a point of criticizing him (contrary to his usual method) for not seeing that Christ suffered from full-blown emotion and therewith fear of death.

The *Enchiridion* (published 1503) works out for ordinary humans everything uncovered in *De taedio Iesu* regarding Christ and the nature of Christianity. Again building on Stoicism, particularly Cicero's *De finibus* and *De officiis*, Erasmus shows in multiple contexts that the Christian journey is not fundamentally about a flesh/spirit either/or but about a both/and consisting inseparably of natural instinct (including emotion), character traits, and situations on the one side ("things indifferent") and spirit/reason (unbending absolutes) on the other. Therewith the contemplative life and the active life are as in Stoicism at all times inseparable. Here again Erasmus radically rewrites Origen. The soul is not something that must attach to either virtue or vice, spirit or evil, but has an independent and material reality. Comprised of things that are "indifferent" the soul "constitutes us as human beings," "seeks what is necessary," and is "the life-giving element." Substantive, inclusive, and variable, the soul is at the very core of what it means to be a human. It is the soul's "natural movements" – and their both/and relationship to spirit – that are of central importance. The "natural movements" are inborn and ineradicable "instincts of nature" and "natural propensities or traits of character." What is spiritual and what is not is relative to a particular person. Spirituality is impossible lacking a careful study of one's own genetic makeup, both physical and mental. The problem is that people just accept their impulses as a given and do whatever comes naturally, deceiving themselves and others. Passions which appear honourable, but which in fact are neutral and indifferent, are "disguised with the mask of virtue." In emphasizing the need to "know thyself" Erasmus is holding in mind Socrates but the frame of thought is very consciously, and demonstrably, Stoic. Socrates had contended that knowing thyself has nothing to do with the body. Nor would Socrates have ever dreamed that spirituality is inseparable from one's particular instincts and traits. Note one thing however: Knowing oneself is only a starting point, something "indifferent." It is not virtue. Natural inclinations, whatever they may be, are nothing a person has earned.

It may be easy to say that all things not spirit or flesh, virtue or vice, are indifferent but what this entails is for most readers, Erasmus recognizes, counter-intuitive and a hard sell. How can it be, first, that the extreme differences between humans are all on the same level – that each and every difference is indifferent? He begins by criticizing here again Origen. Contradicting the views of Gnostics, who held that the variety of human capabilities and social or racial positions is not the result of free will but determined by God, Origen had argued that this diversity does not reflect the capricious actions of an unjust God but the thoroughly just responses of God to the free-will decisions made by rational beings. All humans were in a pre-existent state created rational and good and the diversity comes about because God allowed humans, while in this pre-existent state, free will. The diversity we see is proportionate to the merit won or lost in that pre-existent state. In emphatically rejecting this argument Erasmus refutes in detail Origen's interpretation of the biblical story of Jacob and Esau. The nature that creates human diversity does not (following the Stoics) need any higher explanation. However varied their temperament and situation at birth, humans are not responsible for their differences. Morality has nothing to do with the particular character traits or social situations one is given at birth. In developing the thesis Erasmus brings in Socrates' fable about the charioteer and the good and bad horses, in Plato's *Phaedrus.* What has not been understood is that Erasmus does not argue that the person with a moderate, tractable, and compliant disposition is better than the person with a harsh disposition. Nor did he ever see himself as having a modest and gentle disposition. He makes the point, far from Plato's meaning but fundamental for his entire thesis, that the person with a mild and sociable disposition is no better than the person born with a very rebellious body and harsh disposition. Temperaments are indifferent. Spirituality only begins when one goes beyond (both/and) what one is born with. And yet Erasmus' sympathy is with the bad horse and the person with a rebellious body, which ties with his view of himself and his contention that the greater the handicap the greater the opportunity for virtue – as peerlessly proven by Christ.

Without question the *Enchiridion* does make flesh/spirit contrasts, which Erasmus explicitly ties with Stoic *turpe/honestum* contrasts. But in fact these opposites are throughout framed by something far more fundamental, something at the very heart not only of Stoicism but of Christianity, the unitary both/and: *indifferens/honestum,* indifferent/spirit. Readers have noticed that Erasmus is critical of religious "ceremonies" but have not correctly understood the place of this criticism, the mindset. Ceremonies are indifferents that can reflect, depending on their use, either vice or steps (both/and) on the spiritual path. In fact everything in life is indifferent: family things, social things, economic things, political things. How one deals with indifferents shows what kind of Christian one really is. Take money: from the spirit side of the mind one needs to recognize at every moment that money is worthless while from the indifferent side one needs to work out proper monetary advantage as one holds to spirit. Even if one performs a good action it is "a fault to perform a good action in an improper way," which is the difference in Stoicism between absolute duty (*katorthoma*) and ordinary duty (*kathekon*). A judge, for example, may decide a criminal case appropriately, according to the law, but spirituality is something else. Spirituality requires that the judge also assess his own character traits and decide for or against the death penalty with the "sentiments" of a father and with "immense sorrow."

As all the above indicates, the *Enchiridion* is a philosophical treatise, systematically worked out – not a thrown-together hodgepodge. The author employs rhetorical tools but the work is not, contrary to modern views, that of a rhetorician picking and choosing odd ideas at will for the purposes of debate. Throughout he locates his thought, as in *De taedio Iesu*, by referring to the views on a particular topic of a well known authority – only to rewrite these views in terms of a singular Stoic-based outlook. Consider his treatment of Socrates and Plato. Early in the treatise he refers to Plato's layering of the emotions in the *Republic* and *Timaeus*, showing that Plato would confine food and bodily needs to "a stall like a wild, untamed animal." He also refers to *Phaedo*, where Socrates claims that philosophy is meditation on death in that it is about rejection of the senses and a concentration on reason. Without directly confronting Plato or Socrates Erasmus shows throughout the *Enchiridion* just how limited such views are. Later, in noting that in Stoicism virtue (*honestum*) and evil (*turpe*) contradict each other, he points to Plato's insistence in the *Republic* that the guardians must hold to unwavering principles. And he very explicitly rejects Aristotle's criticism of Socrates for holding in *Protagoras* that "virtue is simply the knowledge of what is to be sought after and what avoided." And yet Erasmus points out the difference, which he more than any of his contemporaries deeply grasped, between Socrates/Plato and Stoicism. Albeit worldly "seeking and avoiding" is one with unbending truth, *honestum*, "seeking and avoiding" is not something that can ever be spun off, as with Socrates, from the absolutes of knowledge and intellect. Truth is not one-dimensional but two-dimensional.

Perhaps nothing displays this mindset more than Erasmus' thought on war, touched on in the *Enchiridion* and detailed later in book after book – and never understood by contemporaries, or for that matter by modern scholars. Directly contradicting scholastic logicizing regarding war, worked out in large tomes with multitudes of logic-based "distinctions," Erasmus holds that there can be no distance between precepts and worldly actions, faith and morals, unbending values and bending values. When Christ disallowed war he meant it and this precept cannot be turned into a mere council. Where this precept is not active in the world of affairs there is no Christianity. Absolutes at all times require appropriate deeds. Lacking the absolutes practices that appear to be expedient and decorous and prudent represent, though covered by a veneer of righteousness, nothing but deceit and evil self-interest. What scholastics call "right intention" in warfare is, in fact, nothing but a logical justification which covers up a precept at the very heart of Christianity. "Right intention" is for them simply a name whereby one can cruelly "whip out his sword, stick it into the guts of his brother, and nevertheless dwell in that supreme charity." Lacking absolute precepts appropriate practices are impossible. Erasmus does not contradict himself where he states "our one aim in life is to take flight from life" and, not far away, "the end and aim of the faith of the Gospel is conduct." Taking flight from life, holding to one type of value, allows one to engage in life, holding to another type of value, in the best possible ways. If a war is now and then necessary this can be ascertained and carried out only by those who hold high the absolutes of Christ's teachings – with undeviating inner resolve and "horror of wars and capital punishment" – at the same time as they respond prudently, appropriately, and expediently to "the immense burden of events," in accord with the bending side of Christ's teachings.

Complementing the two-dimensional military stance of the Stoic wiseman, in day to day affairs Erasmus argues for "the method and rules of a new kind of warfare," soldiering that requires extreme mental strength, that confronts everyday challenges with a certain "state of mind" and "fixed procedures" – which accounts for the title of his work, *Enchiridion militis christiani* (*Handbook of the Christian Soldier*).

Contrast all previous humanist thought with Erasmus' existential concerns, at an early age, with his bodily and mental instincts and traits and from this his all-consuming interest in understanding in detail the workings of the Stoic outlook. While previous humanists had little studied Cicero's philosophical writings, other than *De officiis*, and had seen these writings and Stoicism from the standpoint of rhetoric, Erasmus was deeply interested in Stoic philosophy as such. In *De taedio Iesu* and the *Enchiridion* rhetoric serves philosophy, and not as in previous humanist thought the other way around. Petrarch had opposed at length – in vacillating either/or rhetorical terms – Stoic reason and worldly emotion whereas Erasmus saw, with great insight, that emotion could and should be attached to Stoic natural instinct at birth, *oikeiosis*, and detached from reason (*ratio*). Fifteenth-century humanists tended to ridicule the Stoic wiseman, whom they saw in one-dimensional abstract terms, and even those few who supported him did so for social and political reasons. Niccolo Niccoli saw this wiseman, representing "virtue alone," as a tool by which he could attack nobility as an institution – the power, wealth, and prestige that humanists such as himself lacked. Then too, fifteenth-century humanists had always thought about the differences between the contemplative and active lives in either/or terms. While humanists such as Bruni and Valla had focused on the active life, later in the century a much more autocratic and rigid political situation, tied with the Neoplatonism inspired at Florence by Ficino, led to a focus on the contemplative life. Although brought up in a very different environment, in Holland, Erasmus also focused on the contemplative life in his early work, *On Contempt of the World* (1485–8). But beginning around 1497 with his immersion in Stoicism his outlook radically changed, from then on seeing the contemplative and active lives in unitary both/and terms.

The focus of Italian humanists on one-dimensional abstract doctrines is also evident in the many "mirror-for-princes" treatises set forth in the latter fifteenth century. The purpose of these treatises, inspired in particular by an early work of Seneca, *De clementia*, was to guide princes by setting forth universal precepts. In *The Prince* Machiavelli mounted a frontal attack on such views, showing that rigid abstract doctrines cannot be applied to politics without ruining the state, but what Machiavelli did not see or take account of is of crucial importance. Nowhere does he recognize the two-dimensional Stoicism delineated and illustrated by Cicero (in terms of Roman life) and applied by Erasmus to the world of affairs he knew and to Christianity.

Clearly, many of Erasmus' writings following *De taedio Iesu* and the *Enchiridion* need to be restudied. To what degree are works that have been considered rhetorical in fact built from a philosophy? What needs to be remembered is that the mindset so evident in *De taedio Iesu* and the *Enchiridion* had been deeply implanted before Erasmus had a command of Greek, before his debate with Colet, and before reading Origen, and in response to an existential crisis. And we know from Erasmus' own words in later writings that the physical and mental issues that had brought about this mindset did not disappear over time. If over time he may have developed "the philosophy of Christ" in various ways – depending on audience, situation, and particular purposes – is it not likely that the Stoic platform remained? I have already outlined reasons for believing that Erasmus' extensive writings on war, particularly *Dulce bellum inexpertis* (1515), *Querela pacis* (1517), and *Utilissima consultatio de bello Turcis inferendo* (1530) reflect throughout "the philosophy of Christ" worked out in the *Enchiridion*. Over and over scholars have shown that *The Praise of Folly* is the work of a brilliant rhetorician but was he only this? Elsewhere I will demonstrate in detail that the work is built from a Stoic *honestum/utile* and *honestum/indifferens* mindset – as is also, directly influenced by Erasmus, Thomas More's *Utopia*.

For the moment it can be pointed out that *Ecclesiastes* (1535), one of Erasmus' last works, is all about the types of rhetorical tools preachers need to explicate the Bible and accommodate hearers with diverse needs but the goal – and this has not been understood – is not itself rhetorical. "We persuade," states Erasmus, "the hearer to be willing to embrace what is *honestum* and *utile*"[1] The *honestum* and the *utile* referred to here ties with that described throughout Book 3 of *De officiis* – and the mindset worked out in the *Enchiridion*. *Honestum* (for Erasmus, *spiritus*) is that which is right by itself (*quod per se rectum est*), beautiful (*pulcrum*), and proper (*decorum*).[2] In stating that *honestum* is that which is right by itself (*quod per se rectum est*), Erasmus is repeating a centrepiece of Stoic doctrine. As Cicero puts it in *De finibus*, *honestum* is "quod sit rectum ipsumque per se" (2.50). As for *pulcrum*, *honestum* is a translation of the Greek *τὸ καλόν* and *τὸ καλόν*, as Chrysippus states, is inherently beautiful (D.L. 7.101; cf. *Fin.* 2.47, 49). *Decorum* is one of the four major divisions of Stoic *honestum* (*Off.* 1.94). Erasmus wants readers to embrace that which is inseparably *honestum* and *utile*. The Latin is "nihil esse utile, quod non sit honestum, et quicquid honestum est, hoc ipso esse utile, quod honestum est,"[3] words that mimic those used by Cicero in describing his theme in Book 3 of *De officiis* (3.34). Erasmus ties *honestum* and *utile*

1 *Ecclesiastes*. ASD V-4, 272/541.

2 *Ecclesiastes*. ASD V-4, 312/598–600.

3 *Ecclesiastes*. ASD V-4, 312/593–4. Cf. *Paraclesis* (1516), LB 5, 142A, Olin 101, and *Convivium religiosum* (*The Godly Feast*) (1522), ASD I-3, 249/540–1, CWE 39, 189/41.

to nature: "Virtus secundum naturam est, vitium contra naturam" (cf. *Fin.*3.12).[4] Core features of Stoic *utilitas* include, at one with Stoicism, things that are advantageous (*commoda*) or disadvantageous (*incommoda*),[5] according to nature or against nature, and the necessity of a tie to prudence/justice/fortitude/temperance.

With regard to our individual natures Erasmus emphasizes – as in the *Enchiridion* – that the natural dispositions of humans vary greatly and explains what this means (cf. *Off.* 1.107–20).[6] Here too discussion often centres on "*necessaria,*" things indifferent between *honestum* and *turpe*.[7] For example, the preacher needs to point to the necessities of our nature (such as the need for sex and food) while making listeners see the need not to abuse them but to tie them in actual practice to the virtue that is *honestum*. The fact that one is prone by birth to a particular vice, such as anger, must not be used as an excuse. The real problem is not nature but ourselves. We make what is appropriate in nature inappropriate by not holding to *honestum*.[8]

The origins of all right actions ("fontes omnium recte factorum") are the four philosophical virtues: prudence, justice, fortitude, and temperance.[9] *Recte factum*, or right action, had of course a very technical meaning and Erasmus had uncovered this meaning in his edition of *De officiis* and employed it over and over in the *Enchiridion*. While *kathekon* is "an appropriate act" (in terms of *indifferentia*) *katorthoma* or "*recte factum*" (*Fin.* 3.24, 45) is "an appropriate act perfectly performed" (*Fin.* 3.59). In *Ecclesiastes* as in the *Enchiridion* we find the difference between perfect spirituality and imperfect spirituality, *katorthoma* and *kathekon*, right action and appropriate action, clearly delineated and illustrated. "Natural affections for parents, spouses, and children do not reflect true charity unless we love them at the same time for the sake of God" (Neque enim heroica charitas est, si naturali affectu diligamus parentes, uxorem ac liberos, nisi simul amemus eos propter Deum).[10]

---

4 *Ecclesiastes*. ASD V-4, 368/41–3.

5 *Ecclesiastes*. ASD V-4, 314/631–4, 669–73.

6 *Ecclesiastes*. ASD V-4, 238/976–90.

7 *Ecclesiastes* ASD V-4, 314/642–53.

8 *Ecclesiastes*. ASD V-4, 314/652–3, 398/793–818.

9 *Ecclesiastes*. ASD V-5, 336/502–3

10 *Ecclesiastes*. ASD V-5, 336/1–3. The treatment of parents and relatives is described similarly, and at greater length, in the *Enchiridion* (52) and *The Praise of Folly*, Miller trans. 135, ASD IV-3, 191/202–9, and by Sextus Empiricus (2nd cent. AD) in his description of the Stoic view, *Against the Professors* 11.200–1, LS 59G. See also *Fin.* 3.32, and Seneca, *Ep.* 95/37–46 at 43.

Erasmus' influence in the sixteenth century was phenomenal. Between 1503 and 1536 more than fifty Latin printed editions of the *Enchiridion* appeared and by the end of the century there had been more than seventy editions.[11] Translations had been made into all the languages of Europe. Between 1533 and 1545 there were thirteen editions in English. Readers were undoubtedly inspired, in one way or another, by the fact that the work relates Christianity to their own lives and to particular worldly issues. How various aspects of Erasmus' thought found in the *Enchiridion* and in his many other works were actually understood or appropriated by contemporaries has been much studied with regard in particular to Luther and the Reformation and English intellectual, social, and political developments. But to what degree was the larger meaning of his thought grasped? Moderns have been convinced that his "philosophy of Christ" was merely a way of speaking and had absolutely nothing to do with philosophy as such. Nowhere is it believed that Erasmus was thinking in logical and systematic terms. He was a brilliant rhetorician, not a philosopher. Contemporaries saw the matter similarly. This book has shown just how wrong these views have been.

Of course most early readers of the *Enchiridion* had no way of recognizing the sources of Erasmus' outlook, much less his handling of these sources. Nor could they have easily glimpsed his radical rewriting of non-Stoic authors, not least being fathers of the church, scholastics, and Plato. All of which meant that the larger meaning of the work was not accessible. The fact that *De taedio Iesu* was seldom republished, notwithstanding that the *Enchiridion* was built from it, just illustrates how little was understood about Erasmus' thinking. I know of only one contemporary of Erasmus who demonstrably grasped the Stoic *katorthoma/kathekon* frame of his thought and his employment of the Stoic emphasis on natural instinct (*oikeiosis*) as well as the indispensable relationships to his youthful suffering regarding the nature of his body and mind. That person was the author of *Utopia*, Thomas More.

One might imagine that Erasmus' *katorthoma/kathekon* mindset would have been discerned and appreciated by philosophers but this has never been the case. Towards the end of the century there was considerable interest in Stoicism by philosophers but it was not the Stoicism valued by Erasmus. Far from Erasmus' *katorthoma/kathekon* outlook and inspiration, Justus Lipsius argued in *De Constantia* (1584), employing

11 www.artscouncil.org.uk/media/uploads/Experts_statement_Enchiridion.pdf.

certain works of Seneca, the need to endure worldly calamities without complaint and extirpate emotions. Public affairs are imposed by God and profitable to us and Stoic ideas of fate and Christian belief have much in common.

However much in the centuries that followed Stoicism may have influenced in various ways and to varying degrees philosophical thought, what is striking is the extent to which modern scholarly interest in Stoicism, beginning in the latter twentieth century, has focused on the *katorthoma/kathekon* mindset that had so consumed Erasmus.

Bibliography

Primary Sources

Ambrose. *De Officiis* (*De Officiis ministrorum*). Ed. and trans. Ivor J. Davidson. 2 vols. Oxford: Oxford University Press, 2001.

Aquinas, Thomas. *Questiones disputatae de veritate*. In *Opera Omnia*. Leonine edition. Vol. 22. Rome: Typographia Polyglotta, 1882–.

– *Scriptum super Sententiis*. Ed. M.F. Moos. Vols 3 and 4. Paris: Lethielleux, 1933–47.

– *Summa Theologiae*. Trans. the Dominican Fathers. 60 vols. London: Blackfriars, 1964.

– *The Treatise on Human Nature: Summa Theologiae, Ia 75–89*. Commentary and trans. Robert Pasnau. Indianapolis: Hackett, 2002.

Aristotle. *The Complete Works of Aristotle: The Revised Oxford Translation*. Ed. Jonathan Barnes. Bollingen Series. 2 vols. Princeton: Princeton University Press, 1984.

Augustine. *The City of God*. Ed. and trans. R.W. Dyson. Cambridge: Cambridge University Press, 1998.

– *De diversis questionibus octaginta tribus*. Ed. Almut Mutzenbecher. Turnhout: Brepols, 1975.

– *De mendacio*. PL 40.

– *De natura et gratia*. PL 44.

– *In Ioannis evangelium tractatus*. PL 35.

– *Sermones*. PL 38.

Aurelius, Marcus. *Meditations*. Ed. and trans. C.R. Haines. Loeb Classical Library. London and Cambridge, MA: Harvard University Press, 1916.

Bonaventure. *Breviloquium*. In *Opera omnia*. Quaracchi edition. Vol. 5.

– *Commentaria in quattuor libros Sententiarum*. In *Opera omnia*. Quaracchi edition. Vols 1–4.

– *De perfectione vitae sorores*. In *Opera omnia*. Quaracchi edition. Vol. 8.
– *De triplic via*. In *Opera omnia*. Quaracchi edition. Vol. 8.
– *Lignum vitae*. In *Opera omnia*. Quaracchi edition. Vol. 8.
– *Opera omnia*. Ed. Collegium S. Bonaventurae. 10 vols. Quaracchi, Italy: Collegium S. Bonaventurae, 1882–1902.
– *Vitis mystica*. In *Opera omnia*. Quaracchi edition. Vol. 8.
– *The Works of Bonaventure*. Trans. José de Vinck. 5 vols. Paterson, NJ: S. Anthony Guild Press, 1960–70.

Bracciolini, Poggius. *De nobilitate*. In *Opera Omnia*. Ed. R. Fubini. Vol. 1, 64–83. Turin: Bottega d'Erasmo, 1964.
– "On Nobility." In *Knowledge, Goodness, and Power: The Debate over Nobility among Quattrocento Italian Humanists*, ed. and trans. Albert Rabil Jr, 63–89. Binghamton, NY: Medieval & Renaissance Texts and Studies, 1991.

Bruni, Leonardo. *History of the Florentine People*. Vol. 1. Ed. and trans. James Hankins. Harvard: Harvard University Press, 2001.
– *The Humanism of Leonardo Bruni: Selected Texts*. Ed. G. Griffiths, J. Hankins, and D. Thompson. Binghamton, NY: Medieval and Renaissance Texts and Studies, 1987.
– *Leonardo Bruni Aretino, Humanistisch-philosophische Schriften*. Ed. Hans Baron. Leipzig: Teubner, 1928.

Cicero. *De finibus bonorum et malorum*. Trans. H. Rackham. Loeb Classical Library. 2nd ed. London and Cambridge, MA: Harvard University Press, 1931.
– *De inventione*. Trans. H.M. Hubbell. Loeb Classical Library. London and Cambridge, MA: Harvard University Press, 1949.
– *De officiis*. Trans. W. Miller. Loeb Classical Library. London and Cambridge, MA: Harvard University Press, 1913.
– *De oratore, books I, II*. Trans. E.W. Sutton and H. Rackham. Loeb Classical Library. London and Cambridge, MA: Harvard University Press, 1942.
– *De oratore, book III*. Trans. H. Rackham. Loeb Classical Library. London and Cambridge, MA: Harvard University Press, 1942.
– *On Duties*. Ed. M.T. Griffin and E.M. Atkins. Cambridge: Cambridge University Press, 1991.
– *On Moral Ends*. Ed. J. Annas and trans. R. Woolf. Cambridge: Cambridge University Press, 2001.
– Orator. Trans. G.L. Hendrickson and H.M. Hubbell. Loeb Classical Library. Cambridge, MA: Harvard University Press, 1939.
– *Paradoxa Stoicorum*. Trans. H. Rackham. Loeb Classical Library. London and Cambridge, MA: Harvard University Press, 1942.
– *Posterior Academics*. Book I of Cicero, *Academica*. Trans. H. Rackham. Loeb Classical Library. Cambridge, MA: Harvard University Press, 1933.

– *Tusculan Disputations.* Trans. J.E. King. Loeb Classical Library. Rev. ed. London and Cambridge, MA: Harvard University Press, 1945.
– *Tusculan Disputations 3 and 4.* Ed. and trans. Margaret Graver. In Graver, *Cicero on the Emotions: Tusculan Disputations 3 and 4.* Chicago: University of Chicago Press, 2002.
Cicero [pseudo.]. *Rhetorica ad Herennium.* Trans. Harry Caplan. Leob Classical Library. London and Cambridge, MA: Harvard University Press, 1954.
Clairvaux, Bernard of. *De gradibus humilitatis et superbiae.* PL 182.
– *Opera Sancti Bernardi.* Ed. J. Leclercq, C.H. Talbot, and H. Rochais. 8 vols. Rome: Editions Cistercienses, 1957–77.
– *Selected Works.* Trans. G.R. Evans. Intro. Jean Leclercq. New York: Paulist Press, 1987.
– *Sermon on St. Andrew*: 1.6. PL 183.
Colet, John. *An Exposition of St. Paul's Epistle to the Corinthians.* Ed. and trans. J.H. Lupton. London: Bell, 1874.
Comestor, Peter. *Historia scholastica.* Strassburg: Husner, 1503.
Damascus, John of. *De fide orthodoxa.* PG 94.
Die griechischen Chistlichen Schriftsteller. Berlin: Berlin-Brandenberg Academy, 1897–.
Empiricus, Sextus. *Against the Ethicists (Adversus Mathematicos XI).* Ed. Richard Bett. Oxford: Oxford University Press, 1997.
Epictetus. *Discourses.* Trans. William A. Oldfather. 2 vols. Loeb Classical Library. London and Cambridge, MA: Harvard University Press, 1925.
– *Discourses, Book 1.* Ed. Robert F. Dobbin. Oxford: Oxford University Press, 1998.
– *Enchiridion.* Trans. William A. Oldfather. Loeb Classical Library. London and Cambridge, MA: Harvard University Press, 1928.
Erasmus, Desiderius. *Adagia.* ASD II-4, 5, 6. CWE 30–6.
– *Antibarbarorum liber.* Ed. Kazimierz Kumaniecki. ASD I-1. Trans. Margaret M. Phillips, CWE 23.
– *Christian Humanism and the Reformation: Selected Writings of Erasmus.* Ed. and trans. John C. Olin. New York: Harper & Row, 1965.
– *Collected Works of Erasmus.* Toronto: University of Toronto Press, 1974–
– *Colloquia.* ASD I-3. CWE 39–40.
– *Compendium vitae.* Allen 1, 46–52. CWE 4, 403–10.
– *De contemptu mundi.* Ed. Sam Dresden. ASD V-1. Trans. Erika Rummel, CWE 66.
– *Desiderius Erasmus Roterodamus, Ausgewählte Werke.* Ed. Hajo Holborn and Annemarie Holborn. Munich: Beck, 1933.
– *Disputatiuncula de taedio, pavore, tristitia Jesu, instante supplicio crucis: Deque verbis, quibus visus est mortem deprecari, Pater, si fieri potest, transeat a me calix iste.* LB 5, 1265A–1292A.

– *Dulce bellum inexpertis*. Ed. R. Hoven, ASD II-7. Trans. Denis L. Drysdall, CWE 35.
– *Ecclesiastes*. Ed. Jacques Chomarat. ASD V-4 and 5.
– *Enchiridion Militis Christiani*. Commentary and French trans. A.J. Festugière. Paris: Vrin, 1971.
– *Enchiridion Militis Christiani*. In *Desiderius Erasmus Roterodamus Ausgewählte Werke*, 22–136.
– *The Enchiridion of Erasmus*. Trans. Raymond Himelick. Bloomington, IN: Indiana University Press, 1963.
– *The Handbook of the Christian Soldier/ Enchiridion Militis Christiani*. Trans. Charles Fantazzi, CWE 66, 24–127.
– *Moriae encomium id est Stultitiae Laus*. Ed. Clarence Miller. ASD IV-3. Trans. Betty Radice, CWE 27.
– *Opera omnia*. Ed. J. Leclerc. 10 vols. Leiden: Van der Aa, 1703–6.
– *Opera omnia Desiderii Erasmi Roterodami*. Amsterdam: Brill, 1969–.
– *Opus epistolarum Des. Erasmi Roterodami*. Ed. P.S. Allen, H.M. Allen, and H.W. Garrod. 12 vols. Oxford: Clarendon Press, 1906–58. Translations by various scholars, CWE 1974–.
– *Opuscula: A Supplement to the Opera Omnia*. Ed. W.K. Ferguson. The Hague: Nijhoff, 1933.
– *Paraclesis*. In *Desiderius Erasmus Roterodamus, Ausgewählte Werke*, 139–49. Trans. *Christian Humanism and the Reformation*, 92–106.
– *The Praise of Folly*. Trans. Hoyt H. Hudson. Princeton: Princeton University Press, 1941.
– *The Praise of Folly*. Trans. Clarence H. Miller. New Haven: Yale University Press, 1979.
– *Querela pacis*. Ed. Otto Herding, ASD IV-2. Trans. Betty Radice, CWE 27.
– *Ratio verae theologiae*. In *Desiderius Erasmus Roterodamus, Ausgewählte Werke*, 175–305.
– *A Short Debate Concerning the Distress, Alarm, and Sorrow of Jesus As the Crucifixion Drew Nigh; and Concerning the Words in Which He Seemed to Pray for Deliverance From Death: "Father, If It Be Possible, Let This cup Pass from Me."* Trans. Michael J. Heath, CWE 70, 13–67.
– *Utilissima consultatio de bello Turcis inferendo*. Ed. A.G. Weiler, ASD V-3. Trans. Betty Radice, CWE 27.
Erasmus, Desiderius, ed. *De officiis Marci Tullii Ciceronis libri tres.* [London]: Ioannem Kyngstonem, 1574.
Erfurt, Thomas of. *Grammatica speculative.* London, 1515.
Ficino, Marsilio. *Marsilio Ficino and the Phaedran Charioteer*. Ed. and trans. Michael J.B. Allen. Berkeley: University of California Press, 1981.

– *Marsilio Ficino: The Philebus Commentary.* Ed. and trans. Michael J.B. Allen. Berkeley: University of California Press, 1975.

– *Platonic Theology: On the Immortality of Souls.* Ed. and trans. J. Hankins, W. Bowen, M.J.B. Allen, and J. Warden. 6 vols. Cambridge, MA: Harvard University Press 2001–6.

Filelfo, Francesco. *On Exile* (*Commentationes Florentinae de exilio*). Trans. W.S. Blanchard. Cambridge, MA: Harvard University Press, 2013.

Garin, Eugenio, ed. *Prosatori latini del Quattrocento.* Milan: Riccardo Ricciardi, 1952.

Gellius, Aulus. *Noctes Atticae.* Ed. P.K. Marshall. 3 vols. Oxford: Oxford University Press, 1990.

– *Noctes Atticae.* Trans. John C. Rolfe. 3 vols. Loeb Classical Library. London and Cambridge, MA: Harvard University Press, 1927.

Glossa ordinaria. Editio Princeps. Strassburg: Adolph Rusch, 1480/1; repr. Turnhout, Belgium: Brepols, 1992.

Hales, Alexander of. *Glossa in quatuor libros Sententiarum.* Ed. Collegium S. Bonaventurae. Quarracchi, Italy: Collegium S. Bonaventurae, 1951–7.

Jerome. *Commentary on Ephesians.* PL 26.

– *Commentary on Ezechiel.* PL 25.

– *Commentary on Matthew.* PL 26.

– *Ep. 79.* To Salvina. PL 22.

Kohl, Benjamin G., and Ronald G. Witt, eds. *The Earthly Republic: Italian Humanists on Government and Society.* Philadelphia: University of Pennsylvania Press, 1978.

Laertius, Diogenes. *Lives of Eminent Philosophers.* Trans. R.D. Hicks. 2 vols. Leob Classical Library. London and Cambridge, MA: Harvard University Press, 1972.

Lipsius, Justus. *De Constantia.* Trans. J. Stradling, ed. J. Sellars. Exeter: University of Exeter Press, 2006.

Lombard, Peter. *Sententiae in IV libris distinctae.* 2 vols. Ed. Collegium S. Bonaventurae. Rome: Collegii S. Bonaventurae, 1971–81.

Long, A.A., and D.N. Sedley, comm. and trans. *The Hellenistic Philosophers.* 2 vols. Cambridge: Cambridge University Press, 1987.

Machiavelli. *The Prince.* Trans. George Bull. Suffolk, Eng: Penguin Classics, reissue, 2003.

Migne, J.P., ed. *Patrologiae cursus completus graeca.* 162 vols. Paris: 1857–66.

Migne, J.P., ed. *Patrologiae cursus completus latina.* 221 vols. Paris: 1844–64.

More, Thomas. *The Complete Works of St. Thomas More.* 15 vols. New Haven, CT: Yale University Press, 1963–97.

– *Letter to Martin Dorp.* Ed. Daniel Kinney. CWM 15, 1–127.

– *Utopia*. Ed. G.M. Logan, R.M. Adams, and C.H. Miller. Cambridge: Cambridge University Press, 1995.

Origen. *Commentaria in Epistolam B. Pauli ad Romanos*. PG 14.

– *Commentarius in Matthaeum II. Die griechischen Chistlichen Schriftsteller*, v. 38.

– *Commentary on the Epistle to the Romans Book 1–5*. Ed. and trans. Thomas P. Scheck. Washington, DC: Catholic University of America Press, 2001.

– *Contra Celsum*. Trans. Henry Chadwick. Cambridge: Cambridge University Press, 1965.

– *On First Principles: Being Koetschau's Text of the De Principiis*. Ed. and trans. G.W. Butterworth. New York: Harper and Row, 1966.

– *Origenes Vier Bücher Von Den Prinzipien*. Ed. and trans. into German by Herwig Görgemanns and Heinrich Karpp. Darmstadt, Ger.: Wissenschaftliche Buchgesellschaft, 1976.

– *Selecta in Psalmos*. PG 12.

Petrarch. "How a Ruler Ought to Govern His State." In Kohl and Witt, *The Earthly Republic*, 35–78, and *Opera Omnia*, vol. 1, 419–35.

– *Le Familiari*. Ed. U. Bosco and V. Rossi. 4 vols. Florence, Sansoni, 1933–42.

– *Letters on Familiar Matters: "Rerum familiarium libri" Libri XVII–XXIV*. Trans. A. Bernardo. Baltimore: Johns Hopkins University Press, 1985.

– *Opera omnia*. 2 vols. Basil, Henrichus Petri, 1554; repr. Ridgewood, NJ: Gregg Press, 1965.

– *Remedies for Fortune Fair and Foul*. Ed. and trans. Conrad H. Rawski. 5 vols. Bloomington, IN: Indiana University Press, 1991.

Pico della Mirandolla, Giovanni. *Oration on the Dignity of Man*. In *Renaissance Philosophy: Selected Readings*, ed. and trans. A.B. Fallico and H. Shapiro, 1:141–71. New York: Random House, 1967.

Plato. *Alcibiades*. Trans. D.S. Hutchinson. In Plato, *Complete Works*, 557–95.

– *Collected Dialogues*. Ed. Edith Hamilton and Huntington Cairns. Bollingen Series 61. Princeton: Princeton University Press, 1963.

– *Complete Works*. Ed. John M. Cooper. Indianapolis: Hackett, 1997.

– *Phaedo*. Trans. G.M.A. Grube. In Plato, *Complete Works*, 49–100.

– *Phaedrus*. Trans. Alexander Nehamas and Paul Woodruff. In Plato, *Complete Works*, 506–56.

– *Philebus*. Ed. and trans. R. Hackforth. In Plato, *Collected Dialogues*, 1086–1150.

– *Protagoras*. Trans. Stanley Lombardo and Karen Bell. In Plato, *Complete Works*, 746–90.

– *Republic*. Trans. G.M.A. Grube, rev. C.D.C. Reeve. In Plato, *Complete Works*, 971–1223.

– *Timaeus*. Trans. Benjamin Jowett. In Plato, *Collected Dialogues*, 1151–1211.

Plutarch. *De communibus notitiis contra Stoicos*. Trans. H. Cherniss. In *Moralia*, 13, pt. 2, 622–827.

– *Life of Phocion*. Trans. Bernadotte Perrin. In Plutarch's *Lives*, vol. 8. Loeb Classical Library. London and Cambridge, MA: Harvard University Press, 1959.

– *Moralia*. 16 vols. Loeb Classical Library. London and Cambridge, MA: Harvard University Press, 1927–2004.

Poitiers, Hilary of. *De Trinitate*. In *Corpus Christianorum, Series Latina*, ed. P. Smulders and trans. E.W. Watson, vols 62–62A. Turnhout: Brepols, 1979.

Politian. "A Letter to Bartolomeo Scala in Defense of the Stoic Philosopher Epictetus." In *Cambridge Translations of Renaissance Philosophical Texts I*, ed. Jill Kraye, 192–9. Cambridge: Cambridge University Press, 1997.

Quintilian. *The Orator's Education (Institutio Oratoria)*. Trans. Donald A. Russell. Loeb Classical Library. 5 vols. Cambridge, MA: Harvard University Press, 2002.

Roberts, Alexander, and James Donaldson, eds. *Ante-Nicene Fathers*. 10 vols. Edinburgh: Clark, 1885.

Salutati. *Epistolario di Coluccio Salutati*. Ed. Francesco Novati. 4 vols. Rome: Istituto Storico Italiano, 1891–1911.

– "Letter to Peregrino Zambeccari." In Kohl and Witt, *The Earthly Republic*, 93–114, and *Epistolario di Coluccio Salutati*, vol. 3, 285–307.

Scotus. *Questiones in quartum librum Sententiarum*. In *Duns Scoti Opera Omnia*, vols. 8-21. Paris: Vives, 1891–5.

Seneca. *Ad Lucilium Epistulae Morales*. Trans. Richard M. Gummere. 3 vols. Loeb Classical Library. London and Cambridge, MA: Harvard University Press, 1917–25.

– *De clementia*. Ed. and trans. Susanna Braund. Oxford: Oxford University Press, 2009.

– *De otio, De brevitate vitae*. Ed. G.S. Williams. Cambridge: Cambridge University Press, 2003.

– *Moral and Political Essays*. Trans. J.M. Cooper and J.F. Procopé. Cambridge: Cambridge University Press, 1995.

– *Moral Essays*. Trans. John W. Basore. 3 vols. Loeb Classical Library. London and Cambridge, MA: Harvard University Press, 1932.

Valla, Lorenzo. *De vero falsoque bono*. Ed. M. de P. Lorch. Bari: Adriatica, 1970.

– *On Pleasure/ De voluptate*. Trans. A. Kent and Maristella Lorch Hieatt. New York: Abaris Books, 1977.

Voragine, Jacobus de. Legenda aurea. 2nd ed. 2 vols. Ed. G.P. Magioni. Florence: SISMEL, 1998.

– *The Golden Legend: Readings on the Saints*. 2 vols. Trans. Granger Ryan. Princeton: Princeton University Press, 1993.

Secondary Sources

Abel, K. "Das Propatheia-Theorem: Ein Beitrag zur stoischen Affektenlehr." *Hermes* 111 (1983): 78–97.

Ackroyd, Peter. *The Life of Thomas More.* London: Anchor, 1999.

Annas, Julia. "Aristotelian Political Theory in the Hellenistic Period." In Laks and Schofield, *Justice and Generosity*, 74–94.

– *The Morality of Happiness.* Oxford: Oxford University Press, 1993.

Asmis, Elizabeth. "Seneca's On the Happy Life *and* Stoic Individualism." *Apeiron* 23 (1990): 219–56.

Augustijn, Cornelis. *Erasmus: His Life, Works, and Influence.* Trans. J.C. Grayson. Toronto: University of Toronto Press, 1991.

Bammel, B.P. "Adam in Origen." In *The Making of Orthodoxy, Essays in Honour of Henry Chadwick*, ed. Rowan Williams, 62–93. Cambridge: Cambridge University Press, 2002.

Baraz, Yelena. *A Written Republic: Cicero's Philosophical Politics.* Princeton: Princeton University Press, 2012.

Barlow, J. Jackson. "The Education of Statesmen in Cicero's *De Republica.*" *Polity* 19 (1987): 353–74.

Barnes, Jonathan. "Antiochus of Ascalon." In Griffin and Barnes, *Philosophia Togata 1*, 51–96.

Barnett, Mary J. "Erasmus and the Hermeneutics of Linguistic Praxis." *Renaissance Quarterly* 49 (1996): 542–72.

Baron, Hans. *The Crisis of the Early Italian Renaissance: Civic Humanism and Republican Liberty in an Age of Classicism and Tyranny.* Princeton: Princeton University Press, 1966.

– *In search of Florentine Civic Humanism.* 2 vols. Princeton: Princeton University Press, 1988.

Bartholin, Erasmus, and Lynda Gregorian Christian. "The Figure of Socrates in Erasmus' Works." *Sixteenth Century Journal* 3 (1972): 1–10.

Bäuml, Franz H. "Varieties and Consequences of Medieval Literacy and Illiteracy." *Speculum* 55 (1980): 237–75.

Becker, Carl L. *Everyman His Own Historian: Essays on History and Politics.* New York: Crofts, 1935.

Bejczy, István. *The Cardinal Virtues in the Middle Ages: A Study in Moral Thought from the Fourth to the Fourteenth Century.* Leiden: Brill, 2011.

– "Overcoming the Middle Ages: Historical Reasoning in Erasmus' Antibarbarian Writings." *Erasmus of Rotterdam Society Yearbook* 16 (1996): 34–53.

Bell, Theo. *Divus Bernhardus: Bernard von Clairvaux in Martin Luthers Schriften.* Mainz: Zabern, 1993.

Belting, Hans. *Likeness and Presence: A History of the Image before the Era of Art.* Trans. Edmund Jephcott. Chicago: University of Chicago Press, 1994.

Béné, Charles. *Erasme et Saint Augustine ou influence de Saint Augustin sur l'humanisme d'Erasme.* Geneva: Droz, 1969.

Bestul, Thomas H. *Texts of the Passion: Latin Devotional Literature and Medieval Society*. Philadelphia: University of Pennsylvania Press, 1996.

Blanchard, W. Scott. "Patrician Sages and the Humanist Cynic: Francesco Filelfo and the Ethics of World Citizenship." *Renaissance Quarterly* 60 (2007): 1107–69.

Bosing, Walter. *Hieronymus Bosch, c. 1450–1516: Between Heaven and Hell.* Cologne: Taschen, 1987.

Bossy, John. *Christianity in the West, 1400–1700*. Oxford: Oxford University Press, 1987.

Bouwsma, William J. "The Two Faces of Humanism: Stoicism and Augustinianism in Renaissance Thought." In *Itinerarium Italicum: The Profile of the Italian Renaissance in the Mirror of Its European Transformations*, ed. Heiko Oberman and Thomas A. Brady, 3–60. Leiden: Brill, 1975.

Boyle, Marjorie O'Rouke. *Christening Pagan Mysteries: Erasmus in Pursuit of Wisdom.* Toronto: University of Toronto Press, 1981.

– *Erasmus on Language and Method in Theology*. Toronto: University of Toronto Press, 1978.

Brabant, H. "*Érasme, ses maladies et ses médecins.*" In Margolin, *Colloquia Erasmiana Turonensia*, vol. 2, 539–68.

Brammel, B.P. "Adam in Origen." In *The Making of Orthodoxy: Essays in Honour of Henry Chadwick*, ed. Rowan Williams, 62–93. Cambridge: Cambridge University Press, 2002.

Brennan, Tad. *The Stoic Life: Emotions, Duties, and Fate.* Oxford: Oxford University Press, 2005.

Brooke, Christopher. *Philosophic Pride: Stoicism and Political Thought from Lipsius to Rousseau.* Princeton: Princeton University Press, 2012.

Brown, Robert D. *Lucretius on Love and Sex.* Leiden: Brill, 1987.

Brunschwig, J. "The Cradle Argument in Epicureanism and Stoicism." In Schofield and Striker, *The Norms of Nature*, 113–44.

Brunschwig, J., and M. Nussbaum, eds. *Passions and Perceptions: Studies in Hellenistic Philosophy of Mind*. Cambridge: Cambridge University Press, 1993.

Brunt, P.A. "Cicero's Officium in the Civil War." *Journal of Roman Studies* 76 (1986): 12–32.

Bultot, R. "*Érasme, Épicure et le De Contemptu Mundi.*" In *Scrinium Erasmianum II*, ed. J. Coppens, 205–38. Leiden: Brill, 1969.

Bynum, Caroline Walker. *Holy Feast and Holy Fast: The Religious Significance of Food to Medieval Women*. Berkeley: University of California Press, 1987.

Celenza, Christopher. *Renaissance Humanism and the Papal Curia: Lapo da Castiglionchio the Younger*. Ann Arbor, MI: University of Michigan Press, 1999.

CETEDOC. *Thesaurus Sancti Bernardi Claraevallensis: Thesaurus Patrum Latinorum*. Turnhout: Brepols, 1987.

Chadwick, Henry. *Early Christian Thought and the Classical Tradition*. Oxford: Oxford University Press, 1966.

– "Origen, Celsus, and the Stoa." *Journal of Theological Studies* 48 (1947): 34–49.

Charlier, Yvonne. *Erasme et l'amitié d'aprés sa correspondance*. Paris: Les Belles Lettres, 1972.

Chartier, Roger. "Texts, Printings, Readings." In *The New Cultural History*, ed. Lynn Hunt, 154–75. Berkeley: University of California Press, 1989.

Chomarat, Jacques. *Grammaire et rhétorique chez Erasme*. 2 vols. Paris: Les Belles Lettres, 1981.

– "Pourquoi Erasme s'est-il fait moine?" In *Actes du Colloque International*, ed. J. Chomarat, A. Godin, and J.C. Margolin, 233–48. Geneva: Droz, 1990.

Christ-Von Wedel, Christine. *Erasmus of Rotterdam: Advocate of a New Christianity*. Toronto: University of Toronto Press, 2013.

Clark, Elizabeth A. *The Origenist Controversy: The Cultural Construction of an Early Christian Debate*. Princeton: Princeton University Press, 1992.

Clay, Jenny Strauss. *Hesiod's Cosmos*. Cambridge: Cambridge University Press, 2003.

Colish, Marcia L. "Cicero's *De officiis* and Machiavelli's *Prince*." *Sixteenth Century Journal* (1978): 80–93.

– *Peter Lombard*. 2 vols. Leiden: Brill, 1994.

– *The Stoic Tradition from Antiquity to the Early Middle Ages*. 2 vols. Leiden: Brill, 1985.

Constable, Giles. "The Ideal of the Imitation of Christ." In *Three Studies in Medieval Religious and Social Thought*, 143–248. Cambridge: Cambridge University Press, 1995.

– "The Popularity of Twelfth-Century Spiritual Writers in the Late Middle Ages." In *Renaissance Studies in Honor of Hans Baron*, ed. A. Molho and J.A. Tedeschi, 5–28. Dekalb, IL: Northern Illinois University Press, 1971.

– *Three Studies in Medieval Religious and Social Thought*. Cambridge: Cambridge University Press, 1995.

– "Twelfth-Century Spirituality and the Late Middle Ages." *Medieval and Renaissance Studies* 5 (1971): 27–60.

Cooper, John M. "Aristotle on the Goods of Fortune." In *Reason and Emotion*, 292–311.

– "*Eudaemonism*, the Appeal to Nature, and 'Moral Duty' in Stoicism." In *Aristotle, Kant, and the Stoics: Rethinking Happiness and Duty*, ed. S. Engstrom and J. Whiting, 261–84. Cambridge: Cambridge University Press, 1996.

– "Justus Lipsius and the Revival of Stoicism in Late Sixteenth-Century Europe." In *New Essays on the History of Autonomy*, ed. N. Brender and L. Krasnoff, 7–29. Cambridge: Cambridge Univrsity Press, 2004.

– "Posidonius on Emotions." In *Reason and Emotion*, 449–84.

– *Reason and Emotion: Essays on Ancient Moral Psychology and Ethical Theory.* Princeton: Princeton University Press, 1999.

Courtenay, William J. *Schools and Scholars in Fourteenth-Century England.* Princeton: Princeton University Press, 1987.

Cox, Patricia. "Origen and the Bestial Soul: A Poetics of Nature." *Vigiliae Christianae* 36 (1982): 115–40.

Cox, Virginia. "Machiavelli and the *Rhetorica ad Herennium*: Deliberative Rhetoric in *The Prince*." *Sixteenth Century Journal* 28 (1997): 1109–41.

Crahay, Roland. "Recherches sur le *Compendium vitae* attribué' a Erasmé." *Humanisme et Renaissance* 6 (1939): 7–19, 135–53.

Crouzel, Henri. *Origen: The Life and Thought of the First Great Theologian.* Trans. A.S. Worrall. San Francisco: Harper and Row, 1989.

Dealy, Ross. "The Dynamics of Erasmus' Thought on War." *Erasmus of Rotterdam Society Yearbook* 4 (1984): 53–67.

– *The Politics of an Erasmian Lawyer, Vasco de Quiroga.* Los Angeles: Undena (UCLA Center for Medieval and Renaissance Studies, Humana Civilitas 3), 1976.

– "Vasco de Quiroga's Thought on War: Its Erasmian and Utopian Roots." PhD diss., Indiana University 1975.

Delcourt, M., and M. Derwa. "Trois aspects humanistes de l'épicurisme chrétien." In *Colloquium Erasmianum*, 119–33. Mons: Centre universitaire de l'État, 1968.

DeMolen, Richard L. "Erasmus as Adolescent: 'Shipwrecked am I, and lost, mid waters chill.'" *Bibliothèque d'Humanisme et Renaissance* 38 (1976): 7–25.

– ed. *Essays on the Works of Erasmus*. New Haven: Yale University Press, 1978.

Derbes, Anne. *Picturing the Passion in Late Medieval Italy: Narrative Painting, Franciscan Ideologies, and the Levant.* Cambridge: Cambridge University Press, 1996.

Despres, Denise L. *Ghostly Sights: Visual Meditation in Late-Medieval Literature.* Norman, OK: Pilgrim Books, 1989.

Dodds, Gregory D. *Exploiting Erasmus: The Erasmian Legacy and Religious Change in Early Modern England.* Toronto: University of Toronto Press, 2008.

Doyle, Matthew A. *Bernard of Clairvaux and the Schools: The Formation of an Intellectual Milieu in the First Half of the Twelfth Century*. Spoleto, Italy: Fondazione Centro italiano di studi sull'alto Medioevo, 2005.

Duffy, Eamon. *The Stripping of the Altars: Traditional Religion in England 1400–1580*. New Haven: Yale University Press, 1992.

Duhamel, P. Albert. "The Oxford Lectures of John Colet." *Journal of the History of Ideas* 14 (1953): 493–510.

Dyck, Andrew R. *A Commentary on Cicero,* De Legibus. Ann Arbor, MI: University of Michigan Press, 2004.

– *A Commentary on Cicero,* De Officiis. Ann Arbor, MI: University of Michigan Press, 1996.

Dyson, R.W. *Natural Law and Political Realism in the History of Political Thought: From the Sophists to Machiavelli*. New York: Peter Lang, 2005.

Eden, Kathy. *Friends Hold All Things in Common: Tradition, Intellectual Property, and the Adages of Erasmus*. New Haven: Yale University Press, 2001.

– *The Renaissance Rediscovery of Intimacy*. Chicago: University of Chicago Press, 2012.

Edwards, Francis. *Ritual and Drama: The Medieval Theatre*. Guilford, UK: Lutterworth, 1976.

Edwards, Mark Julian. *Origen against Plato*. Aldershot, UK: Ashgate, 2002.

Ehrman, Bart D. *Lost Christianities: The Battles for Scripture and the Faiths We Never Knew*. Oxford: Oxford University Press, 2003.

Engberg-Pedersen, T. "Discovering the Good: *oikeiosis* and *kathekonta* in Stoic Ethics." In Schofield and Striker, *The Norms of Nature*, 145–83.

Erskine, Andrew. *The Hellenistic Stoa: Political Thought and Action*. Ithaca, NY: Cornell University Press, 1990.

Evans, Gillian R. *The Mind of Bernard of Clairvaux*. Oxford: Oxford University Press, 1983.

– ed. *Medieval Commentaries on the Sentences of Peter Lombard: Current Research*. Vol. 1. Leiden: Brill, 2002.

Fairweather, W. *Origen and Greek Patristic Theology*. Edinburgh: Scribners, 1901.

Fantham, Elaine. "Erasmus and the Latin Classics." CWE 29, xxxiv–l.

Fernandez-Santamaria, J.A. "Erasmus on the Just War." *Journal of the History of Ideas* 34 (1973): 209–26.

– *The State, War and Peace: Spanish Political Thought in the Renaissance, 1516–1559*. Cambridge: Cambridge University Press, 1977.

Ferrary, Jean-Louis. "The Statesman and the Law in the Political Philosophy of Cicero." In Laks and Schofield, *Justice and Generosity*, 48–73.

Field, Arthur. *The Origins of the Platonic Academy of Florence*. Princeton: Princeton University Press, 1988.

Fillion-Lahille, Janine. *Le "De Ira" de Sénèque et la philosophie stoïcienne des passions*. Paris: Klincksieck, 1984.

Fleming, John V. *An Introduction to the Franciscan Literature of the Middle Ages*. Chicago: Franciscan Herald Press, 1977.

Fokke, G.J. "An Aspect of the Christology of Erasmus of Rotterdam." *Ephemerides theologicae Lovanienses* 54 (1978): 161–87.

Fryde, Edmund. "The Beginnings of Italian Humanist Historiography: The 'New Cicero' of Leonardo Bruni." *English Historical Review* 95 (1980): 533–52.

Garin, Eugenio. *Italian Humanism: Philosophy and Civic Life in the Renaissance*. Trans. P. Munz. Oxford: Oxford University Press, 1965.

Gerl, Hanna-Barbara. *Rhetorik als Philosophie: Lorenzo Valla*. Munich: Fink, 1974.

Gerlo, A., ed. *Juste Lipse (1547–1606): Colloque International*. Brussels: Peeters, 1988.

Gerrits, G.H. *Inter Timorem et Spem: A Study of the Theological Thought of Gerard Zerbolt of Zutphen (1367–1398)*. Leiden: Brill, 1986.

Ghellinck, Joseph de. *Le mouvement theologique du XIIe siècle*. 2nd ed. Brussels: Éditions de Tempel, 1948; repr. 1969.

Gibson, Walter S. "Imitatio Christi: The Passion Scenes of Hieronymus Bosch." *Simiolus: Netherlands Quarterly for the History of Art* 6 (1972): 83–93.

Gill, Christopher. "Peace of Mind and Being Yourself: Panaetius to Plutarch." In *Aufstieg und Niedergang der römischen Welt II.36.7*, ed. W. Haase and H. Temporini, 4599–4640. Berlin, 1994.

– *The Structured Self in Hellenistic and Roman Thought*. Oxford: Oxford University Press, 2006.

Gilson, Etienne. "Saint Bonaventure et l'iconographie de la passion." *Revue d'Histoire Franciscaine* 1 (1924): 405–24.

Girardet, Klaus M. *Die Ordnung der Welt: Ein Beitrag zur philosophischen und politischen Interpretation von Ciceros Schrift De Legibus*. Wiesbaden: Franz Steiner, 1983.

Gleason, John B. *John Colet*. Berkeley: University of California Press, 1989.

Glucker, John. *Antiochus and the Late Academy*. Göttingen: Vandenhoeck and Ruprecht, 1978.

– "Cicero's Philosophical Affiliations." In *The Queston of "Eclecticism": Studies in Later Greek Philosophy*, ed. J.M. Dillon and A.A. Long, 34–69. Berkeley: University of California Press, 1988.

Godin, André. "Une biographie en quête d'auteur: le *Compendium vitae* Erasmi." In *Colloque Erasmien de Liège*, ed. Jean-Pierre Massaut, 197–221. Paris: Belles Lettres, 1987.

– "The *Enchiridion Militis Christiani*: The Modes of an Origenian Appropriation." *Erasmus of Rotterdam Society Yearbook* 2 (1982): 47–79.

– *Erasme lecteur d'Origène.* Geneva: Droz, 1982.

Goldhill, Simon. *Who Needs Greek: Contexts in the Cultural History of Hellenism.* Cambridge: Cambridge University Press, 2002.

Gondreau, Paul. *The Passions of Christ's Soul in the Theology of St. Thomas Aquinas.* Münster: Aschendorff, 2002.

Graver, Margaret. *Cicero on the Emotions: Tusculan Disputations 3 and 4.* Chicago: University of Chicago Press, 2002.

– "Philo of Alexandria and the Origins of the Stoic *Propatheiai.*" *Phronesis* 44 (1999): 300–25.

– *Stoicism and Emotion.* Chicago: University of Chicago Press, 2007.

Grendler, Paul F. *Schooling in Renaissance Italy: Lecturing and Learning 300–1600.* Baltimore: Johns Hopkins University Press, 1989.

– *The Universities of the Italian Renaissance.* Baltimore: Johns Hopkins University Press, 2002.

Griffin, Miram T. "Philosophy, Politics and Politicians at Rome." In Griffin and Barnes, *Philosophia Togata 1*, 1–37.

– "Political Thought in the Age of Nero." In *Neronia VI: Rome a l'époque néronienne,* ed. J.-M. Croisille and Y. Perrin, 325–37. Brussels: Latomus, 2002.

– *Seneca: A Philosopher in Politics.* Oxford: Oxford University Press, 1976.

Griffin, Miriam, and Jonathan Barnes, eds. *Philosophia Togata 1: Essays on Philosophy and Roman Society*. Oxford: Clarendon Press, 1989.

Grillmeier, Aloys. *Christ in Christian Tradition: From the Apostolic Age to Chalcedon (AD 451).* Vol. 1. 2nd ed. Atlanta: John Knox Press, 1975.

Halkin, Léon-E. *Erasmus: A Critical Biography.* Trans. John Tonkin. London: Blackwell, 1993.

Hankins, James. "The 'Baron Thesis' after Forty Years and Some Recent Studies of Leonardo Bruni." *Journal of the History of Ideas* 56 (1995): 309–38.

– ed. *The Cambridge Companion to Renaissance Philosophy.* Cambridge: Cambridge University Press, 2007.

– "Humanism and the Origins of Modern Political Thought." In Kraye, *The Cambridge Companion to Renaissance Humanism*, 118–41.

– *Plato in the Italian Renaissance.* 2 vols. Leiden: Brill, 1990.

– ed. *Renaissance Civic Humanism: Reappraisals and Reflections*. Cambridge: Cambridge University Press, 2000.

Hankins, James, and Ada Palmer. *The Recovery of Ancient Philosophy in the Renaissance: A Brief Guide.* Florence: Leo S. Olschki, 2008.

Happé, Peter. *English Drama before Shakespeare,* London: Longman, 1999.

Harnack, Adolf. *The Expansion of Christianity in the First Three Centuries*. Trans. James Moffatt. London: Williams and Norgate, 1905.

Haverals, Marcel. "Une première rédaction du *De contemptu mundi* d'Érasme dans un manuscrit de Zwolle." *Humanistica Lovaniensia* 30 (1981): 40–54.

Heckscher, W.S. "Reflections on Seeing Holbein's Portrait of Erasmus at Longford Castle." In *Essays in the History of Art Presented to Rudolf Wittkower*, ed. D. Fraser and M.J. Lewine, 128–48. London: Phaidon, 1967.

Heine, Ronald E. *The Commentaries of Origen and Jerome on St. Paul's Epistle to the Ephesians.* Oxford: Oxford University Press, 2002.

Heither, T. *Translatio Religionis: Die Paulusdeutung des Origenes in seinem Kommentar zum Römerbrief.* Cologne: Böhlau Verlag, 1990.

Hendrix, Scott H. *Recultivating the Vineyard: The Reformation Agendas of Christianization.* Louisville, KY: Westminster John Knox Press, 2004.

Herlihy, David. *The Black Death and the Transformation of the West.* Cambridge, MA: Harvard University Press, 1997.

Hirvonen, Vesa. "A Nominalist Ontology of the Passions." In *Emotions and Choice from Boethius to Descartes*, ed. Henrik Lagerlund and Mikko Yrjönsuuri, 155–71. Dordrecht, Netherlands: Kluwer, 2002.

Hoffmann, Manfred. "Faith and Piety in Erasmus's Thought." *Sixteenth Century Journal* 20 (1989): 241–58.

– *Rhetoric and Theology: The Hermeneutic of Erasmus.* Toronto: University of Toronto Press, 1994.

Holler, E. *Seneca und die Seelenteilungslehre und Affektpsychologie der Mittelstoa.* Kallmünz: Michael Lassleben, 1934.

Hornblower, S., and A. Spawforth, eds. *The Oxford Classical Dictionary.* 3rd ed. revised. Oxford: Oxford University Press, 2003.

Horowitz, Maryanne. *Seeds of Virtue and Knowledge.* Princeton: Princeton University Press, 1998.

Houser, H.E. *The Cardinal Virtues: Aquinas, Albert, and Philip the Chancellor.* Toronto: Pontifical Institute of Mediaeval Studies, 2004.

Huizinga, Johan. *Erasmus and the Age of Reformation.* New York: Harper and Row, 1957.

Hulliung, Mark. *Citizen Machiavelli.* Princeton: Princeton University Press, 1983.

Hyma, Albert. *The Youth of Erasmus.* Ann Arbor, MI: University of Michigan, 1930.

Inglis, John. "Aquinas's Replication of the Acquired Moral Virtues: Rethinking the Standard Philosophical Interpretation of Moral Virtue in Aquinas." *Journal of Religious Ethics* 27 (1999), 3–27.

Inwood, Brad. *Ethics and Human Action in Early Stoicism.* Oxford: Oxford University Press, 1985.

– "Moral Judgment in Seneca." In *Stoicism: Traditions and Transformations*, ed. Steven K. Strange and Jack Zupko, 76–94. Cambridge: Cambridge University Press, 2004.

– "Politics and Paradox in Seneca's *De beneficiis*." In Laks and Schofield, *Justice and Generosity*, 241–65.

– "Rules and Reasoning in Stoic Ethics." In *Topics in Stoic Philosophy*, ed. Katerina Ierodiakonou, 94–127. Oxford: Oxford University Press, 1999.
– "Seneca and Psychological Dualism." In Brunschwig and Nussbaum, *Passions and Perceptions*, 150–83.
Inwood, Brad, and Jaap Mansfield, eds. *Assent and Argument: Studies in Cicero's Academic Books*. Leiden: Brill, 1997.
Jaquette, James. "Life and Death, 'Adiaphora,' and Paul's Rhetorical Strategies." *Novum Testamentum* 38 (1996): 30–54.
Jayne, Sears. *John Colet and Marsilio Ficino*. Oxford: Oxford University Press, 1963.
Jones, Howard. *Master Tully: Cicero in Tudor England*. Nieuwkoop: De Graaf, 1998.
Kahn, Victoria. *Rhetoric, Prudence and Skepticism in the Renaissance*. Ithaca, NY: Cornell University Press, 1985.
– "*Virtu* and the Example of Agathocles in Machiavelli's *Prince*." In *The Italian Renaissance*, ed. Harold Bloom, 237–60. New York: Chelsea House, 2004.
Kajanto, Liro. "Poggio Bracciolini's *De Infelicitate Principum* and Its Classical Sources." *International Journal of the Classical Tradition* 1 (1994): 23–35.
Kaufman, Peter Iver. "John Colet and Erasmus' *Enchiridion*." *Church History* 46 (1977): 296–312.
Kelly, John. *The Great Mortality: An Intimate History of the Black Death, the Most Devasting Plague of All Time*. New York: HarperCollins, 2005.
Kempshall, M.S. "*De Re Publica* 1.39 in Medieval and Renaissance Political Thought." In *Cicero's Republic*, ed. J.G.F. Powell and J.A. North, 99–135. London: Institute of Classical Studies, 2001.
Kennedy, George A. *Classical Rhetoric and Its Christian and Secular Tradition from Ancient to Modern Times*. Chapel Hill: University of North Carolina Press, 1980.
– *A New History of Classical Rhetoric*. Princeton: Princeton University Press, 1994.
Kidd, I.G. "Moral Actions and Rules in Stoic Ethics." In *The Stoics*, ed. John M. Rist, 247–58. Berkeley: University of California Press, 1978.
Kieckhefer, Richard. "Major Currents in Late Medieval Devotion." In *Christian Spirituality: High Middle Ages and Reformation*, ed. Jill Raitt with B. McGinn and J. Meyendorff, 75–108. New York: Crossroads, 1988.
– *Unquiet Souls: Fourteenth-Century Saints and Their Religious Milieu*. Chicago: University of Chicago Press, 1984.
King, Peter. "Aquinas on the Passions." In *Aquinas's Moral Theory: Essays in Honor of Norman Kretzmann*, ed. S. MacDonald and E. Stump, 101–32. Ithaca, NY: Cornell University Press, 1998.
Knowles, David. *The Evolution of Medieval Thought*. New York: Longman, 1962.

Knuuttila, Simo. *Emotions in Ancient and Medieval Philosophy.* Oxford: Oxford University Press, 2004.

Kohls, Ernst-Wilhelm. "The Principal Theological Thoughts in the *Enchiridion Militis Christiani.*" In DeMolen, *Essays on the Works of Erasmus*, 61–82.

– *Die Theologie Des. Erasmus.* 2 vols. Basel: Reinhardt, 1966.

Kraye, Jill. "Ἀπάθεια and Προπάθειαι in Early Modern Discussions of the Passions: Stoicism, Christianity and Natural History." *Early Science and Medicine* 17 (2012): 230–53.

– "Cicero, Stoicism and Textual Criticism: Poliziano On κατόρθωμα." *Renascimento* 23 (1983): 80–110. Also in her *Classical Traditions in Renaissance Philosophy.* Aldershot, UK: Aldershot, 2002.

– "The Humanist as Moral Philosopher: Marc-Antoine Muret's 1585 Edition of Seneca." In *Moral Philosophy on the Threshold of Modernity*, ed. J. Kraye and R. Saarinen, 307–30. Dordrecht, Netherlands: Springer, 2005.

– "The Revival of Hellenistic Philosophies." In *The Cambridge Companion to Renaissance Philosophy*, ed. J. Hankins, 97–112. Cambridge: Cambridge University Press, 2007.

– "Stoicism in the Renaissance from Petrarch to Lipsius." In *Grotius and the Stoa*, ed. H.W. Blom and L.C. Winkel, 21–45. Assen, Netherlands: Van Gorcum, 2004.

– ed. The Cambridge Companion to Renaissance Humanism. Cambridge: Cambridge University Press, 1996.

Kristeller, Paul O. *Greek Philosophers of the Hellenistic Age.* New York, Columbia University Press, 1993.

– *Renaissance Thought: The Classic, Scholastic, and Humanist Strains.* New York: Harper, 1961.

– *Renaissance Thought II: Papers on Humanism and the Arts.* New York: Harper and Row, 1965.

Kuhn, Thomas S. *The Structure of Scientific Revolutions.* Chicago: Univeristy of Chicago Press, 1962.

Lackner, Dennis F. "The Camaldolese Academy, Ambrogio Traversari, Marsilio Ficino and the Christian Platonic Tradition." In *Marsilio Ficino: His Theology, His Philosophy, His Legacy*, ed. M.J.B. Allen and V. Rees, 15–44. Leiden: Brill, 2002.

Lagrée, J. *Juste Lipse et la restauration du stoïcisme.* Paris: Vrin, 1994.

Laks, André, and Malcolm Schofield, eds. *Justice and Generosity: Studies in Hellenistic Social and Political Philosophy*. Cambridge: Cambridge University Press, 1995.

Landgraf, Artur Michael. *Einführung in die Geschichte der theologischen Literatur der Frühscholastik unter dem Gesichtspunkte der Schulenbildung.* Regensburg: Pustet, 1948.

Lane, N.S. *Calvin and Bernard of Clairvaux*. Princeton: Princeton University Press, 1996.

Lapidge, Michael. "Stoic Inheritance." In *A History of Twelfth-Century Western Philosophy*, ed. Peter Dronke, 81–112. Cambridge: Cambridge University Press, 1988.

Layton, Richard A. "*Propatheia*: Origen and Didymus on the Origin of the Passions." *Vigiliae Christianae* 54 (2000): 262–82.

Leff, Gordon. *The Dissolution of the Medieval Outlook: An Essay on the Intellectual and Spiritual Change in the Fourteenth Century.* New York: Harper and Row, 1976.

Lehmberg, S.E. "Sir Thomas More's Life of Pico della Mirandola." *Studies in the Renaissance* 3 (1956): 61–74.

Lochman, Daniel T. "Colet and Erasmus: The *Disputatiuncula* and the Controversy of Letter and Spirit." *Sixteenth Century Journal* 20 (1989): 77–88.

Long, A.A. "Cicero's Plato and Aristotle." In Powell, *Cicero the Philosopher*, 37–61.

– "Cicero's Politics in *De Officiis*." In Laks and Schofield, *Justice and Generosity*, 213–40.

– *Epictetus: A Stoic and Socratic Guide to Life*. Oxford: Oxford University Press, 2002.

– "Hierocles on *Oikeiosis* and Self-Perception." In Long, *Stoic Studies*, 250–63.

– "The Logical Basis of Stoic Ethics." In Long, *Stoic Studies*, 134–55.

– "Representation and the Self in Stoicism." In *Psychology: Companions to Ancient Thought* 2, ed. Stephen Everson, 102–20. Cambridge: Cambridge University Press, 1991.

– "Socrates in Hellenistic Philosophy." In Long, *Stoic Studies*, 1–34.

– "Stoic Eudaemonism." In Long, *Stoic Studies*, 179–201.

– "Stoic Philosophers on Persons, Property-Ownership and Community." In *Aristotle and After*, ed. R. Sorabji, 13–31. London: University of London, 1997.

– *Stoic Studies*. Cambridge: Cambridge University Press, 1996.

– "Stoicism in the Philosophical Tradition: Spinoza, Lipsius, Butler." In *Hellenistic and Early Modern Philosophy*, ed. J. Miller and B. Inwood, 7–29.

Lorch, Maristella de Panizza. *A Defense of Life: Lorenzo Valla's Theory of Pleasure.* Munich: Wilhem Fink Verlag, 1985.

Lottin, O. *Psychologie et morale aux XIIe et XIIIe siècles*. 6 vols. Louvain: Gembloux, 1942–60.

Lupton, J.H. *A Life of John Colet*. 2nd ed. London: G. Bell, 1909.

MacKendrick, Paul. *The Philosophical Books of Cicero.* New York: Duckworth, 1989.

Madigan, Kevin. "Ancient and High-Medieval Interpretations of Jesus in Gethsemane: Some Reflections on Tradition and Continuity in Christian Thought." *Harvard Theological Review* 88 (1995): 157–73.

– "On the High-Medieval Reception of Hilary of Poitiers's Anti-'Arian' Opinion: A Case Study of Discontinuity in Christian Thought." *Journal of Religion* 78 (1998): 213–29.

Mahoney, Edward P. "Marsilio Ficino and Renaissance Platonism." In *Humanism and Creativity in the Renaissance: Essays in Honor of Ronald G. Will*, ed. C.S. Celenza and K. Gouwens, 231–44. Leiden: Brill, 2006.

Mansfield, Bruce. *Erasmus in the Twentieth Century: Interpretations c 1920–2000.* Toronto: Univeristy of Toronto Press, 2003.

Mansfield, Harvey C. *Machiavelli's Virtue.* Chicago: University of Chicago Press, 1996.

Mara, Maria Grazia. "Colet et Erasme au sujet de l'exégèse de Mt. 26, 39." In *Theorie et pratique de l'exégèse*, ed. Irena Backus and Francis Higman, 259–72. Geneva: Droz, 1990.

Marcel, R. "*L'Enchiridion Militis Christiani*: Sa genèse et sa doctrine, son succès et ses vicissitudes." In Margolin, *Colloquia Erasmiana Turonensia*, vol. 2, 613–30.

Marc'hadour, Germain. "Thomas More on the Agony of Christ." In *Concordia Discors: studi su Niccolò Cusano e L'Umanesimo Europeo Offerti a Giovanni Santinello*, ed. Gregorio Piaia, 487–504. Padua: Antenore, 1993.

Margolin, Jean Claude, ed. *Colloquia Erasmiana Turonensia.* Vol. 2. Paris: Vrin, 1972.

Marrow, James H. *Passion Iconography in Northern European Art of the Late Middle Ages and Early Renaissance.* Kortrijk, Belgium: Van Ghemmert, 1979.

Marsden, Gordon. "Bosch's 'Christ Carrying the Cross.'" *History Today* 47 (1997): 15– 21.

Marsh, David. "Erasmus on the Antithesis of Body and Soul." *Journal of the History of Ideas* 37 (1976): 673–88.

– *The Quattrocento Dialogue: Classical Tradition and Humanist Innovation.* Cambridge, MA: Harvard University Press, 1980.

Mazzotta, Giuseppe. *The Worlds of Petrarch.* Durham, NC: Duke University Press, 1993.

McClure, George W. *Sorrow and Consolation in Italian Humanism.* Princeton: Princeton University Press, 1991.

McClusky, Coleen. "Bernard of Clairvaux on the Nature of Human Agency." *Revista Portuguesa de Filosofia* 64 (2008): 297–317.

McConica, James K. *English Humanists and Reformation Politics under Henry VIII and Edward VI.* Oxford: Oxford University Press, 1965.

– "The Philosophy of Christ." In James K. McConica, *Erasmus*, 45–62. Oxford: Oxford University Press, 1991.

– "The Riddle of Terminus." *Erasmus in English* 2 (1971): 2–7.

McGuckin, John A., ed. *The Westminster Handbook to Origen.* Louisville, KY: Westminster John Knox Press, 2004.

McGuire, Brian Patrick. *The Difficult Saint: Bernard of Clairvaux and His Tradition.* Kalamazoo: Cistercian Publications, 1992.

McNair, Bruce G. "Cristoforo Landino and Coluccio Salutati on the Best Life." *Renaissance Quarterly* 47 (1994): 747–69.

Meiss, Millard. *Painting in Florence and Siena after the Black Death: The Arts, Religion and Society in the Mid-Fourteenth Century.* Princeton: Princeton University Press, 1951.

Mestwerdt, Paul. *Die Anfänge des Erasmus: Humanismus und "Devotio Moderna."* Leipzig: R. Haupt, 1917.

Miller, Jon, and Brad Inwood eds. *Hellenistic and Early Modern Philosophy.* Cambridge: Cambridge University Press, 2003.

Minnich, Nelson, and W.W. Meissner. "The Character of Erasmus." *American Historical Review* 83 (1978): 598–624.

Mitsis, Phillip. "Seneca on Reason, Rules, and Moral Development." In Brunschwig and Nussbaum, *Passions and Perceptions*, 285–312.

Monahan, Arthur P. *From Personal Duties towards Personal Rights: Late Medieval and Early Modern Political Thought, 1300–1600.* Montreal: McGill-Queen's Press, 1994.

Monfasani, John. "Episodes of Anti-Quintilianism in the Italian Renaissance: Quarrels on the Orator as a *Vir bonus* and Rhetoric as the *Scientia Bene Dicendi.*" *Rhetorica* 10 (1992): 127–35.

– "Humanism and Rhetoric." In Rabil, ed. *Renaissance Humanism*, vol. 3, 171–235. Philadelphia: University of Pennsylvania Press, 1988.

– "Toward the Genesis of the Kristeller Thesis of Renaissance Humanism: Four Bibliographical Notes." *Renaissance Quarterly* 53 (2000): 1156–73.

Monsarrat, Gilles D. *Light from the Porch: Stoicism and English Renaissance Literature.* Paris: Didier-Érudition, 1984.

Morford, Mark. *Stoics and Neostoics: Rubens and the Circle of Lipsius.* Princeton: Princeton University Press, 1991.

Mulryan, J. "Erasmus and War: The Adages and Beyond." *Moreana* 89 (1986): 15–28.

Murphy, James J., ed. *Medieval Eloquence: Studies in the Theory and Practice of Medieval Rhetoric*. Berkeley: University of California Press, 1978.

– ed. *Renaissance Eloquence: Studies in the Theory and Practice of Renaissance Rhetoric.* Berkeley: University of California Press, 1983.

Nauert, Charles G. "Humanism as Method: Roots of Conflict with the Scholastics." *Sixteenth Century Journal* 29 (1998): 427–38.

– "Rethinking 'Christian Humanism.'" In *Interpretations of Renaissance Humanism*, ed. Angelo Mazzocco, 155–80. Leiden: Brill, 2006.

Nauta, Lodi. "William of Ockham and Lorenzo Valla: False Friends. Semantics and Ontological Reduction." *Renaissance Quarterly* 56 (2003): 613–51.

Nielsen, Lauge Olaf. "Peter Lombard and His School." In L.O. Nielsen, *Theology and Philosophy in the Twelfth Century: A Study of Gilbert Porreta's Thinking and the Theological Expositions of the Doctrine of the Incarnation during the Period 1130–1180*, 243–361. Leiden: Brill, 1982.

Nussbaum, Martha. *The Therapy of Desire*. Princeton: Princeton University Press, 1994.

Oberman, Heiko. *The Dawn of the Reformation: Essays in Late Medieval and Early Reformation Thought*. Edinburgh: Clark, 1986.

– *The Harvest of Medieval Theology: Gabriel Biel and Late Medieval Nominalism*. Cambridge, MA: Harvard University Press, 1963.

O'Donnell, Anne M. "Rhetoric and Style in Erasmus' *Enchiridion militis Christiani*." *Studies in Philology* 77 (1980): 26–49.

Olin, John C. *The Catholic Reformation: Savonarola to Ignatius Loyola*. New York: Fordham University Press, 1992.

O'Malley, John W. "Erasmus and the History of Sacred Rhetoric: The *Ecclesiastes* of 1535." *Erasmus of Rotterdam Society Yearbook* 5 (1985): 1–29.

– "Grammar and Rhetoric in the Pietas of Erasmus." *Journal of Medieval and Renaissance Studies* 18 (1988): 81–98.

– *Praise and Blame in Renaissance Rome: Rhetoric, Doctrine, and Reform in the Sacred Orators of the Papal Court, c. 1450–1521*. Durham, NC: Duke University Press, 1979.

Overfield, James H. *Humanism and Scholasticism in Late Medieval Germany*. Princeton: Princeton University Press, 1984.

Owst, G.R. *Literature and Pulpit in Medieval England*. 2nd ed. Oxford: Blackwell, 1961.

Pabel, Hilmar M., ed. *Erasmus' Vision of the Church*. Kirksville, MO: Sixteenth Century Journal Publishers, 1995.

– "Exegesis and Marriage in Erasmus' Paraphrases on the New Testament." In Pabel and Vessey, *Holy Scripture Speaks*, 175–209.

Pabel, Hilmar M., and Mark Vessey, eds. *Holy Scripture Speaks*. Toronto: University of Toronto Press, 2002.

Papy, Ian. "The First Christian Defender of Stoic Virtue? Justus Lipsius and Cicero's *Paradoxa Stoicorum*." In *Christian Humanism: Essays in Honour of Arjo Vanderjagt*, ed. A. MacDonald, Z. von Martels, and J. Veenstra, 139–53. Leiden: Brill, 2009.

Payne, John B. *Erasmus: His Theology of the Sacraments*. Richmond, VA: Bratcher, 1970.

Pembroke, S.G. "*Oikeiosis*." In *Problems in Stoicism*, ed. A.A. Long, 114–49. London: Athlone Press, 1971.

Phillips, Margaret Mann. *The Adages of Erasmus: A Study with Translations*. Cambridge: Cambridge University Press, 1964.

– "Erasmus and the Classics." In *Erasmus*, ed. T.A. Dorey, 1–30. London: Routledge, 1970.

Pinborg, Jan. "Speculative Grammar." In *Cambridge History of Later Medieval Philosophy*, ed. N. Kretzmann et al., 254–69. Cambridge: Cambridge University Press, 1982.

Pineau, J.B. *Érasme, sa pensée religieuse*. Paris: Presses universistaires de France, 1924.

Pohlenz, M. *Die Stoa: Geschichte einer geistigen Bewegung*. 4th ed. 2 vols. Göttingen, Ger.: Vandenhoeck & Ruprecht, 1970–2.

Pollnitz, Aysha. *Princely Education in Early Modern Britain*. Cambridge: Cambridge University Press, 2015.

Posset, Franz. "Preaching the Passion of Christ on the Eve of the Reformation." *Concordia Theological Quarterly* 59 (1995): 279–300.

Post, R.R. *The Modern Devotion: Confrontation with Reformation and Humanism*. Leiden: Brill, 1968.

Powell, J.G.F., ed. *Cicero the Philosopher: Twelve Papers*. Oxford: Oxford University Press, 1995.

– "Cicero's Translations from the Greek." In *Cicero the Philosopher*, 273–300.

Pranger, M. Burcht. *Bernard of Clairvaux and the Shape of Monastic Life*. Leiden: Brill, 1994.

Price, Simon. *Religions of the Ancient Greeks*. Cambridge: Cambridge University Press, 1999.

Rabil, Albert. "Cicero and Erasmus' Moral Philosophy." *Erasmus of Rotterdam Society Yearbook* 8 (1988): 70–90.

– *Erasmus and the New Testament: The Mind of a Christian Humanist*. San Antonio, TX: Trinity University Press, 1972.

– "Erasmus's Paraphrases of the New Testament." In DeMolen, *Essays on the Works of Erasmus*, 145–61.

– ed. *Knowledge, Goodness, and Power: The Debate over Nobility among Quattrocento Italian Humanists*. Binghamton, NY: Medieval & Renaissance Texts & Studies, 1991.

– ed. *Renaissance Humanism: Foundations, Forms, and Legacy*. 3 vols. Philadelphia: University of Pennsylvania Press, 1988.

Rebhorn, Wayne, ed. *Renaissance Debates on Rhetoric*. Ithaca, NY: Cornell University Press, 2000.

Reedijk, Cornelis. *The Poems of Desiderius Erasmus*. Leiden: Brill, 1956.

Remer, Gary. *Humanism and the Rhetoric of Toleration*. University Park, PA: Pennsylvania State University Press, 1996.

Reydams-Schils, Gretchen. *The Roman Stoics: Self, Responsibility, and Affection*. Chicago: University of Chicago Press, 2005.

– "Social Ethics and Politics." In *A Companion to Marcus Aurelius*, ed. Marcel van Ackeren, 437–52. Malden, MA: Wiley-Blackwell, 2012.

Rice, Eugene. "Erasmus and the Religious Tradition, 1495–1499." *Journal of the History of Ideas* 11 (1950): 387–411.

– "John Colet and the Annihilation of the Natural." *Harvard Theological Review* 45 (1952): 141–63.

– *The Renaissance Idea of Wisdom*. Cambridge, MA: Harvard University Press, 1958.

Rist, J.M. *Stoic Philosophy*. Cambridge: Cambridge University Press, 1969.

Roest, Bert. *Franciscan Literature of Religious Instruction before the Council of Trent*. Leiden: Brill, 2004.

– *A History of Franciscan Education (c. 1210–1517)*. Leiden: Brill, 2000.

Roller, Matthew B. "Color-Blindness: Cicero's Death, Declamation, and the Production of History." *Classical Philology* 92 (1997): 109–30.

Ronnick, Michele V. "The Raison d'Etre of Fust and Schoeffer's *De officiis* et *Paradoxa Stoicorum*, 1465, 1466." *Medievalia et Humanistica*, ns, 20 (1994): 123–35.

Rosemann, Philipp W. *Peter Lombard*. New York: Oxford University Press, 2004.

– *The Story of a Great Book: Peter Lombard's Sentences*. Peterbourgh, ON: Broadview Press, 2007.

Rudich, Vasily. *Political Dissidence under Nero: The Price of Dissimulation*. London: Routledge, 1993.

Rüegg, Walter. *Cicero und der Humanismus: Formale Unersuchungen über Petrarca und Erasmus*. Zurich: Rheinverlag, 1946.

Rummel, Erika. *Desiderius Erasmus*. London: Continuum, 2004.

– *Erasmus and His Catholic Critics*. 2 vols. Nieuwkoop: De Graaf, 1989.

– *Erasmus' Annotations on the New Testament: From Philologist to Theologian*. Toronto: University of Toronto Press, 1986.

– *The Humanist-Scholastic Debate in the Renaissance and Reformation*. Cambridge: Cambridge University Press, 1995.

– "*Monachatus non est pietas*: Interpretations and Misinterpretations of a Dictum." In Pabel, *Erasmus' Vision of the Church*, 41–55.

– "Quoting Poetry instead of Scripture: Erasmus and Eucherius on *Contemptus Mundi*." *Bibliothèque d'Humanisme et Renaissance* 45 (1983): 503–9.

– "Secular Advice in Erasmus's Sacred Writings." *European Legacy* 19 (2014): 16–26.

– "The Theology of Erasmus." In The *Cambridge Companion to Reformation Theology*, ed. David Bagchi and David C. Steinmetz, 26–38. Cambridge: Cambridge University Press, 2004.

Ruppel, Wendy. "Salvation through Imitation: The Meaning of Bosch's 'St. Jerome in the Wilderness.'" *Simiolus: Netherlands Quarterly for the History of Art* 18 (1988): 5–12.

Russell, Frederick H. *The Just War in the Middle Ages*. Cambridge: Cambridge University Press, 1975.

Salmon, J.H.M. "Stoicism and Roman Example: Seneca and Tacitus in Jacobean England." *Journal of the History of Ideas* 50 (1989): 199–225.

Santinello, Giovanni. *Studi sull'umanesimo Europeo: Cusano e Petrarca, Lefèvre, Erasmo, Colet, Moro*. Padua: Antenore, 1969.

Saunders, Jason Lewis. *Justus Lipsius: The Philosophy of Renaissance Stoicism.* New York: Liberal Arts Press, 1955.

Schär, Max. *Das Nachleben des Origenes im Zeitalter des Humanismus.* Basel: Helbing & Lichtenhahn, 1979.

Schatkin, Margaret A. "The Influence of Origen upon St. Jerome's Commentary on Galatians." *Vigiliae Christianae* 24 (1970): 49–58.

Scheck, Thomas P. "Erasmus's Reception of Origen's Exegesis of Romans." In Scheck, *Origen and the History of Justification*, 129–72.

– *Origen and the History of Justification: The Legacy of Origen's Commentary on Romans*. Notre Dame, IN: University of Notre Dame Press, 2008.

Schoeck, R.J. *Erasmus of Europe: The Making of a Humanist, 1467–1500.* Edinburgh: Edinburgh University Press, 1990.

– *Erasmus of Europe: The Prince of the Humanists, 1501–1536.* Edinburgh: Edinburgh University Press, 1993.

Schofield, Malcolm. *The Stoic Idea of the City*. Cambridge: Cambridge University Press, 1991.

– "Two Stoic Approaches to Justice." In Laks and Schofield, *Justice and Generosity*, 191–212.

Schofield, Malcolm, and Gisela Striker, eds. *The Norms of Nature: Studies in Hellenistic Ethics*. Cambridge: Cambridge University Press, 1986.

Seebohm, Frederic. *The Oxford Reformers: John Colet, Erasmus, and Thomas More.* 3rd ed. London: Longmans, 1896.

Seigel, Jerrold. "'Civic Humanism' or Ciceronian Rhetoric? The Culture of Petrarch and Bruni." *Past and Present* 34 (1966): 3–48.

– *Rhetoric and Philosophy in Renaissance Humanism: The Union of Eloquence and Wisdom, Petrarch to Valla.* Princeton: Princeton University Press, 1968.

Sellars, John. *The Art of Living: The Stoics on the Nature and Function of Philosophy.* Aldershot, UK: Aldershot, 2003.

– *Stoicism.* Berkeley: University of California Press, 2006.

Sépinski, P. Augustin. *La psychologie du Christ chez Saint Bonaventure.* Paris: Vrin, 1948.

Sherman, Nancy. "The Look and Feel of Virtue." In *Virtue, Norms, and Objectivity: Issues in Ancient and Modern Ethics*, ed. Christopher Gill, 57–82. Oxford: Oxford University Press, 2005.

– *Stoic Warriors: The Ancient Philosophy behind the Military Mind.* Oxford: Oxford University Press, 2005.

Sider, Robert D. "*Concedo Nulli*: Erasmus' Motto and the Figure of Paul in the Paraphrases." *Erasmus in English* 14 (1985–6): 7–10.

– "Paul in Erasmus' Paraphrases on the Pauline Epistles." In Pabel and Vessey, *Holy Scripture Speaks*, 85–109.

Skinner, Quentin. *The Foundations of Modern Political Thought.* 2 vols. Cambridge: Cambridge University Press, 1978.

– *Machiavelli: A Very Short Introduction.* Oxford: Oxford University Press, 2000.

– *Visions of Politics.* Vol. 2, *Renaissance Virtues.* Cambridge: Cambridge University Press, 2002.

Smith, John C. *The Ancient Wisdom of Origen.* London: Associated University Presses, 1992.

Sommerfeldt, John R. *Bernard of Clairvaux on the Life of the Mind.* New York: Newman Press, 2004.

Sorabji, Richard. *Emotion and Peace of Mind: From Stoic Agitation to Christian Temptation.* Oxford: Oxford University Press, 2000.

Sowards, J.K. "The Two Lost Years of Erasmus: Summary, Review, and Speculation." *Studies in the Renaissance* 9 (1962): 161–86.

– "The Youth of Erasmus: Some Reconsiderations." *Erasmus of Rotterdam Society Yearbook* 9 (1989): 1–33.

Stacey, Peter. *Roman Monarchy and the Renaissance Prince.* Cambridge: Cambridge University Press, 2007.

Sticca, Sandro. *The Latin Passion Play: Its Origin and Development.* Albany, NY: State University of New York Press, 1970.

Striker, Gisela. "Antipater, or the Art of Living." In Schofield and Striker, *The Norms of Nature*, 185–203.

– "Cicero and Greek Philosophy." *Harvard Studies in Classical Philology* 97 (1995): 53–61.

– *Essays on Hellenistic Epistemology and Ethics.* Cambridge: Cambridge University Press, 1996.

– "Following Nature: A Study in Stoic Ethics." In Gisela Striker, *Essays on Hellenistic Epistemology and Ethics*, 221–80.

– "Plato's Socrates and the Stoics." In Gisela Striker, *Essays on Hellenistic Epistemology and Ethics*, 316–24. Cambridge: Cambridge University Press, 1996.

Stupperich, Robert. "*Das Enchiridion militis christiani* des Erasmus von Rotterdam nach seiner Enstehung, seinem Sinn und Charakter." *Archiv für Reformationsgeschichte* 69 (1978): 5–23.

Thesaurus Sancti Bernardi Clarevallensis. Turnhout, Belgium: Brepols, 1987.

Thompson, Craig R. Review of Chomarat's *Grammaire et rhétorique chez Erasme. Renaissance Quarterly* 38 (1985): 113–17.

Timmermans, B. "Valla et Erasme, defenseurs d'Epicure." *Neophilologus* 23 (1938): 414–19.

Tinkler, John F. "Praise and Advice: Rhetorical Approaches in More's *Utopia* and Machiavelli's *The Prince*." *Sixteenth Century Journal* 29 (1988): 187–207.

Tracy, James D. "Against the 'Barbarians': The Young Erasmus and His Humanist Contemporaries." *Sixteenth Century Journal* 11 (1980): 3–22.

– "Erasmus among the Postmodernists: *Dissimulatio, Bonae Literae*, and *Docta Pietas* Revisited." In Pabel, *Erasmus' Vision of the Church*, 1–40.

– *Erasmus of the Low Countries.* Berkeley: University of California Press, 1996.

– *Erasmus: The Growth of a Mind.* Geneva: Droz, 1972.

– "Humanists among the Scholastics: Erasmus, More, and Lefèvre d'Etaples on the Humanity of Christ." *Erasmus of Rotterdam Society Yearbook* 5 (1985): 30–51.

– "Two Erasmuses, Two Luthers: Erasmus' Strategy in Defense of *De Libero Arbitrio*." *Archiv für Reformationsgeschichte* 78 (1978): 37–59.

Trapp, J.B. *Erasmus, Colet and More: The Early Tudor Humanists and Their Books.* London, British Library, 1991.

Trigg, Joseph W. *Origen: The Bible and Philosophy in the Third-Century Church.* Atlanta: J. Knox, 1983.

Trinkaus, Charles. *In Our Image and Likeness: Humanity and Divinity in Italian Humanist Thought.* 2 vols. London: Constable, 1970.

– *The Poet as Philosopher: Petrarch and the Formation of Renaissance Consciousness.* New Haven, CT: Yale University Press, 1979.

– *The Scope of Renaissance Humanism.* Ann Arbor: University of Michigan Press, 1983.

– "Themes of a Renaissance Anthropology." In Trinkaus, *The Scope of Renaissance Humanism*, 364–403.

Trinkaus, Charles, and Heiko Oberman, eds. *The Pursuit of Holiness in Late Medieval and Renaissance Thought.* Leiden: Brill, 1974.

Tripolitis, Antonia. *The Doctrine of the Soul in the Thought of Plotinus and Origen.* Roslyn Heights, NY: Libra Publishers, 1978.

Tuchman, Barbara. *A Distant Mirror: The Calamitous 14th Century.* New York: Knopf, 1978.

Tuve, Rosemond. "Notes on the Virtues and Vices." *Journal of the Warburg and Courtauld Institutes* 26 (1963): 264–303; 27 (1964): 42–72.

Van Eijl, E.J.M. "De interpretatie van Erasmus' *De contemptu mundi*." In *Pascua Mediaevalia: Studies voor Prof. Dr. J.M. de Smet*, ed. R. Lievens, E. Van

Mingroot, and W. Verbeke, 337–50. Louvain: Universitaire Pers Leuven, 1983.

Van Engen, John, ed. and trans. *Devotio Moderna: Basic Writings*. New York: Paulist Press, 1988.

Vaughn, Pamela. "Cicero and Mario: The Scholar as Activist." *Pacific Ancient and Modern Language Association* 33 (1998): 87–96.

Verbeke, Gerard. *The Presence of Stoicism in Medieval Thought*. Washington, DC: Catholic University of America Press, 1983.

Vickers, Brian. *In Defence of Rhetoric*. Oxford: Oxford University Press, 1988.

– ed. *Arbeit, Musse, Meditation: Betrachtungen zur "Vita active" und "Vita contemplative."* Zurich: Verlag der Fachvereine, 1985.

Viladesau, Richard. *The Beauty of the Cross: The Passion of Christ in Theology and the Arts, from the Catacombs to the Eve of the Renaissance*. Oxford: Oxford University Press, 2006.

Vogt, Katja Maria. *Law, Reason, and the Cosmic City: Political Philosophy in the Early Stoa*. Oxford: Oxford University Press, 2008.

Wakelin, Daniel. *Humanism, Reading, and English Literature 1430–1530*. Oxford: Oxford University Press, 2007.

Walker, D.P. "Origène en France au début du XVIe siècle." In *Courants religieux et humanisme à la fin du XVe siècle et au début du XVIe siècle*, 101–19. Paris: Presses universitaires de France, 1959.

Walsh, P.G., ed. and trans. *Cicero: On Obligations*. Oxford: Oxford University Press, 2000.

Walzer, Arthur E. "Quintilian's 'Vir Bonus' and the Stoic Wise Man." *Rhetoric Society Quarterly* 33 (2003): 25–41.

Ward, John O. "From Antiquity to the Renaissance: Glosses and Commentaries on Cicero's Rhetorica." In Murphy, *Medieval Eloquence*, 25–67.

– "Quintilian and the Rhetorical Revolution of the Middle Ages." *Rhetorica* 13 (1995): 231–84.

– "Renaissance Commentators on Ciceronian Rhetoric." In Murphy, *Renaissance Eloquence*, 126–73.

Waswo, Richard. *Language and Meaning in the Renaissance*. Princeton: Princeton University Press, 1987.

Weiler, A.G. "The Dutch Brethren of the Common Life, Critical Theology, Northern Humanism and Reformation." In *Northern Humanism in European Context, 1469–1625: From the "Adwert Academy" to Ubbo Emmius*, ed. F. Akkerman, A.J.Vanderjagt, and A.H. Van der Laan, 307–32. Leiden: Brill, 1999.

– "The Turkish Argument and Christian Piety in Desiderius Erasmus' *Consultatio de Bello Turcis Inferendo* (1530)." In *Erasmus of Rotterdam: The Man and the Scholar*, ed. J. Sperna Weiland and W. Th. M. Frijhoff, 30–9. Leiden: Brill, 1988.

White, Nicholas P. "The Basis of Stoic Ethics." *Harvard Studies in Classical Philology* 83 (1979): 143–78.

Wind, Edgar. "*Aenigma Termini*: The Emblem of Erasmus." *Journal of the Warburg Institute* 1 (1937): 66–9.

Winkler, Gerhard B. "Die Bernhardrezeption bei Erasmus von Rotterdam." In *Bernard von Clairvaux: Rezeption und Wirkung im Mittelalter und in der Neuzeit*, ed. Kasper Elm, 261–70. Wiesbaden, Ger.: Harrassowitz, 1994.

Winterbottom, M. "The Transmission of Cicero's *De Officiis*." *Classical Quarterly* 43 (1993): 215–42.

Witt, Ronald G. *Hercules at the Crossroads: The Life, Works, and Thought of Coluccio Salutati*. Durham, NC: Duke University Press, 1983.

– *In the Footsteps of the Ancients: The Origins of Humanism from Lovato to Bruni*. Leiden: Brill, 2000.

Wood, Marjorie Curry. "The Teaching of Writing in Medieval Europe." In *A Short History of Writing Instruction from Ancient Greece to Twentieth-Century America*, ed. James J. Murphy, 77–94. Davis, CA: Hermagoras, 1990.

Wood, Neal. *Cicero's Social and Political Thought*. Berkeley: University of California Press, 1988.

– "Some Aspects of the Thought of Seneca and Machiavelli." *Renaissance Quarterly* 21 (1968): 11–23.

Wright, M.R. "Cicero on Self-Love and Love of Humanity in *De Finibus* 3." In Powell, *Cicero the Philosopher*, 171–95.

Zak, Gur. *Petrarch's Humanism and the Care of the Self*. Cambridge: Cambridge University Press, 2010.

Zanta, Leontine. *La Renaissance du stoïcisme aux XVIe siecle*. Paris: Bibliothèque littéraire de la Renaissance, 1914.

Zerba, Michelle. "The Frauds of Humanism: Cicero, Machiavelli, and the Rhetoric of Imposture." *Rhetorica* 22 (2004): 215–40.

Zielinski, T. *Cicero im Wandel der Jahrhunderte*. 4th edition. Leipzig: Teubner, 1929.

Index

Titles of works will be found under the author's name, except for the works of Erasmus.